COSMOPOLITANISM AND EMPIRE

OXFORD STUDIES IN EARLY EMPIRES

Series Editors
Nicola Di Cosmo, Mark Edward Lewis, and Walter Scheidel

Cosmopolitanism and Empire

Universal Rulers, Local Elites, and Cultural Integration in the Ancient Near East and Mediterranean

Edited by
Myles Lavan, Richard E. Payne,
and John Weisweiler

OXFORD
UNIVERSITY PRESS

OXFORD
UNIVERSITY PRESS

Oxford University Press is a department of the University of Oxford. It furthers
the University's objective of excellence in research, scholarship, and education
by publishing worldwide. Oxford is a registered trade mark of Oxford University
Press in the UK and certain other countries.

Published in the United States of America by Oxford University Press
198 Madison Avenue, New York, NY 10016, United States of America.

CIP data is on file at the Library of Congress
ISBN 978-0-19-046566-7

1 3 5 7 9 8 6 4 2
Printed by Sheridan Books, Inc., United States of America

Contents

Preface

THIS volume has its origins in a reading group on ancient cultural history at Cambridge. It was in the course of its regular conversations over claret at Sidney Sussex College that we arrived at the problem of ancient cosmopolitanism, and we would like to thank the University, the College, and all of the participants in the meetings, especially Rebecca Fleming and Robin Osborne. The contemporaneous Gray Lectures of Nicholas Purcell in 2010 encouraged us to pursue the role of aristocratic self-conceptions in the shaping of ancient empires. The American Philological Association in Seattle at 2013 hosted initial discussions of the theme, and Clifford Ando began to make contributions to the project that have continued until its final stages, to its immeasurable advantage.

Thanks to the Fritz Thyssen-Stiftung, the European Research Council, Ruprecht-Karls-Universität Heidelberg, and St. Andrews University, we convened a conference—Imperial Cosmopolitanism: Global Identities and Imperial Cultures in Ancient Eurasia—in the convivial environment of the Internationale Wissenschaftsforum Heidelberg. The meeting was unavoidably complicit in its object of study: "a group of transnational, university types meeting in semi-seclusion, speaking in an exclusive professional sociolect, with some feasting thrown in," as Seth Richardson remarked at the time. It was an example of the dividends cosmopolitanism can yield. Our discussions ranged across Eurasia and over more than two millennia. If the final version of the volume required a greater economy of focus, we remain very grateful to the contributors who did not continue with the project—Matt Canepa, Enno Giele, Amélie Kuhrt, Alex Beecroft, and Lukas Nickel—for their contributions to our thinking.

The volume represents the extensive reworking and refining of the arguments emerging from the conference that took place during subsequent meetings in Cambridge, Istanbul, and Paris. The Neubauer Family Foundation and the University of Chicago supported a week of cowriting on the Bosporus in the spring of 2014, while Trinity College, Cambridge hosted another editorial meeting the following fall. Its enchanting fellows' garden was home to at least one particularly consequential conceptual breakthrough. The University of Chicago's Paris Center supported and hosted a week of workshops and collaborative writing in the fall of 2015 that resulted in the final form of the volume. Sébastian Greppo and Coraline Echasseriau created the ideal, carefree conditions in which to complete the project. We are also grateful to Pierre Briant for an extended conversation at the Collège de France on his concept of the ethnoclass that helped to refine our thinking.

We wish to thank the series editors and the three anonymous readers for their suggestions in shaping the volume. Daniel Gmähle of the Universität Tübingen meticulously proof-read and harmonized the bibliographies. At OUP, Stefan Vranka, Sarah Svendsen, Deepti Agarwal, and Lynn Childress worked hard and long to bring our text to press. Last but not least, the contributors to the volume revised and reworked their texts at multiple stages, and whatever success *Cosmopolitanism and Empire* achieves is the result of their collaborative efforts.

Contributors

CLIFFORD ANDO is David B. and Clara E. Stern Professor at the University of Chicago and Research Fellow at the Department of Classics and World Languages at the University of South Africa. His research focuses on the history of religion, law, and government in the Roman Empire. He is the author of *Imperial Ideology and Provincial Loyalty in the Roman Empire* (2000), *The Matter of the Gods* (2008), *Law, Language and Empire in the Roman Tradition* (2011), and *Imperial Rome AD 193 to 284* (2012), as well as several edited volumes. His most recent monograph, *Roman Social Imaginaries*, is a cognitivist study of metaphor, metonymy, and analogy in Roman legal and political language.

PETER FIBIGER BANG is Associate Professor of History at the University of Copenhagen. He has worked extensively on Roman comparative and world history, dealing with issues of economy, state formation, high culture, and the organization of imperial power. His monograph, *The Roman Bazaar: A Comparative Study of Trade and Markets in a Tributary Empire* (2008), situates the history of Rome in the wider context of pre-modern tributary empires. A booklet, *Irregulare Aliquod Corpus? Comparison, world history and the historical sociology of the Roman Empire* (2014) provides a theoretical manifesto. He has edited volumes on the comparative history of tributary empires, on the idea of universal empire and on the state in the ancient Near East and Mediterranean.

TAMARA T. CHIN is Associate Professor of Comparative Literature at Brown University. She trained in Chinese, Greek, and Latin, and specializes in intercultural contact and exchange, primarily in early Chinese contexts. Her book, *Savage Exchange: Han Imperialism, Chinese Literary Style, and the Economic Imagination* (2014), which received the American Comparative Literature Association's Harry Levin Prize, explores debates over the radically quantitative economic theories that arose during the Han dynasty's (206 BCE–220 CE) expansion of frontiers and markets.

CHRISTELLE FISCHER-BOVET is Associate Professor of Classics at the University of Southern California. She is a specialist in the social and cultural history of the Eastern Mediterranean from Alexander the Great to the Romans, with a special interest in Greco-Roman Egypt. Her book, *Army and Society in Ptolemaic Egypt*, combines documentary evidence with social theory to examine the role of the army in Ptolemaic Egypt. She is now preparing a new book entitled *The Ptolemaic Empire* for Oxford University Press.

JOHANNES HAUBOLD is Professor of Greek at the University of Durham and member of the Academy of Europe. His main areas of interest are Greek literature, especially epic, and the place of Greek literature in a wider Mediterranean and Near Eastern context. He is the author of *Homer's People: Epic Poetry and Social Formation* (2000), *Homer: The Resonance of Epic* (2005), and a commentary on Homer, *Iliad* VI (2010), as well as two edited volumes. His latest book, *Greece and Mesopotamia: Dialogues in Literature*, explores contact and exchange between Greek and ancient Near Eastern literatures from the *Epic of Gilgamesh* to the Hellenistic period.

MYLES LAVAN is Senior Lecturer in Ancient History at the University of St. Andrews. He is a historian of the Roman empire with particular interests in citizenship and imperialism. His monograph, *Slaves to Rome* (2013), explores how the Roman elite conceived of their imperial project. He is currently working on the spread of Roman citizenship, further studies of the language of imperialism in Latin, and the historian Tacitus.

RICHARD E. PAYNE is Neubauer Family Assistant Professor at the Oriental Institute at the University of Chicago. He is a historian of the Iranian world in late antiquity. His research focuses on how the Iranian Empire successfully integrated socially, culturally, and geographically disparate populations from Arabia to Afghanistan into enduring political networks and institutions. His recent book, *A State of Mixture: Christians, Zoroastrians, and Iranian Political Culture in Late Antiquity* (2015), explores the problem of religious diversity within the empire.

SETH RICHARDSON is managing editor of the *Journal of Near Eastern Studies* at the University of Chicago. His work focuses on three areas. First, Richardson is a specialist in the military, political, and social history of the Old Babylonian period (ca. 2000–1600 BCE). Second, he has published articles on violence and the rise of the state in ancient Mesopotamia. Third, he has explored Mesopotamian cultural history from a comparative perspective, working on fields such as liver divination, iconicity, ancestor cult, and changing ancient conceptions of the past.

KATHRYN STEVENS is Lecturer in Classics and Ancient History at the University of Durham. Her main research interests are in Greek and Mesopotamian cultural and intellectual history, with a particular focus on the

Hellenistic period. Her forthcoming monograph examines connections between the intellectual histories of the Hellenistic Greek world and Babylonia, and she has written articles on diverse topics such as Greek geography and Seleucid kingship.

John Weisweiler is Assistant Professor in Late Antique Mediterranean History at the University of Maryland, College Park. He is an expert in Roman and Late Roman social history. He is currently finishing a monograph which traces the changing role played by the senate, the imperial aristocracy of the Roman Empire, in the structures of the Roman state from the Augustan period until the end of the fourth century CE. He is also interested in the relationship between state formation, elite wealth, and the monetarization of social obligation in the Roman Empire.

COSMOPOLITANISM AND EMPIRE

Cosmopolitan Politics

The Assimilation and Subordination of Elite Cultures

Myles Lavan, Richard E. Payne, and John Weisweiler

The first chapter introduces the central themes of the volume. We offer a comparative perspective on the depth and modalities of elite integration from the Neo-Assyrian empire in the early first millennium BCE to the Roman and Iranian empires in the first millennium CE. Our interest is in the ways in which the ruling groups of empires—universal rulers—bridged the distance and difference that divided them from the pre-existing concentrations of power—local elites—on whom they relied. We argue that cosmopolitanism— a complex of practices and ideals that enabled certain individuals not only to cross cultural boundaries, but to establish an enduring normative framework across them—was an indispensable instrument of imperial rule. We distinguish between two forms of cosmopolitan politics, which we term assimilation and subordination. Assimilation works by eliding the cultural difference between universal rulers and local elites, whereas subordination operates by recognising, preserving and organising difference. We conclude with a short history of cosmopolitanism and its associated practices from the rise of the Neo-Assyrians to late antiquity, which illustrates the centrality of these practices in the consolidation and maintenance of imperial networks. Regardless of their differences, each of these empires created transcultural normative frameworks that gave local elites the capacity to act authoritatively and legitimately from the perspective of both the imperial elite and the local population they were encharged to manage, at least in empires that endured.

THIS is a book about empire and difference. The Iron Age empires that developed in the two millennia after the disintegration of the Bronze Age system ca. 1200 BCE were political formations of unprecedented scale and complexity. They projected power over vast distances and ruled over massive, dispersed, and heterogeneous populations.[1] The facts of distance and

---

1. As Mann 1986: 145 observes, "the greater the extent of conquest the more kinship between ruling elites became strained and fictitious."

difference were potential assets. All these empires thrived at least in part through the careful cultivation and management of difference within the populations they ruled—what Jane Burbank and Frederick Cooper have called the "politics of difference" in their analysis of empire in world-historical perspective.[2] Yet distance and difference also posed obvious challenges for the imperial states themselves, strengthening centrifugal forces and dividing the imperial elite which administered the empire from the local elites whose ongoing cooperation remained essential for the exercise of power, in the absence of the technologies that underpin modern states. In addition to developing material structures to overcome these challenges, all these empires also made at least some efforts to bridge the divisions within their populations, particularly those between imperial and local elites. It is these efforts that are the subject of this book.

We offer a comparative perspective on the depth and modalities of elite integration from the Neo-Assyrian empire in the early first millennium BCE to the Roman and Iranian empires in the first millennium CE. Our focus is on the practices that enabled these states and their ruling elites to manage cultural difference. In labeling these cultural forms "cosmopolitan," we aim to reclaim the term as a category for historical analysis. "Cosmopolitan" typically describes persons and polities that freely cross cultural boundaries. We regard the capacities the term encompasses as essential to the consolidation of imperial power. The imperial states and elites of ancient Eurasia developed distinct practices that transcended—rather than erased—difference and drew strength from diversity. In the process, they generated new forms of subjectivity in both the center and the periphery. The vast territories they ruled nevertheless remained irrevocably fragmented by distance and difference. Cultural homogeneity of the kind the modern nation-state produced was beyond the reach of even the most infrastructurally developed of these ancient states.

Four key conclusions emerge from the volume as a whole. The first is the political importance of cosmopolitan practices. Comparative approaches have attracted increasing interest among scholars of ancient empires over the past decade and have transformed our understanding of the political economy of ancient imperial formations. They have shown that enduring empires depended on the creation of robust infrastructures and the redistribution of resources to patrimonial elites.[3] We explore the intersubjective

---

2. Burbank and Cooper 2010. According to Pitts 2010: 213–4, "the problem of managing difference is often seen as the perennial political challenge for empires, although it may be more accurate to say that empires cultivate forms of difference." See also Barfield 2001: 29, Sinopoli 2001: 96–7, Maier 2006: 31, and Stevens and Ando, this volume. Perdue 2007 offers an unusually wide-ranging historical case study in the "imperial management of difference."

3. The literature on ancient empires focusing on the comparative analysis of economic, administrative, and political structures is now vast. The starting point for the economic analysis of inter-elite relations remains

relations of universal rulers and local elites that constituted and sustained imperial networks. This volume focuses attention on the cultural practices that made empire possible.

Second, the volume distinguishes between two forms of elite integration across cultures. No two cosmopolitanisms are identical. From the origins of empire in the late third millennium BCE to its apex in the first millennium CE, we witness imperial elites encountering difference and experimenting with ways of managing it. The imperial elites most successful in creating networks reproducible across time and space innovated cosmopolitan practices that had eluded their predecessors. These practices varied considerably according to the cultural repertoires of rulers and their provincial interlocutors. We nevertheless discern two fundamentally different modalities of integration, which we term assimilation and subordination. The former, which works to create common elite cultures, is familiar because it is epitomized by the paradigmatic empires of Rome and Han China. But other imperial powers such as Achaemenian Persia and Sasanian Iran employed very different strategies which worked by preserving and organizing difference and which were no less effective as mechanisms of incorporation.

Third, the studies assembled in this volume repeatedly explore the limits of integration. Whichever strategy was chosen, the interplay between empire and difference reliably produced unforeseen dilemmas and disequilibria. Clifford Ando elegantly articulates the problem: "A history of cosmopolitanism must therefore pose the question, how difference might be, could be, and was in fact both asserted and contained within a framework of nominal ecumenism, even as one asks how claims to ecumenism were vindicated, in light of the fact of massive difference." This tension recurs throughout this volume.

Lastly, the volume emphasizes the importance of integrative, as opposed to comparative, history. A long tradition of study views its subjects as bounded political systems with their own autonomous trajectories, and aims to uncover convergent or divergent lines of development in societies that never encountered one another or whose trans-regional encounters can be downplayed in the analysis. Such studies have yielded great dividends. Yet recent scholarship has emphasized that institutions and ideas were often transmitted between empires in the Near East and Mediterranean.[4] As Sheldon Pollock has observed, "one thing a comparative history of empire demonstrates is that it is only by looking at past empires that people have learned how to be imperial at all, since empire

---

Haldon 1993. Signal recent works include Bang 2008, Hurlet 2008, Morris and Scheidel 2009, Scheidel 2009, Bang and Bayly 2003, 2011, and Scheidel 2015. Eisenstadt 1963: 33–9 famously regarded the creation and circulation of "free resources" among elites as an essential feature of empires. Bang and Turner 2015 argue for an analytical focus on "patrimonial politics" that comparative studies have tended to neglect.

4. Briant 1994, Canepa 2010a, Rollinger 2012, Martinez-Sève 2014b. Nickel 2013 argues for the central role of the trans-Eurasian encounter with Hellenistic culture in the representational strategies of the Qin empire.

is a cultural practice and not some natural state."[5] Pollock, moreover, suggests that ancient through modern Eurasian empires "formed a coherent category of practice ... continuously re-created through historical imitation, a process that seems to have run along two axes: vertically in time (through historical memory), and horizontally across space (perhaps through what archaeologists have named peer-polity interaction)."[6] We highlight precisely such imperial interaction across time and space. The following articles show Assyrian, Achaemenian, Hellenistic, Roman, and Iranian rulers building empires on the sedimentation that had accumulated over millennia of state and empire formation. Contemporaneous empires such as Rome and Iran, moreover, borrowed from one another.[7]

UNIVERSAL RULERS, LOCAL ELITES, AND CULTURAL INTEGRATION

The empires of Iron Age Eurasia were all geographically extensive, multiethnic states with universal ambitions.[8] Most of these states were monarchies, but a focus on autocratic structures distracts attention from the existence of broader ruling groups that shared their monarch's universal ambitions.[9] Autocrats necessarily depended upon a far-flung administrative and military elite to rule their vast empires. The imperial elites with whom they shared their imperial projects varied in their internal cohesion and their openness to recruits from the periphery. At one extreme, we find the Neo-Assyrian ruling elite with its crisis of confidence that Seth Richardson diagnoses in his chapter, unable to rely on social or ethnic distinction and entirely dependent on personal connections to the king. At the other, we have the apparently closed "dominant ethno-class" that Pierre Briant identified in the Persian empire, secure in its simultaneous social and ethnic distinction.[10] But some form of imperial elite is a structural feature of all these empires. No less than the monarchs, these imperial elites

---

5. Pollock 2006b: 176. See Pagden 1995, Pocock 2005, and MacCormack 2007 for particularly illuminating case studies of the cross-chronological potency of imperial ideologies.

6. Pollock 2006b: 178.

7. Canepa 2009.

8. Doyle 1986: 30 defined empire simply as the "effective control, whether formal or informal, of the subordinated society by imperial society." For Mann 1986: 145, "domination" is the key distinguishing characteristic of empires. But territorial extent, cultural heterogeneity, and universal aspirations are essential features, as the definition of Maier 2006: 31 and 73 emphasizes: "a territorially extensive structure of rule that usually subordinates diverse ethnolinguistic groups or would be nations and reserves preponderant power for an executive authority and the elites with whom this power is shared"; "empires involve.... a motivating universalist ideology," in addition to superior military and communicative technologies and an economic surplus. See Bang and Kolodziejczyk 2012 for a comparative study of universal empire.

9. Winterling 1997, Spawforth 2007, Potter and Talbert 2011, and Duindam, Artan, and Kunt 2011 have analyzed the structures and cultures of the court societies that were at the center of ancient empires.

10. Briant 1988.

saw themselves as *universal rulers*, masters of the world. Ruling over a world of difference was their vocation.

These universal rulers faced similar challenges in seeking to realize their ambitions in a world riven by distance and difference. They developed a range of strategies to overcome them. They invested in infrastructural capacities to mobilize manpower and to facilitate the movement of information, officials, and soldiers across their vast territories.[11] Yet severe technological constraints placed limits on centralization and the reach of the imperial elite. Local concentrations of social power, our *local elites*, inevitably enjoyed considerable autonomy in the day-to-day government of their communities.[12] In most cases, these were patrimonial elites strongly rooted in their societies and usually predating their incorporation into empire. Although the erasure of existing patrimonial elites was always an option open to imperial powers, it was—comparatively speaking—a strategy only rarely applied. All enduring imperial formations depended on engineering some alignment of interest between the imperial elite and a range of preexisting local elites. Material interest certainly played an important role in this alignment. In varying ways imperial elites allowed local elites to appropriate at least some of the rents of empire and explicitly or implicitly underwrote their privileged position within their own societies. It is possible to imagine cooperation based purely on such considerations, but enduring, reproducible networks of local elites never relied entirely on the calculus of material interest. All of these empires made at least some efforts toward the creation of a normative framework shared by universal rulers and local elites, a process we term *cultural integration*.

The process did not necessarily entail the creation of a homogeneous elite culture. The creation of cultural uniformity seems so self-evidently attractive and played so obvious a role in the archetypal empires of Rome and China that it is easy to assume its commonality to all ancient empires. It is an essential feature of Ernst Gellner's famous model of "the agro-literate polity"—which many ancient historians have found useful—which is characterized by the existence of horizontal elite strata superimposed on the vertical strata of laterally insulated communities of agricultural producers.[13] Yet the Iron Age empires of the Near East and Mediterranean varied greatly in the ways in which they achieved the cultural integration of elites. Empires such as Achaemenian Persia aimed at forming purposefully heterogeneous elite networks and established a normative framework that was compatible with cultures with their own cosmologies, political traditions, and languages. The adoption of shared norms and

---

11. On the remarkably complex and efficient communicative apparatuses ancient empires developed, see Kolb 2000, Alcock, Bodel, and Talbert 2012, and Radner 2014c.
12. Goldstone and Haldon 2009: 18–19 stress the imperial state's reliance on a network of local elites.
13. Gellner 1983: 9–11.

symbols did not necessarily require the abolition of difference. Two very different modes of cultural integration deserve to be distinguished—*assimilation* and *subordination*.

Assimilation elides the cultural divide between universal rulers and local elites. Epitomized by Rome and Han China, it is in fact the less common of the two modes of cultural integration. It depends simultaneously on an elite culture that is at least in principle permeable to outsiders and a normative framework that largely ignores local cultural traditions. The imperial state speaks in a universal rather than local idiom, though it must at least start by recognizing local forms of social differentiation before it translates them into its own terms. Perhaps the most obvious mechanism of assimilation is the Roman use of citizenship to integrate local elites into the community of Roman citizens, analyzed by Clifford Ando in this volume. But assimilation also works through broader cultures of inclusion—elite cultures of consumption, sociability, and literacy, among others—that are open to appropriation by outsiders.[14] Taken to their limits, the techniques of assimilation have the potential to erase the cultural divide between universal rulers and local elites altogether. The Roman empire may well have reached that point by the fourth century, by which stage it becomes very difficult to see any cultural difference between imperial and local elites, as John Weisweiler argues in his contribution. More often, however, the assimilation of local elites is only partial. Cultures of inclusion are counterbalanced by cultures of exclusion, as a self-professed imperial elite seeks to preserve its distinction. Myles Lavan illustrates this dynamic in the early Roman empire.

Subordination is a very different mode of integrating universal rulers and local elites. Subordination consists in the recognition and preservation of the cultural differences between universal rulers and various local elites, and the management of difference through categorization. What George Steinmetz calls "ethnographic capital"—the capacity to investigate, classify, and organize the cultural characteristics of subject populations—becomes crucial for imperial rule in the subordinating mode.[15] The key mechanism of subordination is a hierarchical dialogue across cultural boundaries, in which the dominant ascribed identities to their subjects. The imperial elite circumscribe themselves in exclusive, frequently ethnic terms, even if other aspects of their culture are open to appropriation. Imperial interaction with peripheral communities tends to be cast in local rather than universal idioms, inscribing empire into multiple local traditions rather than attempting to speak with one voice to the entire subject population. Local elites, in turn, conceptualize the imperial order according to

---

14. The classic study of cultural assimilation in the Roman empire is Woolf 1998. Lewis 2006: 189–244 traces the distinctive understandings of space on which pan-Chinese aristocratic culture was based.
15. Steinmetz 2008.

their own traditions, as Johannes Haubold and Christelle Fischer-Bovet demonstrate for Hellenistic empires. Hence, there remains a clear divide between a relatively closed imperial elite and multiple, laterally differentiated local elites in the periphery, such as the Babylonian and Greek urban elites distinguished by Kathryn Stevens. But these local elites participated fully in the imperial order. In the process of their integration, they retained their difference, recast in the terms of empire. Richard Payne shows that the Iranian ethno-class created an enduring architecture of power through the organization rather than the erasure of cultural differences among the local elites in a manner reminiscent of their Achaemenian and Seleucid predecessors.

These are ideal types intended to illustrate two fundamentally distinct strategies by which ancient empires integrated universal rulers and local elites. Most historical empires can be observed using both strategies in different times or places. Even empires that relied principally on subordination could seek to assimilate particular groups. The Achaemenians, for example, appear to have incorporated Elamite and Median elites into the otherwise exclusive Persian ethno-class.[16] Conversely, even in the Roman empire—the epitome of the assimilative mode—the techniques of subordination can be seen in interaction with Greek elites of the east.[17]

COSMOPOLITAN POLITICS

Assimilation and subordination are both forms of *cosmopolitan politics*. In employing the term "cosmopolitan" to analyze historical processes of empire formation, the present volume expands on its more familiar, descriptive usage to characterize perspectives, persons, and polities that transcended particular cultures. The term "cosmopolitan" has its origin in Greco-Roman philosophical traditions which can be traced back to the fourth century BCE. Diogenes of Sinope is said to have called himself a *kosmopolitēs*, "a citizen of the universe." Subsequent thinkers, notably the Stoics, articulated a form of Greek citizenship that disrespected the walls of the polis—hitherto thought to constrain human political possibilities—in order ultimately to encompass all of humanity in a community of shared norms. According to Zeno of Kition, inhabitants of various poleis should convene to form "one way of life and one order, like that of a herd grazing together and nurtured by common law."[18] Such a vision of a universal law integrating persons and communities irrespective of their cultural

---

16. Henkelman 2008.
17. The ability of eastern Mediterranean elites to remain Greek while becoming Roman is highlighted by Woolf 1994. The new interest in indigenous traditions generated by subordination to Roman power is brought out by Ando 2010 and Spawforth 2012.
18. Brown 2006, Long 2008a, Konstan 2009.

backgrounds has inspired western philosophers and political theorists to revive these ideals at particular historical junctures. During the Enlightenment, Kant articulated a cosmopolitan law to guide the interaction of peoples and states: foreign visitors were entitled to hospitality in an international order in which relations of reciprocity allowed distinct political communities to coexist peacefully. If the rise of nationalism sidelined this aspiration in the nineteenth and early twentieth centuries, the post-World War II and, especially, post-Cold War eras precipitated a resurgence of cosmopolitan philosophy and political theory. Positive arguments in favor of ethical commitments to all of humanity, the development of transcultural perspectives and the establishment of universal, rationally grounded principles have elevated cosmopolitanism to a normative value, incumbent on individuals, institutions, and states, at least in liberal democracies.[19]

And yet the advocates of cosmopolitanism have only rarely addressed its historically intimate relationship with imperialism. Diogenes criticized the constraints of the polis while the Macedonians dismantled them, paving the way for the expansionism of Alexander and his Hellenistic successors. It was, moreover, under the Hellenistic kings and Roman emperors that the Stoic articulation of cosmopolitanism gained currency, even if, as Tamara Chin shows, its principles did not straightforwardly justify empire. Anthony Pagden has noted an imperialist strain even in the seemingly benign aspiration of Zeno already quoted: whose "law" (*nomos*) was to attain universal assent? For Greco-Roman elites, cosmopolitanism entailed outsiders accepting—voluntarily or involuntarily—their superior norms and modes of existence.[20] Subsequent western thinkers found in such a generous sharing of classical culture—of which they were heirs—a model to be imitated in their own political contexts.[21] Early modern and enlightenment theorists of transcultural order sought to resolve the contradictions that European imperial projects posed to them. If commerce across the seas was natural, even divinely sanctioned, the ethics of how to interact with foreign communities became a problem that animated cosmopolitan theories.[22] Even a thinker as distant from, and critical of, the colonial context as Kant regarded European norms of rationality and judgment as the prerequisites for participation in the cosmopolitan order and excluded inferior, immature, and insufficiently rational peoples.[23] The superior reason of the cosmopolitans could therefore reinforce

19. A number of thinkers critical of cosmopolitanism's tendency to accompany and support imperialist projects propose reworkings of the concept that circumvent its pitfalls: Benhabib 2006: 69–74, Harvey 2009, Sassen 2006, Robbins 2012, Ingram 2013.

20. Pagden 2000: 5–6.

21. Pagden 2000: 7–18.

22. Muthu 2012.

23. Harvey 2009: 23–7. According to a survey of recent scholarship, the apparent humanism of Kant's universal principles "always harbor hidden hierarchies and exclusions—some internal to the concepts themselves, others that arise through their application": Ingram 2013: 75.

their domination over others.[24] Contemporary cosmopolitan visions similarly respond to a particular political context: American global supremacy and, its corollary, the globalization of the institutions of capitalism and liberal democracy. In the aftermath of the Iraq war, the universal laws and principles that have served as the linchpins of the modern cosmopolitan order have come to appear suspect for their roles in supporting interventionism and capitalism. At the same time, cultural cosmopolitanism—the assembling of multicultural experiences and commodities—has also come under critical scrutiny: only the moneyed have access to a range of culturally disparate resources, and the ability to cross cultural boundaries with ease is indispensable to the functioning of the international networks of exploitation characteristic of the era.[25] Proponents and critics alike acknowledge the role of various forms of cosmopolitanism in the maintenance of American, or western, political and economic dominance, while disagreeing on the possibility of recovering its emancipatory potential.

Ancient historians have participated in this cosmopolitan revival without directly addressing themselves to these debates. Some of the most productive lines of inquiry in various subfields over the past twenty-five years have centered on the key questions of cosmopolitan political thought: How are culturally distinct groups integrated into larger normative frameworks? What political institutions are conducive to such a task? How does the emerging mixture of cultures affect the self-conceptions of ruling groups and their subordinate populations? One need only recall the sophisticated literature on the once straightforward topics of Romanization and Hellenization to appreciate the sea change in scholarly priorities toward the relationship of universalism, cultural particularities, and imperialism. There has also been a corresponding growth of research on phenomena that violate modern cosmopolitan norms, such as ethnic and religious exclusion. The term "cosmopolitan," however, performs little analytical work in ancient historiography. The label tends to characterize the openness of a culture to the commodities and ideas of outsiders, or simply its comparative diversity. It is almost always a compliment, a sign that a particular ancient society practiced the same values we—the implied readers of such studies—espouse.

The study of cosmopolitanism in antiquity is thus disjointed. On the one hand, historians are producing ever more insightful studies on the politics of cultural difference. On the other, cosmopolitanism is invoked as a virtue, without further examination of its role in the shaping of the imperial formations that

---

24. It is on account of a failure to acknowledge the cultural specificity of western rationality and its incommensurability with the other ways of comprehending the world that advocates of transcultural reason would negate, that Bruno Latour critiques the leading cosmopolitan thinker Ulrich Beck. Proponents of cosmopolitanism are, in his view, poor anthropologists, or, in our view, poor historians: Latour 2004.

25. For an influential celebration of cultural cosmopolitanism, see Waldron 2000 and for its critics, Brennan 1989, Brennan 1997, Calhoun 2002, and Robbins 2012: 40–1.

gave rise to its theory and practice. A more rigorous use of the term, we suggest, can help to reveal features of ancient imperial political cultures that have remained underexplored. Like other analytical terms derived from Greco-Roman traditions, such as "political," "imperial," or "urban," the usage of "cosmopolitan" should be rooted in our own contemporary political-theoretical discourse, rather than Hellenistic or Roman thought. The aims of historical analysis differ from those of the philosophers, political theorists, and literary scholars who have developed and debated cosmopolitanism in recent decades. It is the value of the concept in elucidating social and political structures and changes rather than its abstract meaning that is of concern to historians.

Cosmopolitanism designates a complex of practices and ideals that enabled certain individuals not only to cross cultural boundaries but also to establish an enduring normative framework across them. The historically particular ideals that led certain groups to transcend distance and difference also compelled them to develop practices that could integrate geographically and culturally disparate populations. Cosmopolitanism might thus be defined as theoretical universalism in practice. Whether a conqueror, a monk, or a merchant, the cosmopolitan regards an encounter with a politically, linguistically, ethnically, and/or religiously distinct group as an opportunity to incorporate its members into their network of political, religious, or economic communities. Recognition of the legitimacy of groups qua groups has therefore been a feature of all historical cosmopolitanisms, but, as only the cosmopolitan had the capacity to recognize, this had the effect of enforcing the subordination of the recognized. Once the encountered group had accepted the terms of integration, the cosmopolitan found himself in an incommensurably superior position, as the author of their shared norms. Such relations were established against a backdrop of disparities of power, with the cosmopolitans in possession of superior political, military, ideological, or economic resources. From a historical perspective, the Kantian ideal of two rational actors agreeing to cooperate in the pursuit of mutually beneficial commerce is an illusion. Successful cosmopolitans established normative frameworks which maximized the trans-regional flow of their sources of power, further reinforcing their own superiority. As enlisted groups could enjoy a high degree of autonomy, a share of the resources in flux, and even relative status within their confines, cosmopolitan networks often proved stable entities that gradually reshaped the identities of their participants—cosmopolitans and their local interlocutors alike—in terms of the normative framework.

As a means of orchestrating trans-regional flows and exercising power through disparate populations, cosmopolitanism was an indispensable instrument of imperial rule. It gave empires a comparative advantage over state formations that either restricted their political ambitions to their own cultural spheres or subjugated populations without integrating their elites. The architects and administrators of empire had, in the first instance, to overcome difference and to derive strength from diversity and multiplicity. The nature and content of the normative frameworks they erected varied enormously, from the cosmologically grounded ethno-hierarchy of the Achaemenian empire of peoples to the essentially juridical, Roman order of republican empire of citizens. But the processes through which they were established were homologous. The imperial context constrained the extent to which local elites could adapt shared modes of representation to their own purposes. As the authors of cosmopolitan cultures, imperial elites determined the range of legitimate expressions and representations. And even the most halting attempt to articulate oneself in terms of the dominant culture on the part of subordinate groups reinforced their inferior position of dependency vis-à-vis imperial elites, the authentic cosmopolitans.

The analytical value of cosmopolitanism for the study of ancient empires resides in its focus on the intersubjective encounters of imperial elites with their subordinates in the cultural domains of language and literature, religion, and identity. At the level of subjectivity, empires generated transcultural experiences: imperial elites crisscrossed the boundaries of various groups, while local elites encountered the culture of the dominant as well as the commodities and ideas that empire brought into circulation. As we have seen, imperial elites often conceived of themselves as universal rulers, and such claims presupposed the capacity to integrate disparate human communities. If at least a rudimentary cosmopolitanism was a prerequisite for expansion, the processes of imperial formation fostered the development of new elite subjectivities that took the management and unification of different cultures as the linchpin of the ruling class. To varying degrees, imperial elites came to define themselves as cosmopolitans.

Cosmopolitanism and empire were not coterminous. As already noted, monks and merchants could construct cosmopolitan networks as expansive and enduring as their imperial counterparts. Early Buddhists and Christians famously piggybacked on the Mauryan, Chinese, and Roman empires to create constellated communities that far surpassed their respective limits. The Sogdian merchants erected a network spanning the inter-imperial spaces between North India, Central Asia, and East Asia, ca. 300-800 CE, making the crossing of cultural boundaries and mixing of religions, literatures, and arts a normative value. The most important intervention in the study of premodern cosmopolitanism has focused on one such non-imperial network: the "Sanskrit cosmopolis" of Sheldon Pollock.[26] In the first millennium CE, communities across South and Southeast Asia from Java to Kabul adopted Sanskrit literary culture as their means of political representation and cultural production. Unlike the comparable trans-regional expansion of Greek, Latin, Chinese,

---

26. Pollock 2006a: 10–19.

and Arabic literary cultures, the Sanskrit cosmopolis emerged without empire, certainly in Southeast Asia. It was a cosmopolitan network that communities, or rather their elites, opted to join. The appeal of this culture derived from its imaginative or aesthetic usefulness: its language allowed actors to conceive and to frame political actions in ways better suited to their circumstances than pre-existing resources permitted. The best-known Sanskrit text, the *Mahābhārata*, was not simply an epic poem, but a "work of political theory," whose terms were transposable to any setting.[27] What made Sanskrit language and literature cosmopolitan was its adaptability to the manifold geographical, cultural, and political circumstances encountered throughout its cosmopolis. Defining and consolidating new forms of political authority, Sanskrit cosmopolitanism was a power-culture, that is, a source of ideological power, complementary to the other sources of social power.

The cosmopolitanisms which emerged in the Near East and Mediterranean were products of imperial actors. It is the role of cosmopolitan practices, theories, and discourses in the making of the hierarchical networks through which empires functioned that is the concern of this volume. If cosmopolitanism could develop without empire, the reverse cannot be said. The real power of cosmopolitan power-cultures resides in their enabling of cultural integration, that is the bridging of the difference and distance that separated imperial and local elites. The combination of cosmopolitanism with military, economic, and political power endowed empires with their characteristic capacity to create stable exploitative regimes across disparate territories and populations. To illustrate the centrality of cosmopolitan politics to the imperial formations of the ancient Mediterranean and Near East, we venture a short history of the role of its associated practices in the consolidation and maintenance of transcultural and trans-regional networks from the rise of the Neo-Assyrians in the early first millennium to late antiquity.[28]

A SHORT HISTORY OF COSMOPOLITAN POLITICS IN THE ANCIENT NEAR EAST AND MEDITERRANEAN

Kings of the Four Quarters: The Origins of Empire in Mesopotamia

The conventional author of empire retains his historiographical position: Sargon of Akkad is the first known conqueror of far-flung territories to have ruled—rather than merely plundered—their populations, although the possibility of earlier trans-regional political formations cannot be excluded

---

27. Pollock 2013: 68–9.
28. This section aims to trace the evolution of the practices of subordination and assimilation, as well as their inter-imperial transmission, not at a comprehensive account of cosmopolitan empire. The crucial empires of the Hittites, Ptolemies, and Parthians, among others, are therefore absent.

given the limitations of the evidence.[29] From the city of Akkad along the Tigris, at the northernmost periphery of Mesopotamian civilization, he conquered the so-called "confederacy" of Sumerian city states ca. 2350 BCE.[30] His successors, above all Naram-Sin, expanded into Elam, the Persian Gulf, Syria, and even Anatolia, reaching the limits of the known world.[31] Naram-Sin accordingly reconceived kingship in terms of universal sovereignty, adopting the titles "king of the inhabited world [*kiššatu*]" and "king of the four quarters."[32] But such designs remained, in the apposite wording of Seth Richardson, "aspirational."[33] The furthest the Akkadians extended their authority from the Sumerian cities was northern Mesopotamia, and their presence in the region of Aššur appears to have been ephemeral.[34] Even in the south, the Akkadian imperial project endured for no more than a century and a half. Its successors pursued far more circumscribed goals, within the confines of the Mesopotamian core. The Akkadians nevertheless realized some of the features that would define subsequent empires in the Near East and the Mediterranean, such as the claim to universal sovereignty and the cosmopolitan practices of subordination and assimilation. The regime of Sargon simultaneously imposed a culturally distinct elite of Akkadians—whose language and political traditions were foreign—on the inhabitants of the south and cultivated cultural commonalities between conquerors and conquered.[35] On the one hand, the Akkadian elite displaced preexisting governors of Sumerian cities (*ensi*), enjoyed juridical privileges vis-à-vis their subjects, and even deprived cities of their walls, the safeguards and symbols of their political autonomy.[36] On the other hand, Sargon occupied the traditional priesthoods, as his Sumerian predecessors had done, and issued bilingual dedicatory inscriptions in Akkadian and Sumerian.[37] The culture of Akkadian elites was, moreover, available to appropriation: Akkadian names became increasingly common in the centuries following the conquest, and the Akkadian language gradually began to supersede Sumerian as what Paul-Alain

29. On possible pre-Sargonic precedents and foundations of Akkadian imperialism, see Steinkeller 1993, together with Westenholz 1999: 40.

30. Westenholz 1999: 30–51, Neumann 2014: 35–8.

31. See Sallaberger and Schrakamp 2015: 105–12 for a historical, geographical reconstruction of the military campaigns as well as the limits of Akkadian rule.

32. Michalowski 1993: 88–9, Michalowski 2010: 152–6.

33. Richardson 2012: 4.

34. The adjective "Akkadian" here refers to the ruling elite rather than an ethnic group, as the relationship between empire and ethnogenesis in early Mesopotamia remains unclear. The same principle applies throughout the volume to adjectives derived from particular empires, such as "Assyrian," "Iranian," or "Roman"; the ethnic valence of each of these terms and their particular contours will be discussed in the relevant sections.

35. The Akkadians described southern Mesopotamia as a region culturally and geographically distinct from their own, *Šumeru*, whence the term Sumer: Steinkeller 1993: 112–13.

36. Westenholz 1999: 38–9, 50–1.

37. Westenholz 1999: 37–8. Foster 1986: 48 suggests the administrative standardization evident under the Akkadians corresponded with an attempt to combine "traditional local theologies into a new imperial theology."

Beaulieu has called "the first cosmopolitan language and culture in the history of the world."[38] These seemingly contradictory tendencies of an imperial elite seeking to identify with its local counterparts while retaining its cultural and political supremacy would reappear as characteristic of the empires that emerged in the first millennium, if not of the immediate successor states of the Akkadians.

For nearly a millennium and a half, the aspirations of Sargon remained a matter of memory rather than practice. No ruler sought to conquer territories beyond Mesopotamia, and only a handful of regimes unified even the Sumerian city states. The kingdom of Ur III encompassed southern Mesopotamia as far north as Akkad and developed, on the basis of Akkadian precedents, a robust, uniform administration composed of urban elites that effectively extracted resources from throughout its core territories.[39] But even though they were able to impose officials and exactions on their northeastern periphery extending from Susa to Nineveh and occasionally to collect tribute from local rulers in the Zagros the reach of the Ur III kings beyond "familiar black-headed people of Sumer and Akkad" was always tentative and short-lived, and their continued use of the Akkadian title "rulers of the four quarters" mere bluster.[40] The subsequent second millennium kingdoms that aimed at Mesopotamian hegemony were even more circumscribed. The dissolution of the Ur III kingdom gave rise to an era of competition among the Sumerian city states for supremacy.[41] It was, however, only with the rise of Hammurabi (r. 1798-1750 BCE) that Sumer was unified in a single kingdom. Its center, Babylon, would remain the symbolic center of the south and reemerge as the hegemonic power in the region under the Kassites (1500-1155 BCE). From Ur III until the eighth-century incorporation of Babylonia into the Assyrian empire, neither empire nor cosmopolitanism is discernible in Mesopotamia, even if expansionary and imperial tendencies were widespread.[42] Trans-regional political unification occurred only exceptionally

38. Westenholz 1999: 33, Limet 2005: 378–9, Beaulieu 2006a: 211. As Foster 2015: 20 emphasizes, the post-imperial diffusion of Akkadian took place precisely because the language was not tied to a particular empire or dominant culture, much like the subsequent rise of Aramaic. Sumerian continued to be spoken as well as written into the first centuries of the second millennium: Woods 2006.

39. Steinkeller 1991: 17 views the Ur III administration as "a unique phenomenon in the history of ancient Mesopotamia," for its efficacy and extent, while Garfinkle 2013: 154 argues the nature of the evidence has led to an overestimation of "the nature of state control and its permanence" and emphasizes the co-optation of local elites.

40. Garfinkle 2013: 163. Neumann 2014: 54–5 stresses the salience of these claims to universal sovereignty among second millennium rulers.

41. Richardson 2013: 8, 16.

42. The Babylonian dynasties continued to harbor imperial aspirations—namely to rule the four quarters and to subjugate the neighboring powers of Assyria and Elam—without realizing them in an actually existing empire: Paulus 2014: 91–3. The expansionist polities of Mitanni and of the Hittites that achieved trans-regional hegemony in Anatolia, Syria, and or northern Mesopotamia in the latter half of the second millennium exhibited imperial tendencies, without forming "empires" of sufficient endurance, cultural heterogeneity, or universalism to meet the definition of the term this volume has employed.

and ephemerally, for instance, under Shamshi-Adad (r. ca. 1809–1776 BCE) in the north, and the regional hegemons of Babylon, Assyria, Mari, Elam, Mitanni, Hittite Anatolia, and Egypt acknowledged the legitimacy of their respective regimes.[43] Characteristic of the era is the skepticism with which the second millennium viewed the Akkadians. Although Sargon was celebrated unambiguously as a conqueror, the gods were believed to have deserted Naram-Sin on account of his ambitions and partly to have delegitimized the project of empire.[44] With the disappearance of political universalism, the problem of difference receded in importance. Rather than seek to integrate distant peoples, cultures, and territories as the Akkadians had envisioned, second-millennium rulers regarded outsiders as inferiors unworthy of their rule and located their legitimacy in the superiority of Mesopotamian culture.[45] And external military powers entering Mesopotamia such as the Amorites and Kassites rapidly assimilated. It was nevertheless out of such a self-satisfied city state, confident of its cultural superiority and disdainful of others, that the most enduring and consequential Mesopotamian empire emerged.

The Assyrians created an empire out of these Mesopotamian political models and structures. In the latter half of the second millennium BCE, the city state of Aššur expanded to encompass the entirety of northern Mesopotamia in a political system that resembled the states of Ur III or Babylonia: culturally uniform, with an intensive administrative apparatus and a single political center. In the ninth century, however, the Assyrians not only conquered territories as far as the Euphrates but also subjected the Aramaean kingdoms beyond, beginning an expansionary era that would ultimately make the eighth- and seventh-century Assyrian kings rulers of an empire extending from the Persian Gulf across the Fertile Crescent to Egypt. They therefore regarded themselves as universal sovereigns and gave plausibility to the claim to rule the four quarters of the earth that had been lacking since the Akkadians.[46] They possessed a much more highly developed cosmopolitan ideology than their third millennium predecessors, abundantly evident in their palatial art, royal inscriptions, and quotidian administrative documents, according to which the god Aššur enjoined the Assyrian kings to bring order to the disordered lands beyond Assyria.[47] The palaces and capitals of the Assyrian kings became cosmic centers where the various peoples, languages, arts, and sciences of the world were to be reunified.

---

43. As Brisch 2011: 717 observes, "most 'imperial' or territorial structures lasted no more than decades and were often threatened by rebellions, economic crises, or internal power struggles." On interstate recognition, see Podany 2010.

44. Brisch 2011: 716, Neumann 2014: 39–40.

45. Michalowski 2010: 157–64.

46. For the development of Assyrian cosmo-geographical conceptions of the world and universal rule in the course of imperial expansion, see Lang and Rollinger 2010 and Zamazalová 2013.

47. Machinist 1993: 84–91, Liverani 2011: 263–4.

In seeking to collect the knowledge of the empire's population, the celebrated library of Aššurbanipal (r. 666-625 BCE) embodied the universalist aspirations of the Assyrians. As Sargon II proclaimed in a palatial inscription, the "expert Assyrians" had taken their rightful place as the "overseers and foreman" of the "people from the four quarters of the world . . . inhabitants of mountains and lowlands."[48]

To rule these disparate populations and territories, the conquerors adopted two distinct strategies. Within the imperial core between the Euphrates and the Zagros, the so-called "land of Aššur," they practiced a politics of erasure: local elites were displaced and deported, and Assyrian officials and administrative structures were installed in their place. Massive deportations of peoples and their mixed resettlement in the core deprived conquered populations of their lands, identities, and traditions, making them mere subjects of the Assyrians in a process of "Assyrianization."[49] In the royal inscriptions, the kings referred to all of their subjects as "Assyrians," expressly denying the salience of their cultural particularities.[50] But as they incorporated territories in Syro-Palestine, Anatolia, southern Mesopotamia, and the Zagros, they subordinated populations through a system of clientage.[51] Local rulers and elites remained in place and retained their cultural identities, as long as they subjugated themselves to the Assyrian kings through oaths and their gods acknowledged the supremacy of Aššur. Ruling classes that abrogated their allegiance or failed to fulfill their obligations to the Assyrians—such as tribute—were Assyrianized, their political traditions erased and their populations and territories integrated into the land of Aššur. The comparative frequency with which Assyrian clients rebelled and had to be assimilated points to the "crisis of confidence" that Seth Richardson sees as characteristic of Assyrian elite culture. The failure of the Assyrians to create a transcultural elite limited their ability to rule distant territories. To compensate, as Karen Radner has demonstrated, the Assyrian kings bound their elites ever more tightly to their persons through the creation of an unprecedentedly robust system of correspondence and surveillance and the use of eunuchs wholly dependent on their ruler.[52] If their failure to overcome the problem of difference led their clients, especially Babylon and Media, to draw on neighboring powers to dismantle the empire in the late seventh century, the Assyrians bequeathed to their successors potent models for the ideological and infrastructural articulation of imperial power.

48. Liverani 2011: 264.

49. Beaulieu 2005: 51, Bedford 2009: 55-6, Radner 2014a: 106. This simultaneously entailed a linguistic Aramaicization that appears to have complemented Assyrian political identities: Beaulieu 2006a: 193-5.

50. Machinist 1993: 90.

51. Lanfranchi 2003: 111-12, Bedford 2009: 45-6, 53-6, Radner 2013: 449-51.

52. Radner 2011: 359-61, Radner 2014b.

The Achaemenian Art of Subordination

The Achaemenian empire—also known by its Greek name as "Persian"—emerged in the course of the conquests of Cyrus the Great (r. 559-530 BCE) and his son Cambyses (r. 530-522 BCE) and the wide-reaching administrative reforms of Darius I (r. 522-486BCE). It was the largest political formation the world had yet seen. Stretching from the Nile and the Balkans in the west to the Indus in the east, its regime encompassed a vast, polyglot population in the tens of millions and endured more than two centuries until the partial disintegration of its territories after Alexander's death. While the Achaemenians drew extensively on Assyrian institutions, the key to the consolidation of Persian power across such culturally and geographically disparate territories was their novel approach to difference, rooted in their distinctive cosmological framework. They perfected the cosmopolitan practice of subordination, which operated in conjunction with the horizontal assimilation of a culturally distinct ruling class.[53]

The Achaemenian kings committed themselves to a cosmological project of restoring the primordial unity of the world and its human population.[54] Royal inscriptions situate their actions within a cosmological struggle between Truth (Old Persian, *arta*) and the divisive force of the Lie (OP *drauga*). The royal capitals and the famous "paradises" (OP *paridaida*) were two sites where these ambitions were realized on a microcosmic scale.[55] Alongside these evocations of lost unity, however, Achaemenian kings also asserted and affirmed the ethnic differences within the empire. Through texts, images, and quotidian administrative documents, the regime articulated its own ethnic identity as "Persian" while organizing the conquered populations into discrete ethnic groups. The Achaemenian kings ruled through the *kāra* of the Persians, "'the people' in times of peace and 'the army' in times of war."[56] The Apadana reliefs from the Palace of Darius at Persepolis represented the empire as a hierarchically organized complex of *dahyāva*, a term that melded the concepts of "people" and "land," ranging from Thrace to Gandhara.[57] The Persian figures are clearly differentiated from other peoples, as the only ethnic group that owed the king no tribute.[58] In the documents of the Persepolis Archive, subject peoples were categorized and administratively organized according to their ethnicity; whether sub-elites or laborers at Persepolis, they were continually defined as Babylonian, Armenian, or Scythian.[59] The adjectives Persian and Elamite—designating the successors of the Neo-Elamite regime who were closely

53. Barjamovic 2012: 47.
54. Lincoln 2012.
55. Lincoln 2012: ch. 1.
56. Lincoln 2012: 407.
57. Lincoln 2012: ch. 6.
58. Kuhrt 2001: 103–9.
59. Henkelman and Stolper 2009: 283, 292–3. See also the argument of Stolper 1984: 310 for the administrative, juridical organization of ethnic groups in enclaves with a high degree of social cohesion: "the many

identified with the Persians from the inception of the empire—were, by contrast, largely absent, as if their ethnic identities needed no reinforcement.[60] The ethnic groups the Achaemenians identified existed prior to their incorporation into the empire, but they obtained more clearly defined boundaries through the acts of interpellation and administrative reorganization evident in the Persepolis Archive. In subordinating these peoples, the Persians also recognized the legitimacy of their culture, language, and religion as well as their elites. They addressed themselves to their subjects in their respective local idioms.[61] They supported local religious institutions.[62] Most important, they co-opted local elites who could retain their political traditions and identities and maintain the confidence of their constituencies, thus overcoming the problem of cultural authenticity the Assyrians had confronted.[63] It was through the reproduction rather than the erasure of difference that the Achaemenians consolidated a network of sub-elites subordinate to the ruling Persians.

The recognition and organization of otherness reinforced Persian supremacy. Much as the kings stood unambiguously above and beyond the subordinate peoples that sustained them in royal rock reliefs, so too did a horizontally integrated class of aristocratic Persians rule over its subjects.[64] In the words of Pierre Briant, a "dominant ethno-class" largely monopolized the highest offices of the empire throughout its territories, with only a handful of—mostly Median—exceptions.[65] His point was that it was simultaneously ethnically and socially exclusive. The satraps who ruled in the place of the kings in provinces were drawn almost exclusively from dynasties genealogically intertwined with the royal house.[66] Based in regional courts that formed microcosms of the royal court, sometimes complete with their own paradises, the satraps coordinated and monitored the activities of varied local elites and sub-rulers over their vast geographical remits, with the assistance of

---

national and ethnic labels used in Achaemenid texts were not merely a device with which vainglorious rulers expressed the vastness of their domains . . . but were also the result of some reality of legal behavior that was necessary for the management of a polyglot, continental empire."

60. Henkelman and Stolper 2009: 275. On the merging Elamite and Persian elite cultures as a defining feature of Achaemenian imperialism, see Henkelman 2008.

61. Stolper 1984: 299–301, Briant 2002: 77. On the symbolics of the trilingual inscriptions and their implied "language ranking," see Finn 2011.

62. Jursa 2007: 77–8, Khatchadourian 2012: 979.

63. Jursa 2007: 78–83. For a case study of elite co-optation that reveals how much could be gained, in material terms, from Achaemenian rule, see Waerzeggers 2014: 113–32, 138–9. The Babylonian Marduk-rēmanni was able not only to consolidate his local position but also to expand his mercantile interests far beyond Mesopotamia, as far afield as Syro-Palestine and the Iranian plateau and to profit directly from the favors of the court in Susa. Jursa 2015: 604 points to the use of elite Babylonian houses, some of whom owed their status to the Achaemenian court, rather than temple institutions themselves.

64. For this representation of the kings, see Root 2000.

65. Briant 1988, Briant 2002: ch. 8, Dusinberre 2013: 77–8, 92, Kuhrt 2014: 119–20. One important Babylonian exception was Bēlšunu the satrap in late fifth century: Stolper 1987.

66. Klinkott 2005: 47–54.

strategically scattered military installations.[67] The ethno-class was relatively small, presumably one key to its cohesion, and in many areas satraps relied directly on the cooperation of non-Persian elites. The satraps of Beyond-the-River, for instance, who administered territories west of the Euphrates, ruled over city states in Cyprus and Phoenicia that possessed their own kings and provinces such as Samaria and Judea that were governed by indigenous aristocrats.[68] In Anatolia and Mesopotamia, too, local dynasts answered to Persian satraps. Only in Egypt—a region the empire failed fully to discipline—do local governors appear to have been Persian.[69] Throughout the Achaemenian period, archaeological evidence for elite practice—such as seals, palatial architecture, religious ritual, and funerary monuments—suggests a relatively clear cultural divide between Persians and the local elites with whom they shared the burdens of government.[70] There are indications of elite emulation, but the predominant pattern is one of continuity and innovation within local traditions.[71] Even the adoption of Persian practices could not undermine the fundamental difference—irreducibly rooted in genealogy—between the ethno-class and its subjects, as the continual reaffirmation of ethnic identities in administrative practice made plain. The Persians derived their trans-regional, transcultural power precisely from their ability to supersede and to organize the different human communities under their rule.

The Seleucids and the Achaemenian Inheritance

After Alexander's conquest of the Achaemenian empire and the fragmentation that followed his death, Seleukos Nikator (r. 305-281 BCE) and his successors seized the bulk of what had been the Persian empire and ruled over it until the second century BCE, when the hitherto dependent Parthian kingdom wrested control of the Iranian plateau from them; a rump Seleucid kingdom persisted until the Roman annexation of Syria in 64 BCE. Its scale and diversity made it the most complex and the most obviously imperial of the Hellenistic kingdoms that emerged from the collapse of Alexander's conquest state.[72] Like its Persian predecessor, the Seleucid empire of the third century BCE was a vast multiethnic conglomerate, encompassing a complex mix of Hellenic, Anatolian, Judean, Mesopotamian, and Persian cultures, to mention only the most important. It bore almost as many faces as the regions it encompassed, and general

67. Khatchadourian 2012: 966–9, Dusinberre 2013. For a provincial paradise, see Knauß, Gagošidse, and Babaev 2013.
68. Briant 2002: 487–90, 713–17. On the nature and evolution of this particularly extensive satrapy, see Stolper 1989: 296–8.
69. Briant 2002: 481–4, Ruzicka 2012.
70. Garrison 1991, Khatchadourian 2012.
71. Dusinberre 2003 sees signs of widespread Persian influence in the material culture of Lydian elites in the satrapal capital of Sardis.
72. See Fischer-Bovet's chapter for an analysis of the Ptolemaic kingdom as an empire.

characterizations of the nature of Seleucid rule have often proven elusive.[73] Unlike its predecessor, it possessed no coherent cosmological ideology through which to articulate a regime; the early Seleucids legitimated by right of conquest, by the "spear."[74] While adopting Achaemenian institutions to their own purposes, the Seleucids introduced a new Greek ethno-class with its own distinct elite culture as well as a novel dynastic cult of divinized rulers.[75] It gave rise to a trans-regional network of self-consciously Greek colonizers who established poleis and the institutions of Greek culture in their colonies, even if they intermarried and shared settlements with the local population.[76] In the Bactrian city of Ai Khanoum, for instance, the Greek colonizers established a polis apart from the preexisting Achaemenian urban center and distinguished themselves through their ceramics, temples, gymnasium, and agora while dwelling alongside local subalterns with their own characteristic mature culture.[77]

The Seleucid imperial elite comprised a relatively closed ruling class of Greco-Macedonian aristocrats in possession of the highest offices. The evidence for the ethnic identity of the court elite—principally onomastic—suggests its members were largely descendants of the initial conquerors.[78] It thus conforms to Briant's model of an ethno-class, albeit with rather more porous boundaries than its Persian predecessor appears to have maintained.[79] Greek ethnicity did not reliably translate into status. Neither individual Greeks nor polis communities appear to have enjoyed particular privileges, apart from opportunities to pursue profitable careers in the king's service.[80] They had, moreover, no monopoly on such opportunities. In Mesopotamia, Persia, and Bactria, local elites with names that clearly distinguished them from Greeks held office at local and regional level, in military, fiscal, and urban administrations, even if

73. Plischke 2014: 315. Its polycentric structure, with highly mobile kings, contributed to the diversity of its structures and local arrangements: Martinez-Sève 2003: 234.

74. Martinez-Sève 2003: 236–9.

75. On the dynastic cults, see Chaniotis 2003 and Canepa 2015.

76. On poleis as Seleucid power bases, see Held 2002, Martinez-Sève 2003: 230, Kosmin 2014: 183–211, and Plischke 2014: 94–139. Mairs 2013: 449 argues intermarriage was "all but universal," while Himmelfarb 1999 emphasizes its rarity in Judea, likely due to its particular religious culture.

77. Martinez-Sève 2014a suggests the local population ultimately rebelled against the Greeks and provoked their flight. Hannestad 2013: 110–11 and Mairs 2014: 98–9, by contrast, describe the material culture of Ai Khanoum as "hybrid."

78. Habicht 1958, long influential, argued that the names of known Seleucid officers from the third century BCE suggested that only about 2.5% were not Macedonian or Greek. Sherwin-White and Kuhrt 1993: 123–5 question the value of the personal names alone as an index of ethnicity, point to the possibility of intermarriage with non-Greek aristocracies, and highlight a few known instances of non-Greek *philoi*, concluding that "this suggests at the very least that the Seleukid ruling group was not an impermeable, unchanging elite rigidly marked off from the ruled purely along ethnic lines." The most recent analysis, however, has confirmed Habicht's thesis: Strootman 2007: 126 reexamined the 41 *philoi* of Antiochos III with known ethnic identities and found that only three were not Macedonians or from a Greek city state. See further Capdetrey 2007: 389–92 and Strootman 2011.

79. So more guardedly Capdetrey 2007: 392.

80. Sherwin-White and Kuhrt 1993: 166 show that Greek cities were subject to tax, military service, garrisons, and governors, with some exceptional poleis enjoying exemptions.

the top stratum remained Greco-Macedonian.[81] The Seleucids systematically intermarried with the aristocracies they subjugated, especially the Persians, a practice that allowed them to forge stable ties with local elites without undermining their own distinctiveness.[82] Such inter-elite relationships were all the more necessary for the distance of the ruling class from its native Macedonia. It was an empire without a homeland.[83] Despite their colonies, the Seleucids depended on culturally distinct local elites no less than the Persians had. [84]

The evidence for Seleucid interaction with local elites is massively skewed toward the Greek cities, thanks to their distinctive epigraphic habit.[85] Babylonia, Judea, and the eastern provinces are the only other regions for which we have any significant evidence for the subjective experience of empire by local populations or for their interaction with Greek colonizers. The surviving material suggests that the Seleucids, like the Achaemenians before them, made extensive use of local idioms in their interactions with their subjects. With the Greek city states, the Seleucid kings conducted an ongoing dialogue of royal letters and city decrees in a markedly Hellenic discourse of euergetism which they shared with the other successor kingdoms and the wider Hellenic world.[86] The very limited evidence for royal pronouncements in Mesopotamia suggests that there the Seleucids inscribed themselves within very different, and distinctly Mesopotamian, traditions.[87] In their dynastic cults, moreover, they incorporated Persian and other local religious elements.[88] That is not to say that local traditions remained unchanged in hermetic isolation. The Seleucid rulers evidently valued ethnographic capital and acquired expertise in local traditions.[89] They collaborated with local interlocutors to find ways to embed overarching Seleucid norms and symbols into existing traditions so as to fix them within an imperial frame.[90] Characteristic of Seleucid rule was the development of distinct idioms to rule different populations that largely retained their local inflections.

But Seleucid polyphony was conducted largely in Greek. Hellenic culture had greater potential as a mechanism of assimilation than Persian culture had in the Achaemenian empire, with its foundations in cultural competences that were

81. Plischke 2014: 42–55, 317.
82. Capdetrey 2007: 124–33, Plischke 2014: 28–32.
83. The implications of this are a leading theme of Kosmin 2014.
84. Capdetrey 2007: 300–306.
85. Martinez-Sève 2003: 226–9.
86. Ma 2002: ch. 4, Bencivenni 2014.
87. See Stevens, this volume.
88. Canepa 2010b: 7–10, Plischke 2014: 162–8, 323–4, and Canepa 2015: 85 emphasizing that while the cults incorporated local religious traditions the royal image was represented "exclusively according to the visual culture of Macedonian charismatic kingship."
89. See Kosmin 2013 on the court's investment in ethnography.
90. See Kosmin 2011 for an excellent case study of the Borsippa cylinder (discussed further by Stevens, in this volume), showing that the "combination of a carefully selected traditionalism and a subdued innovation allowed it to reconfigure age-old Babylonian religious practice for a new and foreign dynasty."

open to appropriation, not least mastery of a written corpus that could be circulated widely. Already relatively widespread before Alexander's conquest, having
spread with and around the Greek diaspora in the Mediterranean, Greek culture was pushed deep into continental Asia by the colonial cities of Alexander
and the Seleucids. Although scholarship once downplayed the appropriation
of Hellenic practices by other subject peoples, recent work emphasizes the
Hellenizing currents among the local elites of Phoenicia, Judea, Arachosia, and
India, which have no parallel in the Achaemenian period.[91] Nevertheless, the
very limited evidence for local elite cultures suggests a strong tendency toward
localism. As Kathryn Stevens shows in this volume, local elites in Greek Asia
Minor and Babylonia inscribed their experience of Seleucid rule in very different
and distinctly local traditions.[92] On the whole, the Seleucids can be seen to have
continued the Achaemenian strategies of subordination—recognizing, preserving, and organizing the diverse cultures they ruled, even though assimilative
tendencies are discernible in the adoption of Hellenic culture in their realm.

Subordination and Assimilation under Rome

The assimilative mode of integrating local elites—previously restricted in scope to
at most a few subgroups—reached its fullest development in the Roman empire.
But even in Roman practice, it took time before assimilation altogether displaced
the familiar techniques of subordination. Having achieved dominance in penin-
sular Italy by the early third century BCE, the city of Rome established hegemony
over the western Mediterranean in the third century by defeating Carthage
in two prolonged wars and then extended it to the eastern Mediterranean in
the second century, displacing the Seleucids and other Hellenistic kingdoms.
Hitherto a littoral power, Rome gradually extended its control into the continental interiors, most notably in temperate Europe where it reached the Rhine
and Danube by the early first century CE. The end of the first century BCE also
saw the establishment of monarchy under the first emperor Augustus. From the
first century CE until the collapse of the western empire in the fifth century CE,
Roman emperors ruled over a population that probably exceeded fifty million at
its height, dispersed across a territory of around five million square kilometers.

As in other empires, locally inflected religious institutions played an important role in underpinning imperial power. The import of local religions into
the imperial center, the export of Roman gods to conquered lands and the acceptance and promotion of a variety of locally rooted ruler cults contributed
to binding local power wielders to the imperial center.[93] But, in other respects,

---

91. Sherwin-White and Kuhrt 1993: ch. 6, Himmelfarb 1998, Bernard 2005, Gardner 2007, Mairs 2014: ch. 3.
92. See also Clancier 2011 on the Babylonian elite and its use of cuneiform culture as means of distinction.
93. The impact of empire on Roman religion is traced by Ando 2008. The export of metropolitan gods to colonies and conquered populations is analyzed by Ando 2007 and Woolf 2009a. The local nature of Roman ruler cult is emphasized by Price 1984 and Fishwick 1987–2005.

relations between the imperial elite and the various local elites of the empire gradually diverged from earlier practice in several important ways. The first is in the sphere of communicative action.[94] Where its most important predecessors had favored the use of local idioms, recognizing local "power-cultures" as such and appropriating their languages and tropes, the Roman empire largely ignored indigenous traditions—at least in the western provinces. There was no real attempt to recognize or exploit the specific ideological resources of the Punic, Iberian, Greek, or Celtic communities that were incorporated into the empire—beyond the elementary recognition of existing elites as fellow aristocrats. Instead the Roman rulers spoke everywhere in Latin, legitimated their hegemony through a universalist discourse of administrative rationality, and expected their interlocutors to reply in kind.[95] The situation was more complex in the east, where Greek was the dominant language among local elites. Emperors and administrators regularly addressed Greek-speaking communities in Greek rather than Latin.[96] Normative texts such as edicts were often issued bilingually and the few surviving transcripts of hearings before provincial governors and even emperors suggest that Roman courts even heard cases in Greek.[97] Roman administrators did not just use the Greek language, they often drew on its distinctive ideological resources to legitimate Roman rule to Greek-speaking populations—typical of the now familiar technique of subordination.[98] But Latin remained the idiom of imperial administration. Significantly, when in the fourth and fifth centuries the eastern half of the empire began to be ruled by a separate government, the governing elite of this "Greek Roman Empire"— to adopt the language of Fergus Millar—continued to communicate with each other and with their subjects in Latin.[99]

The Romans also showed an unparalleled readiness to incorporate subalterns into the metropolitan political community. The most famous example is the extension of Roman citizenship, though the process was gradual and geographically uneven. It proceeded through countless small-scale grants to individual families and communities punctuated by two massive block grants, to the population of Italy in 90-89 BCE and to all free inhabitants of the empire in 212/213 CE.[100] The senatorial and equestrian elite that administered the empire—a small core of approximately a thousand men in the first century, growing to more than four thousand in the fourth—also became progressively more open

94. On communicative action, see especially Ando 2000, Rowe 2002, and Noreña 2011.
95. On Roman claims to legitimacy based on the rationality of rule, see especially Ando 2000.
96. Kaimio 1979.
97. Williams 1975, Coles 1966.
98. See Lavan, this volume, on imperial letters to Greek cities.
99. Corcoran 1996: 22–3, 295–6, 350–2 observes that Latin became more prominent in imperial communications in the east from the later third and early fourth centuries. Millar 2006 highlights the role played by the imperial language in the eastern Roman empire of the fifth century.
100. Sherwin-White 1973 and, for a quantitative perspective, Lavan 2016.

to recruits from the periphery. As late as the first century BCE, the senate was almost exclusively Italian. By the late second century CE, the majority of senators stemmed from families whose origins can be traced to regions outside Italy.[101] But that figure conceals massive regional variation. In principle, high office was open to any Roman citizen with sufficient wealth to meet the property requirement. But it also required imperial permission to stand for office and that required the support of powerful patrons.[102] In practice it took centuries for many provinces to produce more than a handful of senators.[103] Although progress was slow, the equestrian and senatorial orders did gradually develop into a truly trans-regional aristocracy. By the fourth century, the senate had become the political arm of the landowning classes of the Mediterranean world.[104]

The assimilation of local elites was also facilitated by the particular configuration of Roman elite culture, which lent itself to appropriation by provincials.[105] The early Roman emperors witnessed an unprecedented degree of cultural convergence in the territories they ruled, especially in the west of the empire. The depth of change and the degree of homogeneity it produced are hotly debated— as is the extent to which it can be regarded as the product of concerted policy, rather than uncoordinated local initiative. But it is incontestable that the material cultures of the provinces were transformed to a degree that has no parallel among earlier empires.[106] The cultural divide between local elites in different parts of the empire was narrower than ever before. By the second century CE, a Roman official might be transferred from the Atlas to the Rhine and find himself dealing with local notables who drank the same wine, ate from the same tableware, spoke the same language, and had been educated in the same texts. Again, however, the eastern provinces stand somewhat apart because their elites continued to speak Greek and acquired only limited competence in Latin. Even here the differences were gradually bridged. In the second and early third centuries, strategies of distinction that privileged high competence in a stylized, literary form of Greek permeated even western cities.[107] In the fourth century, the expansion of the imperial administration provided a powerful incentive for eastern elites to learn Latin, the language of law courts and administration.[108]

---

101. See Barbieri 1952, Hammond 1957, and the studies assembled in the edited volume of Panciera 1982.

102. Saller 1982: 42–3.

103. Eck 1995-8: 2:280–90.

104. The ways in which the Constantinian reforms reconfigured the relationship between universal rulers and local elites are explored by Heather 1998 and Weisweiler 2014. The best treatments of the institutional structure of the late Roman senate are Garbarino 1988 and Chastagnol 1992. Excellent sociological analyses are provided by Löhken 1982, Salzman 2002, and Skinner 2013.

105. Woolf 1998 remains the most incisive case study.

106. Woolf 1995, Keay and Terrenato 2001, Hingley 2005.

107. Richter 2011.

108. The elite culture generated by schools in late antiquity is mapped by Kaster 1988, Watts 2006, and Cribiore 2007.

Together, these mechanisms of assimilation created ever greater common ground between provincial governors and the municipal elites that they governed, with the result that it becomes ever more difficult to see the cultural divide between imperial and local elites that is so obvious in earlier empires.

The Empire of the Cosmopolitan Iranians

The Iranian empire represented the culmination of ancient Near Eastern patterns of empire formation, as the longest lasting of the territorial extensive states that had ruled from Mesopotamia since the Achaemenians. In 226 CE, Ardashir I conquered the various Parthian kingdoms from eastern Arabia to Bactria to establish an empire that would endure for four centuries, until its dissolution in the face of the Islamic conquests in the 630s.[109] His court called the polity Ērānšahr, "the empire of the Iranians (*ēr*)," a reference to the mythical rulers of the homeland of Zoroaster known from the Avesta.[110] What made the Iranian empire—also known by the name of its ruling house as "Sasanian"—distinct from its Parthian predecessor was a well-developed ideological apparatus that facilitated both the cohesion of an ethno-class and the subordination of their culturally disparate local elites.[111] In naming themselves and allied aristocrats *ēr*, the Sasanian kings of kings claimed to succeed the mythical rulers that had accelerated the restoration of the world through their promotion of the Zoroastrian religion according to its cosmology. The ideas of Iran and of Iranian ethnicity therefore depended on the institutions of what Zoroastrians called the "Good Religion." If priests had practiced rituals and transmitted traditions that could be broadly described as Zoroastrian for upward of a millennium before the rise of the Sasanians, the religion only became institutionalized across the Near East with a hierarchy of religious specialists, a network of religious complexes, and reliable royal patronage in the course of the formation of the empire. Zoroastrian religious officials, their courts, and their fire temples not only assisted the Iranian court directly in ruling its territories but also conveyed and communicated the shared myths, genealogies, and symbols through which preexisting Parthian aristocrats—who practiced highly varied forms of Zoroastrianism—came to reimagine themselves as Iranian (*ēr*) and as the co-rulers of Ērānšahr together with the Sasanians.[112] An ethnogenetic process thus attended the co-optation of the leading aristocratic houses after Ardashir

109. Huff 2008 provides an overview of the consolidation of Ardashir's power, privileging the archaeological evidence.

110. Gnoli 1989.

111. The rise of the Sasanians should nevertheless be viewed against the backdrop of an Arsacid "Konsolidierung" from the first century CE onward: Hauser 2005: 203.

112. For the role of Zoroastrian priests in the administration, see Gignoux 1983 and Shaked 1990; and for the importance of their jurisprudence in aristocratic strategies of economic and biological reproduction, see Macuch 1995 and Macuch 2004. Canepa 2013 underlines the role of fire temples in the articulation of Sasanian power.

I defeated the Parthian kings.[113] In addition to integrating the ancient Parthian aristocratic houses into a trans-regional network, the Iranian court also installed allied aristocratic dynasties in regions whose local elites were not Zoroastrian therefore could not become Iranian.[114] The name of the empire perfectly captured its nature as a complex of territories (*šahr*) in the possession of an ethno-class of Iranians who formed the dominant elite in each of its regions. Although competing interests made antagonism among elites a structural feature of Iranian political culture, such conflicts only rarely jeopardized the foundations of the alliance of aristocrats and autocrats that the idea of Iran, at least until the Islamic conquests.

Beneath the Iranian strata, local elites exhibited cultural specificities particularly challenging to their integration into an empire conceived in Zoroastrian terms. Greek, Arabic, Armenian, Bactrian, and, especially, Aramaic in its various dialects remained dominant in Mesopotamia, Khuzestan, the Caucasus, and Bactria and often served as vehicles for transmitting distinct histories, ideas, and political traditions. Most important, religions at variance with Zoroastrianism such as Christianity, Mandaeism, and Rabbinic Judaism flourished throughout the empire, particularly in its Mesopotamian heartland and along its strategic frontiers.[115] As Richard Payne argues in this volume, the Iranian court confronted the dilemma of irreconcilable cosmologies through the innovation of practices rooted in Zoroastrianism that enabled the Iranians to subordinate and integrate religious communities potentially unconducive to cooperation, notably East Syrian Christianity. The successful overcoming of religious difference facilitated the inclusion of non-Zoroastrian, non-Iranian elites in imperial networks and institutions, albeit in positions inferior to the Iranians, and the recognition of their nobility at a court that considered an aristocratic genealogy the prerequisite for the exercise of power. Armenian and Mesopotamian Christian aristocrats became leading military commanders and fiscal officials, even if they never attained parity with the Zoroastrian Iranians.[116] At the same time, Christian bishops and Jewish exilarchs became representatives of the Iranian court, often undertaking administrative tasks on its behalf.[117] As a consequence, assimilative tendencies are discernible among subordinate groups. To varying degrees, sub-elites reframed their identities and histories in light of the mythical-historical framework of Ērānšahr, participated in the pan-imperial

---

113. The sigillographic evidence demonstrates aristocrats in the service of the court presented themselves as *ēr*, even as they retained distinctive lineages and regional identities: Gyselen 2007: 248–77. Pourshariati 2008: 59–160 provides the most thorough prosopographical account of the Parthian houses, while always emphasizing centrifugal tendencies rather than their continual participation in the project of empire across four centuries.

114. This process is amply documented in northern Mesopotamia and Arabia: Morony 1976: 41, Toral-Niehoff 2014: 68–74, and Payne 2015: 137–8.

115. Debié 2010, Toral-Niehoff 2014: 183–94, Mokhtarian 2015.

116. Garsoïan 2009, Payne 2015: 133–9.

117. McDonough 2008, Herman 2012.

Zoroastrian feasts and festivals and adopted noble genealogies that intersected with those of the Iranians as well as the juridical institutions of aristocratic reproduction.[118] Without themselves becoming Iranian, linguistically and religiously distinct local elites claimed membership in the hierarchical political order the Iranian court created as well as a share of its resources. The political culture that developed on the basis of Zoroastrian institutions successfully integrated cultures that were potentially contradictory with, and even hostile toward, one another under the carapace the cosmopolitan Iranians erected. Their practices of subordination and selective assimilation generated the most politically stable of ancient Near Eastern empires.

CONCLUSION

The normative frameworks the various Near Eastern and Mediterranean empires erected to integrate local elites differed markedly in their ideological contents and in their institutions. The Akkadians relied on a complex of deities and temples that Mesopotamian elites could share, while the Assyrians required universal assent to the god Aššur and his representative, the king. They therefore drew on preexisting religious sources of norms and symbols, and religion played an equally central role in the formation of the Persian, Seleucid, and Iranian ethno-political orders. The Achaemenian and Iranian discourses of ethnicity derived—certainly in the latter case and probably also in the former—from a Zoroastrian hierarchical organization of peoples according to their religious merits and contributions and was communicated, whether in inscriptions or in reliefs, in highly cosmological language. The idioms of local elites, too, were largely dependent on religious norms, symbols, and institutions, and the joining of a variety of deities, discourses, and religions in a single overarching system required the careful management of difference we have seen to have been characteristic of these empires. The Seleucids and Ptolemies introduced a secular normative framework with Hellenic culture as well as the religious institution of divinized kingship—a novelty in the Near East, if not in Egypt. The latter could easily be tailored to accommodate local religious idioms, while the former was hardly incompatible with local religions. Religious discourses continued to play a crucial role in the Roman empire, but the Romans also claimed to establish a rational order founded on administrative and legal norms. Juridical institutions such as citizenship and other privileged statuses provided important mechanisms for according status to local elites. Moreover, the convergence of local aristocratic cultures produced a new pan-imperial idiom for expressing social distinction through a repertoire of cultural symbols that were reproduced

---

118. Garsoïan 1997, Herman 2012, 239–57, Payne 2015.

by imperial and local elites in manifold local contexts throughout the Roman world. Regardless of their differences, each of these transcultural normative frameworks gave local elites the capacity to act authoritatively and legitimately from the perspective of both the imperial elite and the local population they were encharged to manage, at least in empires that endured. The practice of cosmopolitanism translated the fundamental problem of distance and difference into assets, by facilitating the exploitation of ever larger populations and territories.

The chapters that follow present case studies of universal rulers and local elites managing the problems of cultural difference in successive empires. They vary in their focus, their selection of evidence, and their methodology. But they return again and again to a core set of questions. How did universal rulers define themselves in relation to the populations they ruled? How did they invite local elites to see their place in the imperial order? How did local elites refashion themselves in the course of their encounter with the imperial regime?

2

Getting Confident

The Assyrian Development of Elite Recognition Ethics

Seth Richardson

As an urban oligarchy embarking upon an imperial project, Assyrian elites lacked an ideological roadmap for managing the cultural differences they encountered, or for preserving their integrity as a trans-regional class. If rank, prestige goods, and landed estates distinguished the imperial elite, they were primarily bound through their personal oaths of loyalty to the king rather than a shared class consciousness. Competition among elites is thus more visible in their correspondence than consolidation. "Confidence" was something the king conferred instead of the common possession of a self-affirming trans-regional elite. They therefore also were incapable of framing their relations with local, subordinated elites as encounters of groups, and the Assyrian regime appears neither to have valued nor to have acquired ethnographic capital. The legitimacy of both imperial and local elites alike depended on royal confidence, a loyalty to the center that overrode all relations with the province—its sub-elites and subjects—that were necessary to ensure effective domination. Toward the end of their empire, the Assyrian kings began to acknowledge the autonomous legitimacy of local elites and the importance of maintaining their distance from the center. In so doing, they prefigured the development of actual cosmopolitanism.

PROSPECT

The empire Assyria built across the tenth to the seventh centuries BC could draw on some earlier models for establishing control over conquered lands.* But even where precedents for ruling and being ruled were available in principle, they had often not been in practice for generations. Assyria, its provinces, vassals, or enemies had neither dominated nor been dominated for centuries,

---

* All abbreviations follow the *Assyrian Dictionary of the Oriental Institute of the University of Chicago* (CAD), vols. U and W (Chicago, 2010), including the rubric SAA identifying the nineteen volumes of the series *State Archives of Assyria* (Helsinki, 1987-2003). I would like to thank the volume editors, Simonetta Ponchia, and an anonymous reader for their helpful comments which substantially improved this chapter; and Geoff Emberling for the many conversations which helped to bring form to some of its concepts.

and the political culture of the Late Bronze Age had been virtually erased.[1] To a great extent, Assyria not only had to reinvent specific imperial modes and styles for imitation, but even the basic principles of elite identification and emulation. The cosmopolitanism and elite integration achieved in the Neo-Assyrian world was thus relatively modest and sociologically limited when compared to the succeeding Neo-Babylonian and Persian empires. But its impact on a conceptual level was enormous, posing the questions that made cosmopolitan formations a necessary and categorical answer in subsequent empires.

This chapter will begin by exploring the practices of Assyrian political culture for elite integration and assessing their impact. Finding them relatively weak, and not wishing to institutionalize them, I will turn my attention to a bedrock paradox of imperial cosmopolitanism: as much power as provincial elites accrued in adopting imperial ways, those postures consequently undercut their claims to the local political authority and cultural authenticity on which their usefulness to the empire was based in the first place. This unenviable dilemma required vassals and provincial elites to constantly walk a fine line between performances of compliance and autonomy. That then produces further questions: Which act was real? Was control essentially a question of cultural or political authority? To what extent did the Neo-Assyrian empire (or imperialism in general) accommodate this diglossia of power? Did the state prefer this dichotomy as a tactic used to divide and control elites, to set itself up as the final arbiter of power? Or did it ultimately seek to establish a clear and rationalized hierarchy?

This essay will give attention to five issues of Neo-Assyrian elites and cosmopolitanism: first, a survey of the historical setting and relevant scholarship; second, approaches to defining elite identity,[2] initially through a look at both ancient and modern models and metaphors, and then through a specific enumeration of Assyrian ranks and offices; third, the manifestation of cosmopolitanism in attributes, paraphernalia, appurtenance, and practices, as a positive argument for the existence of a cosmopolitan elite; fourth, a negative argument examining countervailing trends, of the insufficiencies and negative feedbacks of the competition and denunciations which prevented a true class formation; and fifth, the foundations that this "ambivalent cosmopolitanism" laid down for future political formations, through questions of authenticity and "confidence" (as a *terminus technicus*).

I will argue that the distribution and perception of the royal "confidence" (Akk. *raḫāṣu*)[3] that marked elite status throughout the Assyrian system was

---

1. Cf. Ataç, forthcoming.
2. On the related but separate issue of personal identity, see Selz 2004 and now Steinert 2012.
3. CAD R, s.v. *raḫāṣu* C v, "1. to trust, to rely, 2. III to make confident, to cause to trust." Importantly, the verb did not emerge in Akkadian until the Neo-Assyrian period itself and remained in use in Neo-Babylonian

an important conceptual tool in the organizational dynamics of the empire. Although imperial elites relied on displays of royal trust as the basis of their local authority, a dilemma developed insofar as the trust of the Assyrian king as perceived by local subjects just as easily led to resentment and *loss* of confidence in those same officials. For imperial elites who walked the fine line between just-enough compliance and just-enough resistance, royal "confidence" as a sole power source often proved unstable. Although I limit myself to an understanding of a non-vernacular Assyrian "cosmopolitanism" restricted to imperial elites[4] (and more visible in its wanting than its presence), the important historical experience of the Assyrian centuries was to set the stage for "autonomous elites" in succeeding empires, with implications for something more like the generalized authority they enjoyed in civil society as much as in government.[5] These post-Assyrian empires would develop cosmopolitan cultures and styles that, to the horrified eyes of any Assyrian king, would have seemed to democratize that most blasphemous elite politics of them all: to "trust in oneself."[6]

ELITE INTEGRATION IN THE NEO-ASSYRIAN EMPIRE

The goal for this workshop was to think seriously about the subjective experience of imperial elites. Much depends, of course, on our understanding of words like "elites" and "empires"; but comparison begins with noting difference. And the largest variance to emerge in the discussions was the relatively low incidence of elite integration in earlier empires, and a higher degree in later ones. So we begin with some implication of a historical development in this area, and questions about how Assyria, as one of the earliest empires, first worked without—but then sought to promote—common elite cultures. Although "imperial cosmopolitanism" sounds to our ears like something every empire ought to want to have, it was in this case very much more difficult than simply deciding on a style of Assyrian chic, since the process was complicated by problems of local authenticity and precepts of personal, rather than group, access to power.

The drive toward cosmopolitan ethics was a long one, and its individual features were not new to Neo-Assyrian imperial times (912-609 BC). Some elements of cosmopolitanism could be said to have been in place as early as the late

---

as well (but not in Late Babylonian). That the verb produced no nominalized by-forms may indicate that its usage never left the sphere of political letters; I am unaware of any negated use of *raḫāṣu* (i.e., to *not* be confident)—only to have confidence in the wrong (i.e., non-Assyrian) authorities. See now also Solans 2014: 104–19.

4. The restricted franchise of this kind of cosmopolitanism is thus very distant from Sheldon Pollock's (1998) global/local dynamic of a "cosmopolitan vernacular."

5. On the rise of this new educated elite, see Richardson 2014a: 465–73.

6. Richardson 2010: 9–10.

fourth millennium, if the possession of exotic, prestige materials by Uruk elites by itself indicates a shared idea of eliteness (or the emulation of their technologies and material culture in Susiana, Syria, and Anatolia). By the Early Dynastic period (ca. 2900–2350 BC), we know more specifically that such goods were circulated between courts through gifting, and that other aspects of elite marking had become regular features of political society: the recognition of language for diplomatic contact, foreign travel as a mark of prestige,[7] interdynastic marriages, commensality, and so forth. Elite emulation was behind imitative palace architecture at Middle Bronze Ugarit, Mari, and Babylon, and elite emulation was behind the exchange of literature, cult, and scientific knowledge between Late Bronze Age Babylon, Egypt, and Hatti.

But these experiences belonged to the limited world of kings and courts, suggestive of a later elite consciousness, but not yet generalized. The regular and geographically diffused interactions of elites of different polities, ranks, and stations that could lead to a cosmopolitan ethic—at least partly autonomous (in sociological terms) of palace authorities—would require the sustained structural conditions that only empires could provide: a conception of otherness produced by regularized interaction over time, the creation of an intermediate official class whose authority drew on both imperial *auctoritas*[8] and local *communitas* (bases of social authority which were often structurally adverse), and the interposition of an ambivalent elite identity to mediate and circumvent that paradox.

Thus we come to the late Neo-Assyrian empire, when these conditions finally pertained. Studies of important households and offices of the period have gradually fleshed out the picture of the stratum of power below the king himself, especially as nodes of semi-independent elite power and identity.[9] Assyria established the foretexts of the Babylonian and Persian cosmopolitanism to follow, rather than reaping the benefits of this social formation itself.[10] To assume any Assyrian consciousness of such a foundational role, however, violates an attempt to examine "subjective experience": it would be anachronistic to think there was an openly recognized contemporary idea that Assyria was laying the groundwork for some future social ideology that it itself employed only haphazardly. Assyrians of the ninth, eighth, and seventh centuries simply could not have known what came next; they were stumbling around in the dark looking for the light switch.[11]

---

7. For a consideration of travel as a polity-building practice in this context, see Ristvet 2011; for a slightly later example set in the Old Babylonian period, see Pappi 2012.

8. On the nature of imperial authorization through the administrative hierarchy, see Postgate 2007: 4–8.

9. E.g., on the household of the crown prince, see Groß 2015; on the magnates, see Mattila 2000; on women in palatial contexts, see Svärd 2015; on high officials, see Grayson 1993.

10. See, e.g., the conclusions of Jursa 2015: 604.

11. Simonetta Ponchia has speculated (pers. comm.) that the eighth-century reforms of Tiglath-pileser III in particular might have formed an important historical moment for the solidification of elite identity and conceptions of "governmentality" in Assyria.

I will briefly set the historical background in terms of ideological developments. The small mercantile city-state of Aššur emerged from a period of political weakness around 1400 BC with four significant ideological renovations. First, Assyria developed an aggrandized historical memory of its brief and modest career as a conquest state under Šamši-Adad I four centuries earlier. This was an "invented tradition" of the first water, and badly out of touch with the political realities of a small territorial Assyria staffed by a few court officers and an oligarchy of first families. Second, this sensibility came to the forefront of the Assyrian cultural imagination against the experience of Mitanni domination and proximity to the Hittite empire. These hegemonies were probably less significant in terms of actual deprivation or oppression and more so in imaginative terms, and that they introduced to Assyrians an imperial "style." Annalistic campaign accounts, deportations and punishments, palatial architecture, the language of vassals and lords—much of the look and feel of (especially Hittite) imperial style formed the *Vorlage* of the Assyrian experience.

A third and unique feature of Assyrian ideology was the development of its anxious chatter about manifest destiny and space. For the five centuries between roughly 1400 and 900 BC, Assyria was for the most part not threatened by other major states, but by a seemingly endless sea of hostile tribes surrounding it in the mountains and plains; only Babylon, itself relatively weak, came out occasionally to act as a proper sparring partner. The Assyrian view of the world reflected— or perhaps produced—a sense of geo-political claustrophobia, the corollary to its nearly obsessive pronouncements about *Lebensraum*. Fourth and finally, Assyria nursed a centuries-old "little brother" complex in relation to Babylonia, the literary and cultural supernova to the south. Assyrians copied and emulated Babylonian political forms, cult, and knowledge arts in such a way as to make clear that their veneration bordered on outright jealousy. These narcissistic injuries, if one may usefully personify states in this way—Assyria's perceived manifest destiny as a once-and-future empire and outfitted with imperial chic, juxtaposed with an awareness of geopolitical weakness and cultural inferiority—these intersections formed the apologetic core and motivating neurosis of the imperial ideology to come, the driving engine to conquer and control.

This 350-word account of five hundred years leads me back to a larger, overall point about cosmopolitanism: by the time the Neo-Assyrian empire began to actually put these ideological energies into systematic practice, its ruling class had little experience of genuine rule. As such, who were its elites? Assyrians drew mostly on the social and political precepts of a regional oligarchy—temple and palace appointees, local landholders, old-money families, and civil officers.[12]

---

12. See Jakob 2003; and now Postgate 2007 and 2014.

These people were probably rather surprised to find, actually, at the end of the tenth century, that the rather artificial-sounding ideas about empire laid down centuries before were in fact becoming actionable. The experience of Assyria's elites over the next three centuries would be one of groping toward a rudimentary sense of cosmopolitanism, unwittingly posing its questions, problems, and advantages as much through mistakes as through any baroque flowering of elite culture.[13] I will illustrate this experience primarily through the lens of Neo-Assyrian letters, avoiding the corpus of royal inscriptions; if elite concerns are our subject, we are not generally going to find them represented in the texts which took the king as their exclusive focus. One problem for readers to consider, however, is that it is often not possible (or systematically feasible) to determine the specific identity of every letter-writer for every text adduced herein. The reader is warned, then, that I have treated these letters as a more or less homogeneous body of evidence for the broader social-political milieu; it may yet be that a systematic analysis on the basis of ethnic or local identity would refine these observations.[14]

This investigation coincides with a good deal of recent work on Neo-Assyrian elite identity. Ariel Bagg (2013), for one, has recently argued for a radically stripped-down understanding of Assyrian influence over imperialized elites, seeing an essentially pragmatic and military (not cultural) approach to domination. Bagg proposes that Assyria was "a world empire without a mission ... a special type of empire" deserving explanation on its own terms, untroubled by projects of acculturation. Since many studies of the Assyrian empire assume that something like "Assyrianization" must be part and parcel of its experience, his conjecture that it might not be so is one worth considering. Beate Pongratz-Leisten (2013) takes a different perspective on the development of elite authority as a consequence of an emerging scholarly elaboration of royal authority. In her view, the implication of elites in elaborating and producing the symbolic systems constitutive of royal authority provided the socio-intellectual basis for their own independent power.[15] A third view is that of Karen Radner in her 2014 edited volume, *State Correspondence in the Ancient World*, in which she contributes a chapter on Assyrian letters. Providing a thorough description of the infrastructure and systems of validation for official Assyrian correspondence, this argument depends on an understanding that the network was, relatively straightforwardly, "instrumental in guaranteeing the cohesion of the empire," partly by circumscribing

---

13. An unscientific but revealing statistic: of thirty-six records in the Oriental Institute library database (http://oi-idb.uchicago.edu) corresponding to the keyword(s) "cosmopolitan(ism)," not one addresses a Neo-Assyrian topic; most relate to Late Bronze Age contexts.

14. Studies in this direction have already been made of letters from later periods; for the Neo-Babylonian period, see Kleber 2012; for late Babylonian times, see Jursa and Häckl 2011 and Jursa, Häckl, and Schmidl 2014. See now also Fales 2015 on idiolects and the possibilities for determining individual identities and voices.

15. Cf. n. 3 above.

authorized communication around, and thus identifying, the limited franchise of ranked elites.[16] This degree of functionality may, however, be more apparent than real, a simulation of the rhetoric of the letters themselves. We may be cautious of imposing a modern idea of "governmentality" on the ancient world, especially where "politics is imagined as a set of institutional structures that can be described adequately by referring mainly to the actions of a few 'actors' at the top of an imperial hierarchy."[17]

My original intention was to focus on a specific problem of Assyrian cosmopolitanism, a dilemma posed for vassal elites in the periphery: How were they to exercise authority on behalf of Assyria when the very delegation of that power compromised their ability to do so by eroding their local cultural authenticity? This was perhaps a nice idea, but Assyrian sources speak little to the "recognition ethics" that an answer would require. Recognition theory calls for globalist or cosmopolitan hegemons to arrive at open acknowledgments of differences with peers and subalterns sufficient to permit rational procedures for regular interaction.[18] As such, "recognition" is hardly a matter of love and affirmation, but a practical and rule-based tolerance; as Richard Payne (this volume) puts it, it is an "accommodation of internally contradictory sets of ideas." Recognition ethics in fact demand that difference be met with skepticism and judgments rendered,[19] as a path to the acceptance of marked differences, and, sufficiently undistorted by ideological concerns, to facilitate elite communications and imperial identity.[20] The recognition problem was first suggested to me by the case of Hezekiah and Sennacherib, in the King of Judah's awkward middle-position between the Assyrians and his own populace.[21] But this story was really a literary product of the Neo-Babylonian and Persian periods, and better speaks to a later time when the forms of recognition and questions of cultural authenticity had come more clearly to the fore.[22]

Indeed: if there is something really interesting about the Assyrian case, it is the relatively *low* incidence of authenticity and cosmopolitan marking. Many

---

16. Radner 2014b: esp. 66 and 2015: 68; see also Liverani 2014: 374, on "concentric belts" of messaging.

17. Bernbeck 2010: 149–50. For Bernbeck, the absence of uniform governmental practices implies not only an undeveloped subjectivity but also an undeveloped political and sociological identity for elites as well.

18. Jurgen Habermas *apud* Turner 2006: 141f.; the argument develops from Hegel, who posits that in a master/slave relationship, the master is barred from receiving recognition as a moral agent from a slave who cannot give it freely.

19. Turner 2006: 143–6: judgment distinguishes cosmopolitanism from mere "descriptive relativism" and "epistemological disinterest"; cf. Fine 2006 on the problem of understanding violence in cosmopolitan contexts, seeing its exercise as part of a "mode of understanding the world." Space does not permit a thorough analysis of the role of violence in the Assyrian world view, but see, e.g., Richardson 2007: 196–200.

20. Turner 2006: 141–2; one could argue that Assyrian identity was shallow along exactly this axis, i.e., in the high degree of ideological distortion of communication.

21. Richardson 2014a.

22. Note, e.g., Dusinberre 2003: 4, that the average Persian "satrap was chronically torn between needing to send the appropriate amount of tribute to the king now, and needing to ensure that the people under his hegemony would be capable of producing tribute again in the future."

scholars studying Neo-Assyrian political language and ideology have grappled with the apparent paradox of the empire's obsessive dipole of political loyalty/disloyalty compared to its overwhelming disinterest in cultural difference. There was a general lack of attention in Assyrian rhetoric, either positively or negatively, to issues of ethnicity, class, language, dress, style, religious practice, and so on. That characterization requires much modification on specific points, and a good deal of secondary literature exists to do just that.[23] But as a general rule, we are presented with an empire which, despite having plenty of neurotic complexes, did not have the definition of Self versus Other, let alone the development of a recognition ethic, at the top of the list. As Reinhard Bernbeck put it recently:

> Assyrian rule does not fit under Foucauldian "governmentality." ... Assyrian officials did not in the slightest way develop an attitude of care for their colonial subjects. The notion of governmentality, however, is based on at least a minimal recognition of the subjected *as subjects*.[24]

Of course, this seems very strange to us: the problems of empires typically have very much to do with the means by which the people who ran the empire defined themselves, identified and distinguished themselves from one another, and harnessed and bounded the competitions that inevitably emerged within the state mechanism.

How could an empire get by *without* this kind of conversation? Indeed, its absence has led many to the conclusion that the "shallow" ideological permeation of Assyrian elite culture had much to do with the rapid and total nature of the empire's collapse; that the one-dimensional or superficial penetration of identity dialogics marks an ideological failure to meaningfully create categories of either "Assyrians" or their Others. All this is much as Bernbeck anticipated. But to stop at that point does not appreciate the historical position of an empire which had the task of creating the constitutive elements of cosmopolitanism in the first place and necessarily engaged in its first steps, however unintentionally. Explicating the historical shape of this challenge and response then becomes the next mission of this particular essay.

Assyrian Cosmopolitanism and Elite Identity

Models and Metaphors, Ancient and Modern

What can "cosmopolitanism" mean in the Assyrian context? A general theory of cosmopolitanism was first advanced by Durkheim more than a century ago,

---

23. See (and compare) Nissen and Renger 1982 and Pongratz-Leisten 2001; and also Fales 2013, Ciffarelli 1995, Feldman 2014, Brown 2014. One specific respect in which cultural recognition was indeed more of a factor was in Assyro-Babylonian relations, to which I return at the end of this chapter.
24. Bernbeck 2010: 154.

as a model to counter ideas about national culture dominant in the context of European nationalism and colonialism. The term has re-emerged today to qualify and modify late capitalist theories of neoliberal globalism which suppose a more integrative and universal social identity than national- or class-based ones. The first theoretical challenge to recognize, then, is that the term "cosmopolitanism" represents a staunchly modern set of precepts which we are here trying to situate in the radically different world of antiquity.[25] Needless to say, such definitional bridging structures as travel, media, and common language[26] were more absent than present in the long-dead world we are looking at. We should have no presupposition that just because ancient empires added territory, that they automatically generated the kinds of social formations we want to think about.

The second theoretical challenge is the duality of the problem before us, in distinguishing as the object of study "elites" as instruments or extensions of the state as a political community, as against "elites" as a class with independent group interests.[27] I believe we ought to cleave to the latter, thinking of a limited form of elite cosmopolitanism in which *individuals* from different places identified themselves and specific others as belonging to an elite class distinct from the mass of humanity under imperial rule which did not participate in their experience. The interests of this group lay neither with (simply) governance, nor the project of creating some kind of open and universal sociocultural community based on a shared morality, the kind of fully cosmopolite world of global citizens envisioned by a George Soros or a Richard Branson. This cosmopolitanism deals with something more than mere state instrumentalism, but well short of a unitary global culture or world order. Its denotative markings identified elite membership and similar (if not common) political-economic interests, and replaced a ubiquity of locally ascribed and subscribed systems of rank, office, and prestige. This latter element is important in its comparative sense, that cosmopolitan elites self-consciously looked to supersede the identities of mere local nobility. What cosmopolitanism does not require is homogeneity across space; indeed, it requires the maintenance of difference (i.e., its "subordination," in the terms of Lavan et al., this volume).

Such theoretical biases are worth considering as we go forward. In fact, one might do well to look around the table at any academic workshop and think a bit about the problems of how a scholarly account of elitism might be scientifically

---

25. E.g., Anthony Giddens, who held that capitalism was a necessary precondition for globalization (*apud* Turner 2006: 141); but cf. Calhoun 2002.

26. The not-uncommon implication that Aramaic as a lingua franca in the Iron Age provided the kind of language contact facilitating the development of an elite sociolect or a common corpora of belles lettres (much less a vernacular language) misunderstands what a lingua franca is and does, which is to enable governance and administration. No Nabatean writer or speaker of Aramaic, for instance, was deploying that language to socially position himself vis-à-vis contemporary elites in Babylonia or northern Syria.

27. Indeed, a number of my colleagues think that the very use of the term "elites" reifies a set of assumptions about clearly defined rank which did not exist in antiquity.

bounded, anyway. There we sit, a group of transnational, university types meeting in semi-seclusion, speaking in an exclusive professional sociolect, with some
feasting thrown in; to increase the level of discomfort, we inevitably engage in
the intramural, invidious comparison and watchfulness that goes along with
cosmopolitan elitism.[28] Scholars may not think themselves to look or feel like
elites—indeed, most are likely to have formed any number of apologetic coun-
ter-narratives to or denials of such a charge—but we must admit that academic
roundtables are probably exactly what many people envision when they think of
elites and elitism today. So we may be further advised to think about theoretical
errors of mimesis in our sometime difficulty (or even unwillingness) to clearly
identify elites as a historical-sociological category.[29]

Assyriologists have thought about Neo-Assyrian elites for a long time. To a
great extent, it has been necessary to do this to push back against official imperial inscriptions and monuments relentlessly celebratory of the state organization, as though it were built and run by the king himself. Obviously, this is not
the case. We might begin, however, to see the outlines of an inchoate debate between Assyria constructing a universalist-globalist identity (i.e., an assimilation
of elites) as against a cosmopolite one by outlining some previous approaches to
the subject. In the first place, an emergent universalism has been seen in Assyria's
production of imagined geographies through cosmological texts[30] and idealized gardens,[31] in an accelerating registration of populations through census
projects,[32] in the administration of loyalty oaths to those same populations,[33]
in the rise of Aramaic as a lingua franca,[34] in experiments and reforms of cult
practice,[35] in a diffusion of trade goods and decorative styles,[36] and in the gath-
ering of knowledge texts at Nineveh.[37] (To this list of universalizing impulses,

28. In the Assyrian context: "If the king does not punish one scribe, [the others] will not get scared" (SAA
XIII 31).
29. Cf. Pongratz-Leisten 2013.
30. See, e.g., Horowitz 1998, Liverani 1999–2001.
31. E.g., Oppenheim 1965, Radner 2000, Thomason 2001, Novák 2002.
32. On the "Harran Census," see Fales 1990 and the relevant texts in SAA XI and the volume introduction,
xxx–xxxv; and on other registrations of military and deportee personnel, see ibid., xxvi–xxx; for other land
grant documents with cadastral and census information, see SAA XII texts 1–67. *Contra* Bernbeck 2010: 153,
there is therefore much more than "just one single document from the whole Assyrian period . . . which focuses
on biopolitics, that is on intricate knowledge qualities and quantities of a subject population." Although such
Assyrian efforts were decidedly limited, occasional, and far from fine-grained, it would be mistaken to dismiss
them as part of a developing interest in precisely such an imperial biophysics; see Richardson 2014a: 477–84.
33. For universal and inclusive terms for whole populations in treaties, see SAA II 8, Zakutu's treaty with
"the entire nation" (UN.MEŠ KUR *gabbu*), Aššurbanipal's treaty with "all Qedarites, young and old," SAA II
10 (restored); cf. SAA XVIII 162; encouraging whole families, wives, sons, elders, etc., to join the "treaty of
Babylon."
34. E.g., Tadmor 1991; but see n. 26 above.
35. Parpola 1993, Porter 2000, Annus 2002: esp. ch. 2.
36. Feldman 2014.
37. Although innumerable "Koyunjikological" studies are available on almost every conceivable aspect of
the Aššurbanipal library, I am not aware of any general, overall treatment of it as a whole; see Fincke 2004 for
a brief overview.

one may add that there was even a corresponding reduction in Assyrian traditions about its own heroic past, since those stories tended to emphasize Assyria's
local particularity.[38]) The building blocs of this scholarship are already in place
should one want to depict Assyria as emerging toward and cohering as (if not
yet realized as) a universal community, and such an argument dovetails nicely
with the empire's explicitly expansionist language.

It is more difficult to make a cosmopolite than a universalist account of the
Assyrian empire, since the methodological presumption of the latter is to see all
sorts of phenomena as disparate parts of one process: the creation of empire as "one
world." Cosmopolitanism is a harder argument to make because the scholarship
is theoretically concerned with making differentiations, with particularizing and
isolating phenomena: one insists on pointing out the ways in which things do not
go together. Universalists must be lumpers, and cosmopolitans must be splitters.
Yet an honest account has to take stock of the fact that this empire (like others)
made feints in both directions simultaneously; and the Assyrian elite experience
has its own clear structures based on group cohesion as well as on distinction and
division. The typologies discussed later test the terms in which particular elite
communities were imagined by the Assyrians, in their own specific and selective
criteria, as against any modern and etic idea of "Assyrianization." Here I will look
at categorical distinctions of loyalty, both descriptive and legal; ethnic ideas of
who counted as an "Assyrian"; membership in the royal household, proximity to
the royal body, or at the royal table; and participation in the state cult.

In the political realm, the elites of the empire were perceived according to
tiers of loyalty: vassals, puppets, servants, the submissive, and so on. These all
appear as stock characters in royal literature: from the faraway kings who had
sent polite and notional greeting gifts, to the fully sworn officials and true believers who stood at the arm of the king, to the craven and mistrusted petty
kings who sometimes rendered tribute—but sometimes did not. The political
community was segmented along axes of compliance and distance.

A legal definition may also apply, since elites may have been marked by who
had taken the *adê*-oaths of loyalty and who had not. Liverani has argued that
adê-oaths may not have been sworn by the entire subject population of the
empire (i.e., in scenes of tens of thousands of people filling city squares), but
only by a few chiefs, sheikhs, and princes in their capacity as royal vassals.[39]
If true, this would mark oath-takers as categorically distinct from other types
of subjects. Doubts about Liverani's position, however, have been multiplying
of late, and the oath may not be as diagnostic of rank as was once thought.[40]
The second and more durable challenge has been that, even if such oaths "were

---

38. Richardson 2014a: 485–94.
39. Liverani 1995.
40. Lauinger 2012: esp. 112, Fales 2012.

composed for all people under Assyrian domination ... they were more concerned with internal affairs,"[41] specifically the royal succession, than they were
with upholding something like law, identity, or an Assyrian way of life. That is,
they were not comprehensive pledges of loyalty, but contracts for the specific
and limited purpose of confirming the crown prince as heir apparent. This is
something short of creating wholesale subjectivity in all its dimensions; but,
as S. Ponchia wonders, it perhaps began to "acquire a more general role ... [in]
forming the mental attitude of the 'subjects of the empire'?"[42] This may be so,
but it would still do little to distinguish elites from other kinds of subjects.

Another differentiation could be made about who was "counted as an Assyrian,"
a stock phrase in imperial descriptions of captive populations incorporated into
Assyria. But though the distinction was sometimes made for legal procedures
(i.e., that some individual was or was not an "Assyrian") and sometimes appears
as an administrative category (e.g., that this or that troop contingent were called
"Itu'eans" simply to distinguish them from "Assyrians"), it cannot be said that
such terms ever attained to a conception of ethnicity, under which identity was an
imbrication of blood, land, and language. And ethnonyms had still less capacity
to form or change notions of class or rank, only something closer to an administrative filing status for one's taxes or residential identity for jurisdictional purposes. In short, to be counted as an "Assyrian" carried little weight or advantage
vis-à-vis other ethnonyms, except insofar as taxes and service were concerned.

Being part of the royal household was another important conceptual metaphor for Assyrian elite status. Space does not permit a full discussion of this
concept, but its importance should be acknowledged. The capacity of the
king's "house" was understood to be enormous—really, a household extending
across the empire: not only his palace and physical household, but his estate
or domain by extension—and thus felt nowhere so keenly as when someone
perceived themselves not to be in it. As one official in Babylonia complained,
"There is no city, no open country, no land, no people, nor a single 'litre' of
bread (for me) in my lord's house."[43] This "oikomorphic" model can be contrasted to a physiomorphic one, in which the king's corporeal form was understood as the mystical body of the empire—and that his ministers and magnates
corresponded to parts of that body, the *sukkallu*-judge as the king's hand, the
turtānu-general as his leg, and so forth, in a physicus of the state.[44] This model

41. Watanabe 2014: 164–5.
42. Ponchia 2014: 523.
43. SAA XVIII 61.
44. Mattila 2000: 7–8; compare to SAA III 14, in which the poetic comparison is made between the cedar tree as the "king's shelter," the cypress as the "shade of his magnates," and the "shade of a sprig of juniper" as the shelter for the lover. The metaphorical distinctions implied by *erēnu/šurmēnu/daprānu* are unclear to me (John Wee, pers. comm., doubts they are particularly evocative), but the language at least is naturalizing, just as the physiognomic model is. On the king's body as a symbol of the cosmos or astral bodies, see Frahm 2013.

identified various elites as extensions of the royal body politic, and it integrated authority without being overly clear about hierarchy (which I imagine is just how the king wanted it).

There are yet other, further possible markers of cosmopolitanism worth considering. One might argue for a sumptuarial model of conspicuous consumption, both literal and figurative, since members of the elite were understood to attend the king's banquet, and where the king controlled the distribution of dress, preciosities, and so on. Or one could define a cultural enceinte within which elites could be distinguished by their relative access to and construction of the knowledge arts that grounded kingship in wisdom. Finally, a theocratic model is also possible, given that the cult of the state god Aššur was officially sustained by the regularly scheduled contributions of taxes to the Aššur temple by governors and officials; indeed, from Middle Assyrian times, this system of cult tithes had been the dominant conception of state income.[45] The eponym system also tied elites into calendars and chronicles. Elites were in the king's household, at his table and in his temple, part of his body and his mind; non-elites were not. All of these models, unlike universalist aspirations, relied on the Assyrian creation of divisions, distinctions, and demarcations of eliteness.

Some of these acculturating experiences were not limited to elites, especially insofar as large conquered groups were also incorporated into the Assyrian domain. A royal inscription of Sargon, for instance, speaks of appointing superintendents who were "competent to teach [common deportees] to fear god and the king," suggesting at least a modicum of interest in Assyrianizing subject people coming to Assyria.[46] Deportee lists, economic documents, and administrative texts show us the reality of a population of resident aliens in the capital city of Nineveh, presumably people of higher rank; this included men from Egypt, Babylon, Arabia, Sidon, Cilicia, Commagene, Samaria, and Elamites. And some degree of acculturation inevitably traveled in an outward direction, too, as the Assyrian army and administrators flowed out to all ends of the empire,[47] a phenomenon partly reflected in Assyrian representations of foreign landscapes as metonyms for Otherness. Thus, by the late high empire, the conditions sufficient to create a more inclusive or common culture had substantially matured. It would be too much to say that something like an "imperial citizen" had fully emerged—only in a limited sense—only to say that, in considering the possibility that various Assyrian terms of eliteness were denominative, one must also remember that these were constantly complicated by trends mixing and leveling throughout the empire.

45. Pongratz-Leisten 2013: 288: the "monthly deliveries to the Ashur temple from all the provinces of the empire" maintained the "social and cultural nexus" of the city as the imperial center; see SAA X 96.

46. Machinist 1992, Paul 1969.

47. Richardson 2011: 50.

The representation of landscapes and experience of travel in imperial Assyrian text and image may be instructive in this regard. The flora and fauna of the natural world were reproduced in gardens at Nineveh, and on its walls as microcosms of empire. In the textual realm, a staple of royal inscriptions was the king's conquest of an adversarial topography, as he crossed high mountains, forded deep rivers, and traversed burning deserts. Meantime, the courier system which permitted the exchange of correspondence itself erased distance. And the business of elites regularly carried them across regional boundaries: when we see a magnate like Remanni-Adad (discussed later) doing business with men from Barzahala, Carcemish, Til-Barsip, Amidi, and so on, we get a sense of the expansive mental maps of Neo-Assyrian elites.[48] One might even say the Assyrian mantic attempts to understand the heavens, floods, earthquakes, weather, and rainbows[49] as ominous messages were all part of an attempt to master topography and environment. All these subjects have been seen as instrumental to a royal ideology in which the imperial king stood at the center of an empire, a world, and a cosmos. And they would be inherently cosmopolitan themes as well, insofar as they removed spatiality as a limiting factor on the elite imaginary. "Space has no meaning for people like us," the underlying message reads; "our community exists in ideological terms, well beyond spatial ones."[50] The postwar English idiom of a "jet set" perfectly encapsulates the idea of a community not bound by the geographic limitations of regular people. To this extent, at least, the experience of elites and other subjects were radically different, and not a shared mentality.

As I build a case for a limited form of Assyrian cosmopolitanism, I do not think it desirable to prefer cosmopolitanism over universalism, or vice versa. Both social ideologies were useful to elites, a multivocalism which permitted authorities to speak to each other and their subjects as different political and social contexts required. States and empires are perfectly happy to let elites who want to imagine themselves as part of an unfolding political macrocosm think they are; and likewise, those who wanted to see themselves as part of one or more exclusive local circles with specific rights and privileges (and even responsibilities) were allowed to think that. This principle of ambiguation not only reaches out to different constituencies but also obscures the locus of authority. Empires like to be omniscient and omnipresent, to monitor others; but they prefer to not be fully visible or accountable themselves.[51] These principles extended to elites

---

48. See also SAA V 250, which documents the coming-together at Kār-Aššur of three high officials, two magnates and four governors for an incipient military campaign; the minimum distance separating these officials in the normal course of their duties would have been more than 300 kilometers.

49. In general and, e.g., see SAA X passim; for earthquakes, see SAA X 10 and 56; weather, SAA VIII 120 and X 42; rainbows, SAA VIII 31; floods, SAA VIII 69.

50. But this social conceit, like the biopolitics discussed above (n. 32), differs qualitatively from the kind of informed toleration of Renaissance "distanciation" and sophistication discussed by Cosgrove 2003.

51. Richardson 2014b.

themselves: though they were part of the apparatus of surveillance over their inferiors, they themselves were watched, and watched one another; the terms on which their privilege was based were never incontestable.

An Inventory of Assyrian Elites

If one looks for cosmopolitan Assyrian elites, it seems obvious to begin with titled officials. At the very top of the administrative structure were the "magnates," the "Great Ones," the *rabûti*, a group of about a hundred men who, as Karen Radner puts it "formed the backbone of the Assyrian empire": provincial governors, advisors (*qēpu*, "trusted one," mostly ministers of foreign affairs stationed in allied states[52]), and palace officials. Radner concludes that the reigns of the kings in the late empire "were marked by an equilibrium of power between multiple advisors whose influence neutralized each other and stabilized the state."[53] These men, the subject of a major study by Raija Mattila in 2000,[54] seem self-evidently to be Assyria's core group, but the small size of the cadre suggests we are dealing with a group with a high incidence of personal, face-to-face knowledge of one another, rather than a cosmopolitan class of thousands of men who identified one another through impersonal and external markings.[55]

Yet there is a pebble in our shoe from the start: even this very small "in-group" was far from homogeneous, and difficult to define sociologically. For one thing, the magnates were set up in positions which were structurally asymmetric: they were in the military, the provinces, the palace, or they were moved between these branches of the imperial administration as "delegates," ministers without portfolio. Their location, retinues, households, proximity to the king, and many other attributes of power discussed earlier were distributed unevenly.[56] Part of this was deliberate, in that the crown relied on the differences of the cadres and the separate channels of information they produced. But even among single classes of officialdom, such as the governors, there was a great deal of difference. It was one thing, for instance, to be governor of wealthy urban Carcemish and quite another to be governor of Suḫu, a desert frontier area far from the bustling centers. As Sargon wrote in one case, replying to a request from a governor to reassign four of his districts to a subordinate: "If you give [these] four districts to [him], would he not become your equal—and what would you be ruling over as governor then?"[57] These disparities means that any assumption of a uniform

---

52. Dubovský 2012.

53. Radner 2011: 375; see also her "Assyrian Empire Builders" website, http://www.ucl.ac.uk/sargon/; cf. the conclusions of Postgate 2007: 28, including the sense that the system was "not bureaucratic, [but] depended on a sense of institutional loyalty and personal interaction up and down the system."

54. Mattila 2000.

55. Postgate 2007, Ponchia 2012.

56. Note the distinction in Esarhaddon's loyalty oath (SAA II 6) between "closer palace groups" and "more remote palace groups" (ll. 214–25).

57. SAA I 1: 31f.

elite class has to account for the competitions and comparisons internal to it; whether this oppositionalism was equilibrious or not is not so clear.

Even the connotations of equal status themselves were potentially problematic, in that the deverbal nouns of parity for "equals" or "peers" in Akkadian, such as *meḥru* and *šāninu*, derived from verbs with semantic implications of confrontation and rivalry rather than, say, ones implying parity, trust, or mutuality.[58] These kinds of structural or semantic critiques of administrative cadres are hardly unique to the Assyrian case, but it is worth pushing back against a presumption of unity or balance in officialdom by introducing the idea, like a grain of sand in an oyster, that elite power was not isometrically structured even at the very top, and that precepts of peerage were ever complicated by notions of antagonism.

To pick more specific categories of people, one might draw the elite/non-elite dividing line around those identified by title or profession in the major texts that directly concerned allegiance to the king: the loyalty oaths (*adê*-treaties), which created one definitive in-group, with especial attention to the wider royal family; and the divinatory queries, which tested the limits and weaknesses of a somewhat wider group. Both types of texts suggest a larger set of people potentially making up an elite stratum, and both genres pay explicit service to some notion of universal subjectivity. Who was named by these texts? The most famous loyalty oath found at Nimrud enjoined the political fealty of specific ethnic groups, magnates, eunuchs, governors, courtiers, the crown prince, nobles, vassals, allies, scholars, prophets, ecstatics, icon-builders, diviners, royal wives, their families, and (in a variety of unspecific terms) all people everywhere;[59] the list in the oath text found at provincial Tayinat, by contrast, reflects more the military-political apparatus of a colonial outpost:

> the governor of Kunalia, with the deputy, the majordomo, the scribes, the chariot drivers, the third men, the village managers, the information officers, the prefects, the cohort commanders, the charioteers, the cavalrymen, the exempt, the outriders, the specialists, the shi[eld bearers(?)], the craftsmen, (and) with [all] the men [of his hands], great and small, as many as there are—[wi]th them and with the men who are born after the *adê* in the [f]uture, from the east . . . to the west, all those over whom Esarhaddon, king of Assyria, exercises kingship and lordship.[60]

---

58. < *maḥāru* and *šanānu* (see s.v. these lemmata in CAD M and Š/1, respectively); see SAA X 294 and 334, XIII 125, XVI 36 and 115, for examples of "colleagues" in contexts of opposition. Another Akkadian verb, *muššulu*, "to make/be of equal rank," was not used in relation to persons other than the king (i.e., that he was similar to other kings, or even to gods). There are not substantially any other Akkadian terms used to describe the emulation or imitation of peers. As Baker and Groß 2015: 85 conclude, a "coded language reflecting a shared set of values and expectations" might be clear in letters between officials and the king, but these expressions are "found far less often in the letters between officials."

59. SAA II 6; but see now Lauinger 2012, Fales 2012, Watanabe 2014.

60. Lauinger 2012; cf. SAA XVII 145, an *adê* which recognizes/confers the political status of a community (see Ponchia 2014); also SAA X 6, XVI 60–61, and XVIII 83 and 102.

The divinatory queries, by contrast, extended their concerns to an even wider range of people; these reflect the setting of the royal city of Nineveh, but also the "completist" concerns of the prophylactic magical procedure being employed (since the queries were concerned with risks to the king from persons who were not necessarily oath-holders—even cooks, confectioners, and tailors). One can take as an example this excerpt from a query in which Aššurbanipal asks

> [will (any) of the] eunuchs (and) the bearded (officials), the king's en-
> tourage, or (any) of his brothers and uncles, his family, his father's
> line, or junior members of the royal line, or the "third men," chariot
> drivers (and) chariot fighters, or the recruitment officers, or the pre-
> fects of the exempt military, or the prefects of the cavalry, or the royal
> bodyguard, or his personal guard, or the keepers of the inner gates, or
> the keepers of the outer gates, or the . . . eunuchs, or . . . or the palace
> superintendents, the staff-bearers (and) the watchmen, or the mounted
> scouts (and) the trackers, or the lackeys, tailors, cup-bearers, cooks,
> (and) confectioners, the entire body of craftsmen, or the Itu'eans and
> the Elamites, the mounted bowmen, the Hittites, or the Gurreans, or
> the Arameans, or the Cimmerians, or the Philistines, or the Nubians
> (and) the Egyptians, or the Šabuqeans, or the eunuchs who bear arms,
> or the bearded (officials) who bear arms and stand guard for the king,
> or any of the exempt, the troops who plotted sedition and rebellion, or
> their brothers, (or) their sons, or their nephews, or their friends and
> guests, or those who are in their *confidence*[61] . . . or any enemy at all,
> whether male or female, whatever their name . . . whether by day or by
> night, in the city or in the country, whether on his throne where he is
> sitting, or on his podium, or while descending from . . . or while going
> out, wherever he wishes to go, or while [. . . ing] his . . . or while drink-
> ing or eating . . . will any human being make an uprising and rebel-
> lion against Assurbanipal, son of Esarhaddon, king of Assyria, or act
> against him in a hostile manner?[62]

Notwithstanding the concluding sections of these lists, which propose to account for external threats from anyone and anywhere, the specified persons,
from the eunuchs to the "friends and guests," identify personnel close to the
king and court (e.g., not all Cimmerians [and especially not those in Cimmeria],
but Cimmerian troops in the Assyrian army and cities). These texts created
a *textual community* of elites, the in-group of sufficient concern to king and

61. Lit., "who hear and know." Cf. below pp. 59–64 on *rahāṣu* as "confidence" and see Richardson 2010: 9–10 on "trust" and rebels, who "trust in themselves."

62. SAA IV 142; for an analysis of the oath-takers, see Ponchia 2014.

crown to warrant contractual and mantic instruments of control[63]—the larger body of persons in the palace, on campaign, and in diplomatic circles who made up the population of people who counted in practice. In a naïve sense, we are directly provided with a list of the people whom the state saw as its elites, though the obligations the lists claim to create cannot have been either as extensive as they pretended or yet inclusive of all the important players.

Looking beyond a strictly metropolitan account, could we propose a functional identification of elites across the empire? The definitional problem scholars wrestle with here is very similar to the one the Assyrians themselves confronted: from a heterodox world of wealthy trading cities, rural villages, venerable temple towns, and pastoralist tribes, the Assyrians faced the task of collating and creating some kind of rational hierarchy out of a myriad of titles and institutions originally created for purely local purposes, and often not directly transposable into the lexicographic categories of Assyrian administration. Was a tribal chief (*nasīku*) to be the equal of a prince (*rubû*)? Should a mayor (*ḫazannu*) of a major city like Babylon really have to defer to the provincial governor (LÚ.EN.NAM) of a backwater province like Parsua? These are largely theoretical questions, and Assyrian documents typically dispense with them by simplifying into divisions of Assyrians versus non-Assyrian,[64] and so such questions of ranking rarely came into the open even as they existed on clay. The questions nevertheless suggest how tangled the situation was in actuality. Assyrians did, however, recognize the categorical *legitimacy* of other elites in other states: the Urarṭians, for instance, were said to have their own magnates, governors, eunuchs, "bearded men," and so forth—called the "mighty ones" of their land.[65] Then again, it is hardly clear that the native Urarṭian terms, whatever they were, in fact transposed so cleanly into Assyrian ones.

One might try to build a typology of elite denotations (see figure 2.1). In addition to the already well-known Assyro-Babylonian titles and offices, sociopolitical terms for important people found in Assyrian letters of the SAA series included ascribed titles, relationships between individuals, community identities, kinship groups from the biological to the metaphorical, and descriptive terms which

63. See esp. Ponchia 2014, who argues that these juridical instruments acquired a new denotative function in the formation of the political community. Pongratz-Leisten 2013: 285–6 takes such lists to argue for the emerging centrality of one group in particular (the scholars), and that such texts structured authority (rather than simply reflecting and documenting existing authority as such); she does not, however, investigate the generative aspect of these lists themselves.

64. Even this strategy may be parsed for gradations by behavior, moral qualities, etc.; see Rivaroli and Verderame 2005; cf. Svärd 2012.

65. SAA V 85, 173, 178–9; see also XV 118, on local magnates in a town on the Babylonian-Elamite frontier. The late imperial encounter with major states clearly beyond Assyria's reach of permanent control (e.g., Urartu and Elam, but also Phrygia, Kush, and Dilmun) may have forced to the surface a form of recognition qualitatively different than that required to deal with subject polities, one in which extreme distance permitted a (safe) fantasy of parallel or peer imperial worlds.

<table>
<tr><td>

ASCRIBED TITLES

king of GN (LUGAL GN): I 1, *passim*
city-lord (LÚ.EN-URU [V xxii]): I 190.[i]
elders (LÚ.*šībūti*): X 112; XV 158
sheikh (*nāsiku*): X 113; XV 280; XVII 150–51.
nobility (*mār banî*): X 118, XIII 60; XI 146
　(LÚ.DUMU-SIG₅); XVII 20, 128; XVIII 56.
prince (LÚ.NUN): VIII 316; XVII 94 as
　"grandee" in a tribal context
leader (*bēlu*): XVIII 68
[ruler] of GN (GN or GN + gentilic): I 226
citizen (DUMU GN): I 1, *passim*

INDIVIDUAL RELATIONSHIPS

associate (*ittika*, lit., "those with you"): I 4.[ii]
colleague (LÚ.*kinattātu*, <*kēnu*, "true, loyal"):
　I 8; LÚ.GABA.RI.MEŠ: X 244; XVI 36.
companion (*ibru*): III 17
benefactor (LÚ.EN.MEŠ-MUN): X 294
great friend (EN *ṭābti*): XVI 48.
protégé (LÚ.*kidinnû*): XVII 48.

COMMUNITIES

of relatives (*kalzi* UN.MEŠ): I 171.
of palaces (*kalzi* é.gal): II p. 37.
scribal collegia (LÚ.A.BA.MEŠ): X 136–42.[iii]
royal entourage (*ina pān* LUGAL): X 226, XVII 16
old families (*qinnāte labīrūte*): XIII 152[iv]
"leading men" (ERIM.MEŠ *maḫrūti*): XVII 22

</td><td>

KINSHIP (REAL & METAPHORICAL)

"brothers" (šeš.m^{eš}): XV 1, 7, 24, 33, 90.[v]
cousins (DUMU-šeš-AD): I 190.
clan (*qinnu*): XVIII 201
members of father's line (*qinnišu* NUMUN
　É-AD): II p. 32.[vi]
little brother (*aḫu qallu*): V 33
of noble descent (DUMU.MEŠ-DÙ.MEŠ):
　X 112; XVII 150
family heads (SAG.DU.MEŠ): X 226
in-law relationship (EN.MEŠ MUN): XVIII 56

DESCRIPTIVE TERMS

"closer" (*qurbūti*) and "more remote"
　(*patûti*) palace groups: II p. 37
"important" men (*kabtu*, lit. "heavy")
　III 11; XVIII 15
"rich man" (LÚ.NÍG.TUK): III 11
the "mighty of the land" (KALAG.MEŠ *ša*
　KUR): V 179
a "loyal family" (*qinnu kēntu*): X 228; cf.
　XV 136, LÚ.*qinnu la pānêšu*.
"leaders" (LÚ.SAG.KAL.MEŠ), XVIII 201;
　XIX 98.

</td></tr>
</table>

---

[i]　i.e., vassal rulers; cf. X 112, where the Assyrian king is called "lord of kings" (EN LUGAL.ME).
[ii]　cf. trans. "his retinue," X 369.
[iii]　cf. "apprentices who [studied] with me" (LÚ.ŠAMAN.LÁ.MEŠ *ša ittiya liginnu* [x x x]): X 160.
[iv]　Distinguished from "common men" (*saklūte*).

[v]　Also XV 162; in some cases, biological brotherhood may be excluded where political fraternity may be meant, also XV 15 and XVII 52, perhaps "colleagues" or "compatriots."
[vi]　cf. dynastic line and "descendants of former royalty" (NUMUN MAN *pānûti*), II 6 (pp. 41–42).

FIGURE 2.1. Examples of Socio-Political Terms of Elite Definition in Assyrian Letters of the Series SAA.

evoked qualities of elite status not readily conveyed otherwise. Such terms are not endless, though their applications start to be once we multiply them by the many places, societies, and professional groups under Assyrian control. The recognition of elite identities preexisting imperial control, therefore, was no simple matter, and only aggravated by the intramural squabbles of competing groups and the men who appear "devoted to nobody."[66] Beyond identifying this as a general structural problem, it is difficult to appreciate its impact, since it is not a problem that any historical empire has ever fully solved. But it underscores the multilogic nature

---

66. SAA XVII 27, *lā ammar* < *amāru*, "to see, to hold in favor"; cf. SAA X 39, 68 ("to whom else would we be devoted?"), 307, XVI 63, XVII 95, 113.

of the identity to be formed: not just between Assyrians and non-Assyrians, but between metropolitans and provincials, officials and private households, civil and temple authorities, colonials and locals, and so on. This was not in any sense a dipole, and we cannot speak convincingly of either an empire-wide public program of cultural "Assyrianization" or emulation by non-Assyrians, although the promotion of something like a civic religion is perhaps demonstrable.[67] Neither is it clear that a discernable priority or hierarchy among elites was a desirable imperial goal, anyway; according to the rhetoric of obeisance, one was only ever "a dog among other dogs,"[68] with any preferential differentiation problematically implying some center of political power other than the king.

There was intense squabbling, suspicion, denunciation, and self-aggrandizement in the correspondence of Assyrian officials, and an atmosphere of unceasing competition and watchfulness. Thus, despite the fact that loyalty to the king—and lack thereof—was the ubiquitous and one-dimensional axis of rhetorical differentiation, one finds a paradox created by its application. On the one hand, some of the deviations from the loyalty principle that the empire thought were problems, such as the self-aggrandizement and self-enrichment of elites, arguably had untapped advantages (e.g., as pressure-release valves for inevitable competition and incentives for the extension of the Assyrian franchise). On the other hand, some of the things the empire thought were solutions, such as loyalty declarations and mandated reporting, created not only a toxic social atmosphere among elites, but inhibited the development of both political resilience and a central Assyrian "style" worth emulating.[69] Thus, the Assyrians did not have a cosmopolitanism yet; they were still dealing with the problems of its general absence and the advantages of its incipience. The site of contestation for cosmopolitanism's emergence, I will argue later, lay in the elaboration of a political notion of "confidence."

Dressed for Success: Marking Elite Style

But first I will make one final positive case for cosmopolitanism's existence in this world, mindful of Peter Bang's observation that there need not have been a consciousness of it in the target cultures we examine: What else might have counted as elite marking in the Assyrian empire? Imperial servants and officials were first of all easily visible by dress and adornment. The king was said to

67. Assyrian imperialism attended to the erection of monuments with the king's likeness in subject cities and around the periphery; the introduction of Assyrian symbols (but not gods) in towns and temples; the imposition of oaths (discussed earlier, pp. 39–40 and 44–46) and display of treaties; and the reproduction of small Assyrian "palaces" by local governors. Such features might aggregate toward something like a "civil religion" of Assyrian rule.

68. SAA XVI 132; also X 109, 218, 239, 294, 309, 359, etc.; cf. XIII 190.

69. Simonetta Ponchia (pers. comm.), however, has suggested to me that denunciations may also have produced a kind of "moral attitude" about the imperial system, i.e., a notion that it *ought* to work fairly (pointing to SAA XVI 64, which proposes rules for royal appeals). Cf. Radner's opinion, discussed pp. 34–35.

"dress and bless" those keeping his treaty,[70] and the literalism of this played out in any number of servants and foreign leaders being "dressed in purple" upon their oaths of allegiance, with silver bracelets put on their arms, and awarded daggers or other prestige weapons.[71] Such appointments made the link between finery and loyalty clear by consistently pairing the phrases "he shall carry a dagger and a ring of gold" to "and he shall keep the watch of the king, my lord."[72] Moreover, Assyrians recognized similar practices among foreign elites, as when they noted jewelry sent by the Urarṭian king to his own vassals,[73] or when messengers from foreign kings were awarded dress in purple and silver bracelets by the Assyrians.[74] The seal of the king[75] and the "cross" of the crown-prince[76] were also distributed to royal servants, visible markers of their station. It is not even too much of a stretch to think that the inscribed eye-stones given by the king to officials were not only status-markers but magical incarnations (if not simply reminders) of the king's omnipresent eye, ever-watchful through (and, more darkly, over) his servants.[77] These sumptuary practices were controlled by the king: there were officials who had not yet been dressed in purple,[78] leaving it as a brass ring still to grasp; and it was clear that if they dressed so without permission, they were malfeasant.[79] The distribution of dress and ornament was a prerogative of the king, and that prerogative was policed.[80] The body was thereby made one of the sites of cosmopolitan identity, manifesting itself in a highly personal way.

Imperial elites were also interested, of course, in property acquisition, especially in the provinces. One of the best-known estate-holders among this class was Remanni-Adad, the chief chariot driver of Aššurbanipal. Remanni-Adad owned dozens of estates—all of them purchased in silver rather than gifted to him—in at least fourteen towns as far apart as Arrapḫa and Ḫarran, distant by

70. SAA I 134, a messenger of the Mannean king.

71. SAA I 134, X 182, XV 90, 91, XVI 63. For goods distributed within a household of a royal relative living in Gambulu (SAA XVII 122), the objects given were mainly for the noble and his wife, but the noble's men were also robed in purple and equipped with bracelets, and the ladies-in-waiting likewise received garments. Cf. X 87, asking whether emissaries should wear "woolen garments" or "white clothing" before the king; but the distinction is unclear.

72. SAA XII 83; also XII 35, 36, XVI 63.

73. SAA V xxiii and no. 31.

74. SAA I 29.

75. Compare to the complaint about a man who is said to have been "lifted up" and "put around your neck like a seal," SAA I 12; and cf. the "sign of the king" (*ittu*) in SAA XVII 52–4, 160; and the shaving of prebend-holders by Sennacherib in SAA XVIII 82.

76. SAA X 30, as a "badge" (*simtu*) and "emblem(?)" (*kizirtu*).

77. SAA X 41, 348; see Clayden 2009; see Oppenheim 1968 on the surveillance-state overtones of the king's "eyes."

78. SAA XI 29. Indeed, we may be able to deduce state control over the commodities like dyed wool, iron, wine, textiles, purple dye, gold, and "luxury items": SAA I 46, V 100–101, XVI 84, XVIII 103, 115, Cole 1996: 41.

79. SAA XVIII 183, on rebels who wear the clothes of the officials they have killed: "These men are not friends, they are enemies!"

80. SAA XVI 63, XVII 129.

500 kilometers. Most of these estates were of modest size, 20, 30, or 60 hectares of land and a house; but some ran up to 600 hectares and several houses. In two cases, he bought entire towns; many of the properties had thousands of grape vines, orchards, pleasure gardens, pools, and people attached to the land; and, mindful of keeping up with important neighbors, Remanni-Adad's pleasure garden in Singara adjoined that of the royal vizier.[81] This is precisely the kind of personal wealth portfolio we would imagine for imperial elites; unfortunately, it is not well-paralleled in other texts, and so it is hard to say whether Remanni-Adad's case is typical or exceptional. One pattern which seems to hold steady is that what elite estates we do know of tended to be, modally, of modest size. Those properties assigned to crown officials were mostly under 40 hectares, with an average of eight people attached, some sheep and an orchard. What we do not know is just how many 40-hectare estates any given official might have.[82] The emphasis of the granting documents was anyway not on the size of a land-holding, but its tax-exempt status;[83] thus the privilege being emphasized was not wealth or its display as such, but that fiscal autonomy had been granted.

The primary concern voiced by most elites was to establish a household more than to acquire multiple estates.[84] The importance of elite residence is most clearly expressed through anxious statements about its absence. "I have no farmer, no farm equipment—no farm," complained one man.[85] Another lower-tier provincial official wrote sarcastically to another higher-up back in the city: "But really you must be in good spirits yourself! You live in your lord's house, you eat bread and drink beer comfortably!"[86] And a third says: "Like a dog, I bound about and roam about. I have no house, no maid, no servant."[87] One reads repeatedly this characterization of elites as dogs (who, important to the metaphor, lived in the street and not in the house[88]), as men without a fixed address; one disgruntled official even protests that he wags his tail for the king.[89] Elite culture was imitative of royal practice in projecting influence from a residence, and this simply could not be effectively done without a convincing house and household.[90] Yet the metaphor also hints at the emergence of

81. SAA VI 296–350.

82. The Harran census documents give estates up to about 100 hectares and 10,000 vines at the largest; with slightly larger numbers when assessing entire villages. SAA XI 221 documents estates for the *sartinnu*, eunuch, cohort commander, scribe, bodyguard, etc., in Barḫalzi, Carcemiš, Ḫindanu, etc.; cf. SAA XI 222, a large (450 ha.+) estate from earlier times, split up and sold off; also SAA XV 316.

83. SAA XII, passim, but especially 6, 8, 9, 19.

84. Postgate 2007: 23–8.

85. SAA X 294.

86. SAA XVII 63.

87. SAA XIII 190; similarly, SAA XVIII 60.

88. At most, a dog at the threshold of the house (SAA XVI 34).

89. SAA XV 288.

90. See also SAA XVII 102.

the independent elites of S. Eisenstadt's model as "free-floating" resources, per Peter Bang's observation. If effective dogs they were to be, then still would they require the trappings of a convincing doghouse.

As mentioned, most estates came along with the people and animals settled on them; retinues[91] and private guards,[92] men in livery, were among the most desirable staff. Carts and chariots were also sought after, in their "latest models," with expensive linen, leather, and wood fittings.[93] One disenfranchised member of the inner circle complained: "People pass my house, the mighty on palanquins, the assistants in carts, even the juniors on mules—and I have to walk!"[94] Commensalism, too, was an important mode of performative interaction between elites: there were dinners between Assyrian and Šubrian officials in Tušḫan;[95] festival invitations for Aramaean sheikhs at Assyrian-held Nippur;[96] and a drinking party turned conspiratorial at Ḫarran.[97] Many letters demonstrate independent contact between elites[98]—indeed, letter-writing itself was one of the premiere arenas of elite practice[99]—audiences granted, messengers exchanged, and alliances built, all unmediated by the king.[100] Public ostentation played its part as well, as wealthy Assyrians could and did make sizeable and highly visible donations of property to important temples[101] or dedicate statues of the royal family.[102] A modest gift-trade developed among elites for hard-to-find goods, as visible status markers—for ostrich eggs to be brought to Nippur,[103] for "that wine that you drink" to be sent from Borsippa in Babylonia,[104] for "luxury goods" (ṣaḫittāte) to be smuggled between Assyrian and Urarṭian elites.[105] And Assyrians shared our conceptual categories of

91. SAA XVII 122.

92. SAA I 11, XIII 20.

93. SAA V 152 and xxix, "with linen above and with *tunimmu*-leather below," i.e., made with not merely functional materials; Cole 1996: 33, carts with *šaššūgu*- and *šakkullu*-wood.

94. SAA X 294.

95. SAA V 32, 34; also I 14, 92, III 31, and XV 359; cf. SAA V xvii, that Rusa of Urarṭu also boasted of giving "meals to the inhabitants of the country."

96. Cole 1996: 27; the plan was to assemble the sheikhs for a conference at the festival (see also SAA X 354); also VII 112, IX 3; cf. the odd passage in SAA X 294 (r. 23f.) about a banquet gone wrong.

97. SAA X 179; see also X 2.

98. SAA I 8, one colleague warning another of "rebellion" beneath him; also, e.g., V 81 and XV 36–37.

99. Radner 2014 and Richardson 2016.

100. SAA V 33, an officer in Tušḫan reports that the nearby governor at Pulua has chided him with: "Why has the messenger of my little brother not come? Is a god visiting him?" The etiquette of subordinate relations thus pervaded officialdom. Also XVII 22: "But the leading men who do not keep the land in order and to whose words the king has listened, after making their views public, are now incessantly sending deceitful messages and fortifying their cities."

101. SAA XII 95–8.

102. SAA XIII 188: Officials of Harran create silver statues of the mother of the king including one for "the streets of Gadisê" (URU.*ga-di-se-e*, probably a place near Harran).

103. SAA XVII 147.

104. SAA XVIII 177: GIŠ.GEŠTIN <*šá*> *tašattû*; also XIII 33, XV 359, XVI 5, XV 358, a fragmentary letter, suggests a practice of sending heralds with "a letter and two jugs of wine."

105. SAA V 100–101.

conspicuous consumption, insofar as their sumptuary displays were encompassed by the verb *akālu*, "to eat."[106]

Our textual and art historical evidence for Neo-Assyria part ways appreciably when it comes to depicting the elite acquisition of prestige goods. Art historians of this period see a great range of emulative practices and cross-cultural sharing of motifs, styles, and materials in palaces, ivories, jewelry, drinking vessels, and so forth.[107] Cuneiformists, on the other hand, would have to admit that a concern for the acquisition or display of such sumptuary goods outside of the royal context was not broadly expressed in texts beyond lists of booty and tribute brought back from military campaigns (and notwithstanding the few examples given above): even the letters tend to comment on the centralization of wealth with the king.[108] In this regard, scholars working with different materials sometimes see quite a different Assyria.

Finally, the epistolary record might also lead us to think that Assyrian elites emulated or competed with one another in their acquisition of cultural erudition.[109] Officers writing to the king were fond of quoting Babylonian proverbs[110] and songs[111]— some of these snippets taking wisdom itself as their subject[112]— and we know of some scholars in private service to such men.[113] Access to wisdom texts at Nineveh was a special mark of rank, foreshadowing the rise of an educated elite as a counterpoise to imperial power in subsequent periods.[114] Again, this was controlled by the king: private acquisition of the divinatory arts was specifically forbidden by the crown. One governor was denounced for not declaring the employment of a diviner according to a royal order (quoted, but unfortunately broken: "Whoever has a scholar in his presence, but hides him from the king and does not send him to the palace, the king's [. . . will . . .] him."[115])

106. E.g., SAA VIII 517, X 294, XVI 63 r. 2–5, and XVII 34; as well as through the idiom "to eat bread under the king's protection," e.g., SAA I 10, XVII 48 and 63, XIX 152. In SB literature, see exs. CAD A/1, s.v. *akālu* v. 2b and 2d; cf. SAA XVI 183.

107. However, Assyrian conceptions did not produce any clear emic categories of their "style" or "taste," though that may not negate their usefulness as analytical terms; see Feldman 2014.

108. But cf. some texts documenting royal distributions of goods to officials, e.g., V 295, VIII 418, X 369, XVIII 131.

109. E.g., the divine hymn SAA III 4 ("wise," *eršu*; "erudite," *mudû*), 32, mentioning "wise bookkeepers [*šassuki enqūti*], who guard the secret [*nāṣir piršti*] of their lords"; these were probably real people, since the hymn mentions them with the magnates and governors.

110. See *passim* in SAA X, but especially SAA X 37, 207, 294 (an odd proverb about being stabbed in the mouth instead of in the back), 353 (attributed to Burnaburiaš); XVII 27, XVIII 1, 117, and 131.

111. SAA X 198.

112. SAA X 23: "An incompetent one [*lā mudê šipri*] can frustrate a judge, an uneducated one [*lā mudê amāti*] can make the mighty worry." SAA X 60 also points to a privileged discourse among scholars by sniffing: "Really, [the one] who has [not already] had (the meaning) pointed out to him cannot possibly understand it."

113. SAA XV 39.

114. SAA XVII 27, in which one official boasts of his "knowledge," *mandītu*.

115. SAA XVIII 131; similarly, X 179. This largely had to do with divination's status as a technical state secret rather than any stricture on scholarship per se. There is at least one other denunciation based on a man's

There is not, despite these flourishes and embellishments, much indication that the elite culture of the Neo-Assyrian period elaborated any widespread and rena-scent immersion in poetry, hymns, or expressive works, much less than that an enlightened elite worked for the good of the state and society thereby (as it was with, e.g., the early modern French nobles called *politiques*).

There was, however, a pervasive concern for "speaking well" or "speaking kindly,"[116] idioms of beautiful speech and diplomatic politesse. Mario Fales has recently discussed these expressions as fixtures of an emerging sociolect of the imperial elite, if not yet quite a classical rhetoric.[117] "Speak kindly with [the city-lords]!", as one diplomat is advised: "Your friend and enemy should not be treated differently!"[118] Although we know little about what might have constituted speak-ing well (especially since it was an explicitly oral phenomenon), a wealth of sec-ondary references suggest that speech was as indispensable a class marker to the Assyrian elite as it was to the English aristocracy in Victorian England.

An explicit conception of Assyrian elite cosmopolitanism is probably in best evidence when we consider the number of foreign elites taken as hostages (*līṭu*) to the capital cities of Kalhu and Nineveh. In addition to the purely political benefits of this practice, here was an acculturation project of the first water.[119] Members of non-Assyrian royal families, opposition leaders, agnatic and cadet-branch loyalists were commonly taken to the Assyrian capitals, sometimes for something like a one-year internship, but sometimes raised to adulthood from as young as five years of age.[120] Sometimes these people arrived as exiles; some-times as tribute under treaty terms, through marriage, or as captives from the battlefield.[121] Their residence was marked by training in language, service in the Assyrian army, oaths of loyalty, acquisition of property, and in some cases even marriage (including into the Assyrian royal family). The purpose was, of course, to develop an international class of imperial elites marked not only by loyalty, but by cultural affinity; we know of several cases in which Assyrianized foreign royalty were effectively reinserted into the imperial periphery as puppet rulers.[122] The Babylonian Bel-ibni, for instance, was famously said by Sennacherib to have "grown up like a puppy in my palace." Notably, this kind of distraint was

---

hire of a scholar to teach his son divination, SAA XVI 65; note also the "renegade scholars" who have defected to the enemy in XVIII 56.

116. E.g., SAA XV 91, 95–96 (*dibbi* DÙG.GA.MEŠ *issišunu dubbu*, lit. "speak good words with them"); XVII 111, and *passim*.

117. Fales 2009; see also now Fales 2015.

118. SAA XV 91; Mannu-ki-Ninua again advised to "speak kindly" to Kullumaneans.

119. See SAA II xx–xxi.

120. SAA XVII 94.

121. SAA X 112, XVII 1, 60–61, 93, 152, and *passim*. See the particular studies of Zawadski 1995, Radner 2012; but surprisingly the subject of hostages in Assyria has not yet enjoyed a thorough scholarly treatment.

122. E.g., a hostage son to be reinstalled in Borsippa (SAA XVII 1); and the lady Barsiptu in a "rehabili-tated" (<*kaṣāru*) Bīt-Dakkuri (SAA XVII 73; cf. no. 68).

practiced on a smaller scale by individual elites as well as by the king. These men were quick to insist that any local notables detained by them were the guests of a host, and not the prisoners of a jailer ("I never take anyone—if he is a hostage or not a hostage!—and imprison him in the garrison of the king, my lord"[123]), but the power relationship could not, of course, be any clearer. Individual elite households thereby made a claim to local authority based on guest-host relations, if not in the didactic sense of promoting Assyrian culture.

The features discussed so far seem in some ways expected categories: Assyrian elites liked to accumulate wealth and nice stuff, and they liked to show it off; like a lot of colonial officers, they had a smattering of education without any substantial intellectual or cultural wherewithal; they spoke in an exclusive speech register marking their class; and their power relations played out through conventions of household etiquette. We could be talking about the administrators and officers of the British Raj here. And yet there does not (yet) develop the kind of class *consciousness* we see in the British Indian case, because the deep historical precedents of a durable elite did not yet exist, as it did on both the British and Indian sides. Assyrian elites were still in the early historical and internal phases of sibling rivalry (with their peers) and separation-individuation (from the king) that would later make an autonomous elite class identity thinkable and workable as an external and extensible category across the coming millennium of Babylonian, Persian, Seleucid, and Roman cultures.[124] The positive argument for Assyrian cosmopolitanism can at most be that it was incipient and stage-setting, rather than critical to the way imperial society was run.

Do Not Envy the Wicked: Class and Competition

And if that is the most that can be said about it, now comes the negative argument. All these status markers got complicated very quickly in the unregulated arena of Assyrian elite competition. Some of the things elites needed to instrumentalize imperial power in their local communities—estates, luxury objects, retinues, and so forth—obligated them to engage in conspicuous consumption to the point of running afoul of jealousy from their peers and denunciation to the king. The very attributes they needed to do their jobs endangered their positions, and sometimes their lives.

"Why does the king, my lord, pay attention to groundless accusations?" mourned one libeled courtier.[125] Invidious comparison in this world was pervasive

---

123. SAA XVII 93: i.e., he bears personal responsibility for them as guests of diplomatic status.

124. Cf. the earlier, nearly ubiquitous concern for individual "good reputations" (*šumu*) indicative of the face-to-face relations of smaller states; see Richardson 2016.

125. SAA V 121. On the atmosphere of intense suspicion and denunciation among rival elites, see also SAA V xxix and nos. 81, 149, and 260, among many others; see also XVII 46.

and without clear rules for dispute resolution. Individual elites were highly sensitive to what others got and what was due to them. This was the case with one man given, he felt, not enough land, complaining that another governor had land, horses, and chariots given to him "befitting his social station" (*ša simtu*)—so why not himself?[126] These jealousies engendered accusations and denunciations in turn. I take as a point of reference a letter from one Lipḫur-Bēl, the governor of Amidu (modern Diyarbakir, about 300 kilometers northwest of Nineveh). He strenuously denied a denunciation ("The royal bodyguard shocked me!") that he had appropriated royal property—a common charge—except as a way to build a "royal palace" for the king there, with 200 stone slabs, the king's likeness "drawn inside," and the king's subjects settled therein.[127] Little could hide, however, that this "royal palace" was just Lipḫur-Bēl's own house. With some sympathy, we must note that this was actually just how the king intended it, that his governors should reproduce the authority of the imperial palace locally in very literal terms. But to live *too* much like a king meant one flew dangerously close to the sun. The trick was to camouflage private assets as royal assets to avoid charges of misappropriation and undue ambition.

An interesting phenomenon was the development of the concept of "squandering" (Akk. *buddudu*), a word unique to the Neo-Assyrian dialect. "The governors have squandered the household of our lord," one letter warns, "and the king does not know!"[128] Charges of wastefulness were a warning sign, a danger zone in which elites were given notice that they seemed to be straying from an appropriate level of opulent display and accumulation into a perceived state of untoward self-enrichment and (more problematic) self-aggrandizement. Thus, normal types of assets in abnormal quantities could be construed as "appropriating as one's own," with bodyguards swelling to the size of private armies;[129] growing holdings in silver, cattle,[130] and labor;[131] entire villages used as personal estates;[132] booty, taxes, and dues claimed under elite authority;[133] the exercise of powers specific to the king,[134] seizure of royal votives to gods,[135] or assertions of

126. SAA XVII 48; cf. no. 46.
127. SAA V 15.
128. SAA XVI 42; see also X 369, XIII 33, XV 55 and 62, XVIII 24. Compare to Kuhrt and Weisweiler (this volume), who both identify the perils of competition as a moral hazard in systems of elitism.
129. SAA I 11.
130. SAA X 369.
131. SAA XV 55.
132. SAA XII 90: Aššurbanipal recovers a stolen village from a eunuch whose "disposition changed and he took that stela away by thievery and took that village for his own."
133. SAA XIII 33, XVII 152.
134. SAA XVIII 125: A certain Hinnumu made speeches in Uruk falsely claiming that the king had put command in his hands and going so far as to make the local cohort commander and eunuch "grasp his feet."
135. SAA XIII 134, about a lamentation priest who removed precious goods of temples and replaced them with other (presumably inferior) objects: "One of the clergymen saw him, but he turned him back and let him go. No one has authority and no one says anything to him!"

independent political status.[136] These last were perhaps the worst of all, because they went beyond merely depriving the king of his treasure and directly into undercutting his authority. One man from Arvad was denounced for using news from court to maintain that the king had actually authorized him to do and take whatever he liked: "He claims: 'They have written to me from the palace: "Do only what is good for you!"'"[137] Charges of disloyalty were bad, but it was even worse if one was seen to be "seeking favor in the eyes of the governors," or too closely mimicking royal authority,[138] and there is little to suggest that individual fame was politically advantageous.[139]

Some of these charges went beyond mere wars of words, revealing individual vendettas and factional squabbling. In one case, for example, the servants of the Chief Cupbearer seized the fields and orchards of another official and chased his servants away.[140] In another case, two Assyrian officers simply borrowed royal cavalry without orders in order to reconquer towns which had broken away from their command to align themselves with a different Assyrian official— simply a turf war between local officers.[141] And the apparatus of the state could be used as a weapon: sometimes routine administrative tasks, such as inventories of cultic payments due or contributions to royal projects, could turn into audits by some individuals and groups working in collusion against others.[142] It was possible to sideline or blacklist rival elites by blocking their access to the king.[143] Denunciations marked this communicative problem, where no rationalized system had been produced to distinguish the proper exercise of elite authority from malfeasance. No mechanism of elite settlement yet existed to stabilize the mistrust generated by the system.[144] Up to a point, this served royal purposes very well insofar as it limited the efficacy of elite insubordination. But at the point at which it inhibited information and resources from reaching the top of the system, or where it disrupted political or military operations in

---

136. SAA XIII 181, A Dakkuri Chaldean chieftain fails to deliver tribute in the name of the Assyrian king, and reportedly says: "I will give of my own accord and establish my own name."

137. SAA XVI 127; cf. XVIII 102, a report on a local "traitor" who (erroneously, as it turns out) keeps "thinking, 'The news of my doings will not reach the palace.'"

138. SAA XVI 32–33, someone who "does not obey the orders of the king, (but) is seeking favour in the eyes of the governors."

139. But note the odd literary piece SAA III 50, unusual for celebrating a non-royal figure, one Na'id-Šiḫu; indeed, the king is said to have "(stood) in his chariot, his eyes filled with tears: 'From now on, officers, Na'id-Šiḫu will be in command of you!'"

140. SAA X 58.

141. SAA XV 69: the insubordination is clear: "They do not openly show that they are running around with them."

142. SAA X 96, a list of governors who had not given their regular offerings to the Aššur temple (cf. X 361); also XIII 138, describing a group cover-up of temple thefts, showing that people were both watching and protecting against being watched.

143. SAA X 361, letters returned to sender from along the post road; the word has come down the line not to forward this man's letters to the king; cf. XVII 59.

144. Burton and Higley 1987, on political transformations of elite disunity into consensus.

the field, it was wildly counter-productive. And most relevant to our subject, the generalized responsibility to report, denounce, and watch created conditions manifestly unfriendly to the creation of cosmopolitan elitehood, which depended on trust and shared knowledge.[145]

AUTHENTICITY AND CONFIDENCE

So what are we left with? I will make two points in closing. The first has to do with an Assyrian sense of the Other. Was there any sign of a developing ethic of recognition that cosmopolitanism requires? Many have written on this,[146] with the opinions running from seeing an Assyria as having a mild distaste for other cultures, up to the point of its having had a moralizing but largely non-ethnographic hostility toward a world of enemies (the pervasive violence of Assyrian imperialism notwithstanding);[147] in sum, an empire with a relative disinterest in the problem of Otherness. Balancing this is a corresponding sense that Assyrian cultural identity was equally weakly formed, expressed outside of royal inscriptions at most by the indication of legal jurisdiction.[148]

There seems little reason to challenge this consensus. One finds very little of the derogation we associate with ethnic distinction, the kind we expect would necessarily precede the curiosity and limited tolerance of a cosmopolitan account. Confusingly, the Assyrians were largely indifferent to the question, at least on clay. The term for "foreigner" was resolutely neutral in meaning simply "citizen of another country (like our country)."[149] The term *aḫû*, which means "strange, foreign, other" was otherwise unmarked: that is, a scholar might mark a list of omens as Assyrian and *aḫû* (commonly translated as "non-canonical" in this context), but then proceed to use and interpret the Assyrian and non-Assyrian omens alike. Or he might distinguish between "suitable" rituals for the king and those which were simply "not ours"—not "unsuitable" or "defective," just "not ours"[150]—and so forth.

Such invective as there was for "barbarians" was, on closer inspection, voiced only for their failure to adopt oaths and treaties of loyalty to the Assyrian king, rather than for any cultural or linguistic traits.[151] And Assyrian

---

145. Fales 2015: 94-95 on watchfulness as a "collective attitude" and "ingrained mental habit" evoked by the term *maṣṣartu*.

146. E.g., Zaccagnini 1982, Fales 1982, Cifarelli 1995.

147. But see Emberling 2014, with literature: some feel "these reliefs indicate an interest in the specific cultural practices of Assyrian enemies."

148. E.g., SAA XVI 64.

149. SAA II 6 (esp. ll. 222–23): a neutral term for "foreigner": DUMU KUR *šanitim*, just "citizen of another country" (cf. l. 339: DUMU KUR *šāninim*, "citizen of a rival country").

150. SAA XVIII 204.

151. SAA X 111: Cimmerians are "barbarians (NUMUN LÚ.*ḫalgati*, a hapax) who recognize no oath sworn by god and no treaty."

behavior was not above reproach itself: one royal adviser asked, on reporting some bad behavior: "If these people, who are Assyrians, refuse to fear the king my lord, how will foreigners behave towards [us]?"[152] Another letter describes Assyrians and Tabaleans sold into slavery and subsequently freed in identical terms, with no distinction made between the groups beyond their ethnonyms.[153] Foreign styles were only "unsuited" (*lā simāti*) to Assyria when and insofar as they were from "enemy" countries.[154] One oft-cited letter upbraids a scribe for writing in Aramaic,[155] but a close read reveals that insisting on Akkadian was a matter of maintaining a systematic format of letter-writing for archival purposes, not an ethnic judgement; virtually all other uses of the word "Aramean" in Assyrian letters are neutral adjectives used to identify towns and scribes writing the language.[156] There are a few cases in which foreigners may have been feminized in an implicitly derogatory way, but even in these rare passages the sense in inconclusive.[157] In the entire corpus of Neo-Assyrian letters, I am aware of exactly one that suggests an articulated "recognition ethic," and it is from a Babylonian rather than an Assyrian: a letter urging the king to respect the customs of a town which had traditionally intermarried with two local Aramean tribes: "The king, my lord, should not act wrongly in this." But in even this case, this was just practical advice on avoiding a rebellion, not a plea for recognition as such.[158] In all, this is not the record of a culture engaged in loads of cultural comparison and introspection; the absence of even negative comments shows that the judgments that cosmopolitan tolerance requires were not being made.

Does this mean the Assyrians had no engagement with the problem? This brings me to my second and final point, the problem of authenticity. Neo-Assyrian letters clearly demonstrate the imperiled position of imperial elites, caught between their royal mandates and the local people they governed, but not along the axis of

---

152. SAA XIII 19.

153. SAA XV 268.

154. SAA X 241: an amulet from the "enemy country" (KUR.*nakire*) is "unsuited to Assyria" (*lā simāti ša* KUR.Aššur^{ki} *šina*).

155. SAA XVII 2: "... if it is acceptable to the king, let me write and send my messages to the king on Aram[aic] parchment sheets'—why would you not write and send me messages in Akkadian? Really, the message which you write in it must be drawn up in this very manner—this is a fixed regulation (*kī pī agannîtimma idat*)!" That the message must be "drawn up" (<*šaṭāru*) suggests that the objection has to do with formatting and archiving, not any qualitative opinion of Aramaic as such. As we know, the empire employed plenty of Aramaic scribes. See Nissinen 2014.

156. SAA XIV 345, an "Aramean Town," and *passim*; cf. XVIII 1, a negated, but equally uninflected, reference, to "non-Babylonians."

157. SAA III 50, a short literary composition in which a young commander reports having "plundered the Aḫlamu-women." See also SAA XVIII 158, Babylonians claiming that they have had enough of guarding the rights of Elamite, Tabalite, and Ahlamite "women."

158. SAA XVIII 113; cf. Cole 1996: 8, in which the Assyrian envoy juxtaposes the status of "enemy" against that of "kinsman" to a sheikh; have they here adopted a local vernacular idiom? Cf. the "happiness" of Babylonia mentioned in XVII 32 and 40, letters which we may rightly imagine are unconcerned with emotional happiness.

cultural authenticity as I had originally imagined.[159] The paradigm case I looked
to is well-known: the encounter at Jerusalem between Assyrian and Judean officials. The biblical scene transpires without the presence of kings Hezekiah and
Sennacherib, showcases the knowledge and ability of their delegates, and directly
opens up the crucial question of credibility. "Speak to us in Aramaic," plead
Hezekiah's officials, "for we understand it well; do not speak to us in the language
of Judah in the hearing of the people on the wall." But the Assyrians, according to
the biblical account, are undeterred: "Has my master sent me to speak these words
only to your master and to you, and not to the men sitting on the wall, who are
doomed with you to eat their own dung and to drink their own urine?"[160]

This moment encapsulates the fraught position of imperial elites, whether
officials or vassals. Obligated to facilitate imperial authority on behalf of a distant king, their ability to effect that authority was bounded by their local credibility. That boundary was a matter of cultural authenticity: the ability of elites
to govern effectively was paradoxically contingent on the local appearance that
they negotiated from some basis of independence. Any impression to the people
for whom elites spoke that they acted more in collusion with the Assyrians
rather than against them would have undermined the authority that permitted
them to help the Assyrians in the first place. This model finds a good deal of
grounding in the long record of local anti-Assyrian rebellions in which competing groups of local elites, even competing branches of local elite families,
formed the axis of compliance with and resistance to the Assyrians.

That said, the question of *cultural* authenticity is much better suited to the
later times in which the Jerusalem account was redacted, when the principle of
empire was more firmly established in the Near East, rather than for the Neo-
Assyrian period in which the story was set, when the modes of signaling basic
political authenticity were still being hammered out. Because if we look at the
writings of imperial elites in Neo-Assyrian times, what we find is an insistence on obtaining "confidence" (deriving from the verb *raḫāṣu*, especially in
nominalized forms) from the king, rather than approbation or recognition from
peers.[161] Displays of royal trust arriving in the form of messengers, bodyguards,
symbols (e.g., the king's seal), or provisions[162] were said to keep the lands in
the king's hands[163] and publicly reiterated his continued support for individual

---

159. For useful contrasts with systems which developed mythologies of elite pasts (Haubold, this volume)
or social precepts such as honor, virtue, and *paideia* (Lavan, also this volume) as strategies of distinction which
might erase local or juridical identities; such developments are largely absent in the Neo-Assyrian case.

160. 2 Kings 18:26–27; see further Richardson 2014a: 478–9.

161. See above, nn. 2 and 4; cf. Pongratz-Leisten's 2013: 293–4 observations on the growing "self-
confidence" of Neo-Assyrian elites—in the positive, English vernacular sense, without reference to *raḫāṣu*; cf.
the illegitimate "confidence in oneself."

162. See Postgate 2007: 8–13, who sees the king's authorization throughout the hierarchy manifested in
direct intervention, letters under royal seal, and specific royal representatives (*ša qurbūti*).

163. SAA XVIII 89; also XV 129 and 213.

nobles and officers. "May I see a sign from the king, my lord," one man begged, "and may we get confident through it!"[164] "I shall 'speak friendly' with them," promises a man charged with establishing Assyrian authority in a newly submitted territory, "give them orders, and make them confident."[165] Or, from an impatient rescript of the king's order to a scholar: "The gist of the rest of the words [of the king's command] is: don't be afraid, but have much confidence and wait for my later report!"[166]

These many entreaties to the king, asking that he "give confidence," might disappear as so much boilerplate language in letters full of niceties and pufferies.[167] What was "confidence"? The quality was essentially tied to the *visibility* of the Assyrian king's support. Legitimate political "confidence" or "trust" could only be given to elites by the king, but it was only useful when other subjects could perceive that it had indeed been given. The centrality of this ethic underscores that whatever veneer of cosmopolitanism elites might have arrogated to themselves was yet fundamentally useless without the trust of the king, given *pars pro toto*. And "confidence" as the root of legitimate political authority is nowhere so clearly demonstrated as when it was inverted or perverted—in the many instances in which rebels, malfeasants, and other political undesirables were said to have committed the unpardonable sin of having had "confidence in themselves";[168] as John Dunn puts it, "the twin of trust is betrayal."[169]

The historical stage at which such an intangible and personal quality as trust might emerge as a crucial political value would be a transformational one, when bridges from personal to institutional politics were being built. One might compare the position of Assyrian "confidence" to the liminal moment at the end of the Roman Republic into the reign of Augustus when "friendship" (*amicitia*) played such a vital role in instrumentalizing political power, with a similar range of hazards and rewards.[170] "[A]s a modality of action," Dunn continues, trust "is essentially concerned with coping with uncertainty over time," especially where the challenge of creating governance changes over time,

> establishing and sustaining structures of government and responsibility which in some measure merit and earn trust. Where such institutions already exist and happen to be operating successfully, it is reasonable for

164. SAA XVII 52-4.

165. SAA XVII 111.

166. SAA X 372.

167. E.g., SAA IV 142, VIII 476, X 372, XV 129, 136, 159, 213, 306, XVI 60, XVII 21, 52-4, 111, 116, 199, XVIII 113, 201, XIX 87, 130. Cf. the "confidence" inspired in the king by the gods, e.g. II 1, III 3, 46, etc.

168. E.g., SAA XVI 60, said of the plotter Sasi.

169. Dunn 1988: 81: "However indispensible trust may be as a device for coping with the freedom of others, it is a device with a permanent and built-in possibility of failure."

170. My thanks for Cliff Ando for suggesting this comparison; one might then further distinguish the political role of "friendship" against its older and more durable use in economic relations of patronage and clientage.

individuals to feel a stolid indifference towards the exertions which have brought them into being and to see them merely as occasions for current confidence. But where they have yet to be established, the need for direct and exigent forms of trust is altogether more importunate.[171]

Creating day-to-day governance over the Assyrian empire—the first imperial formation for centuries—absent an identifiable supra-regional elite class, required relying on and building out from some of the social principles of face-to-face relations as "trust" provided.

But confidence had to be *displayed*. It was not sufficient for governing elites to only travel to gain an audience with the king at far-away Nineveh and thereby obtain "confidence"; they consistently requested of the king that messengers be sent *to them* with *offers* to come to Nineveh, or that the king send the emblems of the palace.[172] Such requests from elites explicitly stated that only in this way would local people acknowledge their clout, because it had been made conspicuous.[173] The public performance of confidence-building practices tied personal devotion to authority—

Now, after I have been twice to the audience of the mighty king, I am beginning to regain my dignity again [*ina bultīya anaḫḫisi*]![174]

—just as the absence of those displays were tied to the collapse of political authority:

I did not even get an audience with the king. . . . If this is the way the king, my lord, regards me, I am finished![175]

The visibility of "trust" was expressed in literal terms: a "devoted person" was one who was "seen by" (<*amāru*) someone, and a huge fund of allied verbiage connected political viability to frontality, as one was understood to stand, literally and metaphorically, in front of the king.[176] (This is in contrast to the

---

171. Dunn 1988: 73, 79–80; also 81, on social existence as dependent on trust, i.e., "the presence or absence of relatively well-founded expectations about the conduct of others."

172. SAA XVIII 201.

173. SAA XVII 116: "The messengers of the king should now quickly come to us. Then *we* will come quickly, see the king, our lord, and [get] confident" (emphasis added). The officials writing request messengers of the king to come with an offer of an audience with the king to "get confident" because they want people to *see* them get invited; no. 117 is similar, hoping that people will not say "the king does not [invite us]"; also X 171.

174. SAA XVII 27, r. 1 (*bultu*, "dignity"); also XVII 95.

175. SAA XIII 190 ("And I perish at my work like a dog!"); also XVI 36 ("As long as the crown prince is here and not going for the audience to Nineveh, how am I to act?") and XVII 140 (Aramean sheikhs near Uruk who become disaffected because they had not "heard anything benevolent," i.e., any news of support, from [in this case] a rebel lord).

176. Especially of the form *mazzāz pānišu* (Sum. LÚ.GUB-IGI), "(the king's) entourage," but lit. "stationed in front," widely referenced in the Assyrian letters, e.g., X 226-7. Cf. SAA XV 136, terming one disloyal family in Marpada as LÚ.*qinnu lā pānêša*, lit., "not in front." The entire language of audiences, gifts, greetings, escorts, messengers, etc. emphasized the idiom of facing/countenancing rather than backing up/supporting; e.g., SAA X,

idiomatic English expression of support and confidence when someone is said
to be "behind you.") The political theater of audiences, arriving letters and gift
exchange implied imperial protection,[177] a social principle of *dignitas* (*bultu*),[178]
an inclusion in the circle of those "speaking kindly,"[179] and the instrumentality
of local reputation for the intermediary elite: "my name has become respectable
under the protection of the king," writes a headman from the Gambulu tribe.[180]

The semantic extension of patronage becomes clearer in those cases in which
the lack or loss of visible "confidence" resulted in problems for local elites. Elites
who were humiliated,[181] discredited, or felt they had been "abandoned" by the
king[182] tied their reputation management issues to their ability to govern,[183] as
when a Babylonian temple officer complained that a rival had "belittled me in
the assembly of my country and made me look stupid before the people of my
country."[184] One might note that expressions for more pedestrian and non-po-
litical issues of "trust" (i.e., as a matter of believing (in) this or that individual
person) usually used the verb *qiāpu* instead of *raḫāṣu*;[185] this helps to distinguish *raḫāṣu* as something broader than mere personal confidence and more
like political credibility.

These "no-confidence" votes were not only personal crises for individual
elites,[186] but problems for Assyrian governance. Some letters of complaint tie
the injustice and rapacity of officials[187] to the alienation of their subjects,[188]
with the most florid problems characterized as "hate" (*zēru*, from *zêru*).[189]

150, "The whole country has turned its face towards the king, my lord"; also 157: men who have "turned their
face to Assyria"; and XVII 33: *ina pān*, "before" as expressing "to be in service." See Postgate 2007: 5.

177. SAA XV 162, XVII 23.

178. SAA XVII 27: refers to men "who are devoted to nobody" (*lā ammar*), <*amāru*, "to see," and by extension "to hold in favor."

179. *raḫāṣu* and *dibbī ṭābūti* are connected in SAA XV 159 and XVII 111.

180. SAA XVII 102; cf. XII 85, an appointment document, the curse formula of which rewards disloyalty
with "bad reputation."

181. SAA XVII 52; in no. 130, a man fears becoming a "laughingstock" (*ṣūḫētīya*) in the local assembly.

182. SAA XVIII 58: "The king my lord must not abandon me!" *lā umaššaranni*; XIII 158: "I may weep
before all lands, but there is no one who would give heart to me. So it is to you alone that I look—you who are my
lord." If one is out of favor with the king, one is (metaphorically) alone.

183. XVIII 192: "The people of Nippur and the whole country have discredited me"; the writers of XVII 120
tie their unpopularity to the fact that they have to order people of the land to work, which results in their being
"sulky" (notwithstanding the opening claim of the letter that "the mood of the people is good.")

184. SAA XVIII 202.

185. SAA XVII 55 and 170, but more common outside of the insistent politics of state letters.

186. Although: SAA XVIII 61: "So, although I have always revered the king, my lord, when I am dead,
where shall they bury me?"; and SAA XVIII 113: an envoy asks the king to send a royal messenger "to give the
city confidence and, for myself, to raise my spirits."

187. SAA XVII 59 (cf. no. 62): The letters of a prefect (LÚ.*šaknu*), Nabu-taklak, are actually being written
by "his delegates" (LÚ.*qīpānīšu*, i.e., the *qēpu*'s), and they are advocating that he be "removed" (*šūṣi*) from office;
the king has asked if he has been unjust (<*ḫabālu*) to them; XVIII 54: Ṣillaya will "kill us all by oppression."

188. SAA XVII 105: local officers are "alienating (*ušennû* <*šanû*, to be different) town after town."

189. See also XVI 29: "the Barhalzeans hate me (*izirrūni*)"; and XVII 55: "he is detested because of this"
(*alla agâ bīš*) and "defecting" (>*maqātu*), both in fragmentary contexts. SAA X 348: in a riot, Babylonians throw
lumps of clay at the cohort commander and his messengers; XII 85.

But other letters make clear that alienation was the cost of compliance, where "confidence" alone had proven insufficient. One man pleads with the king: "The king knows that all lands hate us because of Assyria!"[190] Another loyalist claims to have prayed for the king every morning and evening, but was "despised because of the king . . . and his house has been destroyed because he grasps the feet of the king."[191] That the opposite of "confidence" was "hate"[192] rather than "authenticity" shows us that the core principle of loyalty was compromised and complicated by a boundary of credibility. Elites might be outfitted with credibility, and yet at the same time need to distance themselves from the king to render governance effective—the basic dilemma of compliant colonial elites.

Babylonia offers the best examples of political crises precipitated by this "unenviable dilemma," this contested authenticity, because its cultural ties to and historical contests with Assyria were deeper than other ruled places; and because Babylonia more than other parts of the empire gives a few cases in which the quality of being Babylonian vis-à-vis non-Babylonians (and especially the Assyrians) is occasionally voiced.[193] In one case, the king was told of the absolute devotion of a man named Sin-iddina; but that consequently, the whole of Bīt-Yakin, a Chaldean tribe, loathed him. Then the letter animates the specter of the dead Yakinite rebels' chief: "Were Yakin still alive, one like Sin-iddina would not be shielded!"[194] Bīt-Yakin was a borderland of Assyrian authority, with a long history in the seventh century of intense partisanship.[195] In another case, in the city of Borsippa, the situation was even worse: the king was warned against bringing a local ruler to visit Assyria because "his people will rally against him [*nišēšu ana muḫḫīšu lipḫurū*]—and the people who are not his will rally against him, too!"[196] Another man, Aqar-Bēl-lumur, complains that his Aramean subjects have destroyed what property he had because he worked for the Assyrians—but precisely because the Assyrians had failed to give him even more land! Because he had been thereby exposed as both compliant *and* insufficiently trusted! Aqar-Bēl-lumur calls himself "doubly troubled."[197] Exactly: the dilemma.

190. SAA XVIII 70: the *šandabakku* of Nippur, begging for water, nevertheless fears that "all the lands" would say: "The people of Nippur who grasped the feet of Assyria had their fill of thirst."

191. SAA XVIII 88: this because this Na'id-Marduk, an Assyrian loyalist in Sealand, is said to pray for the king "every morning and every evening . . . [and] his heart is completely devoted to the king, his lord." See also SAA XVIII 181.

192. But also "fear," as in the common encomium: "Fear [<*palāḫu*] not! Be confident!" E.g., SAA XV 306, also X 372.

193. See Larsen's 2000: 117–18 and 123–5 argument for the "internal sovereignty" of the Babylonian cities under the Assyrians, and the particular position of their elders and leading citizens.

194. SAA XVII 43.

195. See esp. SAA XVIII 85–6 on pro- and anti-Assyrian debate there.

196. SAA XVII 82.

197. SAA XVIII 60: *adi 2-šú dalḫāk.*

The experience of imperial governance brought the Assyrians at least to this point of recognition: the individual credibility of their agents in the periphery played a vital role in durable governance. The Assyrians took modest steps to extend elites' freedom of action and establish for them a status modestly separate from the central authority through the extension of "confidence" (or perhaps, better: "respect"). Any cultural basis to this credibility, however, as a matter of a class consciousness or even "party affiliation" type of social sympathy, lagged behind these tactical concessions.[198] The best evidence for the issue is from Babylonia. Because Babylon was nearly unique in the degree to which it put the unenviable dilemma of elites on display, that region became the crucible for the development of elite identities and emulations for the next three centuries. Assyria may have failed to develop or exploit cosmopolitan identities in their ideological and administrative structure, but they began to name the problem. When one looks at elite culture in those next centuries, it is hard not to think that it was opulent, highbrow Babylon that responded to the question posed by its imperial Assyrian predecessor.

198. Fales 2015: 95 opines that any "common spirit" among the rank-and-file and the "king's men" was "utterly dependent on the king's approval and favor, even to the detriment of their colleagues."

3

Empire Begins at Home

Local Elites and Imperial Ideologies in Hellenistic Greece and Babylonia

Kathryn Stevens

Stevens presents four case studies in the self-presentation of local elites and the construction of local cultural memory in the Seleucid empire, two from Babylonia and two from the Greek cities of Anatolia. The cuneiform texts produced by members of the priestly elite in Uruk and the Greek texts inscribed by civic leaders in Lindos and Halikarnassos have at first glance almost nothing in common, but at a more fundamental level they share a "deeply historicizing localism." In different but analogous ways, the two groups write "both themselves and contemporary empires into local histories which stretch back to the distant past." She also shows that the Seleucid rulers collaborated in the process of "assimilating the imperial to the local." Exploring the logic of "localism" for both rulers and ruled in an imperial space fragmented into dynastic kingdoms with rivalrous universal ambitions, she argues that it suited both local elites and their Seleucid rulers "to construct imperial identities . . . which emphasized local particularity and autonomy rather than a broader sense of regional or imperial community." The chapter is a powerful illustration of the effectiveness of local idioms in integrating local elites into a wider imperial order in what we would term a regime of subordination.

INTRODUCTION

εἰς ταὐτὸ συνενεγκὼν τὰ πανταχόθεν. . . . πατρίδα μὲν τὴν οἰκουμένην προσέταξεν ἡγεῖσθαι πάντας, ἀκρόπολιν δὲ καὶ φρουρὰν τὸ στρατόπεδον, συγγενεῖς δὲ τοὺς ἀγαθούς, ἀλλοφύλους δὲ τοὺς πονηρούς.

[Alexander] brought together all regions into a single domain. . . . He instructed all men to consider the whole inhabited world as their fatherland, his camp as its stronghold and garrison, all good men as their kinsmen, and all wicked men as foreigners.[1]

---

1. Plut. *De Alex. fort.* 1.6.

For a brief historical moment, Alexander the Great created an empire which, by the standards of the day, was truly global: it spanned most of the known world, surpassed the territorial reach of all previous imperial formations, linked Europe and Asia, and united under a single ruler areas from Greece to Afghanistan. This short-lived world empire rapidly fragmented after Alexander's death, but the Greco-Macedonian conquest and settlement of the Near East had forever altered the structure of the *oikoumenē*. Although what we call the Hellenistic world consisted not of a single empire but a set of interlocking kingdoms, these were connected by a number of important shared features: a common genesis, the diasporic Greco-Macedonian communities scattered across them all, and sociopolitical and cultural structures exported from the "old" Greek world. All this created what Rostovtzeff called "the unity and homogeneity of the Hellenistic world from the point of view of civilization and mode of life."[2] Moreover, at least in the early Hellenistic period, each of the successor dynasties nurtured the hope of reconquering the whole of Alexander's empire, and rulers presented their own domains in globalizing or universalizing terms, further contributing to the idea of a single world to be won. In the Hellenistic world, we have at once the sense of a single vast space—unified by Macedonian imperialism, Hellenic culture, and the interaction of both with an array of subject cultures—and the reality of a network of competing kingdoms and independent states fighting for supremacy and survival.

How did different Hellenistic local elites experience and negotiate their place in this world of competing "global" empires, and how did imperial elites manage cultural difference to gain and foster their cooperation? As a contribution to the exploration of such questions, this chapter examines a phenomenon which would be opposed to cosmopolitanism on most definitions of the term,[3] arguing that it helped to naturalize empire and maintain the cooperation of culturally disparate elites in the same way as universalist ideologies in other imperial contexts. That phenomenon is localism. Through a case study of

2. Rostovtzeff 1941: 1040.

3. In the extensive modern sociological and anthropological literature on cosmopolitanism, definitions of the term vary considerably (for a useful summary of the main strands, see the introduction to Delanty 2012), but tend to cluster around the philosophical idea of a truly global community defined in moral and/or political terms: e.g., "Cosmopolitanism elaborates a concern with the equal moral status of each and every human being and creates a bedrock of interest in what it is that human beings have in common" (Held 2010: 7); "Cosmopolitanism . . . is centrally concerned with political themes . . . and affiliation to some sort of political structure that putatively covers the whole 'cosmos'" (Inglis and Robertson 2011: 297–8). Such definitions are hard to apply to imperial ideologies designed to express and/or promote subjects' allegiance to a specific imperial formation. Consequently, as the editors of this volume observe, "cosmopolitanism" in this sense is not particularly helpful for thinking about elite self-definition and imperial ideologies in the ancient world, particularly before the advent of Rome. Throughout this chapter I therefore follow their definition of cosmopolitanism as designating "a complex of practices and ideals that enabled certain individuals not only to cross cultural boundaries but also to establish an enduring normative framework across them" (Lavan, Payne, and Weisweiler, this volume).

selected documents produced by local elites in Babylonia and the Greek world, I will argue that the ways in which the different individuals and groups construct imperial identities for their local audiences (and themselves) are similar. Writing both themselves and contemporary empires into local histories which stretch back to the distant past, these elites represent the imperial present as a continuation of the glorious past of their own community, and themselves as the latest in a long line of noble guardians of that community. Thus, they use time rather than space to elide cultural and ethnic difference, and localism rather than universalism to naturalize the experience of contemporary imperialism.

I will further suggest that the similarities between these representations across the two cultures examined, and the extent to which they are sanctioned or supported by ruling powers, reflect not just the particular priorities of separate local groups in the Hellenistic world, but something about Hellenistic imperialism itself. Hellenistic rulers did not simply tolerate but actively participated in the process of casting themselves in local cultural idioms and writing their empires into local histories. The localist ideologies expressed in the documents we will examine do not show us a failed attempt at cultural integration on the part of the imperial center; rather, they are likely to reflect a coherent policy. Investing in the continuation of local cultures was a means of gaining local support, but also of creating a relatively closed imperial elite and reducing the likelihood of large-scale rebellions. Encouraging the reproduction of cultural differences in western Asia effectively discouraged the adoption of the linguistic and cultural tools (in this case, Greek) necessary to become part of the trans-regional governing elite, while encouraging localism in the Greek world might decrease the chance of a united Greek rebellion against Macedonian rule. To use the terminology formulated by the editors of this volume, the case of these Hellenistic elites offers us an example of the subordinating mode of elite integration—at least, from the imperial perspective.[4] From the perspective of the elites concerned, however, it was arguably more a case of assimilation: the assimilation of the imperial to the local.

HELLENISTIC EMPIRES: BABYLONIAN PERSPECTIVES

How did Babylonian local elites represent themselves under Seleucid rule? Any attempt to answer this question is fraught with problems, because of the state of the surviving sources from Seleucid Mesopotamia. A number of caveats are therefore in order. First, we are missing the majority of the source record altogether. The inhabitants of the region spoke Aramaic, and increasingly Greek,

---

4. See Lavan, Payne, and Weisweiler, this volume.

with the latter functioning as the language of Seleucid administration. These languages were typically written on leather or papyrus, which have not been preserved due to climatic conditions in the region. Apart from a few inscriptions on stone or clay, everything in Aramaic or Greek is lost, and with it much of the social, economic, and cultural history of Seleucid Mesopotamia.

What do survive are thousands of clay tablets and fragments, inscribed in cuneiform script with texts in Akkadian and Sumerian—the ancient spoken languages of the region, which in this period survived as written languages of scholarship and liturgy.[5] These languages, and the cuneiform script, were known and used by a small and shrinking circle of specialists connected with the Mesopotamian temples. The cuneiform sources, therefore, derive from a restricted social context, and while they sometimes provide insight into broader political, economic, and cultural phenomena, they give us access first and foremost to the world of a small, elite group. They are also restricted in their geographical distribution, with only two Babylonian cities—Babylon in the north, and Uruk in the south—so far yielding large numbers of tablets from the Hellenistic period. Although the cuneiform sources shed welcome light on what would otherwise be a forbidding expanse of darkness, it is crucial to remember that it is a narrow and fitful beam.

A further difficulty for those who wish to use the cuneiform sources as a window onto the sociocultural history of Hellenistic Babylonia is the conservatism of cuneiform scholarship. Much of cuneiform scholars' activity in the later first millennium centered on the recopying and interpretation of core texts, while new compositions tended to follow traditional formats. Such texts often express archaic or archaizing conceptions which are hard to relate to their first-millennium context. For example, as Francis Joannès has demonstrated, many literary cuneiform texts of the first millennium BCE display "une vision de l'Ouest stéréotypée, volontiers archaïsante."[6] Most of the cuneiform sources from Hellenistic Babylonia are highly traditional, showing strong continuity with earlier periods and little sign of direct engagement with the changing world outside the temples. It is difficult to determine how scholars related these compositions and their contents to the contemporary context—or whether they did so at all. The same difficulty arises with the area of first-millennium cuneiform scholarship which does show major innovation: the study of the heavens. The rise of mathematical astronomy and personal astrology in the later first millennium may well represent in some way a response to the sociopolitical shifts Babylonia experienced under foreign rule,[7] but this is hard to demonstrate in any concrete sense.

5. On the cuneiform sources from late first-millennium Uruk and Babylon, see Clancier 2009 and 2011; for Hellenistic Mesopotamia as a whole, Oelsner 1986 is still the best overall survey.

6. Joannès 1997: 142.

7. On Babylonian astronomy and astrology in the later first millennium and their relationship to broader intellectual and cultural contexts, see Rochberg 1993, Steele 2011 (astronomy), Rochberg 2004: chs. 3–4 (astrology); Brown 2000, Rochberg 2011 (both).

Yet this does not mean that the local elites of Babylonia refused to engage with the contemporary realities of imperial rule and spent their time gazing at the stars or poring over crumbling tablets containing the wisdom of former generations. Although the bulk of the cuneiform documentation from the Hellenistic period relates to the traditional domains of cuneiform scholarship, the new celestial sciences, or the economic life of the temples and their functionaries, a significant minority of texts show us the priestly elites of Babylonia, or at least certain individuals within them, actively engaging with the imperial present. Furthermore, even compositions which on the surface are heavily conservative may articulate contemporary concerns; several studies have shown how a number of apparently antiquarian cuneiform texts from Uruk can be seen to respond to an early Seleucid context.[8] We shall look at two such texts below, while in the next chapter Johannes Haubold examines how Berossos, a Babylonian writing in Greek, used his account of the Neo-Babylonian empire to articulate a model of elite interaction with strong resonances for the Seleucid period.[9]

To begin with more explicit engagement, however, the priestly elite of Seleucid Babylon certainly acknowledged that they were part of an empire which stretched from the Mediterranean to central Asia. Despite the archaizing geographical terms and conceptions of many first-millennium cuneiform texts, precise references to contemporary political geography appear in the Chronicles and Astronomical Diaries. The Chronicles are a somewhat heterogeneous group of documents which record selected historical events, focusing on the actions of kings and/or religious praxis in Babylon or other Babylonian cities, while the Diaries are daily records of celestial phenomena which include reports of selected terrestrial phenomena—again, with a strong focus on the royal house and local cult.[10] Nearly all the Diaries, and the surviving Chronicles from the later first millennium, come from Babylon.[11]

The Hellenistic Chronicles and Diaries regularly refer to movements of people and goods across and beyond the Seleucid empire. One Chronicle from 281 BCE describes Seleucus I marching his forces from Babylonia to Sardis and then making them cross the Mediterranean to "the land of Macedon [Akk. *Makkadunu*], his land."[12] The movement of ruler and troops from the traditional

8. Beaulieu 1992 and 1993, Cavigneaux 2005, Lenzi 2008.

9. Haubold, this volume.

10. On the Astronomical Diaries, see further Sachs and Hunger 1988: 20–36, Rochberg 2011, and Pirngruber 2013; on the Chronicles, see Grayson 1975, Drews 1975, Glassner 2005, Waerzeggers 2012.

11. As shown by Waerzeggers 2012, the Late Babylonian Chronicles, although unprovenanced, almost certainly come from Babylon; those from the Neo-Babylonian period most probably derive from Borsippa.

12. *BCHP* 9 obv. 3'–4'; rev. 1'–3'. Of course, Seleucus never reached Macedon, as he was assassinated by Ptolemy Keraunos in Thrace; his death is also noted in the Chronicle.

Babylonian heartland to the western periphery of Makkadunu, which is first attested in Hellenistic texts and explicitly presented here as the homeland of the new dynasty, highlights the territorial reach of the Seleucid scepter and of the imperial system to which Babylonia now belonged. The next entry in the Chronicle shifts to the eastern edge of the empire, recording something—possibly the arrival of troops or resources—"from the land of Bactria."[13] The huge distances covered in these juxtaposed reports underscore both the size and connectedness of the Seleucid empire, which also emerge with particular vividness in the following report from an Astronomical Diary relating to 273-272 BCE:

> That year, the king left his . . . , his wife and a famous official in the land of Sardis to strengthen the guard. He went to Transpotamia (the province west of the Euphrates) against the troops of Egypt which were encamped in Transpotamia, and the troops of Egypt withdrew before him. Month XII, the 24th day, the satrap of Babylonia brought out much silver, cloth, goods, and utensils' from Babylon and Seleucia, the royal city, and 20 elephants, which the satrap of Bactria had sent to the king, to Transpotamia before the king. That month, the general gathered the troops of the king, which were in Babylonia, from beginning to end, and went to the aid of the king in month I to Transpotamia.[14]

The sweeping geographical coverage and the interlocking journeys of king, satrap, army, and elephants between Sardis, Babylonia, and Bactria convey a sense of a connected imperial space covering much of the known world. But how far did the scholars who described this imperial structure identify with it?

As we shall see, based on the surviving Akkadian sources, the answer is "partially." While acknowledging their status as Seleucid subjects, the priests and scholars of Babylonia do not present themselves as a part of a trans-regional Seleucid imperial elite. Rather, they construct an image of the Seleucid empire in Babylonian-centric terms. Of course, these Akkadian texts were aimed at local audiences; it is possible that in interactions with the imperial authorities, or even in different contexts locally, the same individuals laid claim to a broader 'imperial' elite identity. The group of Macedonian-style burials near Uruk from the third century BC indicate that certain elite individuals in southern Babylonia adopted elements of Seleucid court style.[15] But in the surviving Akkadian texts,

---

13. *BCHP* 9 rev. 8'. There is a break before and after *šá* KUR *Ba-aḫ-tar* ("from the land of Bactria"), but it is likely that the movement of resources is at issue—perhaps elephants, which are recorded as being sent by the satrap of Bactria to the Seleucid king Antiochus I in an Astronomical Diary relating to 273-272 BCE (*AD* -273B rev. 31'-32'; see below).

14. *AD* -273B rev. 29'-32'.

15. Pedde 1991, 1995; Petrie 2002: 104-5; Baker 2013: 52-6. Pedde, followed by Baker, speculates that the tumuli may include those of Anu-uballiṭ/Nikarchos and Anu-uballiṭ/Kephalon (on whom see below).

these men stress their local identity and the interactions of their own city with the ruling power instead of constructing a broader "Babylonian" or "Seleucid" elite identity. While acknowledging the empire's geographical realities and the ethnic background of its rulers, they assimilate them to Babylonian imperial models and structures from the past. These points could be illustrated from various Hellenistic cuneiform texts, but here I will focus on two, from the southern Babylonian city of Uruk.

Anu-uballiṭ/Kephalon, Restorer of the Rēš Temple

The first is an Akkadian building inscription attested on several bricks from the Rēš, Uruk's main temple in the late first millennium BCE. This inscription records restorations made to the sanctuary in the late third century BCE by a local official named Anu-uballiṭ:

> *Anu-uballiṭ ša šumšu šanû Keplunnu māru ša Anu-balāssu-iqbi rab ša rēš āli ša Uruk Enamena papāḫ Anu u Egašanana bīta ša Antu ša Rēš ša ina maḫri Uan-[Ad]ap[a] īpuššu īteniḫma aqqurma ina Nisanni u₄ 2-kám mu 1 me 10-kám ana muḫḫi bulṭu ša Anti'ikusu šar mātāti bēlīya temennašunu labīrūtu urappiš u gaṣṣašunu addu ēpušma bītānu ušaklil erēna ina Maḫdaru? šadû dannu ušēṣâmma uṣallilšunūti dalāt erēni dannūti ina bāb ša papāḫīšunu uretti.*[16]

Anu-uballiṭ, whose other name is Kephalon, son of Anu-balāssu-iqbi, *rab ša rēš āli* of Uruk. Enamena, the shrine of Anu, and Egašanana, the shrine of Antu, in the Rēš temple, which previously Uan/Adapa . . . had built, had become dilapidated. I pulled them down and on 2ⁿᵈ Nisannu, year 110 (Seleucid Era), for the sake of the life of Antiochus, king of the lands, my lord, I widened their ancient foundations and I applied gypsum to them. I built and completed the interior. I brought cedar from Maḫdaru?, the mighty mountain, and I roofed the shrines with it. I installed strong cedar doors at the gates of their cellas.[17]

Like the Astronomical Diaries and Chronicles, this inscription explicitly acknowledges its contemporary imperial world. Anu-uballiṭ's Greek name, Kephalon; the dedication of the building work to the Seleucid king Antiochus (III), "king of the lands,"[18] and the use of the Seleucid calendar leave no doubt

---

16. Editions: Falkenstein 1941: 6–7, with corrections in Van Dijk 1962: 47. Discussions: Kuhrt and Sherwin-White 1993: 151–5, Clancier 2011: 759. Where vowels are indicated, they are rendered as written even where the case appears to be incorrect.

17. The exact meaning of this title, literally "chief of those of the head of the city" is still debated, but the use of *ša rēš āli* elsewhere in temple contexts suggests that it combines elements of civic and cultic administration (Joannès 1988, Beaulieu 1995a: 90).

18. It might be objected that the use of this title—introduced under the Persians and equivalent to the earlier Akkadian universalizing royal title "king of the four quarters" (*šar kibrāt erbetti*)—was by this period "purely traditional" and does not reflect any specific reference to a wider imperial context. It is ultimately

that we are in the Seleucid empire. At the same time, however, the use of the Akkadian language, and the highly traditional format and phraseology, which mirror those used in inscriptions of earlier Assyrian and Babylonian kings, situate Seleucid rule within an almost timeless Mesopotamian imperial landscape. For instance, the claim to be restoring an ancient structure that had fallen into disrepair is a standard trope of Mesopotamian royal building inscriptions, reflecting both practical exigencies (mud-brick structures degrade quickly) and rulers' desire to elevate their own status by presenting their work as continuing or surpassing the deeds of former kings. Thus, Nabopolassar (r. 626–605 BCE) restored "the ziggurat of Babylon, which before my time had become dilapidated and fallen into ruin," while Nabonidus (r. 556–539 BCE) restored the temple of the sun god in Sippar "on top of the foundation of Narām-Sîn, a former king."[19] The use of similar rhetoric assimilates Anu-uballiṭ and his royal patron/dedicatee to generations of previous Mesopotamian rulers and their representatives.

The topos of bringing high-status commodities—in Anu-uballiṭ's case cedar wood—from elsewhere also recalls the building inscriptions of Neo-Assyrian and Neo-Babylonian kings, which regularly boast about the bringing of resources from far-flung regions to beautify the temples and palaces of the heartland. For example, an inscription of the Assyrian king Esarhaddon (r. 680–669 BCE) records: "I roofed it [the temple] with beams of cedar (and) cypress, grown on Mount Sirāra (and) Mount Lebanon, whose fragrance is sweet,"[20] while Nebuchadnezzar II (r. 605–562 BCE) proclaims that "for the roofing of [the sanctuary] Ekua, I sought the best of my cedars which I had brought from Lebanon, the pure mountain forest."[21] Anu-uballiṭ's claim to have brought cedars from the "mighty mountain" Maḫdaru[22] to adorn Anu's temple continues this long-standing *topos*, contributing to the impression that Anu-uballiṭ's activities, and by implication the imperial framework within which they occur, represent a continuation of traditional Mesopotamian practice. Moreover, the center-periphery model implicit in the bringing of this material to Uruk, together with the lack of geographical specificity in Antiochus's title "king of the lands," gives rise to the impression that Babylonia, and indeed Uruk itself, are at the center of "the lands" over which Antiochus rules.

Uruk is also at the center of the identity which Anu-uballiṭ constructs for himself, which is culturally complex, but does not assimilate him to a multicultural

---

impossible to prove the opposite, but without further evidence this seems an overly cynical reading; see below for a further reason why this title may have appealed to both dedicator and dedicatee.

19. Nabopolassar: Langdon 1912: 60, col. i. 32–35; Nabonidus: Schaudig 2001: no. 2.4 I.18–19.

20. Leichty 2011: no. 57, vi. 6–10.

21. Langdon 1912: 126, col. iii. 21–6.

22. The place to which this toponym refers is uncertain (the reading of the cuneiform is not secure), but the "mighty mountain" is clearly not local to the flat, alluvial regions of southern Babylonia. Given that the wood is cedar, if the claim is historical it is likely that somewhere in Syria-Palestine is meant.

imperial elite. Although he advertises the fact that he has a Greek name (whatever its social or cultural connotations), there is no sense of a broader regional or trans-regional imperial community. Anu-uballiṭ's status as a Seleucid subject is expressed through a direct vertical link to the king, "my lord" (l. 11) rather than through horizontal connections with those of similar status elsewhere. He anchors himself within the local temple hierarchy of Uruk, as the son of Anu-balāssu-iqbi and head of the temple clergy.

This is not, however, a parochial or modest move. If the reading of line 7 is correct, the builder of the Rēš whose work Anu-uballiṭ claims to be restoring is none other than Uan/Adapa (Berossos's Oannes), the first of the seven sages who according to Mesopotamian mythology brought wisdom and civilization to mankind before the Flood. By presenting Adapa as the original builder of the sanctuary, Anu-uballiṭ retrojects his city's high status to antediluvian times and links his temple and himself to the most important figure of Mesopotamian wisdom. The Seleucid era by which the inscription is dated may have only begun 110 years previously, but Anu-uballiṭ's cultic and scholarly identity reaches back to the beginning of history itself, neatly subsuming Seleucid rule as a mere moment within the *longue durée* of Mesopotamian history.

The mention of Uan/Adapa may also be significant for another reason. In various cuneiform texts, one of which we will examine later, the sage Adapa is presented as advisor to an antediluvian Mesopotamian king, usually king Alulim (Akk. *Ayyālu*) of Eridu, but sometimes Enmerkar of Uruk.[23] By casting himself as in some sense Adapa's successor, Anu-uballiṭ may be hinting that he should occupy a similar position vis-à-vis the current rulers: the message seems to be that Anu-uballiṭ, and by implication the other members of Uruk's temple elite, are the latest in a long line of priests and scholars who have always protected Uruk's cult and provided advice to its kings, whoever those kings were—just like Berossos's model of the Chaldeans, who guard the kingship of Babylon for all comers.[24] Like the other traditional elements in the inscription, the suggestion of unbroken continuity from antediluvian days to the present glosses over the political and cultural caesuras in Babylonia's recent imperial history. Setting aside the Greek names, it effectively allows Anu-uballiṭ to present himself as a typical Mesopotamian priest/scholar serving a typical Mesopotamian ruler.

This type of deeply historicizing localism, with its emphasis on local history and continuity, arguably plays a role performed in other imperial contexts by ideologies which assimilate the local to the imperial. It elides cultural and ethnic differences (but in this case, between different rulers and empires, rather than between different subjects), naturalizes the current imperial order, and

---

23. Beaulieu 2003: 326–7, with references.
24. Haubold, this volume.

enables local elites to present themselves as part of an aristocratic community which transcends their contemporary local context. The difference vis-à-vis cosmopolitan ideologies which emphasize a trans-regional elite identity is that in this case the aristocratic community in question extends not across space, but back through time.

Royal Advisors and Local Guardians: The Uruk List of Kings and Sages

We see the same construction of a locally focused yet transhistorical identity for both empire and elite in scholarly cuneiform tablets from Hellenistic Uruk. One such is the so-called "List of Kings and Sages."[25] This composition survives on a cuneiform tablet inscribed during the reign of Antiochus IV (165 BCE) by one Anu-bēlšunu son of Nidinti-Anu, a lamentation priest of the Rēš temple (where the tablet was found). The text consists of a list which pairs each king of Mesopotamia with an advisor: a sage (*apkallu*) for rulers of the antediluvian period, and a scholar (*ummânu*) for rulers after the flood. Uan/Adapa appears as advisor to the first antediluvian king, Ayyālu, and after him a (selective) sequence of rulers and sages/scholars leads down through the second and first millennia BCE (see table 3.1).

The last fully preserved entry in the list proper (rev. 3–5) relates to the Neo-Assyrian king Esarhaddon (r. 680–669 BCE), but the Greek name Nikarchos (transliterated into cuneiform as *Ni-qa-qu-ru-šu-ú*) appears in the final line before the colophon. Frustratingly, this line is broken, and no fully satisfactory restoration has been made for the missing signs, but the presence of a Greek name suggests a link to the Seleucid period. Several scholars have even identified the Nikarchos mentioned here with the Anu-uballiṭ/Nikarchos who was governor of Uruk in the earlier third century, and who, like Anu-uballiṭ/Kephalon, dedicated a building inscription at the Rēš "for the life of" the Seleucid rulers.[26] Whether or not this identification is correct, the mention of a Nikarchos shows that the composition engaged with the imperial present as well as the past. Moreover, as Alan Lenzi has demonstrated, several other features of the composition reflect a specifically Hellenistic context.[27]

Three features in particular resonate with Anu-uballiṭ/Kephalon's inscription. First, we see again the construction of an identity for Uruk's scholarly/ priestly elite which is locally focused but temporally extensive. In constructing a scholarly genealogy which goes back to the antediluvian *apkallū*, the Uruk List, like Anu-uballiṭ's inscription, enables the current Urukean elite to view

---

25. Copy: van Dijk and Mayer 1980, no. 89; edition and commentary: van Dijk 1962: 44–52, Lenzi 2008.

26. E.g., van Dijk 1962: 52, Lenzi 2008: 163–5. Lenzi makes the intriguing suggestion that the text of the Uruk List was originally composed in the time of Nikarchos, and that his name was inserted into the list in order to praise and flatter him "in light of his king-like actions" (164). For the inscription of Anu-uballiṭ/ Nikarchos, see *YOS* I 52; Falkenstein 1941: 4–5.

27. Lenzi 2008.

Table 3.1. The so-called "List of Kings and Sages" from Uruk

Obverse

1. [*ina*] *tarṣi Ayyālu šarri Uan apkallu*	[In the] time of king Ayyalu: Uan was sage.
2. [*ina tar*]*ṣi Alalgar šarri Uanduga apkallu*	[In the] time of king Alalgar: Uanduga was sage.
(entries for 5 more antediluvian kings)	**(entries for 5 more antediluvian kings)**
8. [ ] *ina palê Enmekar šarri Nungalpiriggal apkallu*	[...] in the reign of king Enmekar: Nungalpiriggal was sage,
9. [*ša Ištar iš*]*tu šamê ana Eana ušēridu balag siparri*	[whom Ištar] sent down from heaven to Eana. A bronze balang-drum
10. [ ] x xᵐᵉˢ-*šú uqnû ina šipir Ninagal*	its . . . lapis lazuli with Ninagal's work
11. [ ] x kùᵏⁱ *šubat ili amēlūti balagga ina maḫri Ani ukinnū*	. . . the dwelling of the god and mankind, they set up the balang-drum before Anu.
12. [*ina tarṣi* ᵐᵈgiš]-˹*gím*˺-*maš* ˹*šarri*˺ *Sîn-lēqi-unninni ummânu*	[In the time of] king [Gil]gameš: Sîn-lēqi-unninni was scholar.
13. [*ina tarṣi I*]*bbi-Sîn šarri* ᵐidim-maḫ-ᵈmaš *ummânu*	[In the time of] king Ibbi-Sîn, Kabti-ili-Marduk was scholar.
14. [*ina tarṣi Išbi*]-*Erra šarri Sidu šanîš Ellil-ibni ummânu*	[In the time of] king Išbi-Erra: Sidu, or Ellil-ibni, was scholar.
15. [*ina tarṣi Abi*]-*ešuḫ šarri Gimil-Gula u Taqīš-Gula ummânū*	[In the time of] king [Abi-Ešuh: Gimil-Gula and Taqīš-Gula were scholars.
16. [*ina tarṣi* . . .] *šarri Esagil-kīn-apli ummânu*	[In the time of] king [ ]: Esagil-kīn-apli was scholar.

Reverse

1. [*ina tarṣi*] *Adad-apla-iddina šarri Esagil-kīn-ubba ummânu*	[In the time of] king Adad-apla-iddina: Esagil-kīn-ubba was scholar.
2. [*ina tarṣi*] *Nabû-kudurrī-uṣur šarri Esagil-kīn-ubba ummânu*	[In the time of] king Nebuchadnezzar: Esagil-kīn-ubba was scholar.
3. [*ina tar*]*ṣi Aššur-aḫ-iddin šarri Aba-Ellil-dāri ummânu*	[In the ti]me of king Esarhaddon: Aba-Ellil-dāri was scholar,
4. [*ša* ˡú]*Aḫlamû iqabbû Aḫu'qari*	[whom] the Aramaeans call Aḫiqar.
5. [x]-IŠ *Niqaqurušu*	[ ] x Nikarchos.
6. [*ṭuppi*]*Anu-bēlšunu māri ša Nidinti-Anu mār Sîn-lēqi-unninni*	[Tablet] of Anu-bēlšunu, son of Nidinti-Anu, descendant of Sin-lēqi-unninni,
7. ˹*kalê*˺ *Anu u Antu Urukāyu qāt ramānīšu*	lamentation priest of Anu and Antu, Urukean. His own hand.
8. [*Uruk*] *Ayyāru* u₄ 10-kam mu 1 me 47-kam *Anti'ikusu šarru*	Uruk, the 10th day of Ayyāru (II), year 147, king Antiochus.
9. *pāliḫ Ani lā itabbalšu*	He who reveres Anu shall not carry it off.

themselves as the ultimate heirs to the sages' wisdom. Moreover, in this case the link between the scholars of past and present is more explicit and more fully articulated. The scholar who appears in the list as advisor to king Gilgamesh (obv. 12) is Sîn-lēqi-unninni—understood by first-millennium Mesopotamian scholars as the redactor of the *Epic of Gilgamesh*, and more importantly in this context, understood by the tablet's copyist, Anu-bēlšunu, and the other lamentation priests of Seleucid Uruk, as their ancestor.[28]

Second, the Uruk List constructs imperial identities for the Urukean elite in vertical rather than horizontal terms: just as Anu-uballiṭ/Kephalon links himself directly to Antiochus, so the Uruk List matches each scholar directly with a king. This again sets up a transhistorical model for cooperation between kings and scholars. It also integrates all the rulers of Mesopotamia into a coherent sequence which at least in part elides ethnic difference: Assyrian and Babylonian rulers are treated side by side, with no distinction. The Uruk List suggests that Anu-bēlšunu and his colleagues are part of a Mesopotamian scholarly elite who have supported kings for as long as kings have existed. Again, we see the construction of a universalizing imperial framework which subsumes the Seleucids and of a royal/imperial elite which is "temporally" rather than "geographically" extensive.

Third, like Anu-uballiṭ's inscription, the Uruk List foregrounds Uruk and its scholars at the expense of a wider geographical and historical framework, or better, it molds these wider frameworks to put Uruk and its cult at the center. For instance, the longest entry in the list (obv. 8–11) is devoted to Nungalpiriggal, adviser to the Urukean king Enmerkar, who is the first postdiluvian sage and is said to have been sent down from heaven to Eana, the temple of Ištar in Uruk. The following lines are fragmentary but mention the setting-up of the *balag* drum before Anu, whose cult enjoyed a revival at Uruk in the later first millennium and who, during the Seleucid period, was the head of the Urukean pantheon.[29] It was his temple that Anu-uballiṭ and Anu-bēlšunu both served. As Lenzi remarks, the extended mention of Anu's cult in such a prominent position within the list is unlikely to be coincidental and is probably designed to confer antiquity and authority on the contemporary cult and its devotees.[30] Moreover, as noted earlier, Anu-bēlšunu's scholarly ancestor Sîn-lēqi-unninni, who is usually associated with the Kassite period (later second millennium BCE), appears here in a prominent position as the first human *ummânu* and scholarly advisor to Gilgamesh. We have again a vision of past and present

---

28. Lenzi 2008: 162. On Sîn-lēqi-unninni and the Uruk scholarly family who claimed him as their ancestor, see Beaulieu 2000.

29. On the rise of Anu and his cult at Uruk during the Late Babylonian period, see Beaulieu 1992, 1995b; Linssen 2004: 14-15.

30. Lenzi 2008: 161.

which places Uruk and its elite at the center of Mesopotamian history from Alulim/Ayyālu to Antiochus III, and in doing so assimilates Antiochus and his Seleucid predecessors to that Mesopotamian, or better Urukean, vision of history.

Local Voices in the Hellenistic Greek World

Somewhat paradoxically, it is the localism evidenced by these Akkadian texts which enables us to align the Babylonian elites, and their relationships to the Seleucids, with local elites and imperial praxis in the Greek-speaking Hellenistic world. Because the Greek sources are so much more plentiful, our evidence for Hellenistic Greek experiences of empire and elite self-fashioning inevitably shows greater variety than the extant cuneiform sources. Yet it is possible to trace in the Greek material a parallel emphasis on local identities and elite self-perceptions which reach back through time rather than across space.

Various scholars have pointed to the importance of local historiography for Hellenistic poleis, not only in terms of their self-understanding but also as a means of negotiating political and diplomatic relationships with each other and with the imperial powers of the day. To take only a few examples, Angelos Chaniotis, Laura Boffo, and Katherine Clarke have studied the cultural and po-litical operations performed by historiographical inscriptions, which celebrated (or created) on stone a glorious past for communities with little political clout in the present.[31] Clarke has also highlighted the way in which itinerant local his-torians might function as political ambassadors for their communities on the international stage.[32] Within the domain of local historiography, John Dillery has singled out local sacred histories as an important medium of community self-definition and self-promotion.[33] As Dillery puts it, "local historiography was required to help cities define who they were and, further, to help them ar-ticulate their needs and aspirations in the wider context of the power dynamics of the age."[34] In the various types of local historiography that we find in the Hellenistic poleis, there are processes at work similar to those discernible in the Uruk texts: the wider geopolitical framework is ignored or refocused to center on the local context; the local elite look to the distant past to forge an identity for themselves and their community; and the realities of contemporary imperi-alism are muted or molded to fit into this narrative of local pride and prestige. Two well-known inscriptions, from communities with differing relationships to Hellenistic imperial powers, will serve to illustrate these points.

---

31. Chaniotis 1988, Boffo 1988, Clarke 2008: ch. 6.
32. Clarke 2005.
33. Dillery 2005.
34. Dillery 2005: 521.

Local Pride on the Western Edge of the Seleucid Empire

The first example is the so-called "Pride of Halicarnassus" inscription.[35] Erected probably in the second century BCE, when the city was part of the Seleucid empire, this verse inscription gives a proud enumeration of Halicarnassus's contributions to politics, culture, and literature from the earliest times. The poem begins (ll. 1–4) with an address to the local manifestation of Aphrodite, asking her: "What is it that confers honour on Halicarnassus? For I have not heard."[36] It then proceeds to catalogue the famous men Halicarnassus has "brought forth," beginning with the "earth-born men" who supposedly hid the infant Zeus nearby to save him from Kronos (ll. 5–14). The second half of the inscription is a catalogue of famous Halicarnassian writers, from Herodotus to the Hellenistic poet Timocrates; this part of the poem explicitly states that "infinite time will never cease recounting all the proofs of their fame" (ll. 55–6).

Although this inscription belongs to a very different cultural, literary, and epigraphic tradition from that of the Babylonian examples, there are important structural similarities. We see the Halicarnassians constructing an identity for themselves and their city which relies not on their status as part of a contemporary empire, but on their membership of an ancient community which is presented as always having played a starring role on the world stage. As in Uruk, we see the local priestly elite reaching back to the distant past for prestige. Just as Anu-uballiṭ and the Sîn-lēqi-unninni family linked themselves to the primeval sage Adapa, the Halicarnassian elite claim the glory of having hidden the infant Zeus from his father. This retrojects into the mythical past the high status of Halicarnassus and its local cult of Gaia. The foundation narratives and catalogue of authors then provide a series of stepping stones by which the Halicarnassians trace their importance down to the present day—parallel to the list of sages and scholars from Uruk, where Urukean figures appear at key historical moments. Moreover, the twin focus on cultic and cultural achievements as a basis for the city's prestige parallels the evidence from Uruk, where Anu and Adapa, and their human followers, serve as joint sources of local prestige.

The Halicarnassian inscription also subordinates and reframes the wider geographical and historical framework in accordance with the local. Representatives of other localities are mentioned only as bringing settlers to Halicarnassus, giving the impression of a centripetal movement toward the city and making it the center of the world. This impression is achieved not only through the narrow geographical lens of the poem, but through the local appropriation of regional or Panhellenic motifs: Endymion is drawn in from neighbouring Heracleia

---

35. *Editio princeps* and commentary: Isager 1998; revised editions and commentary: Lloyd-Jones 1999a and 1999b; selected literary and historical discussions: Isager and Pedersen 2004, Gagné 2006; Bremmer 2009; Bremmer 2013.

36. τῆς Ἁλικαρνάσσου τί τὸ τίμιον; οὐ γὰρ ἔγωγε | ἔκλυον (ll. 3–4).

under Latmos to become an early coloniser of Halicarnassus, and the city also becomes the setting of Zeus' nourishment by the Curetes.[37] As with Adapa at Uruk, various Greek communities laid claim to the legend of the Curetes; the relocating of Zeus's infant adventures to the shrine of Gaia near Halicarnassus, which goes beyond existing Carian appropriation of the Curetes,[38] parallels Anu-uballiṭ's co-option of the Mesopotamian culture hero for his city.

So strong is the inscription's local focus that the immediate imperial context is not explicitly mentioned. Nonetheless, its presence can be felt in the construction of a paradigm of benefaction and reciprocity between the local community and the wider world: the inscription makes a claim for Halicarnassus's status and worth on the strength of honors received from the most powerful representatives of the divine and human worlds. Lines 13-14 stress the rewards that the local incarnation of the Curetes received from Zeus, with οὐδ᾽ ἄχαριν, "not without recompense," placed emphatically at the beginning of line 13: even the gods honor Halicarnassus, and deservedly so. The last section (ll. 57–60) returns to this theme, this time on the mortal plane. Aphrodite states that the city has received many noble prizes for its naval prowess from the "leaders of the Greeks," Ἑλλήνων ἡγεμόσιν, and the poem ends with the assertion that Halicarnassus can lay claim to the most glorious garlands (στέφανοι) thanks to her "good deeds" (ἀγαθὰ ἔργα). This is the language of euergetism, so often deployed in Hellenistic political discourse between kings and cities, and although no contemporary benefactors are explicitly mentioned here, the implications are clear: Halicarnassus can hold her own even on the Panhellenic stage; she has always received due honors from the gods and the leaders of the Greeks, and whoever those leaders might be, this pattern of honor should continue. Like their Urukean contemporaries, then, the elite of Halicarnassus portray themselves in terms of a glorious local past rather than a multicultural imperial present—but the construction of that past can be seen to respond to the realities of contemporary imperialism.

Lindos, Center of the Oikoumenē

Like the inscription of Anu-uballiṭ, the second Greek example explicitly acknowledges the imperial present, but again shows us a local elite creating links with the past to enhance their prestige and status. This is the so-called "Lindian Chronicle," an inscription on a stele erected in 99 BCE in the sanctuary of Athana Lindia (the local form of Athena) at Lindos on the island of Rhodes.[39]

---

37. Endymion: Bremmer 2009: 305-6; 2013: 69-70. Curetes and Zeus: Isager 1998: 12, Lloyd-Jones 1999a: 4–5; Bremmer 2009: 294-7; Bremmer 2013: 59-62.

38. Bremmer 2009: 297; 2013: 61.

39. *I.Lindos* 2. First edition: Blinkenberg 1912. Other editions and commentaries: Blinkenberg 1915; Jacoby in *FGrH* 532; Chaniotis 1988 T13; Higbie 2003 (essentially following Blinkenberg's text, with translation,

It is difficult to reconstruct the local mood at the time the inscription was created. On the one hand, as Higbie and Dillery stress, Rhodes had effectively lost its independence; deteriorating relations with Rome after Pydna led to a decrease in political and economic power, and the island was now increasingly subordinate to its 'ally'.[40] On the other, Alain Bresson has emphasized that in 99 BC Rhodes was hardly in terminal decline: the island enjoyed continued prosperity and still exercised considerable military clout; relations with Rome had improved, and Rhodes played a significant role in eastern Mediterranean affairs, albeit as Rome's auxiliary.[41] It is therefore hard to know whether the Chronicle is the product of a community feeling the loss of its autonomy and facing an uncertain future, or one with resurgent confidence. At all events, this inscription shows us the Lindians asserting the continued importance of their sanctuary and city in the world of late Hellenistic imperialism.

The inscription begins (A.1-12) with a decree ratifying the proposal of a certain Hagesitimos, from an elite local family whose members often held priestly office:

έδοξε μαστροῖς καὶ Λινδίο[ις· | Ἁ]γησίτιμος Τιμαχίδα Λ[ινδοπολίτας εἶπε·
ἐπεὶ τὸ ἱερὸ]ν τᾶς Ἀθάνας τᾶς Λινδίας ἀρχαιότατόν τε καὶ ἐντιμό[τα]|τον
ὑπάρχον πολλοῖς κ[αὶ καλοῖς ἀναθέμασι ἐκ παλαιοτ]άτων χρόνων
κεκόσμηται διὰ τὰν τᾶς θεοῦ ἐπιφάνειαν, |συμβαίνει δὲ τῶν ἀνα[θεμάτων
τούτων πολλὰ μετὰ τᾶν ἐ]πιγραφᾶν διὰ τὸν χρόνον ἐφθάρθαι, τύχαι ἀγαθᾶι
δεδόχθαι [μ]αστροῖς καὶ Λινδίοις κυρ[ωθέντος τοῦδε τοῦ ψαφίσματος
ἑλέ]σθαι ἄνδρας δύο, τοὶ δὲ αἱρεθέντες κατασκευαξάντω στάλαν [λ]ίθου
Λαρτίου καθ᾽ ἅ κα ὁ ἀρχ[ιτέκτων γράψηι καὶ ἀναγραψάντ]ω εἰς αὐτὰν
τόδε τὸ ψάφισμα, ἀναγραψάντω δὲ ἔκ τε τᾶν |[ἐπ]ιστολᾶν καὶ τῶν
χρηματ[ισμῶν καὶ τῶν ἄλλων μαρτυρί]ων ἅ κα ἧι ἁρμόζοντα περὶ τῶν
ἀναθεμάτων καὶ τᾶς ἐπιφανείας [τ]ᾶς θε<ο>ῦ.[42]

Resolved by the mastroi and the Lind[ians: Ha]gesitimos son of Timachos [citizen of] L[indos, spoke: Since the sanctuar]y of Athana Lindia, which is both most ancient and most hon[or]ed, has [from] the [earl]iest times been adorned with many [beautiful offerings] because of the visible presence of the goddess, and since [many of these] offer[ings, together with their i]nscriptions, have been destroyed over time, with good fortune it

---

but note the criticisms in Gabrielsen 2005 and Bresson 2006). Historical discussions: Higbie 2003, Dillery 2005: 514–19; Bresson 2006; Dillery 2015: 183-192.

40. Higbie 2003: 204-42; Dillery 2015: 190.

41. Bresson 2006, esp. 532-4. Although Bresson's argument about Rhodes' continued vitality is persuasive, he perhaps gives insufficient space to Lindian localism. As he notes, 'il s'agissait ... de montrer le rôle particulier de Lindos... et la contribution d'importance exceptionelle de l'Athana de Lindos'; the specifically *Lindian* rather than Rhodian cast to the Chronicle shows that the Lindians had a strong sense of their separate identity, and leaves space for some anxiety over lost status at Lindos (as opposed to Rhodes), as suggested by Higbie (2003: 242).

42. *I.Lindos* 2 A.1–8, with the restoration in line 4 from Bresson 2006: 539.

has been resolved by the mastroi and Lindians [with the authorization of this decree] that two men are to be sele[cted]. These, after they have been selected, are to prepare a stele of Lartian stone, according to what the archi[tect writes, and inscrib]e on it this decree, and they are also to inscribe, from the [le]tters and the public do[cuments, and other sources of eviden]ce, whatever may be fitting concerning the offerings and the visible presence [o]f the goddess.

After the decree, there follows a long list of the offerings supposedly made by kings, heroes, and locals from the time of the city's foundation down to the Hellenistic period, including among others Menelaus, Amasis of Egypt, Alexander, and Ptolemy I. Each entry records the dedicant, the object, and any inscription on the object. It then cites written sources for the information, which include the works of various local historians and the letters of two priests of Athena, Gorgosthenes and Hieroboulos. The entry for Menelaus (B 62–9) is typical:

Μενέλαος κυνᾶν, ἐφ᾽ ἅς ἐπεγέγρ[απτο·] | «Μενέλας τὰν Ἀλεξά[ν]δρου», ὡς ἱ[στορεῖ Ξεναγό]|ρας ἐν τᾶι ᾱ τᾶς χ[ρονικ]ᾶς συντ[άξιος, Ἡγησίας] | ἐν τῶι Ῥόδου ἐγκωμίω[ι, Ε]ὔδημος ἐν τ[ῶι] Λινδια|κῶι Γόργων ἐν τᾶι ᾱ τᾶ[ν] Περὶ Ῥόδου, Γοργοσθέ|νης ἐν τᾶι ἐπιστολᾶι, Ἱερόβουλος ἐν τᾶι ἐπισ|τολᾶι.

Menelaos: a leather cap, on which had been inscri[bed]: "Menelas, the (leather cap) of Alexander," as [Xenago]ras r[ecords] in the first book of his A[nnalist]ic Acco[unt, Hegesias] in his Encomiu[m] of Rhodes, [Eu]demos in his Lindiaka, Gorgon in the first book o[f] About Rhodes, Gorgosthenes in his letter, Hieroboulos in his letter.

The final part of the inscription describes several occasions on which Athana appeared miraculously to save the Lindians from impending disaster—in two cases from attacks by foreign dynasts; in the third from pollution caused by a suicide in the temple.

In terms of genre and style, the Lindian Chronicle presents us with a different document type again, but once again we can see a local elite telling a similar story. Both the offering list and epiphanies achieve a comparable effect to the Uruk documents. First, they construct a paradigm of royal or imperial behavior with strong contemporary resonance: Alexander, Ptolemy, and, by implication, their imperial successors are simply the latest in a long line of potentates who have come to honor Athana Lindia, her sanctuary, and Lindos itself.[43] Secondly,

43. Reacting against the idea that the Chronicle is in essence a history of the sanctuary, Bresson (2006: 541–6) has suggested that the aim was simply to record all important offerings that were no longer visible. Yet as 'important' implies, and as the decree explicitly states, this was a selective process: the compilers are

they place Hellenistic imperialism within a historical and geographical framework which makes Lindos the center of the world: as Dillery remarks, "historical figures and their deeds are noted only when they intersect with the temple of
Athena at Lindos."[44] Just as in Babylonia, kings and heroes have come and gone,
but Lindos, like Uruk, has always enjoyed center stage. Athana's fame reaches
not only through time but across space: the dedicants in the offering list, whose
homelands are all duly recorded, include representatives of a wide range of localities. Phalaris from Sicily, Amasis of Egypt, the colonists of Cyrene: the roll-
call of ethnics and gentilics spans and transcends the Greek world.

Like their counterparts at Uruk and Halicarnassus, the priestly elite of
Lindos also emerge as the latest in a long line of guardians of their community. First, as we have seen, it was a member of the priesthood who proposed
the creation of this inscription, which is designed to recover and transmit the
community's glorious past. Second, the letters of the priests Gorgosthenes and
Hieroboulos are cited as evidence for the existence of many of the lost offerings,
presenting the priesthood as privileged holders of local memory.[45] Third, the
priests are Lindos's advocates and protectors in the present, even after they have
formally finished their service: the third epiphany recounts how, when Lindos
is being besieged by another Hellenistic dynast, Athana appears to her retired
priest, sending him to the *prytanis* to seek aid from Ptolemy I.[46] The inscription
implies that the Lindian priestly elite will continue their role as guardians of
local memory and status, and that Lindos and its temple will continue to enjoy
favor and benefactions from future rulers.

Localism: The View from the Center

Did the stories these elite individuals and groups told about themselves matter
beyond the local context? And to what extent did imperial rulers engage with, or
respond to, these local narratives? There is some evidence that they did matter,
and that in the Greek world and Babylonia, rulers and elites collaborated to
create this discourse of localism.

To return to Babylonia, it is important to stress once again the one-sided
nature and narrow geographical spread of the surviving sources. It is possible that if we had the Greek or Aramaic sources, our picture of both elite and

---

to record 'whatever is fitting' from the information at their disposal. The focus on royal or imperial behaviour
in both the offering list *and* the epiphany narratives, as well as the geographical coverage, suggests a deliberate
emphasis which it is hard not to relate to the contemporary context. For a recent restatement of the case for
seeing the Chronicle as a work of local historiography, see now Dillery 2015: 183–192.

44. Dillery 2005: 519.

45. Gorgosthenes's letter: *I.Lindos* 2 B 5–7, 13–14, 21–2, 35–6, 40–1, 52–3, 60–1, 66–7, 71–2, 76–2, 80–1, 85.
Hieroboulos's letter: *I.Lindos* 2 B 7, 14, 22, 36, 41, 53, 61, 67, 72, 77, 81, 85–6; C 53–5.

46. *I.Lindos* 2 D 94–114.

imperial viewpoints in Hellenistic Babylonia would be very different; it would certainly be more nuanced and chronologically differentiated. Yet despite the patchiness of the cuneiform record, what survives suggests that Seleucid rulers encouraged and even participated in the writing of Seleucid imperialism into Babylonian local histories.

In the case of Uruk, the situation is admittedly somewhat ambiguous. Beyond the links that Anu-uballiṭ/Kephalon and his earlier namesake claim with the royal court, we have only the tacit evidence that the Rēš temple was lavishly restored during the third century BCE – although the huge scale of the restorations suggests royal investment, or at least support.[47] According to some scholars, the fact that the Uruk building inscriptions are in the name of local governors rather than the Seleucids themselves suggests a waning of royal interest in the city, and/or an attempt on the part of the elite to attract greater royal attention.[48] Yet it is equally possible to take a more positive reading and suggest that this reflects a deliberate Seleucid policy of encouraging local governance and autonomy.[49] The Seleucid king may have provided part or all of the funds, leaving the local elite to see to their correct cultic and ideological deployment.

The only surviving royal inscription from Mesopotamia which is in the name of the Seleucids supports this idea. This is the so-called Borsippa or Antiochus Cylinder, an Akkadian building inscription which records Antiochus I's restoration of the Ezida temple in the northern Babylonian city of Borsippa:

> Antiochus, great king, mighty king, king of the world, king of Babylon, king of the lands, provider for Esagil and Ezida, foremost heir of Seleucus, the king, the Macedonian, king of Babylon, am I. When my heart prompted me to (re)build Esagil and Ezida, I molded the bricks of Esagil and Ezida in the land of Hatti (Syria) with my pure hands, using the finest oil, and for the laying of the foundations of Esagil and Ezida I brought them. In the month Addaru, day 20, of year 43 (27 March 268 BC), I laid the foundations of Ezida, the true temple, the temple of Nabû which is in Borsippa. Nabû, supreme heir, wisest of the gods, the proud one, who is worthy of praise, firstborn son of Marduk, offspring of queen Erua who forms living creatures, look favourably (on me) and, at your supreme command, whose command is unalterable, may the overthrow of my enemy's land, the attainment of my ambition, (the ability) to stand in triumph over (my) foes, a just rule, a prosperous reign, years of

47. Kuhrt and Sherwin-White 1993: 154–5; Baker 2013: 56–7.

48. E.g. Beaulieu 1993: 50 (although he states on p. 48 that the building program was originally contemplated "with the tacit approval, if not active support" of the Seleucid house); Lenzi 2008: 157–8.

49. Clancier 2011: 761.

happiness and the full enjoyment of great old age be a gift for the kingship of Antiochus and king Seleucus, his son, forever. . . . Nabû, supreme
heir, upon your entry to Ezida, the true temple, may the good fortune of
Antiochus, king of the lands, king Seleucus, his son, (and) Stratonice,
his consort, the queen, may their good fortune be established by your
mouth.[50]

The inscription attests to a collaboration between the Seleucid king and the
priestly elite of Borsippa to project a locally centered image of empire, like
that presented by the Urukean elite. Although it contains elements unique
to the Seleucid vision of empire, the Antiochus Cylinder also aligns the
Seleucids with previous Mesopotamian rulers, giving Antiochus traditional
Mesopotamian royal titles, and presenting him as fulfilling the pious duties of
a good Babylonian ruler. Moreover, it focuses on Antiochus's relationship with
Borsippa and its temple (as well as the Esagil temple in Babylon) rather than
Seleucid relations with Babylonia more generally. Just as Anu-uballiṭ's inscription makes the southern city of Uruk the center, the Antiochus Cylinder por-
trays a Mesopotamian empire with Borsippa at its heart.

Thus, it may have suited both the Babylonian elites and their Seleucid rulers
to construct imperial identities that drew connections across time rather than
space, and which emphasized local particularity and autonomy rather than
a broader sense of regional or imperial community. From the perspective of
Babylonia's various local elites, this enabled them to present the empire on
their own terms and even to gain a greater degree of independence and status
vis-à-vis the elites of other cities. From the perspective of the Seleucids, encouraging localism, and hence reproducing cultural difference, may have been
a way of reducing the risk of a united Babylonian rebellion. As Clifford Ando
has emphasized in a Roman context, the existence and maintenance of local
diversity "contributed to the ability of the centre to distract conquered populations from realising solidarity with each other around their subjugation."[51]
Insofar as the maintenance of local diversity reduced the need for cultural
assimilation, it also contributed to restrict access to the (almost exclusively
Greco-Macedonian) elite who occupied the highest levels of imperial administration, perpetuating a hierarchical division between imperial and local elites.
We may therefore be seeing in the Hellenistic cuneiform sources not just the
wishful thinking of a few priests, but the deliberate use of a primarily subor-
dinative mode of elite integration which helped to naturalize Seleucid rule in
Babylonia.

---

50. Rawlinson and Pinches 1884: no. 66 (= BM 36277). Editions and discussion: Weissbach 1911: 132–5,
Kuhrt and Sherwin-White 1991, Beaulieu 2014, Kosmin 2014b, Stevens 2014.
    51. Ando 2010: 18.

And not just in Babylonia. In the Greek world, too, Hellenistic kings acknowledged and encouraged communities' emphasis on local identities and collaborated in the process of assimilating the imperial present to the local past. The correspondence between Hellenistic kings (or their representatives) and Greek poleis provides various examples. One occurs in a letter from Zeuxis, Antiochus III's representative in Asia Minor, to the citizens of Heracleia-under-Latmos, a small city in Caria which had known Persian domination, was subsequently "liberated" by Alexander, and later came under Seleucid rule:

ἀνήνεγκαν τὸ ψήφισμα καθ᾽ ὃ ὤιεσθε δεῖν ἀνακεκομισμέ|νων ἡμῶν
τῶι βασιλεῖ τὴν πόλιν ἐξ ἀρχῆς ὑπάρχουσαν τοῖς προγόνοις αὐτοῦ ...
αἱρεθῆναι | δὲ καὶ πρεσβευτὰς τοὺς ... παρακαλέσοντας τά τε ὑπὸ τῶν
βασιλέων συγκεχωρημένα | [συνδιατηρηθῆν]αι. ... σπεύδοντες οὖν
καὶ αὐτοὶ τὸν δῆμον εἰς τὴν ἐξ ἀ[ρ] | [χῆ]ς διάθεσιν ἀποκατασταθῆναι
καὶ τά τε ἐπὶ τῶν προγόνων τοῦ βασιλέως | [συγκεχ]ωρημένα
συντηρηθῆναι αὐτῶι ... ἐπιχωροῦμεν δὲ ὑμῖν καὶ τὴν πανήγυριν
ἀτελῆ συντελεῖν ο[ὔ] | [τως ὥσπερ] καὶ πρότερον εἰώθειτε ἄγειν.[52]

(Your ambassadors) handed over the decree according to which you thought it was necessary, after we recovered for the king the city that had originally belonged to his ancestors ... to elect ambassadors who ... should ask that the measures granted by the kings be [preserv]ed. ... Since we too are eager that the dēmos be restored to its or[igin]al situation, and that the [conce]ssions made by the ancestors of the king be preserved for it ... we grant you the right to conduct the festival exempt from taxes, [as] you were accustomed to before.

Here, the Heracleian ambassadors and the imperial representative work together, just like the Borsippan elite and Antiochus I, to portray the Seleucid present in terms of the local past. Both Antiochus's rule over the city and the city's status within the Seleucid empire are presented as a restoration of the Heracleians' "original situation," τὴν ἐξ ἀ[ρ][χῆ]ς διάθεσιν. It is not Heracleia's membership of a contemporary Seleucid imperial structure, but the historical privileges it received from previous rulers, which Zeuxis and the Heracleians use to negotiate the city's present privileges. In so doing, both sides gloss over the awkward reality that the Heracleians' "original situation" did not involve Seleucid rule at all. Nor is this an isolated example. John Ma has shown how the creation of a "Seleukid past" for various cities in Asia Minor, visible to us in their correspondence with the kings, allowed both cities and Seleucid rulers to advance their own interests.[53] Periods of Ptolemaic control could be written

52. SEG 37.859 B (excerpted); also edited in Ma 2002: 340–5.
53. Ma 2002: 26–52.

out or referred to obliquely ("the kings" in the Heracleia inscription is likely to be deliberately vague), and, thanks to "local histories which presented an image of royal benevolence and civic gratitude in the form of τιμαὶ ἀξιόλογοι," cities could claim benefactions and kings' loyalty.[54]

CONCLUSIONS

The documents brought together here are a select group, which represent the conceptions and self-presentation of a small set of elite individuals. Any conclusions drawn from them are inevitably restricted in scope, pending a more comprehensive investigation of elite self-presentation across the Hellenistic world. These documents are also in many ways heterogeneous, stemming from different cultural traditions and sociopolitical and intellectual contexts. Yet on a deeper level they can be seen to share similarities—in their localism, its articulations, and the ways in which it naturalizes or otherwise responds to contemporary imperialism. These similarities link the documents and their redactors even across cultural boundaries, and although on the basis of a few case studies they can only be suggestive, they are arguably significant. In the mountains of Asia Minor and the plains of Mesopotamia, Hellenistic local elites were telling the same kind of stories about themselves. These stories emphasized not the global but the local, and they reached out not across space but back through time. This enabled the elites of Halicarnassus, Lindos, Uruk, and Borsippa to present contemporary imperialism as a continuation of their glorious local history, and to identify themselves as heirs to those who had protected their cities since the beginning of time. These stories also seem to have mattered to their rulers, who collaborated with local elites in writing the imperial present into the local past.

Why should these local stories matter to us? First, because each one is part of the elite experience of empire in the Hellenistic period—part of the "imperial subjectivities" which this volume sets out to explore. At the very least, they constitute a reminder that individuals might forge specifically imperial identities not only by laying claim to membership of an empire-wide elite but also by assimilating the imperial to the local in such a way as to sustain and enhance their own status and prestige. But if these stories are also part of a broader pattern, they might suggest that localism as an imperial ideology is particularly characteristic of the Hellenistic empires. In turn, this would imply that the cosmopolitan politics of these empires were characterized principally, or at least significantly, by the "subordinating mode" of elite integration. This would distinguish Hellenistic imperialism from that of imperial systems where the "assimilative mode" of elite integration was predominant, such as the Roman empire.

54. Ma 2002: 38.

Of course, the difference is one of degree rather than kind. Subordinating practices did not cease when Rome absorbed the last of the Hellenistic kingdoms; as Myles Lavan shows, the ecumenical pronouncements of early imperial letters to the cities of the Greek east coexisted with exclusivist rhetoric which created boundaries between rulers and subjects.[55] So too, local elites under Rome continued to tell local stories and assert their identity in terms of the local past; Greek local historiography retained its vitality under the Principate.[56] Yet as Katherine Clarke observes, the most extensive evidence for this type of activity comes from the Hellenistic period.[57] Moreover, in the later Roman empire localism was increasingly matched by universalism, as citizenship and eventually senatorial membership expanded far beyond Rome and Italy. Elites across the empire came to view themselves—and were encouraged to do so—as part of a trans-regional, even "global" aristocracy, for which we see no equivalent in the Hellenistic period.[58]

It is tempting to wonder whether the difference—if it is not simply a result of the distribution of the surviving evidence—might have something to do with the peculiar imperial superstructure of the Hellenistic world. In *On the Fortune of Alexander*, Plutarch lamented that "if the deity that sent down Alexander's soul into this world of ours had not recalled him quickly, one law would govern all mankind, and they would all look toward one rule of justice as though toward a common source of light."[59] Plutarch's point is to contrast those whom Alexander conquered with the rest of the world, which "remained without sunlight" (i.e., Greek law and culture).[60] Yet his statement leads to an important consideration with regard to imperial ideologies and identities within the Hellenistic world. If Alexander had lived longer, there might have been a single Macedonian empire ruling large parts of Eurasia. Instead, his death resulted in an imperial space fragmented between competing dynasties from the same ethnic and cultural background, with diasporic Greco-Macedonian elites scattered across all the kingdoms. Without a true "world empire," and with imperial boundaries constantly shifting, assimilative imperial ideologies which encouraged locals to view themselves as part of Hellenized "Seleucid" or "Ptolemaic" elites might have had limitations and pitfalls for both rulers and ruled. On the one hand, too much Hellenism might from a royal perspective be a dangerous thing, given the ideals of freedom and autonomy traditionally at the heart of "Greekness." The discourse of Hellenism was used by both rulers and cities to

---

55. Lavan, this volume.
56. E.g., Clarke 2005, Whitmarsh 2010.
57. Clarke 2005: 122.
58. Weisweiler, this volume.
59. εἰ δὲ μὴ ταχέως ὁ δεῦρο καταπέμψας τὴν Ἀλεξάνδρου ψυχὴν ἀνεκαλέσατο δαίμων, εἷς ἂν νόμος ἅπαντας ἀνθρώπους διῳκεῖτο καὶ πρὸς ἓν δίκαιον ὡς πρὸς κοινὸν ἐπέβλεπον φῶς. Plut. *De Alex. fort.* 330d.
60. Ibid.

negotiate imperial rule, but with no single kingdom controlling the whole of the Greek-speaking world, it could not function as a unifying marker of a single imperial culture as it did under Rome. On the other hand, for the elites of small poleis in the frontier zones which oscillated between Ptolemaic and Seleucid control, it was a safer strategy to gloss over the precise identity of "the kings" and emphasize past privilege. Identifying strongly as members of the imperial community which had "liberated" them today might invite reprisals from those who would "rescue" them tomorrow. As for the Urukean elite, whose ancestors had after all been local guardians and imperial advisors since before the Flood, they knew that the rule of the latest "kings of the lands" would also come to an end, and that what we call the Seleucid period was really just another chapter in the long and glorious history of Uruk.

Abbreviations

Abbreviations for Classical journals follow *l'Année Philologique*. Assyriological abbreviations follow "Abbreviations for Assyriology," Educational Pages of the Cuneiform Digital Library Initiative, http://cdli.ox.ac.uk/wiki/doku.php?id=abbreviations_for_assyriology, with the addition of:

AD = A. Sachs and H. Hunger, *Astronomical Diaries and Related Texts from Babylonia* (6 vols., 1988–2006). Wien.

BCHP = I. Finkel and R. J. van der Spek, *Babylonian Chronicles of the Hellenistic Period* (forthcoming; preliminary online editions at Livius.org, http://www.livius.org/cg-cm/chronicles/chron00.html).

4

Hellenism, Cosmopolitanism, and the Role of Babylonian Elites in the Seleucid Empire

Johannes Haubold

Haubold offers a case study of how Seleucid Bablyonian elites experienced their place in an empire that was 'universal in aspiration but exclusive in practice'. He focusses on the Babyloniaca, *a fragmentary history of Babylon written in Greek by Berossos, a member of the Babylonian priestly elite. Berossos' failure to establish himself within the Greek canon illustrates the exclusivity of elite Greek culture, despite its apparent openness to appropriation by outsiders. But Haubold shows that Berossos' text also propounds a sophisticated model of empire where success depends on the collaboration of multiple distinct aristocratic networks. The Babylonian 'Chaldeans' may be distinct from the Greco-Macedonian elite that surrounded the king, but they make their own parallel and no less crucial contribution to the maintenance of empire. Where the role of the Seleucids' 'friends' is to take charge of political and military matters around the empire, the 'Chaldeans' guarantee dynastic continuity. Haubold also shows that the Seleucid kings can be seen to have recognised the Chaldeans' special role in sustaining the imperial order, turning to them for support in moments of crisis. The Seleucid empire as described here, capable of recognising the Babylonian elite as such and harnessing it to the imperial order without needing to erode its cultural distinctiveness, presents a typical example of what we term integration through subordination. Haubold's reconstruction of Berossos' model of empire offers a rare insight into how such a regime was experienced by the subordinated.*

As Peter Bang has recently argued, the conquests of Alexander the Great gave rise to cosmopolitanism as a force that shaped the political and cultural landscape of the Hellenistic world.[1] Looking at a range of ideas and institutions, from the cosmopolis of the Stoic philosopher Zeno to the library at Alexandria, Bang suggests that Greek culture provided a global framework

---

1. Bang 2012.

for imperial rule and a mechanism for maintaining supra-regional elite networks: "Hellenism, a badge of nobility, produced a cosmopolitan and trans-
regional aristocratic culture tying together elite groups across culturally and
linguistically very diverse regions."[2] Bang stresses that cosmopolitanism after
Alexander had a distinctly Greek inflection: non-Greeks could join in, but only
up to a point.[3] The obstacles that prevented them from becoming full members of the Greek cosmopolitan elite can be illustrated with reference to the
Letter of Aristeas, a Jewish Greek pamphlet that attempts to validate the translation of the Torah into Greek by attributing it to an initiative of Ptolemy II.
As Bang notes,

> that sort of claim ... could work well enough for groups attempting to
> emulate aspects of Hellenic civilisation to carve out a position for them-
> selves within the ruling order. At the same time it is quite revealing that
> few, if any Hellenic authors outside the Jewish communities ever both-
> ered much about this addition to the world of letters.[4]

Whereas capable "barbarians" were free to adopt the trappings of Greek cosmopolitan discourse, their efforts had little resonance among Greek audiences. At a purely practical level, Hellenistic imperial administrations did,
of course, co-opt the elites of their non-Greek subject populations,[5] but the
question remains whether such measures ever transcended the level of local
accommodation.[6]

This chapter aims to address that question. It asks what models of integration and participation were available to local elites in states that were universal in aspiration but exclusive in practice. Since non-Greek thinkers have left
us no abstract disquisitions on the subject, I will focus on the stories, or as we
might rather say, the mythologies, that enabled them to relate themselves to
the predominantly Greek cosmopolitan culture of the time. My test case is the
Babylonian priestly elites under the Seleucid empire, partly because of my own
long-standing interest in one of their number (more on him in a moment), but
partly also because their example seems to me to be useful for what this volume
tries to achieve.

My argument is in three parts. I start by looking at Berossos's *Babyloniaca* as
an attempt on the part of a non-Greek intellectual to carve out space for himself
and his peers in the wider context of Hellenistic Greek culture. I then argue

---

2. Bang 2012: 75.
3. Bang 2012: 75.
4. Bang 2012: 74–5.
5. Bang 2012: 62, 69; see also Ma 2003.
6. Bang argues that accommodation with non-Greek elites operated within a stable hierarchical system
which further emphasized the distance between Greek "cosmopolitan" and non-Greek "local" culture; see Bang
2012: 70.

that Berossos uses this fairly unremarkable project to propose something much more interesting: according to him, the Seleucid empire relied on two interdependent elite networks, one of them Greek, the other Babylonian. Whereas the Greek "friends" of the king helped him run his empire, the Chaldean priests of Babylon guarded kingship as an institution. In a third step I show that Berossos's vision of Greco-Babylonian cooperation amounts to more than just wishful thinking: the Seleucid kings themselves integrated Babylon and its traditions of empire into their project of maintaining kingship in Asia.

Cosmopolitan Accommodations

Babylonians of the Seleucid period have left behind a rich legacy of cuneiform texts.[7] In the previous chapter, Kathryn Stevens looked at some of the distinctly local—and localizing—strands that run through this material: men like Anu-uballiṭ/Kephalon acquired Greek names and, we presume, a Greek identity of sorts, but their writings in Akkadian remained firmly grounded in local Mesopotamian tradition. Not everyone wrote in Akkadian, however, and even Akkadian scholars did not do so at all times. We have only limited evidence of the literature in Aramaic and Greek which Anu-uballiṭ and his peers presumably also produced.[8] But there is one important exception, the *Babyloniaca* by the priest and historian Berossos.

Berossos was a contemporary of Alexander the Great and a certain "King Antiochus," probably Antiochus I (281-261 BCE).[9] His name looks Babylonian,[10] and his self-portrayal as a "priest of Bel" points to the main temple complex of Marduk in Babylon, the Esagila. Perhaps Berossos left Babylon at some point and settled on the island of Cos, then under Ptolemaic rule (*BNJ* 680 T 5a). That would have been toward the end of his life. The *Babyloniaca* must have been written earlier. We do not know under what circumstances exactly, but Berossos will not have worked in a vacuum, so his reflections are likely to represent—at least in broad outline—the views of his peers at the major Babylonian temples.

The work itself is lost, but we have reasonably extensive fragments which give a good sense of what it was like: Book 1 described the creation of the world and of man. Book 2 traced a succession of rulers from the first king Aloros/Alulim

---

7. Oelsner 1986.

8. We do know that Anu-uballiṭ/Kephalon put up inscriptions in Aramaic as well as Akkadian. He may have had a third name, in Aramaic, which is now lost; cf. Monerie 2012: 342.

9. For a suggestion that the "Antiochus" in question was Antiochus II (261-246 BCE), see Bach 2013. Tatian calls "Antiochus" the third king after "Alexander" (*BNJ* 680 T 2), which Bach interprets as a reference to the child king Alexander IV. However, it seems implausible that a work dedicated to a Seleucid monarch would have claimed a connection with the problematic child king Alexander IV. In other ways, too, Antiochus I is the more likely dedicatee, for we know that he took an interest in Babylon since his time as crown prince and regent of the eastern provinces (294-281 BCE).

10. For a suggestion that Berossos was the temple official Bēl-rē'ûšunu, see van der Spek 2000: 439.

down to the historical Nabonassaros/Nabû-naṣir in the eighth century BCE. Book 3 focused on the more recent history of Babylon: the Assyrian occupation from Tiglath-Pileser III to Sarakos/Sîn-šarra-iškun; the Neo-Babylonian empire; and the Persians under Cyrus the Great and his successors. The work seems to have concluded with the conquests of Alexander (Abydenos *BNJ* 685 F 7; cf. F 1).[11]

We do not know why precisely Berossos composed the *Babyloniaca*. What we do know is that he wrote in Greek and made an effort to address a Greek readership. Book 1 opens with an ethnography of Babylon that would not be out of place in Greek historical and ethnographic literature of the time (*BNJ* 680 F 1b (2)).[12] Also in book 1, Berossos establishes his credentials as a Chaldean sage and conveyor of barbarian wisdom by recounting the creation of the world.[13] In his paraphrase, the standard Babylonian creation account reads strikingly like a piece of Hellenistic Greek physics.[14]

Particularly instructive for Berossos's self-portrayal as a barbarian sage is his account of human creation. This is what his main source, the *Epic of Creation*, had to say about it:

lu-ub-ni-ma lullâ (lú-u$_{18}$-lu-a) a-me-lu
lu-ú en-du dul-lu ilānī-ma šu-nu lu-ú pa-áš-ḫu

Let me create mankind,
they shall bear the gods' burden so that the gods themselves may be at rest.[15]

The speaker in this passage is the god Bel, who advertises to his fellow gods his intention to create mankind. Bel promises to free the gods from the chores of an earthly existence, a standard motif in Babylonian epic. The emphasis is on separating gods from humans, and on putting each group in its proper place. Berossos adopts a different approach:

τοῦτον τὸν θεὸν ἀφελεῖν τὴν ἑαυτοῦ κεφαλήν, καὶ τὸ ῥυὲν αἷμα τοὺς ἄλλους θεοὺς φυρᾶσαι τῆι γῆι, καὶ διαπλάσαι τοὺς ἀνθρώπους· δι' ὃ νοεροὺς τε εἶναι, καὶ φρονήσεως θείας μετέχειν.

[He reports that] this god cut off his own head, and that the other gods used the spilled blood to moisten the earth and form human beings. And that is the reason, he says, why humans are thinking beings and partake in the divine mind.[16]

---

11. For details, see Burstein 1978, Verbrugghe and Wickersham 1996, De Breucker 2010 and 2012, Haubold, Lanfranchi, Rollinger, and Steele 2013.
12. Dillery 2015: 134-6
13. Burstein 1978: 6–7, Haubold 2013a: 148–53.
14. Haubold 2013b.
15. *E.e.* VI.7-8 (Lambert).
16. *BNJ* 680 F 1b (7).

There are uncertainties about the transmitted text of this passage,[17] but there can be no doubt that for Berossos the point of human creation was to make us *like* the gods. The idea would not have been alien to Babylonian readers: in the Akkadian *Poem of the Flood*, also known as *Atra-ḫasīs*, man has understanding (Akk. *ṭēmu*) because he was formed from a god who possessed this quality. The god's flesh also endows us with a spirit (Akk. *eṭemmu*), which serves as a memento of the creation process (OB *Atra-ḫasīs* I.223–30). Berossos, then, is not making a radical break with Babylonian tradition, but he does deviate from his main source so as to echo Greek philosophy and its project of raising man to a higher state of being.

In one sense, then, Berossos's project was not unlike that of the *Letter of Aristeas*. He too aimed to insert himself and his peers into the dominant discourse of Greek cosmopolitan elites. Josephus was sufficiently impressed with the result to claim, self-servingly, that anyone with an interest in Greek παιδεία was familiar with Berossos.[18] In truth, Berossos's attempt at cultural grafting was only marginally more successful than that of *Aristeas*.[19] Bang's basic point still holds: non-Greek intellectuals like Berossos were free to knock on the door of elite Greek culture, but they gained only very limited access to it. Berossos failed to break into the canon of Greek παιδεία, and it is unlikely that he secured for himself, or his Babylonian peers, the status of royal "friend," φίλος.

CHALDEANS AND FRIENDS OF THE KING

The "friends" of the king represented the social, cultural, and military backbone of the Seleucid empire.[20] As Bang points out in his discussion of Hellenistic cosmopolitanism, they formed a supra-local aristocracy, which maintained itself with reference to specifically Greek cultural practices and ideals:

> Greek imperial civilisation was shaped by the transregional dissemination of the social rituals of the polis, such as the athletic contests of the gymnasium, and a literary culture based on poetry, rhetoric and philosophy. It was from this network of Hellenic communities that the Graeco-Macedonian monarchs mostly recruited the members of their courts, their philoi or "friends," to form a supra-local aristocracy.[21]

17. Haubold 2013b: 40–41.
18. *BNJ* 680 T 3 (= Jos. *Ap.* 1.128).
19. De Breucker 2013: 25 concludes that "the impact of the *Babyloniaca* appears to have been limited." For the transmission and early reception of the *Babyloniaca*, see also Schironi 2013 (Polyhistor), Dillery 2013 (Josephus), and Madreiter 2013 (Eusebius).
20. Strootman 2007: 119–180; cf. Savalli-Lestrade 1998, Kuhrt and Sherwin-White 1993: 133, Habicht 2006, Strootman 2011: 70.
21. Bang 2012: 71.

As a rule, the "friends" of the Seleucid king shared a cosmopolitan Greek out-look and background. Non-Greeks were not normally admitted to this net-work. It is possible that Berossos was an exception, but his own work suggests otherwise.[22] For the *Babyloniaca* does not attempt to merge Babylonian cul-ture with Greek to the point where the former can simply become part of the latter. Rather, it suggests that there were elite networks outside cosmopolitan Hellenism that mattered to the long-term success of the empire.

For illustration, let us consider a critical moment in Berossos's account of the Neo-Babylonian empire. In book 3 of the *Babyloniaca* the old king Nabopolassar has died while his son is away on campaign. This is what happened next:

> αἰσθόμενος δὲ μετ' οὐ πολὺν χρόνον τὴν τοῦ πατρὸς τελευτὴν Ναβοκοδρόσορος, καταστήσας τὰ κατὰ τὴν Αἴγυπτον πράγματα καὶ τὴν λοιπὴν χώραν, καὶ τοὺς αἰχμαλώτους Ἰουδαίων τε καὶ Φοινίκων καὶ Σύρων καὶ τῶν κατὰ τὴν Αἴγυπτον ἐθνῶν συντάξας τισὶ τῶν φίλων μετὰ τῆς βαρυτάτης δυνάμεως καὶ τῆς λοιπῆς ὠφελείας ἀνακομίζειν εἰς τὴν Βαβυλωνίαν, αὐτὸς ὁρμήσας ὀλιγοστὸς παρεγένετο διὰ τῆς ἐρήμου εἰς Βαβυλῶνα.

> When Nebuchadnezzar learnt of his father's death not long thereafter, he settled his affairs in Egypt and the rest of the territory and gave control over the captives—Judeans, Phoenicians, Syrians, and the populations settled in Egypt—to some of his friends, ordering them to bring them to Mesopotamia together with the bulk of his army and the rest of the spoils. He himself set out with a few companions and reached Babylon by crossing the desert.[23]

Nebuchadnezzar has just suppressed a rebellion in the western provinces of the empire when news of his father's death reaches him. As Amélie Kuhrt among others has shown,[24] Berossos conceives Nebuchadnezzar as a model for the Seleucids, and the present passage fully bears that out: not only was he a great conqueror of the west, as the Seleucids also aspired to be, but with his dash across the desert he proved himself worthy of his father's throne in a tradition that reaches back to the great kings of Assyria and Babylon, and forward to Alexander the Great.[25]

Yet, Nebuchadnezzar is not the only protagonist in Berossos's account of how the Neo-Babylonian empire was rescued. Out in the west, a group referred to as his "friends" helped to secure his conquests. Meanwhile, another group called

---

22. Kosmin 2013: 206–7 considers Berossos's relationship with the Seleucid court and suggests that it was less close than that of "trusted friends" of the king.

23. *BNJ* 680 F 8a (137).

24. Kuhrt 1987: 55–56; cf. Beaulieu 2006b, Haubold 2013a: 165.

25. Haubold 2013a: 110 n. 125.

"the Chaldeans" ensured a smooth transition back in Babylon. Here is how the text continues:

καταλαβὼν δὲ τὰ πράγματα διοικούμενα ὑπὸ Χαλδαίων καὶ διατηρουμένην τὴν βασιλείαν ὑπὸ τοῦ βελτίστου αὐτῶν, κυριεύσας ὁλοκλήρου τῆς πατρικῆς ἀρχῆς ...

Finding on arrival that the affairs [of the empire] were administered by the Chaldeans and that the kingship was maintained by the best of them, he gained possession of his father's entire realm.[26]

Berossos explains that even Nebuchadnezzar could not have secured his throne without the Chaldeans who preserved it for him. So who are these people, and how do they relate to the military elite earlier described as Nebuchadnezzar's "friends"? As a way into answering these questions, let us have a closer look at the language used to describe their activity—for although the text is transmitted by Josephus, some of the phrasing reveals Berossos's own, specifically Seleucid, agenda.

We may start by noting the term πράγματα as a way of referring to the "affairs" of the Neo-Babylonian empire. Hellenistic sources suggest that the phrasing echoes official Seleucid parlance.[27] There are other parallels with Seleucid imperial discourse: διοικεῖν recalls the office of the διοικέτης,[28] and the idea of "preserving the kingship" for Nebuchadnezzar is reminiscent of a passage in Polybius where the Seleucid general Achaios is said to have performed a similar service for the young prince Antiochus:

Ἀχαιὸς δὲ ... τῶν ὅλων πραγμάτων φρονίμως καὶ μεγαλοψύχως προέστη. τῶν γὰρ καιρῶν παρόντων αὐτῷ, καὶ τῆς τῶν ὄχλων ὁρμῆς συνεργουσης εἰς τὸ διάδημα περιθέσθαι, τοῦτο μὲν οὐ προείλετο ποιῆσαι, τηρῶν δὲ τὴν βασιλείαν Ἀντιόχῳ τῷ νεωτέρῳ τῶν υἱῶν, ἐνεργῶς ἐπιπορευόμενος ἀνεκτᾶτο τὴν ἐπὶ τάδε τοῦ Ταύρου πᾶσαν.

But Achaios ... took the command of the army and the affairs [of the empire] into his hands, and conducted both with prudence and magnanimity. For though the opportunity was favorable and he was eagerly urged by the troops to assume the diadem, he decided not to do so, and preserving the kingship for the younger son Antiochus, advanced energetically and recovered the whole of the country on this side of Taurus.[29]

26. *BNJ* 680 F 8a (138).
27. Ma 2002: 126–7 and index *s.v.*
28. Ma 2002: 135–6.
29. Polybius 4.48.9–10.

Achaios acts in a way that recalls the role of the Chaldeans in Berossos's account: clearly, Berossos read Babylonian history in a Seleucid key.[30] But what can his Seleucid view of the Neo-Babylonian empire teach us about Seleucid imperial elites? Berossos introduces two key players, aside from the king himself: the king's officials—his "friends" in Seleucid parlance—are at the forefront of imperial expansion. By contrast, the Chaldeans "preserve kingship" back in Babylon. In their own way, both groups strive to secure the πράγματα of the king, though they do so in different ways. Berossos portrays the φίλοι as close to the king and as directly involved in his ventures. For better or worse, they play a crucial role in determining the fortunes of the empire, enabling Nebuchadnezzar's accession to power but also murdering the infant king Labashi-Marduk later in book 3:

> τούτου υἱὸς Λαβοροσοάρχοδος ἐκυρίευσε μὲν τῆς βασιλείας παῖς ὢν
> μῆνας θ, ἐπιβουλευθεὶς δὲ διὰ τὸ πολλὰ ἐμφαίνειν κακοήθη ὑπὸ τῶν
> φίλων ἀπετυμπανίσθη.

> His son Labashi-Marduk was king for nine months, while he was still a
> child. Because he displayed much wickedness, the friends plotted against
> him and put him to death.[31]

Berossos explains that there were good reasons for this unwholesome intervention (the baby king was κακοήθης, "depraved"), but the fact remains that the murder of a legitimate monarch is not only a problem in its own right but also leads on to the demise of the Neo-Babylonian dynasty as a whole. For, as Berossos explains, the φίλος who took over from Labashi-Marduk under such murky circumstances was Nabonidus, the last of the Neo-Babylonian kings.

In the *Babyloniaca*, then, the friends of the king intervene very directly in the affairs of the empire, and not always in a salutary way. By contrast, the Chaldeans represent, and protect, an inherited order that is in principle unchangeable. They do not travel with the army and do not involve themselves in the cut and thrust of imperial expansion. And yet, their loyalty needs no prompt: Nebuchadnezzar simply "finds" on returning that the Chaldeans have looked after the affairs of the empire. Moreover, what the Chaldeans preserve for the king is not a personal fiefdom but "kingship" as an abstract concept. The text of the *Babyloniaca* is, of course, fragmentary, but the overall picture of two interdependent elite networks, each with its own function and characteristics, seems reasonably clear.

Elsewhere in his work, Berossos explains how this situation could arise, and derives what we might call a charter for Seleucid elite interaction from precisely the two groups who feature in his account of Nebuchadnezzar: the φίλοι of the king

---

30. For Berossos using Seleucid language and ideas to describe the Neo-Babylonian empire see also Dillery 2013, Dillery 2015: 271-85.
31. *BNJ* 680 F 9a (148).

and the Chaldeans of Babylon. Those two groups, he tells us, used to be one and the same, but they diverged at a crucial moment in human history. The decisive passage comes in book 2 of the *Babyloniaca*, where Berossos describes the great flood that came about during the times of the Chaldean King Xisouthros. For Berossos, the flood was above all a cultural event, and the flood hero Xisouthros remarkable not so much for preserving "the seed of all living creatures" (as the *Gilgamesh Epic* has it) but rather for rescuing all human writings, "beginnings, middles and ends."[32] The narrative unfolds in several stages: first a god appears to Xisouthros in a dream and informs him of the impending flood; as part of his preparations, Xisouthros is to bury all human writings in Sippar, city of the sun. Xisouthros carries out these orders and then embarks on a ship, together with all animals, his own family and—important for our purposes—his closest φίλοι:

τὸν Κρόνον αὐτῶι κατὰ τὸν ὕπνον ἐπιστάντα φάναι μηνὸς Δαισίου πέμπτηι καὶ δεκάτηι τοὺς ἀνθρώπους ὑπὸ κατακλυσμοῦ διαφθαρήσεσθαι. κελεῦσαι οὖν [διὰ] γραμμάτων πάντων ἀρχὰς καὶ μέσα καὶ τελευτὰς ὀρύξαντα θεῖναι ἐν πόλει Ἡλίου Σι[σ]πάροις καὶ ναυπηγησάμενον σκάφος ἐμβῆναι μετὰ τῶν συγγενῶν καὶ ἀναγκαίων φίλων ... τὸν δὲ οὐ παρακούσαντα ναυπηγήσασθαι σκάφος ... τὰ δὲ συνταχθέντα πάντα συνθέσθαι, καὶ γυναῖκα καὶ τέκνα καὶ τοὺς ἀναγκαίους φίλους ἐμβιβάσαι.

Kronos appeared to him in his sleep and said that on the fifteenth of the month of Daisios mankind would be destroyed by a flood. He therefore ordered him to bury the beginnings, middle parts, and ends of all writings in Sippar, the city of the Sun. And after building a ship he was to embark on it with his family and close friends.... He did not disobey and built a boat ... and loaded it with all he had been told and brought on board his wife and children and close friends.[33]

When they first appear, the φίλοι of Xisouthros are slipped in almost as an afterthought, but they become important after the flood: when the waters recede, the king and his family disappear, and a voice from heaven instructs their companions to become "god-fearing" and to re-establish human civilization by digging up the archive of pre-flood literature. What we have here is not just an etiology of the Chaldeans as a body of priestly experts but also a template for how they relate to the Seleucid king, the ruling elite of Greco-Macedonian friends of the king, and the empire as a whole: as φίλοι of Xisouthros, the Chaldeans inherit the task of maintaining the kingdom and ensuring dynastic continuity. In practice, Berossos suggests, this need not entail close contact with the

---

32. For the *Gilgamesh Epic*, see SB *Gilg.* XI.27. For Berossos, see *BNJ* 680 F 4b (14–17) and the discussion in De Breucker, *BNJ ad loc.*; Haubold 2013a: 159–60; Dillery 2015: 253-64.
33. *BNJ* 680 F 4b (14).

rulers themselves, or indeed with their military elites (we recall the narrative of Nebuchadnezzar and his western campaign). But it does entail a shared vision for the empire which goes beyond the historically grounded localism that Kathryn Stevens discusses elsewhere in this volume. In effect, Berossos offers a charter for participation in the Seleucid empire which includes both Greek and Babylonian elites.

Maintaining the Kingdom

Berossos, we have seen, envisages the Neo-Babylonian empire as relying on two distinctive elite networks: the generals and courtiers of the king whom he calls his "friends" and the Chaldeans of Babylon. Berossos himself invites us to read this arrangement in a Seleucid key. If we follow him, we can say, with only slight simplification, that according to him, the role of Antiochus's Greek elites was to take charge of political and military matters around the empire, whereas the Chaldeans guaranteed dynastic continuity. This is a compelling vision in its own right, and one that casts an interesting light on what a leading Babylonian thinker made of the Seleucid empire and his own role in it. But what relation, if any, does Berossos's model of elite interaction have with real-life politics? Would the Seleucid kings and their "friends" have recognized it as meaningful and relevant to them?

Prima facie that seems unlikely, given the gap in culture and outlook between the Babylonian temples and Seleucid Greeks. To the Greeks, the Babylonians were "barbarians," a notion which could accommodate respect for their esoteric wisdom but otherwise left little room for cultural rapprochement. Aristotle, for one, had no qualms about declaring all barbarians natural slaves.[34] Babylonian authors tend to be more guarded, but at least one extant text, the *Ptolemy III Chronicle*, suggests that the distaste for the other may have been mutual: it describes an invading Ptolemaic army as "Hanaeans clad in iron who do not fear the gods."[35] At one level, this is, of course, an attempt to create a shared enemy for Babylonians and Seleucid Greeks.[36] But at another, it shows how invading Greeks could appear from a Babylonian perspective.

There can be no doubt, of course, that Greeks and Babylonians found ways of coexisting in Seleucid Mesopotamia. They sometimes intermarried (the family of Anu-uballiṭ/Kephalon is an example), and they certainly interacted. Politically, however, the two communities remained clearly distinct,[37] and their different political status was understood to reflect different cultures. Thus, one

---

34. Aristotle, *Politics* I.2–7.
35. *BCHP* 11, ll. 6–7.
36. Haubold 2013a: 134–5.
37. Van der Spek 2009.

late Babylonian chronicle refers to the (Greek) "citizens" of Babylon as people "who anoint themselves with oil like the citizens of Seleucia"—an allusion perhaps to the gymnasium and the nudity that, shockingly to most Babylonians, was on display there.[38]

Berossos's mythology of the Chaldeans suggested how these cultures could nonetheless work together in the interest of the empire. But did his Greek readers share his view of Greco-Babylonian cooperation? Even if we accept that Berossos spoke for most members of the Babylonian temple elites (and we must allow for the possibility that some of them would have disagreed), there remains the question of what Antiochus and other Greek readers would have made of his proposals. Did Berossos's model of elite interaction have any purchase in the world of Seleucid *realpolitik* or was it simply the product of wishful thinking? In the final part of my chapter, I argue that—however we assess the impact of Berossos's work—he did articulate something important, and real, about how the Seleucid empire worked. Like Nebuchadnezzar in the *Babyloniaca*, real-life Seleucid kings from Antiochus I to Antiochus III turned to their Chaldean elites at moments of crisis. Rather than reviewing all the relevant evidence here, let me single out one example that seems to me to be particularly instructive.

Just after his defeat at the hands of the Romans, and still smarting from the disastrous treaty of Apamea, Antiochus III came to visit Babylon. When he arrived in the city, the empire was at a low ebb: Antiochus had just lost a major war and with it vast amounts of military equipment, manpower, money, and territory. His reputation too had taken a knock: Antiochus had styled himself a conqueror king in the tradition of Alexander, so a defeat of this magnitude was not an easy sell. Antiochus had conducted much of his western campaign, as already his earlier reconquest of the east, under the banner of recovering what was rightfully his:[39] to Seleucid observers, his wars were not just acts of bravado but signaled a restoration of the empire after decades of uncertainty. Now that his aims had turned out to be unattainable, the future of the empire as a whole, its very shape and purpose, came into question. How bad things had got may be seen from the fact that, just a few months later, Antiochus was dead, killed while attempting to press money from a temple in Elam. But first he visited Babylon.

The episode is recorded in loving detail in an *Astronomical Diary* of 188/7 BCE.[40] The *Astronomical Diaries* were a curious set of texts which recorded routine celestial observations but also included notes on the weather, the economy, and brief accounts of important political events.[41] The passage about

38. *BCHP* 14, esp. ll. 2-4, with van der Spek's note *ad* l. 4.
39. Ma 2002: ch. 1; but see Kosmin 2014a: ch. 5 for the Greek campaign as a war of expansion.
40. *AD* -187 (Sachs and Hunger).
41. Edition in Sachs and Hunger 1988-2006; Del Monte 1997 prints the historical sections with Italian translation and commentary. For discussion of the historical sections, see also van der Spek 1993 and Pirngruber 2013.

Antiochus's visit to Babylon is precisely such an account, though it is exceptionally long and detailed: clearly, Antiochus's visit was of some importance—
at least from a Babylonian perspective. The result of all this attention to detail
is an amazingly rich text, and one which would deserve a chapter all of its own.
Here I want to focus on just two of the objects that are presented to Antiochus
in the course of his visit: a 1,000 shekel crown made of gold and the cloak of
Nebuchadnezzar.

To take the crown first, John Ma points out that crowns constituted a standard way of honoring victorious kings in the Hellenistic world, often combining
symbolic value with very real material worth.[42] Antiochus, of course, was far
from victorious at this point in time, and he desperately needed money. Under
such circumstances, it was relevant that the Babylonian crown had a significant
value, as the author of the *Diary* stresses. But at least equally important was the
symbolic significance of the object: the top official (*šatammu*) and governing
assembly of the Esagila bestowed on Antiochus a powerful token of kingship.
In so doing, they expressed not only their own continued allegiance to the king
but also that of the city of Babylon and—presumably—much of the surrounding
territory besides.[43]

This is a stunning gesture, but there is more to come. After the 1,000 shekel
crown, and a series of other gifts, the narrative culminates in the cloak of
Nebuchadnezzar being brought out from the magazines of Esagila. Once
again, the gesture is transparently legitimizing, but this time the effect is more
pointed: the cloak is not simply handed to Antiochus but recovered from the
archives of Babylon, where it had been stored for safekeeping since the days of
Nebuchadnezzar. This is not just a piece of clothing, however precious. Rather,
it is a token of precisely the mythology of elite interaction that I have been discussing in this chapter: the king has fought a war, with the help of his (Greek)
φίλοι. But now something else is needed, something that only the Chaldeans
can provide.

It is not entirely clear what Antiochus does with the cloak of Nebuchadnezzar—
perhaps he puts it on, or perhaps he merely marvels at it. Either way, the king
accepts his place in the tradition of universal kingship which Berossos describes, and he also accepts the peculiar role of the Chaldeans at the heart of
his empire: these men were not close to him personally or culturally, and he
is not likely to have encountered them on a regular basis. But when the king's
fortunes were at their lowest ebb, they had something to offer that not even the
king's most loyal courtiers could provide: a war had been lost, but the kingdom
had been maintained.

---

42. Ma 2002: 204.
43. For the *šatammu* and the assembly of the Esagila, see Clancier 2012.

CONCLUSION

Scholars have often suggested that the Seleucid empire was held together—to the extent that it did hold together—by discrete acts of accommodation between a cosmopolitan Greek center and non-Greek local elites.[44] The picture that emerges is one of integration through subordination, to use the conceptual framework proposed by the editors of this volume.[45] In this chapter, I have argued for a rather more complex alliance of the local and the global. Defining tokens of empire—objects as well as stories—were kept in the archives of Babylon whence they could be retrieved at times of crisis. The Chaldeans as guardians of the archives thus came to see themselves, and to be seen by their Greek masters, as guardians of kingship *par excellence*, alongside the ruling elites of the king's "friends." Berossos explained to the Seleucids how this situation had arisen and how it could work for them; and in broad outlines at least, they seem to have embraced it.

To be sure, the Seleucids did not elevate Babylonian culture to the same level as Greek, nor did they attempt to create a composite ruling class of the sort that might impress historians of the later Roman empire.[46] But they too grappled with the challenge of holding together a disparate empire. Berossos's mythology of the king, his "friends," and the Chaldeans suggests a fully worked out model of elite participation, which we see reflected in historical events such as Antiochus III's visit to Babylon. What Babylonians thought about their role in the Seleucid empire clearly mattered to the Seleucids, and it should matter to us too: we need to know more about the stories that non-Greeks of the Hellenistic period told their masters—both about themselves and about the states in which they lived. And we need to know how their stories informed social and political practice in the Hellenistic empires if we are to understand better what sustained them, and what cosmopolitan legacies they left behind.

44. For an eloquent articulation of this view, see Ma 1999, 2003.
45. Lavan, Payne, and Weisweiler, this volume.
46. Weisweiler, this volume.

5

Toward a Translocal Elite Culture in the Ptolemaic Empire

Christelle Fischer-Bovet

It has long been thought that Ptolemaic rulers generally interacted with Egyptian and Hellenized subjects in distinct cultural languages; on the conventional view, they primarily relied on what we call 'subordination' rather than 'assimilation' in integrating local elites. Fischer-Bovet's paper challenges this conventional view of a clear boundary between indigenous and Graeco-Macedonian cultural spheres. She shows that from the early years of the dynasty onwards, kings orchestrated transcultural moments which brought together different ethnic groups. This is visible in the introduction of a cult of queen Arsinoe II, who was revered as benefactor for 'all mankind', and in the creation of a new cultural memory of Persian invaders as common enemies of Greek and Egyptian populations. From the mid-third century, the court's efforts to create a trans-local elite intensified. The trilingual decrees issued by Egyptian priests neatly encapsulate the paradoxes of integration. On the one hand, the fact that these texts were written in hieroglyphic, demotic and Greek brought out the cultural differences between Egyptian and Graeco-Macedonian elites. On the other hand, by employing a diplomatic medium otherwise employed by Greek city-states, Egyptian priests constituted themselves as a poliadic community on the Hellenic model. Similarly, the forms of dynastic ritual and the festivals mentioned in these decrees show that Greek and Egyptian elites increasingly revered the same gods and shared the same calendar. These practices of 'assimilation' created a translocal elite culture whose participants defined themselves not through their ethnicity but through their association with the royal court.

INTRODUCTION

After the death of Alexander, the former Persian empire was divided into several states which are traditionally called kingdoms since their rulers chose the title "king" (*basileus* in Greek). In the cases of the Seleucids and the Ptolemies, this title could resonate as the Hellenistic equivalent of the Persian title "Great king."[1] These rulers indeed seized any opportunity to control new regions beyond the Greek world. Strootman underlined how the Ptolemies and the Seleucids adopted and adapted Near Eastern ideologies of universal empire, as Alexander before them.[2] The expansionist policies of the Ptolemies, even if they were not always successful, can be evidenced at least until the mid-second century BCE and again under the last queen, Cleopatra VII.[3] The empire reached its largest extension under Ptolemy III and Ptolemy IV, when they controlled territories around the Eastern Mediterranean extending from Cyrenaica to Thrace, including Coele-Syria, Cyprus, and islands in the Aegean, as well as territories in Lower Nubia.[4] If one accepts M. Doyle's definition of "empire" as "a relation in which one state controls the effective political sovereignty of another political society" and of "imperialism" simply as "the process of establishing or maintaining an empire," then the Ptolemaic state was indeed an empire.[5] The extension of the territories under imperial control and the degree of control vary at lengths from one empire to another and also within the same empire over time, as in the Ptolemaic case. Yet the term "empire" remains a useful heuristic tool because it identifies a particular type of state that shares in common a set of ideological, economic, military, and political characteristics such as the concept of universal kingship, large share of the taxes invested in warfare, a larger army than one necessary for defense alone, and provinces headed by governors, to name only a few.[6] Moreover, imperialism was not an alien concept to the population living in Egypt, the core of the Ptolemaic empire. The New Kingdom can be characterized as an imperialistic moment of Egyptian history, when kings expanded their control to Syria-Palestine and to Nubia thanks to the implementation of a standing army. Such a perception of the Egyptian past was certainly still a component of Egyptian cultural memory by the time of the Ptolemaic takeover.[7]

It is generally accepted that the Ptolemaic dynasty, which was Macedonian in origin, developed a double or Janus face: it co-opted and adapted Egyptian culture to facilitate a dialogue with the Egyptian population and its priestly

---

1. Bang 2012, Strootman 2014b: 46. I would like to thank the Institute for Research in the Humanities at the University of Wisconsin-Madison and the von Humboldt Foundation, Germany (Freiburg-im-Bresigau) for providing the time and material necessary for writing this chapter.

2. Strootman 2014b: esp. 44, 51–52.

3. Hauben and Meeus 2014, e.g., Meeus 2014 on Ptolemy I.

4. For a survey of Ptolemaic history, see Hölbl 2001 and Huss 2001; for Ptolemaic expansion, see the current work of Andrew Meadows, e.g., summarized in Meadows 2012.

5. Doyle 1986: 45; on premodern empires, see, e.g., Burbank and Cooper 2010, who start with Rome but acknowledge previous empires (4) and Bang and Scheidel 2013.

6. This description draws on Mann's model to explain state formation through four sources of social power: ideological, economic, military, and political. See Mann 1986, see also the refinement of this model by Goldstone and Haldon 2009.

7. Manning 2003: 40 stresses that the projection of power outside Egypt under the Saite dynasty (664–525 BCE) goes back at least to the New Kingdom; see below on the concept of cultural memory.

elite and used Greek culture to interact with the Greek and with the Hellenized population in Egypt and beyond it. But such an interpretation only partially represents the ruling strategies of the Ptolemies. Thanks to the growing collaboration between papyrologists, demotists, and ancient historians, recent scholarship has shown more and more frequently that the two faces were in fact less independent of each other than previously thought.[8] Drawing on this research, two complementary aspects can be emphasized. First, the Ptolemies may not have thought of their coercive power in terms of domestic policies in Egypt and of foreign policies in the rest of their territories, but rather in terms of networks of individuals who belonged to the diverse local elites and through whom their power was projected, and at best through whom it penetrated society more deeply. The development of such networks necessitated the translation of Ptolemaic power into localist idioms, for instance, in royal stelae erected in Egyptian temples and in decrees voted by poleis in order to honor the royal figures. As in other contributions to this volume (e.g., Haubold), one of the central questions is whether these interactions transcended the level of local accommodation. Second, while the Ptolemies were shaping their royal ideology in line with their imperial ambitions, the kings created opportunities for transcultural moments and places to emerge and for some individuals to bridge places and cultures: at times they also used universalist idioms.

From the point of view of the elite groups in the Ptolemaic territories, the challenge was to create a connection with the new ruler in order to maintain their superior position or to strengthen it.[9] In this way they also shaped the formation of the empire, its political ideology, and cultural overtone. The allegiance to a particular dynasty, who claimed above all to protect them, was translated by elites into a discourse that emphasized the benevolence of the king and the queen, as well as of their royal officials, in exchange for honors granted to them, sometimes related to the worship of the kings and of the queens.[10] The cult of the Ptolemaic kings developed differently in the two main cultural spheres, Greek and Egyptian, yet with some overlaps too often overlooked. It can be argued that the royal family, its councilors, and the local elites were particularly keen at selecting overlapping cultural symbols and that all participated, to various degrees depending on their asymmetrical power relation, in constructing a translocal Ptolemaic elite culture. Such an encounter between cultures has triggered numerous recent studies, for example, on the Egyptian Isis and the Greek Aphrodite and their associations with the Ptolemaic queens, as well as their potential universal character in providing protection (notably the protection

---

8. Koenen 1993. The bibliography is vast, see, e.g., the contributions in the recent volume on royal cult by Iossif, Chankowski, and Lorber 2011.

9. For such a definition of local elites, see Dreyer and Mittag 2011: 10–11.

10. See part I for this so-called language of euergetism.

of sailors) and care for the population.[11] But this chapter focuses mainly on the analysis of steles that bore witness to the interaction of the king, the royal family, and elite groups. It aims to identify the characteristics of cosmopolitanism in the Ptolemaic empire across time and to assess how the two ideal types of cosmopolitanism suggested as heuristic tools in the present volume, "assimilation" and "subordination," worked simultaneously in the Ptolemaic case.[12]

The two parts of the chapter identify two different steps in the emergence of a translocal elite culture and aim to explain the mechanisms at work. By "translocal culture" I mean a culture that stresses—and tries to facilitate—the connection between at least two places and the traditions and cultural memories attached to each.[13] The first part focuses on the earliest strategies of communication and negotiation that developed between the Ptolemies and the local elites, where the localist idioms dominated and cultural differences were maintained (subordination). Yet some elements hinted at a universalist view or at least carried with them the possibility of universalism (assimilation). Then the second part turns to the trilingual decrees of the Egyptian priests honoring the king in order to demonstrate how localist idioms were adapted and how transcultural moments and places were created. Finally, this investigation shows how some elements belonging to different cultural spheres, in particular the appeal for Greek decisional tools and for Egyptian religion, were conflated in the late Ptolemaic period, notably through the agency of individuals whom one may characterize as translocal.

THE LOCALIST MODE OF EXPRESSION

The earlier examples of interaction between the Ptolemaic kings and the local elites down to the mid-third century BCE were usually expressed in a localist mode of expression, in which the local populations incorporated the changing reality into their mode of expression and interpreted it from their local perspective. This mode continued throughout the period while other possibilities clearly opened from the mid-third century.

Greek and Hellenized Cities

During the troubled decades following Alexander's death, cities from around the eastern Mediterranean developed strategies to negotiate with the generals

---

11. Barbantani 2005, Bricault 2006, Demetriou 2010, Plantzos 2011, Llewellyn-Jones and Winder 2011, and Caneva 2014.

12. The acknowledgment of a simultaneity resembles one of the approaches to cosmopolitanism proposed by Breckenridge et al. 2002: 13, 48, where they theorize the "both-cosmopolitan-and-vernacular" as an option where the choice between the two is rejected.

13. See the analysis of transcultural practice and space in Ptolemaic Egypt by Moyer 2011b or the reflection on the circulation of Sanskrit poetry conceived as participating in a translocal culture in Breckenridge et al. 2002: 10; on cultural memory, see part I.

who soon became kings and who monopolized military power but not ideological power. In a well-known episode of the *Life of Demetrius*, Plutarch describes with consternation how the Athenians, delivered from the rule of Demetrius of Phalerus in 307 BCE by Demetrius Poliorcetes, voted for the latter honors which would have been inconceivable a few decades earlier. He and his father Antigonus received the title of kings and of Saviour-gods, a priest was elected every year for their cult, and two tribes called after their names were created.[14] Not all the Athenians agreed with these decisions, as reported later by Athenaeus, but voting divine or quasi-divine honors to kings became part of the process of negotiations between poleis and kings, often referred to as the language of euergetism.[15]

The Ptolemies participated in the same kind of negotiation of political and ideological power. Later in the third century, when Athens was independent but threatened by Demetrius's successors, the kings of Macedonia, the city constantly tried to find support from other more distant kings, such as the Ptolemies.[16] Polybius reports that the Athenians consented "to every variety of decree and proclamation however humiliating."[17] In this context, they added another tribe (*phyle*) called "Ptolemais" to honor Ptolemy III Euergetes (224 BCE), and it is almost certain that he was granted Athenian citizenship, as were perhaps Ptolemy I and certainly Ptolemy II before him, and as were his successors.[18] Royal officials were also granted citizenship in Athens or in cities under Ptolemaic control, in a world where most powerful individuals became "suprapolis players," to borrow John Ma's expression.[19] The decision process and the vote of honors still conformed to the institutions of the city and Athens was at the same time asserting some ideological control over the kings and their officials by granting them citizenship.

Honorific decrees to the Ptolemies were even more common on the part of poleis in the territories they controlled, such as in Itanos in Crete, as a way of communication. During the first year of rule of Ptolemy III, in 246 BCE, the citizens dedicated a sacred enclosure to the royal couple and decided that the king and the queen should receive sacrifices on their birthdays, accompanied by a race.[20] The reasons for these honors are said to be the continuous benevolence

---

14. Plu., *Demetr.* 8–10.

15. Ath. 253c–f reports that the honors Demetrius was granted in Athens were disapproved by Demachares, Demosthenes's cousin, and by Douris of Samos; on the ithyphallic hymn for Demetrius sung while he returned to Athens in 291 BCE, see now Chaniotis 2011. On the language of euergetism, see Bertrand 1990, Ma 2002, and also Bencivenni 2014.

16. On Athens and the Ptolemies, see Habicht 1992.

17. Plb. 5. 106. 8, translation by Paton, Walbank, and Habicht 2011.

18. IG ii² 2314, Col. I 40ff.; Osborne 1981–3: vol. III, T101 and T102 (Ptolemy IV), T105 (Ptolemy V), T118 (Ptolemy VI).

19. E.g., Ma 2013: 295; for instance, Thraseas of Aspendos, the strategos of Cilicia and later of Coele-Syria, was granted the Athenian citizenship, see Habicht 1992: 76.

20. Syll.³ 463 = Austin 2006: no. 265; Ptolemy ceded land that he owned in the city center, which suggests a royal initiative, see Viviers 2011: 45, or at least a partial royal initiative.

of the king, his father Ptolemy II and his ancestors. Yet as also noted by Michel Austin, there is no evidence of Ptolemaic involvement in Itanos before Ptolemy II.[21] The citizens shaped their history (perhaps encouraged by royal officials) in order to create the appearance of a long connection with the Ptolemies and to include themselves in a long-lasting imperial tradition.[22] They also incorporated this relationship into their own history in a tangible way by placing the stele inscribed with the decree in the sanctuary of their goddess, Athena Polias. Finally, by establishing new holidays on royal birthdays, they altered their own calendar to participate in royal celebrations of an imperial character, since these were celebrated throughout the empire (see later discussion of the synodal decrees).

Egyptian Priests

If one turns to Egypt proper, the same principles were at work but the dialogue took place with the priestly families who composed the Egyptian elite. Even before Ptolemy became king officially, and later under Ptolemy II, one means for negotiating power relations was for the new ruler to reaffirm his generosity by guaranteeing donations of land and revenues to the temples. He also supported the cult of regional gods in exchange for the benevolence of the gods and the collaboration of the priests. The nature of this relationship was initially cast into localist idioms, in hieroglyphic sacerdotal decrees engraved at the initiatives of the priests on steles and erected within the precincts of Egyptian temples. In the Satrap Stele (311 BCE), the Egyptian priests of a given temple integrated Ptolemy Satrap into their local history while in the Pithom Stele (ca. 264 BCE) and the Mendes Stele (257 BCE), they incorporated Ptolemy II into their own world. The erection of most of these early steles was triggered by one or several royal visits to the temples of the region.[23] Some of these steles enumerated a series of events and reported the content of royal decrees, whereas others commemorated mainly one decision (e.g., the Sais Stele, discussed later). The priests represented their relationship with the new dynasty in the same way as they did with previous pharaohs. An extreme instance of localism is the Famine Stele, supposedly a royal decree of King Djoser of the Old Kingdom addressed to a governor in Elephantine but which was written in the Ptolemaic period, probably by the priests of the temple themselves under the reign of Ptolemy V.[24] Their localist point of view goes as far as not to mention the Ptolemies but instead to refer only to Djoser, who describes his

21. Austin 2006: note to no. 265.

22. On the construction of a Seleucid past by Greek poleis, see Stevens, this volume, with Ma 2002: 26–52.

23. Respectively, Cairo General Catalogue 22182, 22183, and 22181; for references to earlier editions, translations, and bibliography, see Gozzoli 2006: 126–44; on the Satrap Stela, see Manning 2010: 96–7; on the royal visits and the date of the Mendes stele, see Clarysse 2007: esp. 204 n. 7.

24. Lichtheim 1980: 5, 94–103, Gozzoli 2006: 126–52 and 261 for the Famine Stele.

donations to the temple of Khnum according to the god's will in order to end a famine.

It is notable that in the sacerdotal decrees dated to the reigns of Ptolemy I and Ptolemy II, at least three elements that departed from a localist perspective appear tangentially. They became important thematics on which a translocal culture could develop. The first two were closely related: the integration of deified royal figures in the Egyptian temples and rituals and the conceptualization of these figures as sources of welfare to all mankind. The third one emphasized the necessity of fighting against the enemies coming from the east (the "Asiatics"), and even perhaps the need of creating new provinces, in order to bring back the stolen statues of the Egyptian gods.

The narrative section of the Mendes Stele mentions that Ptolemy II was generous toward all the Egyptian temples and in particular toward the temple of Ram, god of Mendes, which he visited, and that he returned to the royal residence (in Alexandria) where he married his sister Arsinoe. The central section of the text, however, turns to the death of the queen in year 15 (270 or 268 BCE) and to the subsequent establishment of the cult of Arsinoe and of her cultic statue in each Egyptian temple, including in the local temple of the Ram god.[25] The thematic of the welfare for all human beings appears here already. For the Egyptian priests Arsinoe was like a goddess "on account of her benevolent thoughts for all mankind,"[26] a term rarely used in these sacerdotal decrees but more frequent under the following kings (discussed later). The stele adds that the king chose bodyguards from among the Egyptian elite, notably of the Mendesian nome, and built a canal connecting the region to the Red Sea.[27] Then the text focuses again on local privileges, especially fiscal ones. In the Pithom Stele, Arsinoe was presented as a good councilor for the king regarding foreign enemies and a town was renamed Arsinoe, in which a temple was established for the Brother-Sister Gods (*Theoi adelphoi*), that is, for the cult of Ptolemy II and Arsinoe as a royal couple, which existed in parallel to the cult of the queen alone. With the cult of Arsinoe, the local was connected to the regional, and even beyond, since her cult also developed throughout the Ptolemaic empire, where it followed Greek rituals.[28] The creation of the Arsinoeia, a Greek festival for the deified queen in Alexandria which was also attested later in the chora (Egyptian countryside), was one example of these spatial connections through special celebrations.[29] It is

25. See translation of this section of the stele, with bibliography, in Collombert 2008: 83–4 and in Thiers 2007: 190. I thank Damien Agut-Labordère for sharing his expertise with me on the hieroglyphic text.

26. Translation of S. Birch after the translation by Brugsch-Bey (1875) *Records of the Past*, series 1, vol. 8 (online); Collombert 2008: 84 translates this as "ses actes de bienfaisance pour les gens."

27. On the bodyguards, see Fischer-Bovet 2014: 162 n. 7.

28. See the introduction of the cult of Arsinoe-Aphrodite by the admiral Callicrates Hauben 2013: esp. 48 and n. 58 and her role as protectrice of the sailors in Barbantani 2005; on her cult in Cyprus, Fulinska 2012 and more generally on Arsinoe, Carney 2013.

29. Fraser 1972: 1:229, Collombert 2008: 97–8, Perpillou-Thomas 1993: 155–8.

remarkable that pigs were sacrificed at her festivals, like for Isis and Osiris, who are the only Egyptian gods to whom pigs could be sacrificed.[30]

On the basis of the Mendes Stele, it has been generally accepted that the cult of Arsinoe was not conceived as purely Greek but as a means to bring the populations attached to either Greek or Egyptian cultures closer together. In the Pithom Stele, as we mentioned already, she is presented as a councilor to the king for the protection of Egypt. Collombert has recently challenged this assumption through his analysis of the chronological information provided by the Sais Stele (ca. 263/2 BCE), another stele regarding the introduction of the cult of Arsinoe in Sais. According to him, there was a time gap of about five years between her deification in 268/7 BCE (year 18 of the Macedonian calendar) in Alexandria shortly after her death—where she was worshipped according to a Greek ritual—and the introduction of her cult in the Egyptian temples.[31] However, he accepts that the introduction of Arsinoe in the Egyptian temples actually made the two population groups feel closer ritually and culturally and that an Egyptian councilor probably suggested the "translation" of Arsinoe's cult into the Egyptian cultural sphere. Even if there was such a time lag, its brevity suggests that the figure of the queen had always been thought of as one that could easily pass from one culture to the other. In any case, by the time of the Mendes Stele, the Egyptian priests presented the development of her cult as one cult and made no allusion to previous cultic honors granted to the queen. The transport of a Heliopolitan obelisk to the Arsinoeion of Alexandria by Ptolemy II complements the transcultural character of the deified queen.[32]

The third set of elements that depart from a localist perspective are those that include, at least partly, the Egyptian elite in the war effort and imperial ambitions of the Ptolemaic dynasty. Common points between Greek and Egyptian traumatic cultural memories of their encounters with Eastern empires were used by the priests to open a dialogue with the king.[33] The connection between the local and the world outside Egypt is made clear in the Satrap Stele and the Pithom Stele: the Persians were conceived as past common enemies, while anti-Persian ideas among the Egyptians had already been noted by Herodotus more than a century before. In the Satrap Stele, "Xerxes the enemy" was accused by the priests of Buto of having confiscated land from their temple. The texts on both steles report that statues of Egyptian gods found in Syria and Palestine (only Syria in the Satrap Stele) were brought back after military expeditions by Ptolemy—while he was still satrap—and by Ptolemy II. The Egyptian priest Manetho also reported

30. Perpillou-Thomas 1993: 156.

31. Collombert 2008: esp. 98–9, 84 n. 1, and 97 on the debated dates.

32. Plin. *H. N.* 36. 14. 67–8; Thiers 2009: 36–7.

33. On collective memory as the commemoration by a community of certain "objects" or "lieu de mémoire" and cultural memory as an externalization and objectivation of texts, images, and rituals, see Agut-Labordère 2016 with references to Nora 1989: 7 and Assmann 2010: 122.

the story of an Egyptian king, Amenophis, looking for statues in his *Aegyptiaca*.[34] However, Agut-Labordère has recently showed that while the Persians were the "villains" in the Greek tradition, the Assyrian invasions have remained the traumatic period in Egyptian collective memory.[35] This explains why the sacerdotal decrees of the Satrap and Pithom steles did not point specifically to the Persians as the robbers of the gods' statues, whereas the trilingual decrees honoring Ptolemy III and Ptolemy IV adapted the Egyptian cultural memory by accusing the Persians of the plundering (see part II). There is in fact no direct evidence for the Persians stealing the statues of Egyptian gods, while the seizure of gods' statues was well attested in Near Eastern history.[36] This latter tradition perhaps prompted the Ptolemies to bring back statues and inspired the Egyptian priests to suggest the Macedonian kings should do so, or at least to acknowledge their actions this way afterwards. Perhaps Alexander the Great's decision to return the statues of the Athenian tyrannicides Harmodius and Aristogeiton, stolen by the Persians during the Persian Wars and found by the Macedonian king in Susa, was also a model for the Ptolemies.[37] Alexander's action was a demonstration of Macedonian philhellenism to the Greeks, and it illustrates the ongoing constructions of common grounds between Greek and Macedonian cultural memories.

Moreover, the Pithom Stele describes in details the festivities organized by Ptolemy II so that the priests could identify the statues which he had returned, while additional royal gifts accompanied the statues of the gods. The text reports the return of the local god of the nome but also mentions a general edict of the king proclaiming that the Egyptian gods were supporting his Syrian campaign and that the gods considered him as ruler of Egypt and all the foreign countries.[38] The cities of the Delta were militarily strategic, so it is not surprising that the kings visited this region in person and that Ptolemy II spent his time traveling there just before his last campaign against Syria in 257 BCE.[39] The local elites of these

34. Gozzoli 2006: 136; on Manetho, see below.

35. Agut-Labordère 2016: section 2.3 discusses two literary texts preserved on papyrus from the Roman period in which the Assyrians are accused of stealing sacred objects (the *Story of King Djoser and his chancellor Imhotep*, P. Carslberg 85, and the *Prophecy of the Lamb*, P. Wien D 10,000) and follows Ryholt 2009: 237 on the identification of three traumatic periods in Egyptian collective memory, the Assyrian invasions, the Hyksos era, and the Amarna Age. On the construction of anti-Persian memory by Ptolemy I and the perception of the second Persian occupation by the Egyptian elite as a time of disorder but also of collaboration, see now Colburn 2015.

36. Briant 2003 shows that there is no Persian document regarding stealing Egyptian gods' statues against Winnicki 1994: 155–69 who gathers the possible allusions to Persian plundering in Egyptian documents. One can add the newly published P. Carlsberg 555 verso in Ryholt 2012: 143–55; on the Near eastern tradition of stealing statues, see Winnicki 1994: 151–5 and Gozzoli 2006: 135.

37. Arr., *An.* 3.16.7–8, 7. 19, Plin. *H. N.* 34.69–70; Winnicki 1994: 154 n. 25 gives references to other versions where Seleucid kings would have finally sent back the statues; on Xerxes as a robber of statues in Greece in Seleucid texts, see Briant 2009: 31.

38. See also Agut-Labordère 2016: section 3.2.

39. Clarysse 2007: 206–7 also notes that Ptolemy II spent the Macedonian New Year of that year in Memphis.

towns, especially those where steles have been erected (Buto in the Western Delta, Mendes and Pithom in the Eastern Delta), were aware of their geopolitical importance, as were for instance the citizens of Itanos in Crete, as mentioned earlier. The visits of the king and the commemoration of his decisions by the priests participated in a dialogue that reactivated the memories of an imperial past during the New Kingdom and included the Egyptian elite and population in the current imperial project. The conceptualization of the empire was not limited to the Mediterranean world, since even the foundation of Ptolemais on the Red Sea was mentioned in the Pithom Stele in connection with the hunt for war elephants.

Translocal Culture and Ideology

This section explores how the themes emphasized in the earliest medium of communication between the Egyptian priests and the first two Ptolemies, that is, the sacerdotal decrees, and the medium itself, developed in the next three generations (ca. 240s to 180s BCE). Additional decisions were made by the priests and the royal administration, who both played with overlapping symbols and elements of cultural memories which were adapted and sometimes distorted. They resulted in the construction of translocal media, moments, and places where the accumulation of cultural memories and the emergence of a translocal elite culture could occur. This is reminiscent of the concept of "middle-ground" on which Ian Moyer has recently drawn in order to study the relations between the Egyptian priests and the kings.[40]

The Trilingual Decrees

In contrast with the types of sacerdotal decrees examined earlier, the trilingual decrees, also called synodal decrees, were drafted by the Egyptian priests gathered in a synod in collaboration with the royal administration. The most famous is the Memphis decree on the Rosetta stone, but there were at least ten of them voted by the priests between 243 BCE and 182 BCE to thank the kings for their benefactions by granting them new honors.[41] The texts were supposed to be engraved in three scripts, though the Greek is sometimes missing, in all the Egyptian temples of the first three categories. Therefore, it is not surprising that fragments from multiple provenances have been preserved.[42] These trilingual

40. Moyer 2011a: esp. 116 on the idea of middle-ground as used by White 1991 about Indians and Europeans.
41. Table with references in Clarysse 2000: 42–3 and a possible eleventh decree in 162/1 under Ptolemy VI; the bibliography is enormous, see Pfeiffer 2004 and Pfeiffer 2010 and the new decree of Alexandria by El-Masry, Altenmüller, and Thissen 2012; for an introduction to these texts, see, e.g., Gozzoli 2006: 145–52 and Thompson 2012: 110–28.
42. The debate remains open on the mutilations of some of these decrees, see Moyer 2011a: 124 and El-Masry, Altenmüller, and Thissen 2012: 182.

decrees were in fact written only in two languages, Egyptian written in both hieroglyphics and in Demotic (the cursive script used at the time), and Greek usually placed at the bottom.[43] There is no doubt that the hieroglyphic version was composed last in an archaizing language typical of the hieroglyphs of the Ptolemaic period, which only a handful of priests could read and write. It normally came first, just below the relief that represented the king (and often also the queen) honoring the gods, according to the traditional Egyptian iconography, as was the case in the sacerdotal decrees discussed earlier. The question, however, of whether these texts were first conceived in Demotic Egyptian or in Greek has been closely tied to the larger debate in the scholarship over the supremacy of royal or priestly power and the idea of the Egyptianization of royal power between the time of the Canopus decree (238 BCE) and that of the Memphis decree (196 BCE).[44]

In an important article on these decrees, Willy Clarysse has shown that the debate had been framed anachronistically according to the idea of a medieval state-church competition, and he has argued that Hellenized priests had composed the decrees and that there is in fact no evidence for the decrease of royal power or the Egyptianization of the dynasty.[45] This last point has now been confirmed by the recent discovery of the full text of the Alexandria decree (243 BCE), which was the first of the trilingual decrees and to which the Canopus decree alluded. The many acts of benevolence of Ptolemy III toward the priesthood in 243 BCE were as numerous as those of Ptolemy V recorded in the later Memphis decree, as can be seen in the synoptic view of these three decrees in table 5.1. In contrast, the Canopus decree of 238 BCE has less of them simply because it was not necessary to reiterate all the decisions taken five years earlier. At first sight, each language and script brought with it its particular vocabulary and conception of the world but the form and formulas were those of an honorific decree by a Greek polis, as emphasized by Clarysse. He may have overestimated, according to Moyer, the assimilation process of the priests, by pointing to these decrees as being essentially Greek, since they also expressed Egyptian concepts using Greek words, such as the term *phyle* employed for the first time to designate a sacerdotal group. But Clarysse also suggests that the priests and the royal officials were not two separate groups and that the same families were involved

---

43. This configuration of the texts was not always the same. Sometimes one of the languages was written on the side or the Greek was missing, see table in Clarysse 2000: 42–3.

44. See a survey of past views and bibliography in Clarysse 2000.

45. Clarysse 2000: 56; central to this last point is that the non-application of the reform of the calendar proclaimed in the Canopus decree, is not, in his view, the reflection of a nationalist opposition on the part of the Egyptian priests, since even the king did not apply it in his civil administration. Bennett 2011: 42–50, 179–86 argues that a few anomalous Macedonian-Egyptian double dates can be explained by the application of the Canopic calendar down to the reign of Ptolemy VI. I thank Cathy Lorber for pointing this this to me; for the opposite view, see Hauben 2011.

Table 5.1. Comparison of three trilingual decrees about the cult of the Ptolemies in the Egyptian temples (Some items have been reordered to illustrate parallels across texts; the letters indicate the original sequence within each text)

Alexandria (243 BCE)—Ptolemy III	Canopus (238 BCE)—Ptolemy III	Memphis (196 BCE)—Ptolemy V = Rosetta
1. Date with eponymous priests, Macedonian and Egyptian months (ll. 1-3)	1. Date with eponymous priests, Macedonian and Egyptian months (ll. 1-3)	1. Date *with pharaonic titulature*, eponymous priests, Macedonian and Egyptian months (ll. 1-3)
2. Decree (ψήφισμα)	2. Decree (ψήφισμα)	2. Decree (ψήφισμα)
3. The priests gathered in *Alexandria* for the feast of the king and of the Theadelphia, in the temple of Isis and the Gods Theadelphoi (ll. 3-5)	3. The priests gathered in *Canopus* (near Alexandria) in the temple of the Benefactor Gods	3. The priests gathered in *Memphis*
4. Since (ἐπειδή) the king	4. Since (ἐπειδή) the king	4. Since (ἐπειδή) the king and the queen
4.a. increased the revenues of the temples and maintained the current revenues	4.a. and the queen are generous toward the temples and the Gods	4.a. are generous toward the temples and the Gods, the population of Egypt and gave income to the temples
4.b. lightened and remitted some taxes		4.b. abolished taxes and debts, and installation taxe and the yearly trip of the priests to Alexandria
4.c. remitted arrears, so that the "people" (*laoi*) and all the others be prosperous		4.i. granted tax-exemptions to temples
4.d. released many men who were in prison for years		4.d. dispensed justice to everybody
4.e. led an expedition on the first year of his reign; captured many men, horses, elephants, warships, and was victorious (ll. 10-12)		4.e. amnestied soldiers who deserted

4.f. *brought back the statues of the Gods* from temples in Syria, Phoenicia, Cilicia, Babylonia, Persia, and Susiana + sacrifices, and libations

4.g. preserved peace in Egypt in fighting for it in far-flung regions
4.h. *improved the lives of human beings* (ἀνθρώπων)

4.i. took care of Apis, Mnevis, and other sacred animals more than his predecessors + sepultures + installation of the new ones + ceremonies, sacrifices, panegyries, and all what is necessary

4.j. he built new temples and restored others + gods will give them kingship and every other goods forever (l. 21)

5. Ἀγαθῆι τύχηι (with good fortune!)

6. It has been decided (δεδόχθαι) by the priests to
6a. increase the existing honors in the temples for Ptolemy and Berenice, their parents the Brother-Sister Gods and their parents the Savior Gods
6.b. erect statues of the king and the queen

4.c. *brought back the statues of the Gods*

4.d. and the queen provided food during period of shortage

4.b. and the queen take care of the sacred animals

5. Ἀγαθῆι τύχηι (with good fortune!)

6. It has been decided (δεδόχθαι) by the priests to
6a. increase the existing honors in the temples for the king and his ancestors

---

4.f. defended Egypt on earth and sea
4.g. besieged and seized Lycopolis
4.h. punished the rebels in Memphis

4.j took care of the sacred animal
4.c re-establish the cults

4.k. restored the temples Gods will give them kingship and every other goods forever (l. 21)

5. Ἀγαθῆι τύχηι (with good fortune!)

6. It has been decided (δεδόχθαι) by the priests to
6a. increase the existing honors in the temples for the king and his ancestors
6.b. erect statues of the king in Egyptian style in each temple of Egypt

(continued)

Table 5.1 Continued

Alexandria (243 BCE)—Ptolemy III	Canopus (238 BCE)—Ptolemy III	Memphis (196 BCE)—Ptolemy V = Rosetta
6.c. build shrines for them with the other gods in the temples of first category	6.c. establish a fifth tribe of priest for the Benefactor Gods	6.c. establish a cult for the king and the queen in an additional chapel
6.d. organize procession of their portable shrines during the "great panygyries"/festivals of the local gods	6.d. establish a new feast for the royal couple the day when the Isis star raises and to reform the calendar: 364 ¼ instead of 365	6.e. add the royal couple to the titles of the priests and to their ring
6.e. to place the ten royal diadems with ureus according to the scripts on their shrines, like the uraeus on the other shrines (ll. 22-7)	6.b. attach all the priests to the royal cult through their titles, documents, and seals	
and since it pleased the priests . . .	and since the princess Berenice died during the session	
6.f. establishment of a festival for the king's birthday, for the day he received kingship and the queen's birthday, every month and year (ll. 28-31)	6.e. eternal honors for Berenice (the daughter) in all temples: feast, procession of boats, a statue with the proper crown, hymns, and a new kind of bread (+mummification)	6.d. celebrate the birthday of the king and the inauguration/crowning day
6.g. offerings received during these three festivals (heortai) days will go to the priests (ll. 32-4)		
6.h. individuals who desire to build a *private chapel of the Benefactor Gods* (Ptolemy III and Berenice) are authorized if they celebrate the festivals *according to the rules*, each year and each month.		6.f. to authorize individuals to build a *private chapel* in theirs houses
7. Decree inscribed on a stone stele in hieroglyphs, demotic and Greek, in each temple from 1st, 2nd, and 3rd categories, in the most visible place	7. Decree inscribed on a stone or bronze stele in hieroglyphs, demotic, and Greek, in each temple from 1st, 2nd, and 3rd categories, in the most visible place	7. Decree inscribed on a stone stele in hieroglyphs, demotic and Greek, in each temple from 1st, 2nd, and 3rd categories *beside the statue of the ever living king*

in the priestly milieu and in the royal administration, a view on which Moyer draws when he analyzes these milieux through the concept of middle ground.[46]

Building on the emphasis made by these two scholars of the priests acting as a "fictive polis," to use Moyer's expression, I examine how the Egyptian priests, the kings, and his Greco-Macedonians *philoi* chose a Greek diplomatic medium in order to reinforce both the ideological power of the king and of the priests.[47] It is not possible to establish to what extent these two networks of local elites overlapped at that time, but they did overlap to a large extent in the second and first century BCE (discussed later). I argue that these steles purposely offered a double meaning, not because they were written in two languages, but because the main elements of the content of the decrees were framed in such a way that they could be interpreted at the same time as preserving the cultural differences between the ruler and the Egyptian elite (the subordination mode of cosmopolitanism) and as ignoring cultural differences (the assimilation mode) by playing with existing and newly created symbolic overlaps. The presence of the three scripts, or in some cases of the space assigned to each language, made these steles conspicuously different from the earlier sacerdotal decrees. These scripts illustrated above all the need for communication, as already stressed by Willy Peremans, rather than "aggressive nationalism" or the imposition of royal orders.[48] They could even remind the lower strata of the population, who could see them within the precincts of the temples, of the new spaces, times, and traditions emerging from the combined benevolence of the kings and decisions of the priests recorded on the steles. In the specific examples examined later, which regard several aspects of the royal and dynastic cults and return to the thematic of the stolen statues of the Egyptian gods, I show how these new spaces, moments, and traditions constructed a translocal culture.

The Royal and Dynastic Cults

The decisions made by the priests gathered in synods concerned the introduction and organization of the royal and dynastic cults in the Egyptian temples, as can be seen in table 5.1. There is no mention of a higher centralizing official coordinating these cults throughout the Ptolemaic empire.[49] In Alexandria, a courtier close to the king was appointed priest of the Greek cult of Alexander and of the deified Ptolemies, usually for one year.[50] This function was eponymous, meaning his name and function and the names and functions of the priestesses of some of the queens were used to date Greek and Egyptian official

---

46. Clarysse 2000: esp. 54–6; Moyer 2011a: 120.
47. On the hellenistic *philoi*, see, e.g., Strootman 2014a: 117–35, 165–84 with bibliography.
48. Peremans 1985: 261.
49. Bagnall 1976: 71.
50. Clarysse and Van Der Veken 1983.

documents, immediately after the regnal year of the king. In the Greek city of Ptolemais in Upper Egypt, other eponymous priests took care of the cult of Ptolemy I, the founder of the city and of other deified Ptolemies, while there could be local eponymous priestesses of Arsinoe in the provinces, as for instance in Idalion on Cyprus.[51] Yet in Cyprus, at least since 203 BCE, all the cults of the island, including the royal cults, were overseen by the governor (*strategos*) of the island who was from then on also the high priest (*archihiereus*).[52] The royal and dynastic cults may at first seem to form an incoherent system with many faces, but this should not be surprising. Multiplying the number of individuals who held such honorific titles and functions strengthened the relationship of the local elites with the unifying figures of the king and his family, who all personified imperial expansion. Like the citizens of the Greek poleis, the Egyptian priests, acting as a polis, included the king and his family in their rituals. The initiative was presented as local but the trilingual decrees make it implausible that the Ptolemies had no say at all in it. Similarly, royal and dynastic cults in Greek cities were presented as being civic initiatives, but the distinction between civic or spontaneous cults, on the one hand, and dynastic or imposed cults, on the other hand, may be an overrated distinction, as this dichotomy seems partly artificial.[53]

Royal Festivals and the Creation of Translocal Space and Time

Central to the argument of the emergence of translocal events or practices is the establishment of festivals and the encouragement of the development of private worship of the same royal figures. Even if their cults and their representations could take different cultural forms, the festivals initially created in an Alexandrian context to honor the king and his family were added to the Egyptian festivals, as is clear from these decrees. Three important points can be made about the transcultural nature of these festivals. First, it is noticeable that in 243 BCE, the year of the Alexandria decree, the priests met in the capital for the feast of Ptolemy and the Thealdelphia, in other words for the Ptolemaia in honor of Ptolemy I, the first instance of which was lavishly described by Callixeinus, and for the festival of the Brother-Sister Gods in honor of Ptolemy II and Arsinoe II.[54] The occasions chosen for the meetings of the

---

51. Bagnall 1976: 72 on a Phoenician inscription from Idalion (Cyprus), 254/5 BCE with bibliography. Three dating systems were used: Ptolemy II's regnal year, the era of Kition, and the canephorate (priesthood) of Arsinoe.

52. Bagnall 1976: 73.

53. Palagia 2013 has recently demonstrated that the Ptolemies provided the cult images to the cities; see also the note above about Itanos; for a critique of the dichotomy between spontaneous and imposed cults, see Lozano 2011 on Roman imperial cults.

54. The account of the Great Procession is narrated in Athenaeus, 5.197c–203e; commentary of this passage in El-Masry, Altenmüller, and Thissen 2012: 77, 81, l. 17–18 who also note that the date of the Theadelphia did not match the date known in other documents, see Perpillou-Thomas 1993: 154–5.

priests were indeed usually the celebration of birthdays, of the king's inauguration day, of a victory at a battle, or of the successful repression of a revolt.[55]
Second, the temples where they gathered were not chosen arbitrarily but could
facilitate these translocal encounters. In December 243 BCE, they met in the
temple of Isis and the Brother-Sister Gods (*Theoi Adelphoi*), which was next to
the Royal palace.[56] In 238 BCE, they met in Canopus for the birthday of Ptolemy
III, a celebration which had been included in the Egyptian feasts in the decree
of 243 BCE. The temple was that of the new Benevolent Gods (*Theoi Euergetai*),
that is, Ptolemy III himself and Berenike II. Third, the priests of Egypt were not
the only local elite groups to meet for the feast of Ptolemy and the Thealdelphia
of 243 BCE but delegates of cities from all around the empire came to see the
king and present requests for these occasions.[57] The Thealdelphia probably occurred purposefully close in time to the feast of Ptolemy in order to allow these
various local groups to participate in both festivals—no doubt to impress them
with multiple demonstrations of ideological power. In other words, the feasts
enabled the connection of a multitude of places and local groups with the royal
figures at a symbolic level, but were also festive interruptions of daily life. The
ideological power of the kings and of the priests benefited from the careful spatial and chronological arrangement of these feasts where the multitudes of the
empire could meet. Those who could not gather where the court was in order to
celebrate the event could still do it elsewhere at the same time, as made clear in
the decrees (in Table 5.1, 6.h and 6.f).

The cult of the king and queen as the Benevolent Gods (*theoi euergetai*) had
been created earlier during the year 243 BCE but clear directives were needed
regarding their cult statues in the Egyptian temples.[58] The Benevolent Gods
became "gods who share a temple" (*sunnaioi theoi*) with the gods of each
Egyptian temple and their statues intended to participate in the procession
on holidays.[59] The next synodal decisions voted in 238 BCE in Canopus, at
the end of the Third Syrian War, embellished their cult with the creation of a
fifth sacerdotal "group" dedicated to the Benevolent Gods and called in Greek
phyle (tribe). Moyer has shown in detail the significance of this term which
belonged to the vocabulary of the Greek poleis and convincingly suggests that

55. El-Masry, Altenmüller, and Thissen 2012: 71 and Pfeiffer 2004: 111–12.

56. Goddio 1998: fig. 7.8; the priests met in the same temple again when they voted the decree of Philae II
in 186 BCE. The two other known venues for the synods are the temples of the *Theoi Euergetai* (Ptolemy III and
Berenike II) in Canopus and the temple of Ptah in Memphis, see El-Masry, Altenmüller, and Thissen 2012: 174.

57. SEG 18 1936 with Bousquet 1986: esp. 27; in this letter of Ptolemy III to Xanthos in Lycia, the king
mentions the embassy of their delegates who came for the *Ptolemaia* and the Thealdelphia, therefore at the
same time as the Egyptian priests, see Kayser 2012: 433. The feast of Ptolemy, therefore must correspond to the
Ptolemaia.

58. El-Masry, Altenmüller, and Thissen 2012: 115–27 commentary to §15–19; Kayser 2012: 436 on ll. 22–3
of the Greek version. On later developments of the dynastic cults, see, e.g., Lanciers 2014.

59. Kayser 2012: 436–7 about ll. 22–3; El-Masry, Altenmüller, and Thissen 2012: commentary to §16–17.

the priests actually imagined themselves as a political body, "active participants in the creative process."[60] Even Athens, which was not under Ptolemaic
control, added a thirteenth *phyle* to honor Ptolemy III toward the end of his
reign and the capital of the empire, Alexandria, was in fact divided into five
phylai.[61] Besides the symbolic meaning that emerged from the overlaps created
by distorting Greek and Egyptian traditions, the selection of new individuals
to enter the fifth *phyle* strengthened the loyalty of a larger pool of the local
priestly elites. The principle is not dissimilar to that of the Roman emperors
increasing the number of senators.[62] Similarly, Ptolemy III and his successors
increasingly collaborated with the priesthood of the god Ptah in Memphis, in
whose temple the trilingual decrees of 217, 196, and 182 BCE were voted.[63] A last
point worth noting when exploring the development of the royal and dynastic
cults as translocal cults is the death of the young princess Berenike, daughter
of Ptolemy III and Berenike II, during the meeting of the priests in Canopus.
This loss resulted in decisions being taken by the Egyptian priests regarding
her mummification and her deification but her cult was also integrated in some
Greek poleis across the empire. The inscription mentioning the foundation of
Arsinoe in Cilicia indicates the establishment of the cult of the king, Arsinoe
II and Berenike.[64]

The Birthday of the King as the Beginning of Good Things for All Mankind

The production of a unified time is also evident in the celebrations of the king's
and queen's birthdays and the king's inauguration day, not only every year but
also every month (though on a smaller scale). The Ptolemies were shaping time
across space according to royal matters, but in a different manner than the creation of a Seleucid era by their rivals.[65] For Françoise Perpillou-Thomas, the celebration of the king's birthday seems to be influenced by the Egyptian conception of kingship.[66] Accordingly, the population brought gifts to Alexandria but
also to other places, thus offering the produce of agricultural work in exchange
for justice and benevolence. More important, the decree of Alexandria states
that the birthday of the king and his inauguration "happened to have initiated
many good things for human beings" (l. 29, *pantes anthropoi*). The equivalent of

60. Moyer 2011a: 121–4, quote on 124.
61. Moyer 2011a: 123 also notes the overlaps between the five tribes of the Archaic Greek period and of the
Old Kingdom.
62. See Weisweiler, this volume.
63. Thompson 2012: 136–43; Agut-Labordère 2016: section 3.2; El-Masry, Altenmüller, and Thissen
2012: 174 for the list of venues; see also the presence of Ptah in the titulatures in Leprohon 2013: 175–89.
64. SEG 39 1426, ll. 32–33 with Habicht and Jones 1989: 325, 336: a similar formula is found in the Canopus
decree (OGIS 56, l. 54), which serves of *terminus postquem*.
65. On the Seleucid era, see Kosmin 2014a: esp. 100–103 and his forthcoming works.
66. Perpillou-Thomas 1993: 159–61.

the expression "all human beings" was used in Demotic and even in hieroglyph-ics.[67] This expression was similarly employed for Arsinoe II in the hieroglyphic text of the Mendes Stele (discussed earlier). This could be the "universaliza-tion" of the expression used in the decree of the League of the Islanders naming Ptolemy II as the source of good things for the Islanders (Nesiotai) and the other Greeks.[68] In the Canopus decree, Ptolemy III's birthday was once again "the beginning of good things for all human beings," both in Greek (l. 26) and in Demotic (l. 26) but the translation into archaizing hieroglyphics reflected a more local perspective: "all human beings in Egypt" (l. 14).[69] It did not explic-itly distinguish, though, between the different ethnic groups living in Egypt. Yet the different linguistic versions of line 15 of the decree of Alexandria were somehow ambiguous. After the presentation of Ptolemy III as triumphant over his enemies—an allusion to the Third Syrian War—the Greek text states that "he improved the life of human beings" (l. 15, *anthropoi*). The Greek text has been reconstructed on the basis of the similar expression in the Greek, Demotic, and hieroglyphic titulature of Ptolemy V in the later Memphis decree. But in the Alexandria decree, the Demotic text simply records that "he improves their lives," with "their" referring to the inhabitants of Egypt, while the hieroglyphics remain unclear.[70] The titulature of the Egyptian kings were composed of five names: for instance, the so-called Horus name of Ptolemy III was "the one over whom gods and men rejoice," while Ptolemy IV's "two-ladies name" was "Savior of mankind."[71] My aim is not to establish whether this universalist claim was influenced by a Greek or an Egyptian (or even a Macedonian or a Persian) con-ception of kingship but to argue that these traditions overlapped sufficiently to be adapted. Dynasties that succeeded Alexander traditionally cared for all the Greeks and the kings who ruled over Egypt traditionally cared for the inhabit-ants of their country, therefore kings ruling over wider areas were accordingly benevolent to all mankind. Providing many good things (*polla agatha*) for all mankind was a mark of the Ptolemaic political ideology that was reflected in the

67. El-Masry, Altenmüller, and Thissen 2012: 136, 212, commentary and text to §98; Greek is partially restituted after the Demotic text, l. 36.

68. Syll.[3] 390, translation in Austin 2006: 256; see also Lavan and Weisweiler, this volume with a reference to Ma 2002: 187–88 on "horizontal generalization" in the Hellenistic world, usually to all Greeks but sometimes to all men.

69. Pfeiffer 2004: 112 provides parallels, notably the birth of the Roman emperor Augustus; the hiero-glyphic text for "of Egypt" seems missing in Pfeiffer's quotes and on p. 111, l. 14, see El-Masry, Altenmüller, and Thissen 2012: 104 for the full expression in the Canopus decree. I thank Emily Cole for sharing her expertise with me on the hieroglyphic texts, see also her dissertation, Cole 2015, esp. chapter 7.

70. On the Alexandria decree, see El-Masry, Altenmüller, and Thissen 2012: 103–4, commentary to §11, l. 52 where the editors ponder how to reconstruct the hieroglyphics: "men/women (of Egypt?)"; on the Memphis decree, see OGIS 90, l. 2, translation in Austin 2006: no. 283, l. 17 of the Canopus decree shows the same sort of ambiguity, with the Greek text referring to the safety (*soteria*) of the people and the Demotic and hieroglyphic versions referring to the inhabitants of Egypt.

71. Alexandria decree, §1; see list of titulatures in Leprohon 2013: 175–89.

languages of the trilingual decrees and of their titulature, but also went beyond these contexts.

Indeed, the ambition of Ptolemy III as a universal ruler, who had launched a military expedition as far as Mesopotamia in 246/5 BCE, was evident to a larger audience. As Stanley Burstein noticed it in a petition from the mid-third century Fayyum, a region about 150 km southwest of modern Cairo, the king is addressed as "the great king [*basileus megalos*] . . . you who rule the whole inhabited world [*oikoumene*]."[72] At the same time, the trilingual decrees encouraged individuals to set up private altars to the royal couple in their homes in order to perform the celebrations described in them.[73] These festive moments were, of course, available to all subjects of the Ptolemies and were not restricted to the Egyptian population, and all mankind could thus participate in the celebration of the royal family, anywhere on the right days. In addition, their images were flexible enough to receive multiple associations, for instance, Aphrodite-Berenike could share a private altar with the Syrian goddess, as noted in a petition to the king from the Fayyum where a woman has built such an altar in the house where her husband, a soldier, was billeted.[74]

The Return of the Statues Carried Away by the Persians

The acknowledgment of common interests between the Egyptian priests and the kings regarding expansionist policies reached a higher level in the trilingual decrees than in the sacerdotal decrees, in which only hints of them were visible (discussed earlier). The theme of bringing back the statues of the Egyptian gods seem to be an innovation of the Ptolemaic period, although there could be a precedent under one of the last native pharaohs, Nectanebo I (380–362 BCE).[75] It had been argued that this had never happened but Winnicki has shown that some statues were certainly brought back and that the return of the statues was not a topos but had really occurred.[76] Indeed, it is hardly plausible that the celebrations of the statues' return did not really take place if they are mentioned in the sacerdotal decrees (with some details) and in the synodal decrees, as well as in the royal inscription of Adulis about Ptolemy III's expedition against the

72. PSI V, 541, l. 1, ll. 7–8; I thank Stanley Burstein for drawing my attention to this text, see his forthcoming work on Ptolemy III; see also, for instance, the decree of Canopus, ll. 12–13 of the Greek, where the king and the queen "have provided good government [*eunomia*] to all those in the country [*chora*] and to the other subjects of their kingdom (*basileia*)," translation in Austin 2006: no. 271.

73. It was thought to be a later development visible in the Memphis decree of 196 BCE but it is in fact already attested in the decree of 243 BCE, see El-Masry, Altenmüller, and Thissen 2012: 143–6, commentary on §24; the so-called queen vases were certainly one aspect of these cults and were found throughout the empire, made of faience, typically Egyptian, and with a Greek iconography, see, e.g., Rowlandson 1998: 30, fig. 3.

74. P. Enteux 13 (222 BCE) translation in Rowlandson 1998: 28–9, no. 5.

75. Klotz 2009: 298 with sources.

76. Winnicki 1994: esp. 169 "the stereotype phrase seems rather to be the attribution of abduction of divine images to the Persians"; he suggests that Egyptian statues in the Levant were brought back. Alternatively, one could argue they were fabricated.

Seleucids. However, the symbolic meaning of the stolen statue was developed in the trilingual decrees of Alexandria, Canopus, and Raphia as well as in the Adulis inscription, by specifically accusing the Persians, also called Medes, of having committed violence and carried away the Egyptian gods.[77] This justified and facilitated the construction of an imperial culture, in this case turned especially against the Seleucids as "successors" of the Achaemenid Persians by the kings, their councilors, and Egyptian priests among the latter.[78] They entangled several cultural traditions that fitted particularly well together for their many audiences: the mean Persians, the carrying away and return of gods' statues, and the care for sanctuaries.

Trilingual Decrees, Translocal Constructions

The new cultural constructions that emerge from the trilingual decrees connected time and space and unified them around the royal figures, even if only on special occasions, yet regularly and frequently. There was no creation of a Ptolemaic era, but equivalence was made between the Macedonian and Egyptian calendars and the eponymous priests in Alexandria were part of the dating formula. In the Memphis decree of 196 BCE, it is stated that the Egyptian New Year was to be celebrated to honor the king and the queen.[79] The kings and queens came to Memphis regularly for this event at least from the time of the reconciliation of the children of Ptolemy V in 164 BCE, which also offered the possibility for them to receive petitions from the population.[80] Their presence at the Egyptian New Year was perhaps the result of the decision in the Memphis decree, which can also be interpreted as a conscious act of unifying time around the king. Their presence at this date may also have happened sporadically in the past, as, for example, the year of the erection of the Mendes Stela (257 BCE).

While in the case of the Roman Principate the limits of the assimilative type of cosmopolitanism need to be emphasized by historians (see Lavan, in this volume), in the case of the Ptolemaic empire the preeminence of the subordinate type should not to be exaggerated. Certain elements that were commemorated in the trilingual decrees could be simultaneously read as reflecting a localist and a universalist perspective. The benevolence of the kings and of the honors granted by the priests offered the possibility to their authors of concentrating their attention on the cultural similarities. Their actions and decisions followed a principle of mutual inclusion: first, the inclusion of the king and queen in the Egyptian temples; second, the inclusion of the Egyptian priests into the worship of the king; this was the Egyptian version of the worship of the king by Greek

---

77. Gozzoli 2006: 135–6, El-Masry, Altenmüller, and Thissen 2012: 164–9.
78. On anti-Seleucid propaganda, see also Agut-Labordère 2016: part III.
79. OGIS 90, ll. 49–51.
80. Thompson 2012: 140–1, 199–200.

poleis and by members of the gymnasium; third and above all, the inclusion of the Egyptian elite in the dialogue of euergetism that was shaping the rest of the empire and was used beyond it. For the first time with the decree of Alexandria, as early as 243 BCE, the Egyptian priests could "play" the same diplomatic game as cities.

It remains partly unexplained why there were no longer any synodal decrees under the sons of Ptolemy V, and both the cancellation of the annual journey of the priests to Alexandria in the Memphis decree and the ever-growing importance of the priesthood of Ptah in Memphis have often been proposed as elements of an answer. Alternatively, there was perhaps no longer a need for such meetings and decrees, since the principles they had established regarding the ruler cults were by then well in place.[81] Moreover, associations honoring the king and called *basilistai* or *philobasilistai* seem to have become more common in the Egyptian chora.[82] Yet the concept of a multilingual medium and the structure of a Greek honorific decree to convey the decisional process were not abandoned. The so-called Stele of Ptolemy VIII, a bilingual hieroglyphic and Greek text engraved on a monumental stele recently discovered in underwater excavations, was in fact an honorific decree by the Egyptian priests of the temple of Khonsu-Heracles and Amon-Gereb in Heracleion near Alexandria.[83] Like in the earlier steles during the satrapy of Ptolemy and the rule of Ptolemy II, the perspective is that of the local priests of Heracleion and the text is recorded on their initiative. There is no decision on their part made as the members of a fictive polis. An allusion to the journey of Khonsu-Heracles in the "islands," which may allude to Ptolemaic (past?) ambitions in the Mediterranean, according to Thiers, is the more explicit connection made beyond the local.[84] The aim of the priests was to make visible the privileges which the king granted to them during his visit. Despite the localist perspective of this text, one of their privileges, the right of asylum for their temple, was a right that resonated in both Greek and Egyptian cultures.[85]

Translocal Individuals?

The analysis of the trilingual decrees has shown how the king, his family, and the Egyptian priests became the central figures who intertwined cultural memories and traditions. If the king was a translocal figure, activating the transfer, association, and distortion of cultural elements, he was not alone. There were perhaps

---

81. For the same argument see Gorre and Véïsse 2016, who also emphasize that the royal administration had penetrated the temple administration by the second century.

82. Fischer-Bovet 2014: 287–90 with bibliography.

83. First edition by Thiers 2009.

84. Thiers 2009: 16, ll. 16 and 29.

85. Thiers 2009: 47 n. 149 *contra* Rigsby 1996: 541 and 548 for whom there is no perilous Egyptian equivalent to the concept of asylia.

not many Egyptians at the court in the early period, but they played an important role by pointing to elements of convergence in the Greco-Macedonian and
Egyptian cultures, as did for instance the Egyptian priest Manetho of Sebennytos
in his *Aegyptica*.[86] Of course, individuals at court could be interested in other
cultures to various degrees and for various reasons. A good example of this is
the contrasted attitudes of the two most important military commanders of
Ptolemy II, Patroclus of Macedonia and Callicrates of Samos, as brought to light
by Hauben.[87] Patroclus's military career is well known as a general (*strategos*) and
the leader of the Ptolemaic fleet during the Chremonidean War, but none of his
actions suggest a particular interest in bridging Greek and Egyptian culture.[88]
In contrast, little evidence was preserved of Callicrates's military career, but his
inscriptions report how active he was in the construction of the Ptolemaic political ideology. He was most famous for the introduction of the cult of Arsinoe-
Aphrodite Euploia Zephyritis near Canopus and his dedication of two monumental statues of Ptolemy II and Arsinoe II in Olympia, and he was even mentioned
in Posidippus's epigrams.[89] More surprising perhaps, the same man also built a
shrine to Isis and Anubis.[90] For Bing, Callicrates "sought to mediate between old
Hellas and the somehow strange new world of Ptolemaic Egypt, bridging the gap
between the two whether by bringing Greek tradition to bear on his Egyptian
milieu or by spreading abroad his ruler's new politics."[91] Callicrates was truly a
translocal figure. Even if there were only a handful of such men close to the king,
they could have a strong effect on long-term political ideology.

In addition, offsprings of mixed marriage certainly played an important role
in bridging the cultures but how this actually occurred is sometimes difficult to
detect in the sources. In the second century BCE, Dioscourides, the prime min-
ister of Ptolemy VI, had long been thought to belong only to the Hellenic milieu
until the careful edition of the inscriptions on his Egyptian sarcophagus by
Collombert. His mother had an Egyptian name and he was priest of Horembeb,
though this function seems rather to have implied administrative rather than
cultic functions in the temple.[92] One can also think of Dionysios Petosarapis
among the high elite members at the court, whose attempt at a coup d'état is
described by Diodorus.[93] The actual encounter of multiple cultures through

---

86. GrHist 609; Dillery 1999: esp. 111 and now Dillery 2015; Legras 2002; there may have been more
Egyptian "experts" hidden at the court behind Greek names or as offspring of mixed unions, see also Moyer
2011b: 16–19 against Habicht 1958.

87. Hauben 2013.

88. On his career, see Hauben 2013: 53–64; the fleet had Egyptian soldiers on board, so he was certainly
exposed to other cultures.

89. Hauben 2013: 47–52.

90. SB I 429; see Thiers 2006: 285–6, 291, no. 6.

91. Bing 2003: 244.

92. Collombert 2000, Gorre 2009: no. 50, and Gorre 2007: 240–2.

93. Diod. 31.15a. 1–4 with Mcging 1997: 289–95 and Véïsse 2004: 28–32, 99–112.

individuals slightly lower in the hierarchy is visible in the case of Dorion. Born to an Egyptian priestly family with ancestors perhaps of Hellenic origins on the paternal side, he illustrates how Egyptian priestly families integrated the Ptolemaic government through a military career.[94] Only his hieroglyphic funerary inscriptions reports his Egyptian priesthood, while a Greek honorific decree addresses him as a *strategos* (here to be understood as "governor of a nome") and priest of the association (*plethos*) of the saber-bearers (*machairophoroi*).[95] This latter function confirms his current (and past) affiliation to the army. The politeuma of the Idumeans and the Idumeans in Memphis voted honors to thank him for his benefactions, borrowing the formulas of a Greek honorific decree, as the Egyptians priests had done before them during the synods. The Idumean community was particularly grateful for his help with the repair of its temple, the so-called Apolloneion, certainly the Hellenic name for their Semitic god. If Egyptian culture seems at first excluded from this particular document, it should be noted that Dorion, like his homonymous father before him, was a priest of Horus-Khenty-Khety (in Athribis) and that the *interpretatio graeca* of Horus was Apollo.[96] This hardly seems a pure coincidence. The sources may not give the practical details of these transcultural moments but still offer important hints.

As a governor of a nome, Dorion also held the title of "kinsman" (*suggenes*) of the king, one of the several titles that formed the honorific court titulature created by Ptolemy V in order to mirror positions at the court and to strengthen the loyalty of his officials.[97] This fictive kinship extended to members of the Egyptian elite who held the function of governor, at least from the last decades of the second century BCE on.[98] Moyer has demonstrated how the kinsman's *mitra*, a sort of headband visible on some of their representations, was a mark of alliance with the king despite the asymmetrical power relation and was in fact a "transcultural emblem . . . that circulated between Greek and Egyptian contexts, rather than an independent element of the identity of one or the other discrete culture or ethnicity."[99] This set of examples, which is far from exhaustive, suggests that in the case of the Ptolemaic empire, co-opted local elites could transcend, at least sometimes, the level of local accommodation. The distance between Greek "cosmopolitan" and non-Greek "local" culture was not always

---

94. Thompson 1984, Gorre 2009: no. 54, and Gorre 2007: 242–5.

95. Greek honorific decree, OGIS II 737 = SB V 8929 (112 av. J.-C., Memphis) and hieroglyphic funerary inscription, Cairo General Catalogue 22137.

96. On Apollo in Egypt, see Henri 2013.

97. Mooren 1975, 1977, Strootman 2014a: 165–84. The court titulature may have been created at the end of Ptolemy IV's reign, see Abd el-Fattah, Abd el-Maksoud and Carrez-Maratray 2014.

98. See Gorre 2009: 469–70, table 5 on the growing number of priests who become officials.

99. Moyer 2011a: 125–37, quote on 133, and Moyer 2011b for a detailed analysis of several Egyptian families which cannot be treated here, notably those of Teos in Tanis, Apollonios in Edfu, see respectively Gorre 2009: nos. 80, 81, and nos. 4–7 and Fischer-Bovet 2014: 326–7.

emphasized by a hierarchical system.[100] The extent to which the downsizing of the Ptolemaic empire in the second century BCE explains these developments still requires further work.

The families of Platon and Callimachus (not the poet) in the late second and first century BCE confirm this Ptolemaic tendency from a different angle. These were Alexandrine families well established at court whose members became closely entangled with Egyptian families and culture in Upper Egypt. They represented, to quote Coulon about the family of Platon, the "exceptional bi-culturalism" of the high officials in the first-century Egyptian countryside.[101] Several members of Platon's family, all called Platon, held the governorship of several nomes.[102] The last member of the family known to us was prophet of several Egyptian gods, though these functions seem to have been a counterpart to his judicial functions in the region, and thus he was perhaps also the governor of several nomes. The hieroglyphic texts of his statue, in the style called "striding draped male figure" commonly used by this group of officials, also records his involvement in temple building and his role as an oracular interlocutor of the god Amon in Thebes.[103] The family disappeared after the troubled period in the region around 88 BCE and the return of Ptolemy IX to power. Slightly later, another Alexandrine family whose male members are all called Callimachus was administrating the region, and the last of them was responsible (*epistates*) for the finances of the Peri-Theban nome and *strategos* of the Thebaid under Cleopatra VII.[104] He was also overseer of the Red and Indian Seas and held the court title of "kinsman" (*suggenes*) of the king. In order to thank him for his benefactions toward Thebes, "the priests of Amonrasonther, the elders (*presbyteroi*) and all the others" voted to honor him in 39 BCE and recorded their decisions in a bilingual Demotic and Greek honorific decree very similar to the trilingual decrees by its form, content, and even iconography of the relief.[105] Callimachus has acted "as a father for his homeland (*oikeia patris*) and for his own children" (l. 12) and is to be called "savior of the polis" (l. 26), with Thebes called a polis and its priests and elders acting, in fact, as a council. He was to receive three statues to be erected on his birthday, one in stone from the priests and two from the polis (bronze and stone) and his birthday was to be celebrated every year and that day named after him. He was honored for his "humane feelings" (*philanthropia*, l. 9) and his actions marked by "benevolence" (*euergesia*, l. 9), in particular the maintenance of the sanctuaries, and his help during a

---

100. See the question of Haubold, this volume, n. 6, in a dialogue with Bang 2012: esp. 70.
101. Coulon 2001: 85.
102. Coulon 2001: 85, Gorre 2009: no. 24.
103. Bianchi 1978 with Kaiser 1999 for the correction of the dating of some of the statues.
104. Blasius 2001: 95–8 with previous bibliography; Ricketts 1982–3.
105. SEG 24 1217; Greek text in OGIS I 194; Blasius 2001: 96 gives a partial translation in English; Heinen 2006 with earlier bibliography; see also Moyer 2011a: 125.

famine, guided by an oracle of the god Amon that took place publicly.[106] By imitating the king who acts generously toward all men, these high officials betrayed the emergence of a translocal culture, even if the medium, that is the stele, responds to a local context. Callimachus had long been interpreted as a viceroy threatening royal power, but in fact his actions and the decisions of the priests and of the elders reflect the spread of the Ptolemaic political ideology of communication and exchange, a complex construction that developed through the association of different cultural traditions and their overlaps.

Conclusion

In conclusion, this analysis of the negotiation between the Ptolemies and their local elites and the mode of integration that developed between them has identified three important elements. First, both types of cosmopolitanism, subordination and assimilation, existed in the Ptolemaic empire. The assimilative mode of integration tends to be overlooked in the Ptolemaic case. In fact, even media that at first sight seemed to participate in the subordination type, such as the trilingual steles, also erased some cultural differences and showed a certain openness to outsiders (assimilation). Second, the emergence of an integrated elite culture was above all "royal," evolving around the figures of the king and of his family. Only next came the Hellenic overtone of this culture as a "connector" that did not deny other cultures but accommodated the accumulation of cultural traditions and memories and their connection through overlapping symbols. Third, this Ptolemaic elite culture was not exclusive but rather inclusive, or more precisely "cumulative," even if this accumulation was only clearly visible in particular times, places, and media as well as in particular groups of the population. I have argued that the trilingual decrees, as the results of a search for cultural overlaps on the part of the kings and the local elites, were such media and that above all, by establishing festivals and means to worship the king and the queen, they produced further instances of translocalism.

---

106. On the parallel between the famine here and that mentioned in the Canopus decree, see Heinen 2006.

6

What Is Imperial Cosmopolitanism?
Revisiting Kosmopolitēs *and* Mundanus

Tamara T. Chin*

To a volume otherwise concerned with social and political practice, Tamara Chin contributes a literary-philological study of theories of cosmopolitanism that reexamines its traditional Hellenistic genealogy. Diogenes the Cynic, though apocryphally admired by Alexander, embodied a defiantly anti-imperial world-citizen (kosmopolitēs) grounded in ethical priorities incompatible with world-rule. Philo introduced a kosmopolitēs *who adhered to a religious constitution that was also at odds with Roman imperial rule. By contrast, the Roman Stoics who articulated a cosmopolitan theory compatible with empire drew more on the Socratic tradition of universalism than on Diogenes. Rather than* kosmopolitēs, *Cicero regarded himself a* mundanus, *a "Universian," with the capacity to establish—and implicitly to enforce—universal, rationally grounded laws. This disengaged the problem of horizontal relations of power (man of the universe) from vertical relations of power (anarchic or anti-imperial citizen of universe). Histories of "imperial cosmopolitanism" that take cultural pluralism—rather than egalitarian citizenship—as world-citizenship's signifying element thus rely on one of two distinct traditions. Chin sharpens our image of this culturally specific conception of cosmopolitanism through a comparison with contemporary Chinese debates that occurred within a comparable framework of imperial expansion, reiterating the need for greater awareness of vested histories of ancient and modern translation.*

COMPARE two modes of narrating cosmopolitanism. First, in a pedagogical mode, cosmopolitanism is an ethical ideal with a conventional history beginning with Hellenistic and Kantian philosophy. Second, in a performative mode, cosmopolitanism can be used to describe a variety of

* I would like to thank Anthony Long, Boris Maslov, and the editors of this volume for their comments on versions of this chapter.

practices (literary, religious, etc.), regardless of the actual historical use of the term itself.[1] These two modes are situated, dynamic, and dialogic. Thus, to give an example to be addressed in the coda, the idea of cosmopolitanism officially entered China in modern translation, with the neologism *shijie zhuyi* 世界主义 (lit. "world-ism"); however, comparable concepts were immediately translated back, in a performative mode, to characterize an array of ancient Chinese practices, terms, and historical periods. Within this doubled narrative of ancient cosmopolitanism, "imperial cosmopolitanism" (or "cosmopolitan empire") has become perhaps the most pervasive and least transparent figure.[2]

This chapter seeks to defamiliarize imperial cosmopolitanism by revisiting its conventional, pedagogical Greco-Roman beginnings in an array of terms and phrases that we now conflate with the cosmopolitan or world citizen (e.g., *kosmopolitēs, politēs tou kosmou, civis mundi*). Exploring extant uses prior to the sixth century CE, in the context of alternate formulations, it proposes that these terms were not necessarily interchangeable. Lexical patterns suggest a more important distinction between the person who was politically or religiously at odds with imperial rule (primarily, the *kosmopolitēs*) (part I) and a more abstract notion of belonging to an enlarged cultural and ethical world that was compatible with empire. This was articulated through a range of other terms and phrases (e.g., Gk. *politēs tou kosmou, kosmios*; Lat. *civis mundi, mundanus*) (part II). To speak of imperial cosmopolitanism—whether in the context of Rome or Han China—one must therefore sidestep the former anti-imperial tradition that is so often taken as its etymological origin.

PART I: COSMOPOLITANS AGAINST EMPIRE

Modern histories of cosmopolitanism often begin with Diogenes the Cynic's (fl. mid–fourth century BCE) coining of the term "cosmopolitan" (κοσμοπολίτης, hereinafter *kosmopolitēs*), and approach Cynic and Stoic cosmopolitanism as the earliest stages of a shared concept. Strangely, no surviving Stoic text includes Diogenes's term.[3] Although many Hellenistic and Roman Stoic authors drew from Cynic teachings and paid close attention to language, none of the many extant formulations of what we now call Stoic cosmopolitanism actually

1. I appropriate these terms from Homi Bhabha's account of narrating nationhood. See Bhabha 1994: 139–70. One might also draw on Reinhart Koselleck's distinction between conceptual and social history. See Koselleck 2002.
2. On the politics of the modern definition and analysis of ancient empire, imperialism, and colonization, see Dietler 2010.
3. Results obtained from the *TLG* and *Brepols* databases. There is, to my knowledge, no scholarship addressing this.

invoke the *kosmopolitēs*.[4] Stoic uses of the two terms that are commonly seen as synonymous with the *kosmopolitēs*, the "citizen of the world" (πολίτης τοῦ κόσμου, hereinafter *politēs tou kosmou*) and the Latin *civis mundi*, are more rare than one might expect. Epictetus (ca. 50–ca. 135 CE) uses the former once, and Cicero (106–43 BCE) the latter twice. Moreover, Epictetus and Cicero introduce Socrates (469–399 BCE), not Diogenes, as the respondent to the question of natal origins, using another neologism: "I am a 'Universian'" (Gk. *kosmios*; Lat. *mundanus*, "man of the universe"). By contrast, evidence survives of contemporary uses of the term *kosmopolitēs* outside the Stoic tradition. The earliest and most sustained surviving elaboration of the *kosmopolitēs* comes in Philo of Alexandria's (ca. 30 BCE–45 CE) interpretation of Hebrew Scriptures. Although Philo engaged with early Stoicism, his *kosmopolitēs* inhabited a world defined by Mosaic Law.

Diogenes as Kosmopolitēs

Studies of Cynic cosmopolitanism have focused on Diogenes's legendary quip in Diogenes Laertius's third-century CE *Life of Diogenes*: "When asked where he was from, he said '(I am) a cosmopolitan' [ἐρωτηθεὶς πόθεν εἴη, "κοσμοπολίτης," ἔφη]."[5] Since this single association of Diogenes (or any Cynic) with the term comes without context in a series of aphoristic answers to anonymous questions, modern scholars have drawn on other elements of Diogenes's biography to reconstruct its meaning. Some have emphasized the negative construction of Diogenes's cosmopolitanism: he pitted the *kosmopolitēs* against the *politēs*, rejecting the narrow citizenship of his natal Sinope in favor of a world in which he remained "Citiless, homeless, bereft of homeland / A beggar, wanderer, living life from day to day."[6] Others suggest that the *kosmopolitēs*—in etymology and practice—positively redefined rather than rejected the *politēs* (citizen). Although Diogenes lived in exile after defacing his city's currency, he reappropriated the language of political citizenship. When he stated that "the only true *politeia* [polity, commonwealth] was the one in the universe [*en kosmō*]," he asserted an ethical approach to politics.[7]

Two interrelated issues complicated this debate. First, problems of transmission, doxography, and reliable attribution permeate scholarship on Hellenistic philosophy in general. Second, unlike the Stoics, Diogenes did not produce formal philosophy. He parodied existing philosophical practices and rejected systematization in favor of a habitual *parrhesia* ("saying everything,"

---

4. On Stoic studies of language and grammar, see Schenkeveld 2007, Brunschwig 1994.

5. D. L. 6.63.

6. D. L. 6.38, e.g., Husson 2011: 159–63, Schofield 1999: 141–5, Goulet-Cazé 1982: 229–31.

7. D. L. 6.72, e.g., Branham 2007, Nussbaum 2002, Höistad 1948: 141–3, and esp. Moles 1996.

free-speech) that scandalized the rich, the powerful, and the revered. His spectacularly exhibitionist lifestyle and bodily practices—sleeping in a wine-jar, masturbating in the market-place, imitating mice, reducing his possessions to the beggar's wallet—provided the main patterns for his radical ethics of self-examination, self-sufficiency, and self-mastery that prepared him for any exigencies of fortune.[8] Thus, Marie-Odile Goulet-Cazé and Malcolm Schofield have argued that the doxographic section of Diogenes Laertius within which Diogenes embraces laws for the city, and the true commonwealth of the universe, reflects efforts of Stoics to turn Diogenes into a more constructive political philosopher.[9]

This danger of making Diogenes's quip into a concept—into an abstract cosmopolitan*ism*—might be clarified by looking at the two extant associations of Diogenes with the term *politēs tou kosmou*. Lucian's (125–ca. 180 CE) satiric play *Sale of Lives* predates Diogenes Laertius. The scene of utterance is a slave market in which Zeus and Hermes attempt to sell off as slaves Greece and Rome's most famous philosophers. When it comes to Diogenes, the joke turns on Hermes advertising him as "a manly creature, an excellent and noble creature—a free creature." The perplexed prospective buyer has to confirm that Hermes is indeed "selling a free creature" (πωλεῖς τὸν ἐλεύθερον) before interrogating Diogenes.

> Ἀγοράστης: τὸ πρῶτον, ὦ βέλτιστε, ποδαπὸς εἶ;
> Διογένης: παντοδαπός.
> Ἀγοράστης: πῶς λέγεις;
> Διογένης: Τοῦ κόσμου πολίτην ὁρᾷς.

> BUYER: First of all, my good friend, where are you from?
> DIOGENES: Everywhere.
> BUYER: What do you mean?
> DIOGENES: You're looking at a citizen of the world.[10]

On the one hand, Lucian's Diogenes uses the term "citizen of the world" simply to gloss "everywhere" (*pantodapos*). On the other, his pronouncement defines for the buyer what he is "looking at," dictating the terms through which he should be evaluated. He parodies one of the basic transactions that constitute the citizen-slave opposition. From the dramatic position of enslaved noncitizen, he asserts his "free" status by becoming a (world) citizen. The term "citizen of the world" effectively reformulates the buyer's introduction of him as a "free life" for sale. What matters here is not what Diogenes's self-identification

---

8. On Diogenes's radical use of improvisation and of linguistic and bodily acts, see Branham and Goulet-Cazé 1996.

9. Goulet-Cazé 2001: 217–20, Goulet-Cazé 1982, Schofield 1999: 141–5.

10. Luc., *Vit. Auct.* 8.4. Translations are mine unless otherwise stated.

as a world citizen means (from "everywhere"), but what it subversively does. Diogenes does not provide a theory of exile but rather subverts the slave-citizen hierarchy in the face of his own profound *non*-freedom.[11] Julian (331/332–363 CE), the last non-Christian Roman emperor, similarly ties Diogenes's self-reference as a *politēs tou kosmou* to his noncitizen status.[12] Since the *kosmopolitēs* only appears once in the Cynic archive, they provide the only other comparable associations of Diogenes (or any Cynic) with the *politēs tou kosmou*. As in Diogenes Laertius's case of the *kosmopolitēs*—and unlike in the writings of Cicero, Epictetus, and Philo—Lucian and Julian stage the world citizen as an embodied verbal response by, and exclusively about, Diogenes. In both cases the utterance is a strategic, parrhesiastic power reversal, not part of a generalized concept.[13]

Diogenes thus inspired a biographical tradition that identified the *kosmopolitēs* and the *politēs tou kosmou* with his embodied self, and that narrated his consistently anarchic antagonism of rulers, masters, and emperors. Diogenes-meets-Alexander was a classic theme in their respective apocryphal traditions: "Stand out of my sunlight," the recumbent philosopher commanded the visiting Alexander; "Are you the Alexander whom they call a bastard?"[14] As in his exchanges with slave-buyers, Diogenes subverts through imperious mimicry the discourse of power. These infamous confrontations belong to a

---

11. Although Diogenes Laertius does not stage Diogenes's self-identification in the slave market, the parallel rhetorical formulation with Lucian's satire is worth noting. Diogenes's scandalization of slave market protocols was clearly a trope. According to Diogenes Laertius, both Eubulus and Menippus wrote works entitled the "Sale of Diogenes." In the latter, Diogenes's response to a slave buyer's question about what he could do was: "rule men" (ἀνδρῶν ἄρχειν). As with Diogenes's (world) citizenship in Lucian's satire, Diogenes appropriates the idiom of the master–slave relation. One might compare the first-century CE *Life of Aesop*. Aesop, up for sale in the slave market, responds to the questions "where are you from?" and "where were you born?" with "from the flesh" and "in my mother's belly." Aesop's purchaser later muses: "I didn't realize I had bought myself a master." *Vit. Aes., Vit. G,* 25, cf. 28. On the parallels with, and potential influence of, the Aesopic tradition, see Kurke 2011: 139, 207–8, 355.

12. Julian's *On the Cynic Herakleios* responds to the Cynic Herakleios by contrasting Diogenes with the impiety of the new Cynics (who were often associated with Christians). Julian argues that when Diogenes refused to worship the Pythian god he was not impiously avoiding initiation but rather shunning the Athenian citizenship requirement for initiates, by birth or through legalization procedures:

> [S]ince he considered himself to be a citizen of the world [νομίζων αὑτὸν εἶναι τοῦ κόσμου πολίτην], and with his great mind he saw fit to take as his fellow-citizens all the divine beings who together administer the whole universe, and not those occupying parts of it. (Jul. *Or.* 7.25)

As in the other two cases, the citizen of the world is not a generalized term. Diogenes again applies it strictly to himself. Julian also frames the problem of birthplace as one of citizenship status. Without Athenian origins, Diogenes was not a citizen and hence not eligible for initiation. Although Lucian and Julian were not disinterested sources of Cynic doxography (O'Meara 2002), they provide the only other comparable associations of Diogenes (or any Cynic) with the *politēs tou kosmou* besides the single appearance of *kosmopolitēs* in the Cynic archive.

13. One might pursue Michel Foucault's discussions of *parrhesia* and Diogenes's anti-Platonic "game of philosophical being-true" in the face of Alexander's exercise of political power in this broader context. See Foucault 2011, esp. 285–98.

14. D. L. 6.38; D. Chr. *Or.* 4; cf. D. L. 6.32, 45, 63, 68, 79; Arr. *An.* 7.2; Plu. *De Alex.* 331F.

broader tradition of "philosopher meets king" tales in which philosophical kingship (self-mastery) trumps political kingship (world mastery). During the decades that Diogenes allegedly styled himself the first *kosmopolitēs*, Alexander the Great was embracing a larger *kosmos*, including Sinope, as the "King of Kings" (*basileos basileōn*) and—as he was later known—the first "world ruler" (*kosmokratōr*).[15] As Seneca observed, "Much more powerful, much richer in land [*locupletior*] was [Diogenes] than Alexander who then possessed everything; for what he would not accept was more than Alexander was able to give."[16] Alexander pronounced that he "would have liked to have been Diogenes if [he] had not been born Alexander," but Diogenes rebuffed his every overture.[17] From Diogenes's perspective, a cosmopolitan emperor such as Alexander was thus a laughable oxymoron (*kosmopolitēs* and *kosmokratōr*). Diogenes used (or coined) his term not as a concept so much as a dramatic, parrhesiastic act of self-identification.

Philo's Kosmopolitēs

Since Diogenes's famous term was not recorded until the third century CE, Philo of Alexandria's eight allusions to the *kosmopolitēs* are the earliest on record. Modern scholarship on cosmopolitanism generally overlooks Philo.[18] However, early Christian writings took up Philo's *kosmopolitēs*, and together they represent a distinct tradition that developed at the same time, and within the same *oikoumene*, as that of the Hellenistic and Roman Cynics and Stoics. Somewhat confusingly, the two passages in von Arnim's canonical *Stoicorum Veterum Fragmenta* that attribute the word *kosmopolitēs* to a Stoic author are taken from Philo's *On the Creation of the World According to Moses*. Von Arnim attributes these passages to the early Stoic Chrysippus (ca. 280–ca. 206 BCE) not because Philo directly quotes or cites him, but because they likely show Chrysippus's influence on Philo.[19] As recent scholars have pointed out, Philo used Stoic vocabulary and themes as philosophical building blocks, but he did not seek to record Stoic doctrine.[20] He loosely and creatively appropriated select Stoic concepts for his exegesis of the Torah:

> The beginning [section of Moses's laws], as I have said, is most awesome in encompassing universe's creation [κοσμοποιίαν], with both the universe

15. Stoneman 2008: 96–7. *Historia Alexandri Magni* MS A, the earliest extant version dating to the third century CE, records the divine decree before Alexander's birth that an Egyptian man would become world-ruler: Αἰγύπτιον ἄνθρωπον κοσμοκράτορα βασιλέα (1.12.8); and Aristotle's later greeting to Alexander: Χαίροις κοσμοκράτωρ (1.16.5).

16. Sen. *Ben.* 5.4.

17. D. L. 6.32. They reportedly died the same day in 323 BCE. D. L. 6.79.

18. Husson 2011: 159–60, and Long 2008a note, but do not pursue, Philo's use of the term.

19. *SVF* 1, xix, Pearson 1905; cf. Long 2008b.

20. On Philo's departures from Stoicism, especially in asserting the active creative principle of God, and the inadequacy of the human basis of Stoic moral values, see Radice 2009, Lévy 2009, Long 2008b.

in accord with the law, and the law with the universe, and the man who follows the law is at once constituted a cosmopolitan [κοσμοπολίτου] who guides his actions towards nature's will, according to which the entire world is also regulated.[21]

If we say that the first founder [i.e., Adam] was not only the first human but also the only cosmopolitan [μόνον κοσμοπολίτην], we will be speaking the greatest truths. For the world was his household and city.[22]

Since every city with good laws has a constitution, it was inevitable that the cosmopolitan [τῷ κοσμοπολίτῃ] used the same constitution as that of the whole world. This itself is the correct reason of nature, which by its more authoritative term is "ordinance" [θεσμός], since it is divine law [νόμος θεῖος], according to which each was apportioned his duties and lot.[23]

Philo's appeal here to the *kosmopolitēs* and to the "correct reason of nature" that is also divine law employs the kind of Stoic themes that are elaborated later in this chapter. However, the divine law is that of the Jews and in this fundamental sense, Philo's cosmopolitan and the world he inhabits differ radically from those of Diogenes, Cicero, or Epictetus. These passages belong to his discussion of *Genesis* (here part of Moses's laws). In the first instance the *kosmopolitēs* is any "man who follows the law" (*tou nomimou andros*) of this perfect world created by God. In the second and third, he is Adam, the "only cosmopolitan," who lives according to a world-encompassing divine law. Between these two passages, Philo criticizes those who admire the "world and not the creator of the world," and who impiously assume God's "great inactivity" instead of his role as "Creator and Father." Stoics had ascribed to the universe a passive principle that referred to matter and an active principle that referred to God, both of which constituted parts of it. Philo departed from this by insisting on God's infinite powers and first creation of the universe (*kosmopoiia*). As the title of his book suggests, the universe that his cosmopolitan inhabited was specifically in accord with Mosaic Law, and elsewhere Moses is identified as another *kosmopolitēs*.[24] Philo does not use the formulation *politēs tou kosmou* (or *kosmios*) and there

21. Philo *Opif.* 3, *SVF* 3.336.
22. Philo *Opif.* 142, *SVF* 3.337.
23. Philo *Opif.* 143, *SVF*, 3.337.
24. In a similar vein, when discussing the diminutive number of God's exiled but chosen people, Philo's *On the Migration of Abraham* contrasts the universe and the wise cosmopolitan (ὁ κοσμοπολίτης σοφός) that were filled with great and good things, with the crowd of other men that largely experienced evil things (Philo *Migr.* 59). In two further instances, Philo identifies the *kosmopolitēs* with Moses. As the cosmopolitan who took the world as his town and homeland, Moses was exemplary in his "desire for a nature that knows no body" (Philo *Mos.*, 1.157). Moses led the exiled Jews from Egypt as a cosmopolitan (*kosmopolitēs*) who was not a registered inhabitant of any city—he took "not a part of the earth, but the whole world as his portion" (Philo *Conf.* 106). For a distinct account of God as the only true *politēs*, see Philo, *Cherub.* 120–1.

are only a couple of exceptions in which he does not explicitly identify the *kosmopolitēs* with Adam, Moses, or followers of Mosaic Law.[25]

Philo's *kosmopolitēs* differed from the Stoic citizen of the world. Philo's was descent-restricted, whereas Stoic citizenship of the rational universe was open to all. Philo's divine citizenship is of a universe whose religious constitution was at odds with Roman imperial rule; by contrast, the Roman emperor, as much as his slave, could participate in Stoic ethics. More like the Cynic Diogenes (the *kosmopolitēs* who rebuffed Alexander), Philo's *kosmopolitēs* is a citizen of a non-imperial universe. Philo used Stoic themes when he described the harmony between natural and divine law but ultimately restricted his *kosmopolitēs* to a single descent group who had followed Mosaic Law in the face of exile, violence, and political regulation. Philo recorded the complex and dynamic relation of Alexandrian Jews to the Roman empire. He himself held multiple privileged citizenships—of Alexandria, of Rome, and of Alexandria's Jewish community—but records his own embassy to Gaius Caligula after the violent pogroms of 38 CE, when fellow Alexandrians invaded synagogues to install images of the emperor.[26] Caligula did not respond well ("Are you the god-haters who do not take me to be a god?").[27] Although Philo does not introduce his *kosmopolitēs* directly

25. The subjects of the following passage from *On Special Laws* are the "practitioners of wisdom in Greek or barbarian lands" (*Hellēsin ē para barbarous askētai sophias*) who observe nature and rise above their passions, whom some have identified with the Stoics (e.g., Lévy 2009):

> While settling their bodies on the land below, they equip their souls with wings, so that in perambulating the ethers they can gaze at the powers there, as was necessary through this for those becoming cosmopolitans [κοσμοπολῖται] who have understood the world to be a city, and its citizens companions in wisdom, registered by their virtue, which provided the pledge for the common administration of the government. (Philo *Spec.* 45)

This passage is part of Philo's discussion of the Fourth Commandment for which he uses these cosmopolitans as evidence by analogy that only the wise can carry out daily feasts. These cosmopolitans, whoever they are, are thus analogs to those able to obey Mosaic Law. The explication of the *kosmopolitai* as citizens of a commonwealth due to their wisdom and virtue suggests that he may be alluding to an early Stoic or Cynic concept. The passage from *On the Giants* differs somewhat from the other seven. As in the preceding quotation, it associates the *kosmopolitēs* with the philosopher, but unlike in any other case, this *kosmopolitēs* is inferior to, or a step on the way to becoming, the "men of God." Philo's three-rung typology ascends from "those born of the earth, who are hunters after the pleasures of the body," to "those born of heaven who are men of skill and science and devoted to learning," to the final group:

> Men of God are priests and prophets [θεοῦ δὲ ἄνθρωποι ἱερεῖς καὶ προφῆται], who have not seen fit to appear amongst the commonwealths of the universe and to become cosmopolitans [κοσμοπολῖται], but stepping above all sensory things, have moved to the apprehended universe, and they live there registered in a commonwealth of uncorrupted and incorporeal ideas [ἀφθάρτων <καὶ> ἀσωμάτων ἰδεῶν πολιτείᾳ]. (Philo *Gig.* 61)

Cosmopolitans (*kosmopolitai*) are second-rung heaven-born lovers of learning (i.e., the philosophers). They are superior to the earth-born pleasure-seekers, but superseded by the priests and prophets born of God. Philo goes on to explain that Abraham, when named Abram, was a "man born of heaven" but progressed and became a "man born of God" when he became Abraham.

26. See Schwartz 2009. On the anti-Jewish violence of 38 BCE, see Philo *Flacc.*, *Legat.* 120–31, Gruen 2002: 54–83.

27. Philo *Legat.* 354. Caligula also attempted to install a statue of himself in the Temple of Jerusalem.

into these historical scenes, the Mosaic Law governing the religious universe of the *kosmopolitēs* had increasingly to be asserted in the face of attack.[28]

Early Christian writings iterated Philo's use of the *kosmopolitēs*, but the term did not become part of the formative Christian lexicon. Treatises that were not accepted into the New Testament use it in reference to Adam, Abraham, or their kin.[29] The *kosmopolitēs* does not appear at all in the New Testament, perhaps due to Philo's association of it with a specific descent group. Pauline "cosmopolitanism" looked to a different term. In his famous address to the non-Jewish Ephesians, Paul (ca. 5 BCE–ca. 67 CE) used the term "fellow-citizens" (*sumpolitai*) to explain how they, too, could now gain access to God through Jesus Christ: "You are no longer strangers and foreigners but fellow-citizens with the saints" (Ephesians 1:18–20). Although derived from the classical verb *sumpoliteuō* ("to live together as fellow-citizens"), this noun is first attested in the late first century BCE and his is the earliest recorded use of the plural form.[30] St. Paul's fellow citizenship with strangers and foreigners is conceptually closer to the Stoic formulations, addressed in part II, than to the *kosmopolitēs* of Philo or Diogenes.

PART II: COSMOPOLITANISMS UNDER EMPIRE

Kosmios, Mundanus, Politēs Tou Kosmou, Civis Mundi

Most accounts of Stoic cosmopolitanism take Diogenes's *kosmopolitēs* as etymon and conceptual origin. However, Cicero and Epictetus associated their abstract theories of the world citizen with Socrates's *kosmios*, not Diogenes's *kosmopolitēs*. Nor did they adopt Diogenes's flagrantly anti-imperial stance. Cicero's *civis mundi* and Epictetus's *politēs tou kosmou* become generalized subjects of theory. Cicero, a New Academy skeptic, clearly draws on Stoic philosophy in the earliest surviving formulation of the cosmopolitan subject. *On the Laws* provides an exposition of the early Stoic ideal of a cosmic city grounded in natural law governed by right reason and shared by a community of gods

---

28. The Jews in Hellenistic Egypt formed a "voluntary ethnic corporation" (sometimes called a *politeuma*) and lived by Greco-Egyptian common law. They were allowed—but not compelled—to use Jewish law. The maintenance of, and participation in, temples to their ancestral God appears to have been central to the observance of Jewish law. See Schwartz 2001: 220 and Schwartz 2009: 42–4, which present Philo as an integrationist who acknowledged his doubts about the benefits of Roman rule.

29. *Constit. Apost.* 7.34, cf. 7.39, 13.12, 8.41. The Apostolic Constitutions were not accepted into the New Testament but formed a fourth-century manual for clergy. The seventh book was based on treatises for Jewish-Christians that were popular around 100 CE; cf. fourth-century Did. Caec., *Comm.* 33.186 on the transcendental *kosmopolitēs*. On Philo's influence, see Runia 2009: 210–30.

30. St. Paul goes on to refer to the devil as the world-ruler (*kosmokratōr*) (Ephesians 6:12). During subsequent centuries when secular legends of Alexander the world-ruler (*kosmokratōr*) were proliferating as a shining archetype of the Roman and Byzantine cosmocratic cosmopolitan, many Christians (including Didymus Caecus) echoed St. Paul's call to the Ephesians to arm themselves against the dark forces of the world-ruler.

and men, and pursues its relevance to Roman institutions. In praising philosophy as the guide to these principles, Cicero describes the process by which the philosopher, "the person who knows himself," becomes a "citizen of the world" (*civis mundi*):

> And when he has studied the heaven, lands, seas, and the nature of all things ... and has (so to speak) got a grip on the god who guides and rules these things and has recognized that he is not bound by human walls as the citizen of one particular spot but a citizen of the whole world [*civem totius mundi*] as if it were a single city—then in this perception and understanding of nature, by the immortal gods, how will he know himself.[31]

Self-knowledge, not assertive self-identification (as in Diogenes's case), is at stake. To become the philosopher who can establish human laws in accordance with the true providential law of nature, the anonymous ideal subject must first achieve a long series of philosophical tasks, including recognition (*agnouerit*) of himself as "citizen of the whole world." Both of Cicero's two iterations of the *civis mundi* include the modifier "whole" (*totius*). In both cases it highlights his use of the citizen of the world to contrast part and whole: here, belonging to "one particular spot" on the human map must give way to membership of a universal city governed by natural law and right reason. Although Cicero does not pronounce himself as a citizen of the world, his authorship of *On the Laws* implicates him as one. He disembodies and abstracts the term; his long series of conditional acts makes world citizenship available to any hardy philosopher.

Cicero's *Tusculan Disputations* offers a philosophical lineage for this cosmopolitan idea, but does not acknowledge the Cynics among the great Hellenic philosophers that his new Latin philosophy must build on (and one day render redundant). In defending the life of exile, he lists sixteen of the "most eminent philosophers" who lived permanently abroad, including Stoics (e.g., Cleanthes), Peripatetics (e.g., Aristotle), Academics (e.g., Xenocrates), New Academics (e.g., Carneades), and Epicureans.[32] Cicero states there are countless others, but the absence of Diogenes from ensuing passage suggests that the Cynic *kosmopolitēs* belongs to an alternate tradition:

> itaque ad omnem rationem Teucri vox accommodari potest: "Patria est, ubicumque est bene." Socrates quidem cum rogaretur, cuiatem se esse diceret, "mundanum" inquit; totius enim mundi se incolam et civem arbitrabatur.

---

31. Cic. *Leg.* 1.61. Following Zetzel 1999: 127.
32. Cicero discusses the Epicurean Albicus at the end of *Tusc. Disp.* 5.108.

Thus Teucer's saying, "A homeland is wherever one [lives] well" can be adapted to every case. Indeed when Socrates was asked where he was from, he used to say he was a "Universian"; for he considered himself as a resident and citizen of the whole world.[33]

Three aspects of this passage are important. First, it is here Socrates who invokes the larger world in response to the question of where he was from (*cuiatem*), not Diogenes (cf. ποδαπὸς in Lucian; πόθεν in Diogenes Laertius). Second, Cicero's nominalization of the adjective *mundanus* (lit. "person of the world," "Universian") is previously unattested, and appears to be a Latin translation for Socrates's own (ostensibly novel) Greek term. As addressed below, Epictetus and Plutarch (46–120 CE) provide the Greek term *kosmios* (κόσμιος) for Socrates's self-description. Here, Cicero uses *civis mundi* as part of a more self-evident phrase used to explicate the cognate *mundanus*. Indeed the *civis mundi* is hard to separate out from the rest of the clause—Socrates is a citizen and resident of the whole world (*totius . . . mundi se incolam et civem*). Crucially, Socrates's term lacks the "citizen" (*civis, politēs*) element that Diogenes drew on in his verbal acts of power reversal. The exiled or wandering *mundanus*, like the *civis mundi* of Cicero's *On the Laws*, takes issue with affiliation with only one "particular spot." The type of political constitution is not here at stake. Third, Cicero forges a philosophical genealogy for this abstracted idea (Socrates's *mundanus* and *civis mundi*) that precedes and bypasses the Cynics.

Epictetus's *Discourses* (composed by his student Arrian [92–175 CE]) ostensibly builds on Cicero's discussion of Socrates-as-Universian. The following passage is commonly cited in analyses of Stoic cosmopolitanism:

If what philosophers say about the kinship of god and men is true, what other way is left for men than that of Socrates, who never said to anyone who inquired where he was from that he was an Athenian or a Corinthian, but that he was a "Universian" [εἰ ταῦτά ἐστιν ἀληθῆ τὰ περὶ τῆς συγγενείας τοῦ θεοῦ καὶ ἀνθρώπων λεγόμενα ὑπὸ τῶν φιλοσόφων, τί ἄλλο ἀπολείπεται τοῖς ἀνθρώποις ἢ τὸ τοῦ Σωκράτους, μηδέποτε πρὸς τὸν πυθόμενον ποδαπός ἐστιν εἰπεῖν ὅτι Ἀθηναῖος ἢ Κορίνθιος, ἀλλ' ὅτι κόσμιος]. So why do you say that you are Athenian, and not simply from that corner into which your meager body was flung at birth? Otherwise it is clear that you [claim to be] from [the place that] has greater authority [ἀπὸ τοῦ κυριωτέρου] and encompasses not only that corner of yours, but also your whole household and, to put it plainly, [the place] from where your race [τὸ γένος] descended, from your ancestors to yourself,

33. Cic. *Tusc. Disp.* 5.108. Cf. Douglas 1985: 164. On *Tusculans* 5, see Gildenhard 2007: 203–5, 269–75. Gildenhard reads the *Tusculans* as a political engagement with the realities of Caesar's tyranny that sought a "new ethics for Rome's traditional oligarchy."

and from this you call yourself Athenian and Corinthian. Whoever has attended closely to the administration of the universe and has learned that "the greatest and most authoritative and most comprehensive of all is the system comprised of humans and god, and from that [god] fell seeds not only to my father or grandfather, but to all things produced and growing on earth—above all to rational beings; [and whoever has learned that the rational] alone by nature shares communion with god, entwined with him through reason [κατὰ τὸν λόγον]"[34]—why should he not say that he is a Universian, why not a son of god? [διὰ τί μὴ εἴπῃ τις αὐτὸν κόσμιον; διὰ τί μὴ υἱὸν τοῦ θεοῦ] Why fear what happens amongst men? But will kinship with Caesar [πρὸς μὲν τὸν Καίσαρα ἡ συγγένεια], or with another of the powerful in Rome, be enough to provide for a life of security, without any indignities or fears at all—so that to have god as maker and father and guardian will no longer keep us free from pains and fears? And how, one asks, might I eat if I have nothing? And how about the slaves and the runaways, on whom do those who have escaped their masters rely? On their household slaves or silver dishes? No, on themselves.[35]

Scholars commonly translate *kosmios* as "citizen of the world," and thereby tie it to Diogenes's formulation. However, as in the case of Cicero's Latin *mundanus*, Epictetus simply nominalizes the Greek adjective *kosmios* (lit. "man of the universe," "Universian"), replacing the citizen with the person. Like Cicero's *civis mundi* (in *On the Laws*), this Universian can call himself such when he has achieved a philosophical understanding of the providentially organized universe. Epictetus's Universian more explicitly rejects mere affiliation to imperial power ("the place that has greater authority"); kinship (*sungeneia*) between "god and man" and entwinement with reason (*logos*) is better than "kinship (*sungeneia*) with Caesar, or with another of the powerful in Rome" because, Epictetus suggests, even those with no standing or citizenship within empire will be protected. Epictetus had been a slave before his career as a philosopher, and here even the slave and runaway can become a Universian and son of god. One might note that the roughly contemporary first-century CE pseudographic Epistles of Heraclitus of Ephesus contains a similar iteration of the slave, but using the phrase *kosmou politēs*. The ninth epistle is addressed to Hermodorus, who has been exiled from Ephesus for attempting to give citizenship status to freedmen: "As for an Ephesian man, if he is good, he is a citizen of the world" (*kosmou politēs*); "Nor did [god] shut out the sun's light from slaves, since he

---

34. Likely a quotation from Poseidonius or another Stoic. D. L. 7.138.
35. Arr. *Epict.* 1.9.1–6.

enrolled all men as citizens of the world" (*kosmou . . . politas*).[36] Epictetus's discussion does come closer to the Cynic critique of power; however, unlike Diogenes, he does not anarchically preclude the emperor or master from also being the ethical subject (and Universian). In this sense, his cosmopolitanism remained compatible with empire.

This (possibly Roman) tradition of Socratic cosmopolitanism (*mundanus, kosmios*) invoked by Epictetus and Cicero is generally overlooked in modern genealogies of cosmopolitanism. Epictetus's Stoic mentor Musonius Rufus had defended exile by praising Socrates's claim that the universe (*kosmos*) was the "common fatherland of all humans," and by arguing that a person should "consider himself to be a citizen of the city of Zeus comprised of humans and gods."[37] Apart from Epictetus's *Discourses*, Plutarch's *On Exile* provides the other extant instance of the *kosmios*, holding Socrates up as a model for saying he was "not an Athenian or a Greek but a Universian" (*kosmios*).

Unlike Cicero, neither Epictetus nor Plutarch glosses the Universian (*mundanus, kosmios*) as the citizen of the world/universe (*civis mundi, politēs tou kosmou*). However, on the single occasion that Epictetus (or any surviving Stoic) employs the term *politēs tou kosmou*, he foregrounds the part/whole opposition underlying Socrates's *kosmios/mundanus* and Cicero's *civis mundi*.

> Study who you are: first of all, a human being, that is one who has nothing more authoritative than volition, but who holds everything else subordinate to that while keeping it unenslaved and sovereign. Consider, then, from what creatures you are separated by possessing reason. You are separated from wild beasts, you are separated from sheep. You are a citizen of the world [*politēs tou kosmou*] and a part [*meros*] of it, not one of the subordinate parts, but one of the foremost. For you are capable of understanding the divine administration and of reasoning out what follows from it. What is the profession of the citizen? To treat nothing as a purely private interest and to deliberate about nothing as though one were detached [from the world as a whole], but as the hand or the foot, if they had reason and the capacity to attend to the world's [natural] constitution would never exercise impulse or desire except by reference to the whole.[38]

Epictetus's generalized citizen of the world embodies the figure of the synecdoche—a vision of the social whole in every part. His organic metaphor of

36. This work is attributed variously to Jewish and Cynic traditions. However, this invocation of the citizen of the world seems more compatible with Cynic or Epictetus's formulations. On this work, see Attridge 1976: 3–39.

37. Ruf. Rh. 9.

38. Arr. *Epict.* 2.10.1–4, following Long 2002: 200, 233. Cf. Arr. *Epict.* 2.5.26.

the "hand or foot" makes the citizen of the world a remedy for social detachment. Unlike Cicero, Epictetus embraced Diogenes. Diogenes's rebarbative words and exemplary lifestyle permeate the *Discourses*. However, Epictetus associated his *kosmios* with Socrates and he does not associate his *politēs tou kosmou* with Diogenes. Epictetus's framing distinction between human beings, who possess capacities of volition (*prohairesis*) and reason, and wild beasts that do not, reflects his more traditional approach to the human/beast divide. Diogenes's rhetoric, by contrast, had thrived on reversing the hierarchies of man and beast. He embraced his own dog-like (*kunikos*, hence Cynic) lifestyle and epithet, notoriously finding in mice his inspiration for adapting to circumstance.[39]

Thus, the few surviving instances of *civis mundi* or *politēs tou kosmou* occur not as terms to explicate, but as one of a set of synonymous formulations that describe a concept: how any possessor of correct reasoning, regardless of nationality, shares with the gods a universe governed by natural law. The absence of the term *kosmopolitēs* from the extant Stoic corpus does not mean Stoics never used it. However its absence, taken together with the repeated staging of Socrates's *kosmios/mundanus* as the significant neologism, does suggest the Stoics did not find the *kosmopolitēs* particularly important and useful. The only extant use of *kosmopolitēs* outside the Cynic and Jewish traditions comes fairly late, when the Neo-Platonist Proclus (412–485 CE) called Homer a cosmopolitan (*kosmopolitēs*): "It is not easy to give an account of Homer's parents or his place of birth ... [S]ince every city tends to lay a claim on the man he might reasonably be called a cosmopolitan [κοσμοπολίτης λέγοιτο]."[40] This follows the Stoic emphasis on the indifference of the world citizen to ethnic or regional affiliation, more familiar to modern notions of cosmopolitanism.

Epictetus's conception of the world citizen as an abstract unit of a rational whole accords with a set of well-known passages that are commonly cited as examples of Stoic cosmopolitanism but that do not use the term *politēs tou kosmou*. These include Cicero's notions of degrees or steps (*gradus*) of fellowship in *On Duties*; Hierocles's (fl. ca. 100 CE) concentric circles of affiliation that proceed outward from the self, to family, neighbors, fellow city dwellers, and all humanity; the ideal city of Zeno's (ca. 490–ca. 430 BCE) *Republic* in which "the wise [*spoudaious*] alone are citizens, friends, kindred and free"; and the Stoic notion of *oikeiosis*, variously translated as "appropriation," "endearment," or "recognition and appreciation of something as belonging to one."[41] They

---

39. E.g., D. L. 6.22. Cf. D. L. 6.24, 6.40.

40. Procl. *Chr.* 99.

41. Cic. *Off.* 1.53–60, Plu, *Alex.* 329A–B, Hierocl. 61.8. See Ramelli 2009: 125–6, n. 40; D. L. 7.33. On the reliability of the fragment concerning Zeno, and for an argument that Zeno's vision addressed the status of outsiders within the changing fourth-century BCE classical polis, see Richter 2011: 58–74. On *oikeiosis*, see Striker 1983, Richter 2011: 74–80. On literary cosmopolitanism in the first centuries of the Common Era, see Whitmarsh 2001b.

collectively produce a positive theory of the world citizen subject (*civis mundi, mundanus, politēs tou kosmou, kosmios*) as, variously, the wandering exile, the member of a universal city of gods and men governed by natural law and right reason, and the inseparable part of a larger social community than one's *polis, deme*, or *ethnos*.⁴² The Christian Roman Emperor Constantius II (r. 337–361 CE) later applied this multi-constituency notion of *politēs tou kosmou* to Themistius (317–ca. 390 CE), a non-Christian public philosopher whose Hellenic *paideia* remained supportive of Christian empire. On adlecting Themistius to the Senate of Constantinople, he praised this outsider who had chosen to live in the imperial capital as "an exceptional citizen of our city, whom one might with good reason salute as a citizen of the World [κόσμου πολίτην]."⁴³

Although not identified with the imperial order itself, these diverse formulations of what we now call cosmopolitanism were not seen as incompatible with empire. In contrast to the Philonic and Cynic *kosmopolitēs*, Cicero's *civis mundi* was harnessed to the improvement of political rule. Epictetus, writing a generation after Philo, differentiated the Roman empire from the (non-Judaic, Providential) god's rational *kosmos*, within which the slave, too, might become a *kosmios* and "son of god." However, as with Cicero and other Stoics, Epictetus made the part-versus-whole opposition the kernel of the *politēs tou kosmou*. Even when differentiated from imperial citizenship, this abstracted Stoic world citizenship does not appear incompatible with empire. Retrospectively, the now forgotten term "man of the Universe" ("Universian," *kosmios, mundanus*) disengaged the problem of horizontal relations of belonging (*man/person* of the universe) from vertical relations of power (*citizen* of the universe). One might contrast the Stoic model of multicultural cosmopolitanism (Socrates as *kosmios*, not Athenian) with Philo's descent-based *kosmopolitēs* and Diogenes's disaffection with his famously multiethnic natal city of Sinope. Sinope was the busy Black Sea terminus of caravan routes from India, home to Assyrians, Paphlagonians, Greeks, and Persians. However, Diogenes's self-identification as a *kosmopolitēs* likely had more to do with Sinope's political submission to Greek, Persian, and Alexandrian empires, than with its multiethnic harmony.⁴⁴

Cosmopolitan Emperors and Empires

Somewhat surprising in this survey is the absence of the actual terms *kosmopolitēs, politēs tou kosmou, civis mundi*, or *kosmios/mundanus* from the

42. Long 2002: 232–7. Nussbaum 2002 finds the core of Cynic and Stoic cosmopolitanism "in recognizing the equal and unconditional moral worth of human grounded in reason and moral capacity." Cf. Nussbaum 1997. Schofield argues that Cynic and Stoic cosmopolitanism lay in seeing the universe as a city common to men and gods. See Schofield 1999: 144.

43. Them. *Or.* 22c. For the Greek text, see Downey 1974: 127. For a discussion and translation, see Heather 2001: 97–117.

44. On Sinope, see Doonan 2004, esp. 69–92; Robinson 1906, esp. 150–258.

two historical scenes that modern historians most commonly use as a template for "imperial cosmopolitanism," namely Marcus Aurelius and Alexander. Emperor Marcus Aurelius's (121–180 CE) *Meditations* cite Epictetus and implicitly appropriate the Stoic notion of *politēs tou kosmou* for his model of enlightened imperial rule: "My city [*polis*] and fatherland is, for myself as [Marcus Aurelius], Rome; for myself as a human being, the world [*kosmos*]. Therefore only those things that are useful to both cities [*polesin*] are good for me."[45] Marcus adapts the Socrates-as-*kosmios/mundanus* ideal found in Epictetus, Cicero, and Plutarch: but now the emperor, rather than the wise man or slave, is the subject of cosmopolitan ethics.

Ancient sources also recorded Alexander's imperial policies in other terms: the concord (ὁμόνοια, "oneness of mind") and "partnership with one another" (κοινωνίαν πρὸς ἀλλήλους) among the diverse nations he conquered, rather than world citizenship.[46] Arrian (composer of Epictetus's *Discourses*), Quintus Curtius Rufus, and others recorded the marriages of Macedonian conquerors (especially Alexander) to the local women of conquered nations, but the association of this intermarriage policy with Stoic cosmopolitanism comes from Plutarch. Writing four centuries after Alexander's death, Plutarch's idealizes the emperor as the wise ruler who concretizes through world conquest Zeno's dream of a philosophical commonwealth:

> The much-admired *Republic* of Zeno, who founded the Stoic sect, is aimed at this one main point, that our arrangement for habitations should not be based on cities or peoples, each one distinguished by its own special system of justice, but we should regard all men as citizens and members of the populace, and there should be one way of life and order [εἷς δὲ βίος ᾖ καὶ κόσμος], like that of a herd grazing together and nurtured by a common law/pasturing. This Zeno wrote, picturing as it were a dream or image of a philosopher's well-regulated republic [εὐνομίας φιλοσόφου καὶ πολιτείας], but it was Alexander who gave effect to the theory. For he did not, as Aristotle used to advise him, treat the Greeks as a leader would, and the barbarians as a despot/master would [δεσποτικῶς], caring for [the Greeks] as friends and kin, but treating [barbarians] as animals or plants, [as that] would have filled his leadership with numerous wars, exiles, and festering discords. But believing that he came as god-sent governor for everyone and mediator for all—forcing by arms those he did not bring together by argument, bringing them from everywhere into one, as if mingling together in a loving-cup their ways of life, customs, marriages, and habits of life—he instructed all to think of

---

45. Marc. Aur. *Med.* 6.43.
46. Arr. *An.* 7.11.5–12; Plu. *De Alex.* 330E. Cf. Plu, *Alex.* 47.3.

the whole inhabited world as their fatherland [ἀλλὰ κοινὸς ἥκειν θεόθεν ἁρμοστὴς καὶ διαλλακτὴς τῶν ὅλων νομίζων, οὓς τῷ λόγῳ μὴ συνῆγε τοῖς ὅπλοις βιαζόμενος, εἰς τὸ αὐτὸ συνενεγκὼν τὰ πανταχόθεν, ὥσπερ ἐν κρατῆρι φιλοτησίῳ μείξας τοὺς βίους καὶ τὰ ἤθη καὶ τοὺς γάμους καὶ τὰς διαίτας, πατρίδα μὲν τὴν οἰκουμένην προσέταξεν ἡγεῖσθαι πάντας], his camp as their acropolis and garrison, the morally good as their kin, the morally bad as foreigners; to distinguish Greek and barbarian not by cloak and light shield nor by scimitar or jacket, but to take virtue as the sign of Greekness, vice that of the barbarous; and to regard clothes, food, marriages, habits of life as common to all, blended together by blood-ties and children [ἀλλὰ τὸ μὲν Ἑλληνικὸν ἀρετῇ τὸ δὲ βαρβαρικὸν κακίᾳ τεκμαίρεσθαι· κοινὰς δ᾽ ἐσθῆτας ἡγεῖσθαι καὶ τραπέζας καὶ γάμους καὶ διαίτας, δι᾽ αἵματος καὶ τέκνων ἀνακεραννυμένους].[47]

Four aspects of this passage are important. First, Plutarch's version of Zeno's lost *Republic* differs somewhat from other fragmentary sources: he uses *kosmos* to mean social order ("there should be one way of life and order"), rather than god's rational universe.[48] Second, this social order is violently imperial. Although Zeno invoked "all men as citizens and members of the populace," Alexander alone is the god-sent governor (*theothen harmotēs*) who unites the world by force of arms or argument. The primary social distinction his empire addresses is ethnic: that between Greek versus barbarian, not citizen versus emperor/ruler (as with Diogenes's anti-cosmocratic *kosmopolitēs*). Third, this multiethnic (or post-ethnic) imperial order is the ethical order. Any virtuous person is now the "Greek"; any bad person, the *barbaros*. The Greek is no longer defined by birth or by democratic citizenship; he is the virtuous imperial subject. Finally, Plutarch's simile of Alexandrian empire as a loving-cup (or "mixing vessel of friendship," *kratēri philotēsiōi*) for different "ways of life, customs, marriages, and habits of life," "blended together by blood-ties and children" (*di' haimatos kai teknōn anakerannumenous*) makes racial and cultural fusion, rather than the pursuit of wisdom, the means to the new moral order. Both Marcus and Plutarch's Alexander conflate *kosmos* with empire; they draw on the tradition of Socrates's multi-polis belonging (*kosmios, politēs tou kosmou*), rather than that of Diogenes's contestatory citizenship of an anti-imperial universe (*kosmopolitēs*). From this perspective, Marcus's appropriation of Epictetus seems less egregious than Alexander and Emperor Julian's celebrations of the anti-cosmocratic Diogenes.

47. Plu. *De Alex*. 329A–C. Largely following Schofield 1999: 104, 109.
48. Plutarch's version of Zeno's city as a paradigm for a world community—as well as its imagery—differs from earlier representations of Zeno's ideal for the bounded classical polis. See Schofield 1999: 104–5, Richter 2011: 63–74.

One might summarize the two stances as follows. First, that of the anti-imperial (or un-imperial) cosmopolitan excluded the possibility of the emperor becoming the cosmopolitan ethical subject. In the Cynic instance, the cosmopolitan was exclusively embodied in the anarchic Diogenes; in Philo's writings, cosmopolitans were the followers of Mosaic Law. Whether an accident of the surviving archive or not, all extant uses of the term *kosmopolitēs* are associated with Diogenes or Philo. In both cases, the true *kosmos* was at odds with the imperial order and asserting oneself as world *citizen* (*kosmopolitēs*) upset vertical relations of power. Second, an abstracted cosmopolitanism remained compatible with empire. This primarily Stoic tradition emphasized the ethical extension of horizontal relations of belonging beyond a particular place to a larger social community. Cicero and Epictetus celebrated Socrates-as-Universian (*mundanus, kosmios*)—but not Diogenes-as-*kosmopolitēs*—as a template for the universal wise man, and they used the phrases *politēs tou kosmou* and *civis mundi* in similar ways. Some highlighted a gap between empire and the providential *kosmos*, but this tradition generally did not preclude either the attempt to close the gap, or the emperor from playing the cosmopolitan wise man. Emperors and their chroniclers did associate imperial policy with Stoic cosmopolitanism, but used terms or metaphors other than *kosmopolitēs* or *politēs tou kosmou*—such as Alexander's "loving-cup" of intermarriage.

Narratives of imperial cosmopolitanism thus might better look to Socrates's Universian (*kosmios*), and not to Diogenes's *kosmopolitēs* of conventional etymology. Retrospectively, this distinction between the anti-imperial *kosmopolitēs* and an abstracted imperial cosmopolitanism accrues greater importance in the later contexts of European empire. These later genealogies matter because they help to make visible, however schematically, some of the politics of inherited notions of cosmopolitanism that are then read back into antiquity.[49] By the end of the nineteenth century, Alexander scholarship and imperial ideology were mutually imbricated and the trope of Alexandrine cosmopolitanism circulated in British and French colonial discourse and historiography.[50] By contrast, in the influential tradition of Immanuel Kant's *Toward Perpetual Peace* (1795), cosmopolitanism's explicit opposite is not cultural narrowness, nationalism, or dynastic statism, but imperialism. As in the case of Diogenes's *kosmopolitēs*, cross-cultural contact is not necessarily the sign of cosmopolitanism.[51] Kant explicitly distinguished between cosmopolitan hospitality and forcible entrance, that is, the colonial or "*inhospitable* behavior of the civilized states in our part

49. On the need to attach a contingent genealogy of cosmopolitanism to the history of contact, empire, and the internationalization of commerce, see Anderson 1998.

50. Vasunia 2013: 33–90.

51. The universal hospitality of the host governs this cosmopolitan public right. In Kant's account, China's restrictions on European attempts to force trade and entry become a figure of the preservation of cosmopolitan law.

of the world, especially the commercial ones" in foreign lands, such as China.[52] Let us end by following Kant's gaze beyond the Mediterranean and Near East.

CODA

Cosmopolitanism (*shijie zhuyi*) entered Chinese through the modern translation of Western texts. Any pursuit of Chinese "imperial cosmopolitanism" must therefore take into consideration the tradition/definition on which the translation was based (e.g., Stoic *kosmios*, Kant's *Kosmopolitisches Recht*), the semantic field of the modern term, and the modern politics of, and criteria for, establishing ancient linguistic and historical equivalents. *Shijie zhuyi* (cosmopolitanism, lit. "world-ism") and *shijie ren* 世界人 (cosmopolitan, lit. "world person") took the modern Chinese loan-word *shijie* 世界 ("world") for their etymology, but generally occluded the "citizen" (*politēs*) element (cf. *kosmios/mundanus*).[53] Some also borrowed the classical Chinese term for empire, *tianxia* 天下 (lit. "All under Heaven"), for cosmopolitanism.[54] Early twentieth-century Republicans celebrated "cosmopolitan nationalism" (*shijie guojia zhuyi*) as a defense against foreign imperialism. With the establishment of the People's Republic of China in 1949, more turned to Karl Marx's use of *Kosmopolitismus* to refer to the natural tendency of capital to transcend national borders and to his critique of "bourgeois cosmopolitanism" (*zichan jieji de shijie zhuyi*).[55] Capital itself is "despotic" and "autocratic" in Marx; and in Negri and Hardt's more recent redefinition of empire as global capitalism, the cosmopolitan capitalist has become by definition "imperial."[56]

This interpretation of cosmopolitanism strictly in terms of commerce—in relation to profit-seeking trade across the cultural and political borders of

52. Kant 2006: 82–4. Kant grounds cosmopolitan law (*Kosmopolitisches Recht*)—the right of every human to visit another country without being treated with hostility—in "the right of common possession of the surface of the earth." Inhospitality is the cosmocratic violence of the guest, exemplified by imperialist and colonial expansions into America, Africa, and East India. Kant's cosmopolitan community comprised not world citizens, but a federation of states that would redirect resources from war to moral cultivation. See Cheah 2006.

53. Although the common *shijie gongmin* (lit. "world citizen") is sometimes used, the "citizen" (*gongmin*) element is dropped for the abstract noun cosmopolitanism (i.e., *shijie zhu yi*).

54. The standard modern Chinese term for empire is the modern neologism *di guo* 帝國.

55. Marx 1991: 449. Guo Moruo translated Marx's *Capital* into Chinese in 1931, after others had already begun to translate his other writings. Marx refers to "cosmopolitan swollen-headedness," "cosmopolitan blackleggism," "cosmopolitan orgies," "hypocritical, bourgeois cosmopolitanism." Drawing on Soviet debates, but citing Marx and Engels, Chinese editors and journalists of *Renmin Ribao* (*People's Daily*), writing on the eve of the founding of the People's Republic of China in 1949, emphasized the distinction between bourgeois cosmopolitanism and the working-class solidarity of proletarian "internationalism" (*guoji zhuyi* 国际主义). See, e.g., "*Zichan jieji de shijie zhuyi ji qi fandong zuoyong*," *Renmin Ribao*, September 30, 1949, and "*Shijie zhuyi yu guoji zhuyi*," *Renmin Ribao*, July 15, 1949. On the earlier twentieth-century discourse of cosmopolitanism in China—including the use in some contexts of *tianxia*—see Shen 2009; on Lu Xun's critique of the term, see Wang Hui 2010. These competing modern interpretations of cosmopolitanism need to be taken into account when engaging modern Chinese versus Europhone historical scholarship.

56. Hardt and Negri 2001.

empire—unexpectedly resonates with the ideological conflicts of Han dynasty China (206 BCE–220 CE). During the largest-scale territorial expansion in China's history, the new figure of the expansionist economist came to challenge the traditional classically-trained official as the proper imperial adviser. Thus, although the Tang dynasty (618–906 CE) is China's best known "cosmopolitan empire" for its openness to diverse cultural and religious groups (i.e., in the Stoic and Alexandrian tradition), the Han dynasty offers an alternate starting point to that of the *kosmios* or the *kosmopolitēs* for negotiating ancient and modern discourses about imperial cosmopolitanism.

Modern scholarship in English and Chinese tends to identify Han imperial cosmopolitanism with Confucian or classicist universalism. Han scholars and officials drew on traditional texts, including the Five Confucian Classics, to conceive universal empire in terms of *tianxia* ("All under Heaven," empire, world), *yitong* (unified rule) and *hua* (moral transformation, cultural assimilation, or sinicization). However, this was only one of two major competing forms of Han imperial cosmopolitan ideology that date from the last two centuries BCE, when Former Han Emperor Wu 漢武帝 (r. 141–87 BCE) expanded the Chinese empire by 1.5 million square miles into modern-day Inner and Outer Mongolia, Xinjiang, Guangzhou, Vietnam, Korea, and eastern Central Asia (as far as the Ferghana Valley). These positions respectively promoted restrictive versus expansionist ideals of *tianxia* 天下 ("All under Heaven").[57] *Guanzi's* 管子 "Qingzhong" 輕重 (lit. "Light and Heavy," "Ratios of Value") economic dialogue, compiled ca. 100 BCE, is the most important textbook of expansionist economics that Emperor Wu's advisers drew from in stimulating state markets to finance imperial expansion. The *Guanzi* promoted *tianxia* as the larger "world" to be conquered by military or economic strategies. By contrast, critics of Emperor Wu's expansion saw *tianxia* as the already unified "empire," delineated above all by the moral and ritual values encoded in traditional classical texts.[58] Both positions are elaborated in Huan Kuan's 桓寬 (fl. 60 BCE) *Debate on Salt and Iron* (*Yantielun* 鹽鐵論), a text which clearly sided with the critics of Emperor Wu.

The *Guanzi's* ideal ruler aimed to conquer the world (*tianxia*) by mastering the quantitative laws of market price, that is, the strategies or "rules for Light and Heavy" (*qingzhong zhi fa* 輕重之法), which transcended cultural or political contexts. The *Guanzi's* economic idiom creatively employed new and traditional terms. Most prominently, the phrase "Light and Heavy" (*qingzhong*),

---

57. For an expanded discussion of these texts, and their literary and historical contexts, see Chin 2014. On translating *tianxia* and empire in a Chinese context, see also Nylan 2008, Chang 2007, Pines 2002, Yates 2001. For a discussion of "intersecting" cosmopolitanisms in a later Buddhist text, see Beecroft 2010.

58. For modern theorists who differentiate a *universalism* that imposes its ethical program on others from a *cosmopolitanism* that negotiates multiple ideals, both versions of *tianxia* may too closely resemble the former. See, e.g., Anderson 1998, Appiah 2006.

generally used for standard weight or fluctuation in currency value, took on the meaning of "price ratio" or "relative value," especially in technical relation to its novel proposal that the quantitative relation between commodities and money in circulation determines price. (This proposal is now often taken as the world's earliest explicit articulation of a "quantity theory of money").[59] By first buying and selling the right goods at the right time the cosmocratic leader can then march his armies into economically weakened states. In the following, Guanzi explains how fiat currencies can be used to "connect" economies of foreign lands.

> Duke Huan said: "The four *yi* [四夷 i.e., all foreigners] have not [politically] submitted [themselves] and I worry that their political transgression will spread through the world and harm me. What path of action should I take for this?"

> Guanzi replied: "... Since the Yuzhi [i.e., Yuezhi/Kushans in Central Asia] have not paid court, I request our use of white jade discs as money [請以白璧為幣乎]. Since those of the Kunlun deserts [modern-day Xinjiang and Tibet] have not paid court, I request our use of lapis lazuli and *langgan* gems as money [請以璆琳琅玕為幣乎].... Since a white jade held tight unseen against one's chest or under one's armpit will be used as a thousand pieces of gold, we can obtain the Yuzhi eight thousand *li* away and make them pay court. Since a lapis lazuli and *langgan* gem (fashioned in) a hair clasp and earring will be used as a thousand gold pieces, we can obtain [i.e., defeat] [the inhabitants] of the Kunlun deserts eight thousand *li* away and make them pay court. Therefore if resources are not commandeered,[60] economies will not connect, those distant from each other will have nothing to use for their common interest [遠近無以相因] and the four *yi* will not be obtained and come to court."[61]

This new *Qingzhong* world (*tianxia*) is cosmopolitan in the sense that the laws of the market are universal. The cosmocrat's fiat universal equivalent (here gold) makes diverse local products (patterned white jade, lapis lazuli, gems) into exchangeable forms of money (*bi*).[62] Once connected to this culturally

---

59. The text also playfully introduces personifications of its economic principles, such as Mr. Great Extravagance (*Tai she* 泰奢) and Mr. Calculate-y (Guiyi 癸乙 [taking *gui* 癸 for *kui* 揆]), who personifies the action fundamental to *qingzhong* policies, namely continually estimating or calculating the ever-fluctuating ratio of money and commodities in circulation in order to buy and sell at a profit.

60. Lit. "goods have no ruler" (物無主), i.e., the ruler needs to harness unused resources. Alternately: "if no commodity is made preeminent," following Guo Moruo and Ma Feibai.

61. Ma 2008: 560.

62. Uncoined gold and copper coinage were the two established forms of currency during early Chinese empire

transcendent global *qingzhong* economy whose rules the Guanzian has mastered, the foreigner will eventually be forced to politically submit ("pay court"). Unlike the Stoic or Confucian philosopher, who seeks to bring (or "assimilate") everyone from every cultural or ethnic background into their respective communities of the wise, the Guanzian cosmocrat subordinates all precisely by hoarding his knowledge of *qingzhong* strategies. He is disinterested in changing or preserving moral or cultural norms; he transforms commodities, not people. Cosmology (or Heaven) plays little or no part in this political economy. Although the dialogue is set in the pre-imperial Warring States era, its geopolitical horizons (including the Kunlun Mountains and Yuezhi/Kushans in Central Asia) are anachronistically those of the expansionist Han imperial period when the "Qingzhong" text was composed.[63]

This "cosmopolitan" imperial economics is pitted against the more traditional Chinese notion of universal moral and civilizational transformation (*hua* 化) in the *Debate on Iron and Salt*. Composed during the first-century BCE political backlash against Emperor Wu's activism, the dialogue dramatizes a court debate between Emperor Wu's strategist and the "Classical Scholars" (*wen xue* 文學) who seek to replace his materialist values and failed "methods of calculation" (*ji shu* 計數). The work sympathizes with these Classicists who repeatedly demand *fan ben* 反本, a punning phrase that simultaneously refers to a "return to agriculture" and a "return to fundamental values" (lit. "return to the root"), that is, the values encoded in traditional classical texts.[64] The Classical Scholars interpret *tianxia* restrictively as empire or the Central States (in contrast to Guanzi's larger "world"). Unlike Emperor Wu's adviser, they promote *yitong* (一統 "unified rule").[65] The Classical Scholars want the Han empire to become the idealized archaic Central States of the Five Classics that spreads its domain through moral suasion: "The Duke of Zhou [a paragon in classical texts] cultivated virtue and the Yue and Shang clans [i.e., foreigners] came. They followed goodness like shadows or echoes. If in government one is devoted to using virtue to make close alliances, what does one have to worry about the other not being transformed [*hua*]?"[66] The salient division is that between those with and without knowledge of the ritual propriety (*li* 禮) and moral righteousness

---

63. The text takes as its main speakers the historical Duke Huan of Qi 桓公 (685–643 BCE) and his eponymous adviser Guanzi (Guan Zhong 管仲 [685–645 BCE]).

64. The debate took place soon after Han Emperor Wu's death. The author, Huan Kuan, makes his clear sympathies with the Classical Scholars in the final chapter.

65. Wang 1983: 160, 531. According to the *Debate on Iron and Salt*'s Classical Scholars, the Emperor should be satisfied that "the empire is unified" (天下一統), instead of waging expansionist wars against the Xiongnu in the northwest; now that "the Central States have become unified" (中國為一統), he should focus instead on the unrest within the borders. Outside the *Debate on Salt and Iron*, unified rule does become associated with expansionist enterprise. According to the second-century BCE *Shiji* (*Records of the Grand Historian*), Li Si tells the future Qin Emperor that he has the might and talent to "destroy the feudal lords, to accomplish the imperial enterprise, and to bring the empire under unified rule." See *Shiji* 87.2540.

66. Wang 1983: 525.

(*yi* 儀) encoded in classical texts, that is, between the morally (rather than ethnically) superior Central States (the Hua 華, Xia 夏, Zhou 周) and the benighted foreigner (e.g., Yi 夷, Di 狄). Subordination of subject to ruler (and wife to husband) is constitutive of this moral order. Cosmopolitan in the sense of open to all people (rather than a respect for differences), the Classicist *tianxia* depends on "conversion" (*hua*) to its universal system of text-based moral-cultural values. With the historical rise of the classically trained bureaucracy, the Classicists' cultural cosmopolitanism (later known as Confucian universalism) became increasingly identified as the only Chinese imperial paradigm.

Modern theorists rightly argue the need to contextualize the conceptual genealogy of cosmopolitanism in international frameworks of cultural contact, and especially within the social history of empire.[67] This chapter has argued that this conceptual history is further complicated by the problem of translation, that is, by the conflation of distinct (and rhetorically particular) locutions within antiquity, between antiquity and modernity, and in the translingual negotiation between various antiquities and modernities of unequal status.[68] The ongoing enterprise of comparing (often connected) cosmopolitan empires draws on the cosmopolitan spirit of cultural or regional inclusiveness (i.e., the spirit of the Stoic *kosmios* or the Classical Scholar's *tianxia*). For example, in differentiating two modes of historical integration across ancient Mediterranean and Near Eastern empires—assimilation versus subordination—this volume crucially focuses on the historical imperial response to cultural difference. To this, this chapter has sought to re-engage the more conflicted imagination—the subjunctive what-ifs and would-thats of those whose neologisms and ethical worlds were forgotten, short-lived, unrealized, re-appropriated, or actively stamped out in establishing a pedagogical narrative of imperial cosmopolitanism.[69]

---

67. On historicizing cosmopolitanism in relation to cultural contact and histories of universalism, see Anderson 1998. On cosmopolitanism and empire, see, e.g., Cheah 2006, Pagden 2000, Nussbaum 1997, Breckenridge 2002.

68. On the politics of translation under conditions of unequal exchange, see Liu 1995.

69. On this subjunctive or minor mode, see Gandhi 2014.

7

"Father of the Whole Human Race"

Ecumenical Language and the Limits of Elite Integration in the Early Roman Empire

Myles Lavan

Lavan analyses Roman efforts to integrate local elites in the eastern provinces of the early Roman empire. He reviews the many sources of difference—legal, cultural and ethnic—that divided local populations from each other and from their Roman rulers, highlighting in particular the gap between the imperial elite and local elites in the east of the empire. He shows that Roman rulers and civic elites engaged in a dialogue of decrees and letters that worked to bridge that gap by imagining an empire in which 'the whole human race' was equally subject to the emperor. The chapter illustrates the importance of discursive practices in bridging the divide between imperial and local elites even in an empire normally taken as the model of integration. It also demonstrates that assimilation and subordination were not mutually exclusive. Rome is our exemplar of the assimilative mode and assimilation can certainly be seen at work in the west of the empire, where the Romans largely ignored existing cultural traditions. In the east, however, they can be seen continuing earlier practice, recognising and appropriating an existing discourse of power to speak to a particular, culturally distinct sub-set of subjects.

THE Roman empire is often presented as the paradigmatic example of cultural integration in an imperial context. By the fourth century CE, as John Weisweiler shows in the next chapter, it is certainly difficult to draw a line between imperial and local elites, as the former becomes the "political arm of the landowning classes of the Mediterranean world." But it is all too easy to take the process of elite integration for granted for the earlier period, ignoring the many forms of difference that divided provincial elites from their Roman rulers (and each other) and the imaginative work that was required to overcome them. This chapter explores efforts to represent the propertied classes of the east of the empire as privileged members of the imperial order in the first century CE. I focus on the east because that is where the problem of difference was most acute, with most local notables marked off from their Roman rulers along multiple axes of difference, including culture, ethnicity, and legal status. The chronological focus allows me to bring out the contrast with the fourth-century empire discussed in the next chapter and significant continuities with earlier empires.

I begin by developing the ideas adumbrated in our introduction about the limits of integration in the early empire, highlighting the persistence of diversity and indeed its accentuation by Roman administrative practice. The imperial state cultivated difference within the subject population and also imposed several overlapping hierarchies of persons and communities, most notably by distinguishing Roman citizens from non-citizens and Italians from provincials. I also show that the imperial elite that governed the empire remained relatively exclusive in its social, juridical, cultural, and ethnic profile and viewed itself as such: its members saw themselves as elevated above the "allies" they ruled. The second half of the chapter explores efforts to bridge the divide between the imperial elite and provincial elites in the east of the empire. I focus on one key medium of communication between the two groups, the letters written by Roman emperors and provincial governors to Greek cities and associations. These letters are remarkable for their recurring references to imperial concern for "all men" or "the whole human race"—a strikingly ecumenical rhetoric which implicitly denies the relevance of the legal, cultural, and ethnic differences within the population of the empire. The letters simultaneously deploy an aristocratic rhetoric of honor and virtue which "recognizes" the merits that the propertied classes of the east would have claimed for themselves. The combination of ecumenical and aristocratic language was ideally suited to appeal to the Greek-speaking, largely non-citizen families that dominated the cities of the east by inviting them to view themselves as members of a global aristocracy. But its importance can only by appreciated if we grasp the very real differences that this vision obscures.

Difference and Hierarchy

Processes of political and cultural integration are certainly among the most striking features of the early Roman empire when seen in historical perspective. The most famous is the gradual extension of Roman citizenship, historically the key distinction between the imperial people and its allies and subjects, to individuals and communities in the provinces. The Roman state had enfranchised freed slaves, immigrants and some conquered peoples from early in its history, though citizens remained a minority of the population of Italy until the first century BCE. Following the Italian revolt in the co-called Social War of 90–88 BCE, Roman citizenship was granted en masse to all of Italy south of the Po and later extended to the area between the Po and the Alps in 49 BCE.[1] The next stage was the enfranchisement of the provinces. From the first century BCE, growing numbers of non-Italians became Roman citizens by serving in the Roman army, by holding magistracies in their own communities, by virtue of a special imperial grant to themselves, their family, or their city or as ex-slaves freed by Roman citizens. The process continued until 212 or 213 CE, when the otherwise infamous emperor Caracalla took the radical step of granting citizenship to all or almost all the free inhabitants of the empire.[2]

The first century of the Principate also stands out for the breadth and depth of cultural change across the vast territory ruled by Rome. This reveals itself in an unprecedented convergence of material culture across the Mediterranean and deep into temperate Europe.[3] The Roman empire is also remarkable for the mobility of persons and things, facilitated by the central sea which distinguishes it from earlier, continental empires. Some groups in particular—administrators, soldiers, traders, and cultural experts (philosophers, *rhetors*, physicians), not to mention slaves—traveled vast distances and often spent much of their lives far from where they were born.[4] Commodities such as wine, olive oil, and grain were moved across the Roman world in unprecedented volume, driven by the need to supply staples to the major cities of the empire and to the army on the frontiers.[5] The great cities of the empire were multilingual agglomerations which drew their populations from all over the empire, none more so than Rome itself.[6] Writers both ancient and modern have described the city of Rome as the world in miniature (often by exploiting the fortuitous assonance of *urbs* and *orbis* in Latin).[7]

Yet these signs of integration should not be allowed to obscure the persistence of local difference. Given the technological constraints of the preindustrial world, this massive territory inevitably remained highly heterogeneous, particularly outside the cities. This can be glimpsed in, for example, the evidence for the survival of many local languages.[8] Even at the elite level, there were notable differences between highly urbanized and less urbanized zones, such as between the south of France (Gallia Narbonensis) and the other northwestern

---

1. Sherwin-White 1973.
2. Sherwin-White 1973 with Lavan 2016 for a quantitative perspective.
3. Woolf 1995 and Woolf 2012: 222–6. See also Ando 2000, esp. ch. 9, on the penetration of everyday life by Roman administrative rituals.
4. See, e.g., Moatti 2006 and the papers in Compatangelo-Soussignan and Schwentzel 2007, Carroll 2006: ch. 8 on four western cities, Verboven 2009 on traders abroad, and Scheidel 2004 and Scheidel 2005 for an attempt to quantify human mobility in Italy.
5. Harris 2000.
6. See Noy 2000 on the evidence for immigration to the city of Rome
7. Edwards and Woolf 2003. Cf. Christ 1938: 81–3 for the trope in ancient texts.
8. See, e.g., Harris 1989: 175–90 on the persistence of languages other than Latin and Greek.

provinces. Even more pronounced was the divide between the west, where the dominant language was Latin, and the east, where it was Greek. Even within regions, we see not just the persistence but the intensification of local identities under Roman rule.[9] The Roman imperial state assumed and indeed worked to reinforce the heterogeneity of its population, structuring the provinces into a mosaic of small autonomous communities most of which (Roman and Latin communities excepted) were expected to adhere to a distinct normative order rooted in local traditions.[10]

The empire also established a hierarchical ranking of persons and communities that reflected its origins as a conquest state. Central to Roman law was the distinction between those who were Roman citizens (*ciues Romani*) and those who were not (*peregrini*). The boundary between citizen and non-citizen was certainly permeable, as I have already observed. But it is important not to exaggerate the scale of enfranchisement in the first century. Even in 212, on the eve of Caracalla's universal grant and after three centuries of enfranchisement, it is highly unlikely that more than a third of the free population of the provinces were Roman citizens.[11] The epigraphic evidence shows that there were still a significant number of non-citizens among the municipal elite, at least in the east of the empire. Even in the second century CE, some of the wealthiest individuals in the east—great benefactors like Opromaoas of Lycia or Menodora of Sillyon—were not Roman citizens.[12] The citizen minority enjoyed a range of concrete privileges which elevated them above the rest of the population of the empire, not to mention the symbolic importance of citizen status. In the public sphere, for example, Roman citizens were shielded from summary beating or execution by a governor or other magistrate by a right of appeal. Non-citizens enjoyed much more limited protection against the use of violence by the Roman authorities. Even when convicted of a crime, citizens might hope to be treated with greater leniency than non-citizens.[13] In the private sphere, non-citizens faced a number of disabilities, including being unable to inherit from a Roman will, which excluded them from the circulation of capital through legacies, an important mechanism of horizontal cohesion among the citizen elite.[14]

Roman administrative practice also created a distinction between Italians and provincials. In the early Roman Principate, Italy was marked off from the rest of the empire symbolically by not being called a province (hence

9. Whitmarsh 2010.
10. Ando 2015c: 53–5.
11. Lavan 2016.
12. Opramoas spent more than a million denarii (four times the senatorial census) on benefactions to around thirty cities (Kokkinia 2000). Menodora commemorated benefactions amounting to a total of either 350 or 700 thousand denarii, between one and three times the senatorial census (*Inscriptiones Graecae ad Res Romanas Pertinentes* III: 800–2 with Coulton 1987: 175).
13. Garnsey 1970: ch. 11.
14. Kaser 1955–9: 576.

"provincial" means non-Italian) and practically by not being subject to a provincial governor, instead being supervised directly by magistrates in Rome.[15] Residents of Italy also enjoyed a number of legal privileges, most notably in the fiscal sphere.[16] They were exempt from the *tributum*, the most important tax the Roman state exacted from its subjects, which was levied exclusively on the provinces.[17] Citizen communities in the provinces (though not citizens in peregrine communities) enjoyed the same privilege, by virtue of the "Italian right" (*ius Italicum*). The discrepancy was obvious and potentially meaningful. As the Christian Tertullian put it, liability to tribute was a "mark of enslavement" (*nota captiuitatis*).[18]

These are real distinctions grounded in law and administrative practice. There was also a subjective but still important distinction between Italians and other ethnicities. Like the Persians and Hellenistic Greeks and Macedonians before them, the Italians formed a great imperial diaspora.[19] That diaspora had its origins in the second and first centuries BCE, when individuals probably numbering in the region of a hundred thousand settled abroad to capitalize on the economic opportunities opened up by empire. They were reinforced by a massive program of colonization carried out by Julius Caesar, Augustus, and others in the second half of the first century BCE which saw the foundation of around a hundred colonies outside Italy, with several hundred thousand Italian colonists.[20] The Italian diaspora was further swelled, though at a slower pace, by emigration and colonial foundations in the first century CE. These Italians and their descendants could and did claim to be more "Roman" or "Italian" than other provincial citizens. They were also disproportionately represented in the two imperial aristocracies, the equestrian and the senatorial orders. There were other distinctions created by the Roman state, including those between more and less privileged cities and between men of higher and lower social rank, but these should suffice to illustrate the difficulty of imagining "all men" as equal subjects of the empire.

MASTERS OF THE WORLD

The processes of integration outlined above did not erase the distinction between imperial elite and local elites that had characterized earlier empires, even if the line did become blurred in a few regions. The responsibility, the prestige, and the profits of ruling the empire were largely the preserve of an

15. Eck 1979.
16. Other privileges discussed further at Lavan 2013a: 76.
17. Brunt 1981, Neesen 1980.
18. Tertullian *Apology* 13.6.
19. Purcell 2006.
20. Brunt 1971: ch. 15.

office-holding elite drawn from two aristocracies, the senatorial and equestrian orders (supplemented by the slaves and freedmen of the emperor's household). As late as the first century BCE both orders were overwhelmingly composed of Italians. Access to the imperial elite was in principle open to wealthy families in the provinces through the grant of Roman citizenship, admission to the equestrian order, and then recruitment to administrative and military posts. But the process was gradual, and ever slower toward the top of the social hierarchy. The limited evidence at our disposal suggests that men of provincial origin became a majority in the equestrian order in the second half of the first century, but remained a minority in the senate until the end of the second century.[21] Moreover, the recruitment of provincials, particularly to the senate, was highly selective. A disproportionate number of provincial senators came from veteran colonies with a strong Italian element and otherwise from a small number of highly urbanized sub-regions, such as southern France, southeastern Iberia, and later Western Anatolia and northern Tunisia. For most of the first two centuries CE, the senate remained far from the trans-regional aristocracy it would become by the fourth century.

Its members continued to espouse a distinctly imperial identity. This is most evident in literary texts. Much of what we know of as Latin literature was produced by, or at least for, the office-holding elite. Many authors were senators who held office in Rome and the provinces; many more were equestrians. Most of the rest moved in the same social milieu, writing in Rome with the support of senatorial or equestrian patrons.[22] Latin literature does offer some parallels to the ecumenical rhetoric I will discuss in the second half of this chapter, but they are relatively rare. The most famous is a passage from the encyclopedic *Natural History* written in the 70s CE by Plinius Secundus ("Pliny the Elder"), an equestrian from north Italy who pursued a career in the emperor's service, holding numerous military and civil offices in the provinces. Opening a survey of the geography of Italy, he interjects an encomium of the peninsula:

> I know that I might be judged ungrateful and lazy-minded—and rightly
> so—if I were to mention in so brief and cursory a fashion the land that is
> simultaneously the nursling and the parent of all other lands, chosen by
> divine will to make heaven itself more famous, to herd together scattered
> empires [*imperia*], to soften men's manners, to unite so many peoples'
> dissonant and feral tongues in dialogue in a common tongue, to bring

---

21. Duncan-Jones 2006: 189–90 and Devijver 1991 on the *equites* (the latter based exclusively on equestrians in military service); Hammond 1957 on the senate, to be supplemented with Panciera 1982 and Eck 1995–8: ii:289–96. Halfmann 1979 demonstrates the rarity of senators from the eastern provinces in the first century.

22. See White 1993: 211-22 for the predominance of senators and equestrians among known writers of Latin verse.

civilization [*humanitas*] to man, and—in short—to become the common fatherland [*patria*] of all peoples in the whole world.[23]

This is heady stuff. Pliny credits Italy with a divine mandate to create a single universal empire that will produce the political and cultural integration of the whole human race. It is worth pointing out that this is a description of a project, not of the state of affairs in the first century CE as Pliny saw it. In any case, the frequency with which this particular passage is quoted should be cause for concern. It is in fact a highly idiosyncratic text, not just in its precocious vision of a single *patria* for all mankind but also its interest in the cultural changes brought about by Roman rule and its identification of Italy, rather than Rome or the Roman people, as the imperial power.[24]

Far from espousing an ecumenical vision of an undifferentiated community of subjects, the overwhelming majority of Latin authors insist on internal divisions within the population of the empire.[25] It is striking that Latin of this period lacks an umbrella term for all the subjects of the empire.[26] The closest equivalent is the phrase *omnes gentes* ("all the peoples"), but that evokes ethnic diversity simultaneously with political unity, implicitly distinguishing the *gens Romana* from other peoples.[27] *Provinciae* ("the provinces") is often used in similar contexts, the provinces standing by metonymy for their inhabitants, but it excludes Italy, implicitly dividing periphery from center. The terms available to denote persons as opposed to groups are even more obviously discriminatory. *Peregrini* ("foreigners") encompasses all free persons who are not Roman citizens, strikingly making no distinction between those within the empire and those outside it. *Provinciales* ("provincials") denotes the inhabitants of the provinces, as opposed to Italy. By far the most common term is *socii* ("allies"). This originated as a term for the Italian peoples that Rome subordinated but did not formally annex and soon became an umbrella term for all non-citizens under Roman hegemony; by the second century CE it would become capable of encompassing citizens in the provinces as well.[28] It remains the term most often used to denote the populations administered, protected, or abused by provincial governors well into the second century. According to Quintilian, the good orator does not allow "the complaints of the *allies*" to go unpunished, referring to provincials'

---

23. *nec ignoro ingrati ac segnis animi existimari posse merito, si obiter atque in transcursu ad hunc modum dicatur terra omnium terrarum alumna eadem et parens, numine deum electa quae caelum ipsum clarius faceret, sparsa congregaret imperia ritusque molliret et tot populorum discordes ferasque linguas sermonis commercio contraheret ad conloquia et humanitatem homini daret breuiterque una cunctarum gentium in toto orbe patria fieret.* (Pliny *Historia Naturalis* 3.39)
24. Lavan 2013b: 207–8.
25. Lavan 2013b, esp. 17–19, 25–72, 243–4.
26. See further Lavan 2013b: ch. 1.
27. Sherwin-White 1973: 437–46, Lavan 2013b: 34.
28. Lavan 2013b: ch. 1.

right to bring extortion charges against former governors (*Institutio Oratoria* 12.7.2). Pliny the Younger praises Trajan for reforming the supply of provincial grain to Rome so that it was no longer "plundered as if from the enemy territory with the *allies* complaining in vain" (*Panegyricus* 29.3). Suetonius writes that Augustus in a moment of crisis kept existing governors in office to ensure that "the *allies* were kept under control by tried and experienced men" (*Augustus* 23.2). Fronto lists among the emperor's duties "to use edicts to restrain the faults of the *allies*" (*Ad Antoninum de eloquentia* 1.5). The "allies" are always implicitly, and often explicitly, contrasted with the Roman citizen body or the imperial center. The term itself, with its connotations of association, emphasizes their exclusion from the Roman *res publica*. Only in the fourth century, after Diocletian's provincialization of Italy, do the terms *provinciae* and *provinciales* acquire new currency as terms for the whole population of the empire.[29]

Roman writers do not just distinguish the Roman people (or some more exclusive community) from its subjects, they regularly insist on Roman supremacy. This is most striking when it is articulated in the language of chattel slavery. Throughout my period *dominus/-a* ("master"/"mistress") is the most common epithet for the Roman people and the city of Rome, with Roman writers boasting of the supremacy of the "master people" (*populus dominus*) and "mistress city" (*urbs domina*).[30] Perhaps most famously, Vergil—whose epic poem the *Aeneid* quickly established itself as perhaps the single most widely read and most influential text in the Latin literary corpus—had the god Jupiter promise supremacy to "the Romans, *masters of the world* [*rerum dominos*], the togate race" (*Aeneid* 1. 282). For most Latin authors throughout this period, to be Roman was to be part of an imperial people. It was an exclusive identity which presupposed the existence of a subject population.

ECUMENICAL RHETORIC

Despite the relatively exclusive composition and identity of the imperial elite, its members did in some contexts seek to bridge the divide that separated them from local elites throughout the empire. The question of how provincial elites were invited to see their place within the Roman order is obviously a massive subject with an extensive bibliography.[31] A full account could not limit itself to the official pronouncements of the emperor and other agents of the imperial state. It would have to engage with administrative practice as well as discursive

---

29. Lavan 2013b: 69–70.
30. Lavan 2013b: 91–2.
31. Key studies include Ando 2000, on the communicative actions of the Roman state and their role in eliciting provincial loyalty, Noreña 2011, on the imperial values propagated by imperial coinage and their role in reinforcing local elites' strategies of distinction in the Latin west and Meyer-Zwiffelhoffer 2003 on governors' interactions with local notables in the east.

production, images as well as texts, the private as well as the public sphere. That is obviously impossible in the compass of a single chapter. I focus instead on one particularly important site of dialogue with the local elites in the east of the empire—the letters of Roman emperors and provincial governors to Greek cities and associations, always written in Greek.

Like Republican magistrates before them, the Roman emperors engaged in an ongoing exchange of imperial letters and civic decrees. In so doing, they were continuing a tradition that had been established under the Hellenistic kings.[32] Hundreds of cities and some private associations wrote individually to the emperor on a wide variety of occasions—such as his accession, the adoption of a successor, birth of a son, or a notable victory—and apparently always received a response.[33] The imperial replies survive in relatively large numbers, because many individuals and communities chose to monumentalize the emperor's words by inscribing them on stone. We have copies, sometimes fragmentary, of some three hundred imperial letters to communities in the east of the empire.[34]

The letters are remarkably homogeneous in both form and content from the reign of Augustus well into the third century CE. From the perspective of this chapter, their most striking feature is their ecumenical perspective on the Roman empire. The letters tend to concentrate on the personal relationship between the emperor and the particular community in question, but when they do broaden their focus to the rest of the empire, they turn to a set of markedly ecumenical categories. From the very beginning of the Principate, Roman emperors write of their concern for "all the cities" (πᾶσαι αἱ πόλεις), "the inhabited world" (ἡ οἰκουμένη), "all men" (πάντες ἀνθρώποι), and "the whole human race" (τὸ πᾶν τῶν ἀνθρώπων γένος)—all categories which obscure the divisions within the population of the empire.[35] At the same time, the Greek equivalents of the terms which Latin texts use to denote a category of imperial subjects— "the allies," "the provinces," "the provincials," "the foreigners"—are notably absent. The same ecumenical rhetoric can also be found in the letters and edicts of provincial governors from the reign of Augustus. They describe the emperor as the beneficent ruler of all mankind and give no hint of any divide within the population of the empire. In 10 BCE, for example, Paullus Fabius Maximus, governor of Asia under Augustus, issued an edict proposing that all the cities of Asia realign their calendars so that the year would begin with Augustus's

---

32. Welles 1934, Bertrand 1990, Ma 2002, Bencivenni 2014. For the Republican antecedents to the imperial letters, see Sherk 1969.

33. Oliver 1989: 11–15; see further Millar 1977: 410–34, Millar 1988, Eck 2009, and Eilers 2009.

34. The majority are collected by Oliver 1989. Most of the rest are catalogued by Anastasiadis and Souris 2000: 2–12. Subsequent discoveries can be found by consulting the indices of *L'Année Epigraphique*. On the individual and group agendas that determined which texts were monumentalized, and the distortions they may have introduced into the surviving corpus, see Eck 1995–8: ii. 359–82 and Lavan 2013b: 215–16 and 233.

35. See Lavan 2013b: 222–6. Examples can also be found by using the lexical index to imperial constitutions in Anastasiadis and Souris 2000.

birthday. Justifying this unprecedented honor, he writes: "[Augustus] has given to *the whole world* [πάντι τῶι κόσμωι] a different appearance, [a world] which would have met its ruin with the greatest pleasure, if Caesar had not been born as the common good fortune of *all men* [τὸ κοινὸν πάντων εὐτύχημα]."[36] Some fifty years later, Paullus's son Paullus Fabius Persicus, himself governor of Asia under Claudius, issued an edict shoring up the finances of the temple of Artemis at Ephesus. In an elaborate preamble which expounds on the duties of a good governor, he professes to be inspired by the example of the emperor: "I am incited to this policy by the example of the most excellent and truly just ruler who has embraced *the whole human race* [πᾶν τὸ τῶν ἀνθρώπων γένος] under his particular care."[37] Shortly after the proclamation of Galba, the prefect of Egypt, Tiberius Iulius Alexander, issued a long edict responding to a number of petitions complaining of abuses by Roman officials. It too opens with a preamble professing the concern felt my both emperor and prefect for their Egyptian subjects. The prefect assures Egyptians that they "may more confidently hope for everything pertaining to your security and happiness from the Emperor Galba Augustus, who has brought light to us for the safety of *the whole human race*" (ἐπὶ σωτηρίᾳ τοῦ παντὸς ἀνθρώπων γένους) and goes on to say that "the gods have reserved the security of *the world* [οἰκουμένη] for this sacred age."[38]

The universalism of these imperial pronouncements is not unqualified. The emperors and governors may obscure the juridical, ethnic, and cultural divisions within the population of the empire, but they do so only to replace them with the social distinctions that were embedded in the Hellenistic discourse which they had adopted.[39] The aristocratic language of honor and virtue pervades the imperial and presidial letters to Greek cities. Vespasian commends a synod of athletes for their honor and ambition (τὸ ἔνδοξον καὶ φιλότιμον, Oliver 1989: no. 37). Hadrian notes the "antiquity and nobility" (ἡ ἀρχαιότης καὶ ἡ εὐγέν[εια], Oliver 1989: no. 62) of the city of Delphi and the "ancient nobility" of Cyrene (τῆς παλαιᾶς ... εὐγενείας, Oliver 1989: no. 121), classes Didyma among the "honoured cities" (τὰς εὐδ[οξούσας πόλει]ς, Oliver 1989: no. 87) and praises Aphrodias as "worthy of honour" (τειμῆς οὖσαν ἀξίαν, Oliver 1989: no. 69). Antoninus Pius praises Coronea for acting "as befitting Greek men" (πρέποντα Ἕλλησιν ἀνθρώποις, Oliver 1989: no. 115). Marcus Aurelius and Lucius Verus promise to protect Borea's honor (ἀξίωμα, Oliver 1989: no. 167) and praise the Athenian Areopagus as the "oldest and most honourable" among the Greeks (πρεσβύτατον [τῶν ἐν τοῖς Ἕλλησι συνεδρίων καὶ] ἐνδοξότατο[ν], Oliver

---

36. Sherk 1969: no. 65, 7–9.

37. Smallwood 1967: no. 380, 5–17.

38. Smallwood 1967: no. 391. Mourgues 1995b argues compellingly that the solar imagery indicates that the edict was originally composed while Nero was emperor, and hastily amended after news of Galba's accession

39. The importance of a shared aristocratic honor-culture in the Roman empire is well illustrated by Lendon 1997 and Meyer-Zwiffelhoffer 2003.

1989: no. 173). Marcus Aurelius notes the Athenians' honor (δόξη, Oliver 1989: no. 184). Septimius Severus commends Aezani as an honorable city (πόλις ὄντες ἔνδοξος, Oliver 1989: no. 213).

Individuals too are singled out for praise. Claudius commends Diogenes of Antioch as having being worthy (ἄξιος) of Roman citizenship (Oliver 1989: no. 28). Antoninus Pius praises Meleager of Balbura for his pursuit of honor (φιλοτιμία, Oliver 1989: no. 159) and commends the reputation (ὄνομα) of Valerius Zoilus (Oliver 1989: no. 154). A particularly striking feature is the letters of recommendation that individuals and communities solicited to testify to the standing of their most distinguished citizens.[40] The most famous examples are in the dossier of texts honoring Opromoas, a second-century CE Lycian magnate, which were inscribed on the walls of his funerary monument at Rhodiopolis.[41] The dossier includes almost forty letters written by Antoninus Pius and other Roman officials to the Lycian League and its component cities, all testifying to Opramoas's standing. Like other communities in the east of the empire, the Lycians looked to the Roman emperor as the final arbiter of local distinction.

The combination of ecumenical and aristocratic rhetoric was a potent mix. The ecumenical element promoted elite cohesion by obfuscating the juridical, cultural, and geographic distinctions that divided local elites from each other and from their Roman rulers. The aristocratic element simultaneously worked to preserve, even reinforce, the strategies of distinction they employed to distinguish themselves within their local communities. It invited those who regarded themselves as preeminent in honor and virtue—whatever their legal status or cultural or ethnic identity—to see themselves as part of an empire-wide, even universal, aristocracy.[42]

A LOCAL IDIOM?

It is worth dwelling on the fact that this ecumenical vision is expressed not just in Greek rather than Latin, but in a highly stylized discursive form, the royal letter, which the Roman emperors had inherited from the Hellenistic kings. The ecumenical categories themselves—"the whole human race" and "all men"—are relatively novel, without parallel in the surviving royal letters.[43] But a close reading of the earliest Roman examples suggests that the innovation came not from the emperors themselves but from the provincial communities to which they were responding.

---

40. Kokkinia 2003.
41. Kokkinia 2000.
42. Here I betray the influence of Nicholas Purcell's incisive Gray Lectures at the University of Cambridge in 2010.
43. There are no parallels in Welles 1934, Lenger 1980, or Hatzopoulos 1996.

Josephus in his *Jewish Antiquities* quotes the text of an edict which Augustus issued in 12 BCE in response to an embassy from the Jews of Asia complaining of maltreatment by the Greek cities in which they lived. Augustus reaffirms the privileges of the Jews and provides for the publication of his edict: "I order that the decree that was given to me concerning the piety which I observe to all men (ὑπὲρ τῆς ἐμῆς εὐσεβείας ἧς ἔχω πρὸς πάντας ἀνθρώπους) and in appreciation of C. Marcus Censorinus [then governor of Asia], along with this edict, be very prominently erected in the place dedicated to me by the Koinon [provincial assembly] of Asia."[44] The fact that the reference to his piety to all men occurs within a clause describing the content of the Jews' decree suggests that Augustus is reproducing the language with which the Jews of Asia (like any Greek polis or association) had addressed themselves to him in their edict.

Shortly after Augustus's death, the new emperor Tiberius wrote a letter to the city of Gythium in Laconia, again in response to an embassy:

> [Tiberius Caesar] Augustus son of [the deified] Augustus, *pontifex maximus*, holding tribunician power [for the sixteenth time], to the ephors and city of the Gytheates, greetings. The ambassador sent by you to me and to my mother, Decimus Turranius Nicanor, delivered your letter in which were recorded the laws you had established for veneration of my father and honour to us. I praise you for this; I consider it proper for all men [πάντας ἀνθρώπους] in general and for your city in particular to maintain exceptional honours which are due to gods for the great benefactions of my father to the whole world [εἰς ἅπαντα τὸν κόσμον], but I myself am content with the more moderate honours which are proper for men. (Oliver 1989: no. 15, ii)

Like Augustus, Tiberius uses ecumenical language, telling the citizens of Gythium that it is proper for "all men" to give divine honors to the late Augustus on account of his benefactions to "the whole world." The two instances of ecumenical language occur within the accusative and infinite construction governed by προσήκειν ("it is fitting that . . .") with which Tiberius expresses his approval of the city's actions as reported in its letter. This suggests that Tiberius too is reproducing the language of the text to which he was responding.

A few years later, in 19 CE, Tiberius's nephew and adoptive son Germanicus issued an edict in response to an effusive acclamation he had received at Alexandria:

> Germanicus Caesar, son of Augustus, grandson of divine Augustus, proconsul, proclaims: The good will which you ever display when you see me I accept gladly, but those invidious divine acclamations of yours I reject

---

44. Josephus *Jewish Antiquities* 16.165. On its authenticity, see Pucci Ben Zeev 1998.

absolutely. For they are suitable to him alone who is truly the saviour and benefactor of the whole human race [μόνῳ τῷι σωτῆρι ὄντως καὶ εὐεργέτῃ τοῦ σύνπαντος τῶν ἀνθρώπων γένους], namely my father and his mother, who is my grandmother. The deeds reputed as mine are but an additional working of their divinity. Thus if you do not obey me, you will compel me not to appear among you. (Oliver 1989: no. 17, trans. Oliver)

Germanicus styles Tiberius the savior and benefactor "of the whole human race." But he is obviously repeating language the Alexandrians had used in their acclamation. The use of ὄντως ("truly") indicates a correction. The Alexandrians had acclaimed *him* "saviour and benefactor of the whole human race"; he tells them that title is appropriate only to his father the emperor.

Confirmation that the impetus for this ecumenical language came from the periphery rather than center can be found in the fact that precisely the same universal categories—"all men" and "the human race"—are commonly associated with the emperor in city decrees and in private and public dedications to the emperor from throughout the Greek east. From the beginning of the Principate, individuals and communities in the east were eager to elide the important distinctions within the population of the empire and represent the emperors as the benefactors of all their subjects.[45] An honorific decree of the provincial assembly of Asia refers to Augustus as "father of the fatherland and of *the whole human race*" (πατρὸς τῆς πατρίδος καὶ τοῦ σύνπαντος τῶν ἀνθρώπων γένους)—a formulation which expands on the title *pater patriae* awarded to Augustus by the Roman senate by extending the scope of the emperor's paternal concern from his *patria* to all mankind.[46] A private dedication to Augustus and Tiberius at Olbia uses the same formula: "to the father of the fatherland and of *the whole human race*" (πατρὶ πατρίδος καὶ τοῦ σύμπαντος ἀν[θρ]ώπων γένους).[47] Another decree of the *koinon* of Asia from Halikarnassos, celebrating the birthday of a first-century emperor (probably Augustus or Gaius), styles the emperor "both father of his own fatherland the goddess Rome and Fatherly Zeus and saviour of *the common human race*" (πατέρα μὲν τῆς [ἑαυ]τοῦ πατ[ρ]ίδος θεᾶς Ῥώμης, Δία δὲ πατρῷον καὶ σωτῆρα τοῦ κο[ι][ν]οῦ τῶν ἀνθρώπων γένους).[48] A decree of the city of Kos from 4 CE praises Augustus for his benefactions "to *all men*" ([ταῖς εἰς πάντας ἀνθρ]ώπους εὐεργεσίαις).[49] A private dedication to Claudius at Hyllarima in Caria styles the emperor "saviour and benefactor of *all men*" (τὸν

45. See further Ando 2000, esp. chs. 8 and 9.
46. *Inscriptiones Graecae ad Res Romanas Pertinentes* IV 1756.101-102. See further Ando 2000: 403.
47. *Inscriptiones Orae Septentrionalis Ponti Euxini* I² 181.
48. *Ancient Greek Inscriptions in the British Museum* 894.
49. *Inschriften von Olympia* 53.

πάντων ἀνθρώπων σωτῆρα καὶ εὐεργέτην).⁵⁰ A decree of Maroneia in Moesia praises him as "founder of new benefits for *all men*" ([κ]τίστης νέων ἀγαθῶν ἄπασιν ἀνθρώποις).⁵¹

This sample of Greek texts honoring the emperors is intended only to illustrate the ubiquity of the universalizing categories "the human race" and "all men" in the civic discourse of the cities of the east. The individuals and communities in the east of the empire who produced these texts were reconfiguring a rhetoric of power that had been developed to describe the relationship between the Greek cities and the imperial powers to which they found themselves subject, first the Hellenistic kings and later the Roman Republic. The ecumenical tropes of the Augustan period have antecedents in the representation of "the Romans" as the "common benefactors" of Greek cities throughout the second and first centuries BCE and in what John Ma has called the "generalising idiom" in the dialogue between the Seleucid kings and their subjects, according to which the king was represented as the benefactor of "all Greeks."⁵²

But truly ecumenical categories such as "all men" and the "whole human race" remain extremely rare in the Hellenistic period. As noted above, they never appear in the substantial corpus of royal letters. The only parallels are in a handful of texts produced by subject communities. Most of these come from the Ptolemaic kingdom. The so-called Canopus decree of 238 BCE, an honorific decree passed by a synod of the priests of the temples of Egypt, claims that the birth of Ptolemy III "was the origin of many good things for *all men*" (ἡ καὶ πολλῶν ἀγαθῶν ἀρχὴ γέγονεν πᾶσιν ἀνθρώποις).⁵³ A decree of the city of Alexandria dating to 176-175 BCE praises Ptolemy VI on the grounds that "he bestowed benefactions on our city Alexandria and *all men*" ([εὐηργέτησε τὴν πόλιν ἡμῶν Ἀλεξαν[δρεί]αν καὶ πάντας ἀνθρώπους).⁵⁴ A petition to Ptolemy VI and Cleopatra II (161-160 BCE) praises them for their consideration "for *all men*" (δι᾽ ἣν ἔχετε ... πρὸς πάντας ἀνθρώπους εὐγνωμοσύνην).⁵⁵ It is striking that the best evidence for a shift from a Panhellenic to a truly ecumenical rhetoric in the Hellenistic tradition comes not from the Seleucid empire but from Ptolemaic Egypt. The first example is from one of the trilingual synodal decrees that Christelle Fischer-Bovet analyzes in her chapter, a new form developed by the Egyptian priests in the later third century BCE, which blended elements of the traditional hieroglyphic sacerdotal decree with the civic decree of Greek cities such as Alexandria. Perhaps it was the Egyptian priests who first styled

50. *Hyllarima Inscriptions* 17.
51. *Supplementum Epigraphicum Graecum* LIII 659.
52. Romans as "common benefactors": Erskine 1994; Seleucids: Ma 2002: 187–8.
53. *Orientis Graecae Inscriptiones Selectae* 56. On this decree and its context, see Fischer-Bovet, this volume.
54. *Sammelbuch griechischer Urkunden aus Ägypten* VI 8993.
55. *P Paris* 29.

kings benefactors of "all men," inviting them to overlook the important distinction between Greeks and non-Greeks in Ptolemaic Egypt.

In any case, my point is that the ecumenical rhetoric of the Roman emperors represents the elaboration of a discourse of power native to the Greek east. In the aftermath of the battle of Actium, the inhabitants of poleis all over the Greek world turned to an existing but under-exploited cosmocratic rhetoric to represent the unprecedented power of the Roman emperor and simultaneously to invite the emperors to collude in ignoring the distinctions between citizens and noncitizens or Italians and non-Italians which would mark them as subalterns. Because the Roman emperors continued the dialogue of letter and decree which they had inherited from the kings, this ecumenical style was first reproduced (and implicitly endorsed) by Roman emperors in their responses to civic decrees and then gradually established itself within the rhetoric of imperial pronouncements.

This collaborative creation of a new discourse of power is a good example of what John Ma has called "empire as interaction."[56] It also has parallels in the practice of earlier empires to which Rome is normally contrasted. Paradoxically, this ecumenical rhetoric can be seen as yet another example of the now familiar strategy of subordination, whereby imperial states adapted local languages and ideological resources to legitimate themselves to different cultural groups within their ambit. It is unfortunate that we do not know whether this language extended to pronouncements issued in Latin to communities in the west in this period. In the epigraphic corpus, imperial pronouncements in Greek massively outnumber those in Latin, not least because western cities seem to have favored bronze for the monumentalization of the emperor's words, where eastern cities used stone.[57] Letters to western cities are especially rare; in comparison to some three hundred Greek letters from the east, we have only six Latin examples from the west.[58] It remains uncertain whether western cities communicated with the emperor as often as their eastern counterparts.[59] Even if they did, it is possible that the correspondence followed a different set of conventions, at least in the early empire. Although the sample is very small, the surviving Latin letters are uniformly shorter and more functional than the Greek letters, with their elaborate professions of mutual regard.[60] It is thus quite conceivable that the imperial state modulated its voice in the east of the empire to adjust to an existing

---

56. Ma 2002: ch. 4. It is also an important qualification to the unilateral model of communication propounded by Carlos Noreña in his important recent study of "the diffusion of imperial ideals" in the Latin west, which argues that developments in imperial rhetoric normally diffused from the imperial court to provincial communities (Noreña 2011).

57. Eck 2009: 198–202. Bronze was obviously vulnerable to being melted down for other uses.

58. Lavan 2013b: 226 n. 53.

59. Eck 2009: 198, Millar 1977: 418.

60. Mourgues 1995a: 106–9 and 121–2 argues for a strong contrast in the style of diplomatic correspondence between the Latin west and Greek east.

discursive tradition, in ways that recall the attention showed to local idioms by earlier imperial states.

CONCLUSION

In the early Roman empire, the integration of local elites remained a challenge. The divide between imperial and local elites was particularly sharp in the east of the empire, where the Roman state recognized and actively preserved a distinct cultural tradition. The men who administered the provinces, all Roman citizens, predominantly Latin-speaking and disproportionately Italian or of Italian extraction, depended on the support of propertied classes who spoke Greek, saw themselves as Greek and often lacked Roman citizenship. The letters and edicts that Roman rulers addressed to Greek communities do try to bridge those differences by situating their addressees within a global aristocracy of virtue that pays no heed to legal, cultural, or ethnic difference. But it is crucial not to confuse the world evoked by this ecumenical rhetoric with reality. That would obscure the creative work it is doing in seeking to bridge the real differences within the population of the empire—and the fact that those differences were in other respects accentuated by Roman practice.

The chapter also illustrates some of the methodological problems that beset the historical project we are engaged in. This book aims to take the subjective experience of empire seriously by exploring how imperial and local elites saw their place within different imperial orders. Any such study must proceed by the analysis of texts and images. But there are obvious limits to what can be achieved by a discursive history of this sort for any ancient empire, given the exiguity of the evidence. The challenge is to make useful generalizations about particular historical contexts without obscuring the complexities and contradictions in the surviving material (or forgetting the vastly greater volume of discourse that is entirely lost to us). We should assume that in the complex societies which we are examining important topics such as the boundaries of the political community were subjects of debate and contestation, not consensus. We should also remember that discursive space is not homogeneous or continuous, but rather articulated into distinct discourses each embedded in its own social and institutional context and subject to its own regulations and conventions. We should expect to find divergent, even contradictory, discourses coexisting in any given context. This is exemplified here by the contrasting visions of empire presented by imperial letters to Greek cities, a particularly stylized form, penned by professionals chosen for their literary competence who obviously composed with a strong sense of the long tradition in which they were writing, and Latin literature (itself a heuristic simplification which conflates different genres with their own distinct trajectories). Any adequate analysis of the subjective experience of empire has to take account of both these discourses and the tensions between them.

8

Making Romans

Citizens, Subjects, and Subjectivity in Republican Empire

Clifford Ando

The history of Roman citizenship is conventionally told as an emancipatory story. On this reading, the gradual extension of the franchise slowly erased the distinction between conqueror and conquered. Ando complicates this narrative by taking a long-term perspective which embraces both the republican and imperial periods and illustrates several massive discontinuities in the history of citizenship. He shows that the enfranchisement of aliens originally served not as reward but as punishment for defeated communities. The second century BCE saw a key departure with the innovation of conferring citizenship on office-holders in some subordinate communities. Ando highlights the paradox that this effectively devolved the right to create citiens to alien populations, while underlining its effect in reproducing local structures of social differentiation. It integrated local elites into a wider community that was exclusive and distinctly imperial in form. On this reading, the universalization of citizenship by the emperor Caracalla in 212 can thus not simply be seen as logical continuation of earlier practices. Rather, citizenship fulfilled radically different functions in different periods of Roman history.

I

In their thought-provoking invitation to the colloquium from which this volume originates, the editors invited participants to reflect upon "the role of cosmopolitan ideologies as an integrative force" in assorted aristocratic empires, the question being how such ideological structures mitigated other factors—of language, dress, culture, ecology, and distance, to name but five—that will otherwise have worked to disjoin the disparate and heterogeneous populations in ancient imperial states. Arrayed against this integrative force the editors' opening chapter sets "the exclusivist self-understandings of the imperial elite." How did these tensions work out in practice, across time? The challenge, as the editors put it, "is to take the subjective experience of empire seriously."

This chapter responds to their summons by attempting to integrate two stories that seem to belong together, but which also seem in important ways discontinuous. Each concerns the languages and significance of citizenship in the Roman empire: in one case, the history of republican citizenship in an imperial state and, in the other, the history of imperial citizenship in republican empire. But if it is clear where the two stories end—that is, in a world empire of universal citizenship—important questions regarding the historical and normative salience of the universalization of citizenship cannot adequately be addressed until we understand how that world came to be. In other words, we must eventually weave the histories of imperial and republican citizenship together, and that turns out be hard to do.

This is perhaps a surprising claim. The history of Roman citizenship has often been told, as a chapter in the history of both colonial cultural change and law. It might well seem ground well-ploughed, indeed, not worth plowing again. Indeed, so it once seemed to me. Some fifteen years ago in a work of historical ideology critique, I made the argument that contemporary histories of political belonging in Roman antiquity should be more capacious than they had been theretofore, which was to say, they should embrace more than the language and institutions of the law.[1] Histories of imperial politics that reduced political belonging to a problem of law and so indexed political change to the spread of Roman citizenship risked a simplistic and misleading processualism. Instead, I argued, varied forms of cosmopolitanism or universal citizenship as ideals achieved their first meaningful articulations during the Roman period in attempts by provincials to assert the primacy of a distinction between those inside and those outside the empire. They did so using the language of Roman propaganda, both because it was the normative language available to them most directly crafted to make universalist claims, and because doing so gave their claims purchase upon those who had rendered that language normative in the first place.

Today that judgment is worth revisiting, for at least two reasons. First, substantial normative claims have been advanced in recent years on the part of both cosmopolitanism and contemporary republicanism, both of which amount to more-or-less self-conscious recuperations of Roman ideals, articulated in the language of citizenship. On a theoretical level, this research raises questions about the extent to which the language of political belonging and legal tribunals are effective means and fora for overcoming postcolonial difference. On a historical level, one is invited to ask how far such doctrines can be abstracted from their imperial roots and recursively redeployed to dismantle the power relations that they once articulated and sustained.

---

1. Ando 2000.

Second, the field of empire studies has made significant advances over the last two decades. Historians of the ancient world now have vastly more sophisticated apparatus for situating metropolitan discourses and instruments of social differentiation, like those of citizenship in particular and the law more generally, within the social world of colonized populations.[2] This chapter draws on such work in order to pose questions of the following kind: How should we understand the relationship between metropolitan citizenship and cosmopolitan ideology? What were the functions of citizenship within Roman imperial governance? How did imperial citizenship affect structures of politics and political belonging at a local level? And what sort of politics was possible, in an imperial state in which all deemed persons were citizens?

To aid intelligibility, let me quickly sketch the argument of the chapter. The story of Roman citizenship is often told as an emancipatory one, in which the gradual extension of the franchise to noncitizens slowly erased the juridical distinction between conqueror and conquered. To tell the story in this way elides a number of distinct problems related to the functioning of metropolitan citizenship in imperial states. Early in its imperial project, for example, Rome imposed citizenship on conquered populations wholesale. In that period, citizenship cannot have functioned to differentiate conqueror and conquered, nor was it understood as a reward. Later, when grants became more selective, Rome used citizenship as a reward for local elites who de facto governed on Rome's behalf. But Rome also encouraged communities to select their leaders by democratic means. The result was that the power to grant Roman citizenship was effectively delivered into electorates composed nearly wholly of aliens, and that the difference between imperial and local citizenships merely calqued highly particularized, local forms of social differentiation. The unity of the imperial elite and indeed of the polity thus created bears a distinctly imperial cast.

To take up the terms employed by the Introduction, the history of Roman citizenship as granted through the operation of local politics reveals even Rome, "so often seen as the cosmopolitan empire par excellence,"[3] to have employed both assimilation and subordination even at the dawn of universal citizenship. We find ourselves considering the dynamics of what Seth Richardson terms the "diglossia" of imperial politics, which "required vassals and provincial elites to constantly walk a fine line between performances of compliance and autonomy."[4] This chapter's focus on the operation of local electoral politics allows us

2. Recent texts with extensive bibliographies include Burbank and Cooper 2010, Pitts 2010, Pitts 2012, and Benton and Ross 2013.

3. Lavan, Payne, and Weisweiler, this volume.

4. Richardson, this volume.

to consider the operation of subordinationist practices in a very fine-grained way. In so doing, this chapter offers a reminder of how distinctly imperial Roman culture remained, and how constrained its politics were by the material effects of its size and the inefficiency of communications and transportation technology regimes.

II

Let me commence with some remarks on the primary form of evidence available to us for writing histories of Roman citizenship. It consists in the use of Roman names or, perhaps, the advertising of one's Roman status via the use of Roman names on forms of monumental writing intended for permanent, public display. I focus on two aspects only of such texts.

First, it is the use of a Roman name that advances the claim to citizen status. Roman names in the classical period had a distinctive form, consisting of three parts (*praenomen, nomen, cognomen*), to which one might append notice of the name of one's father and the voting unit at Rome of which one was a member.[5] The use of three names thus flagged one's status as juridically Roman, even if other parts of one's name or other formal characteristics of the text flagged one's status as an enfranchised indigene: unique names, translations of non-Latinate or non-Italian names, bilingual texts, and so forth.[6]

The formal qualities of Roman nomenclature were regarded as so distinctively Roman that the Roman emperor Claudius is described in the same breath as having executed aliens for usurping Roman citizenship and likewise having forbid persons of alien status from usurping Roman names.[7] Likewise, when on one occasion the same emperor granted citizenship to Gallic indigenes who had long since usurped it, he also issued the following allowance:

> quod benificium is ita tribuo, ut quaecumque tanquam cives Romani gesserunt egeruntque, aut inter se aut cum Tridentinis alisve, rata esse iubeam, nominaque ea, quae habuerunt antea tanquam cives Romani, ita habere is permittam.

> I so grant this benefit to them that whatever they have done or transacted as if they were Roman citizens, either among themselves or with the Tridentini or with others, those things I order to be legally valid, and

---

5. I state this with all due caution regarding the historical variations in the form of Roman names: the three-name form was the norm only in a particular historical period, though as it happens, the best-attested one. For a survey, see Salway 1994.

6. For some examples, see *ILA* 2.3.9077a, from Faubourg Bel Air, with the unique "Munnesius"; 2.3.9214, from Castellum Arsacalitanum, a bilingual text; and 2.3.10036, from Beni Ziad, containing the Numidian "Sufidius."

7. Suetonius *Claudius* 25.3.

the names which they have previously had as if they were Roman citizens, I permit them to retain.[8]

Beyond such contingent documentation, we also possess normative texts that require one to state one's name or have it displayed in a specific form in order to access the rights and perform the duties of citizenship. These include statutes from Rome of the late second century BCE, specifying the form of one's name to be employed when enrolling for jury duty, as well as municipal charters from Spain in the late first century CE:[9] in both cases, one is required to provide *praenomen, nomen,* patronymic, voting tribe, and *cognomen*. It merits observation that the requirement to specify Roman voting unit applies even in Spain of the first century CE, at a place and time when the franchise as a component of citizenship had surely lost all practical meaning. This is a problem to which I will return.

The second aspect of these texts on which I wish to comment concerns the work they perform—the work metropolitan citizenship performs—in colonial politics. Granting metropolitan citizenship to select individuals within provincial populations elevated them above the communities in which they had theretofore resided. Their entry into a relationship of juridical equality with other Roman citizens was accomplished, indeed, was rendered meaningful, by the simultaneous exclusion of others. The point may be obvious, but it is not banal.

As a related matter, Roman law, which is to say, the law of the community into which they had been elevated, disallowed the continuance of certain social and economic relations with those alien in respect to the metropole.[10] The grant of Roman citizenship was thus understood to atomize individuals in respect of their immediate political and social contexts; it alienated them from the political, cultural, and religious structures that rendered poliadic localism meaningful. But if these new elites, who were local and yet Roman, were to be useful as agents of metropolitan interest, they had to remain at least partially embedded in local life.[11] Restraints and controls on the process of alienation were therefore enacted in the Flavian municipal law, and a generic acknowledgment of the existence of such controls is stated in a very late grant of citizenship preserved in Morocco and granted empire-wide application in Caracalla's decree of universal citizenship.[12] There, the phrase *salvo iure gentis,* "with local law preserved," is presumably intended to keep the new citizen sufficiently

8. *ILS* 206, translation after Sherk 1988: no. 52. On the use of fictions contingently to efface legal and cultural difference, but always by assimilating non-Roman to Roman, see Ando 2015a.

9. *Lex repetundarum* (*Roman Statutes* no. 1), line 14; *Lex Flavia municipalis* (González 1986: ch. 86).

10. Gardner 2001.

11. Again, see Richardson, this volume.

12. Morocco = the so-called *Tabula Banasitana,* Euzennat and Marion 1982: no. 94. The edict of Caracalla = *P.Giss. 40,* from the edition in Kuhlmann 1994.

embedded and powerful within his local community to render this status as agent of Rome effective. But one should also observe that its brevity bespeaks a common understanding.

This atomization in respect to the local might also be described as a form of interpellation by the center. Such a description is most appropriate to the moment of direct address that occurred in grants of citizenship, and the political impact of this moment was no doubt amplified by the transformation at once imposed and undertaken in the form of a change of name. The act of interpellation was subsequently repeated at regular intervals in the various rituals that constituted the life of the citizen, especially the census.[13] Grants of citizenship thus contributed to the birth of a distinctive form of imperial subjectivity, by which individuals came to be known to themselves, and to understand their relations with others, in light of the extraordinarily precise but also limited way in which they were known to government.[14]

This characterization of metropolitan citizenship brings to mind Anthony Pagden's critique of liberal cosmopolitanism.[15] Pagden recalls the long-standing pattern, by which cosmopolitanism has emerged as a meaningful doctrine in political discourse only in contexts of empire, in those moments, in other words, when some hegemon has sought through soft or hard power to establish itself in superordinate relation to other foci of political belonging, now rendered merely local in the context of empire. Pagden thus posed the question whether liberal cosmopolitanism should not be understood as equally the spawn of the hegemonic position claimed for itself by Anglo-American liberalism and liberal institutions.[16]

Rome occupies a special place in this history, because in universalizing its citizenship (at least, according to its lights), it bequeathed to subsequent European empires a most remarkable ideal, of empire as a project that ends in the erasure of juridical distinction between conqueror and conquered. To say this is, of course, to remind ourselves that historically, cosmopolitanism has generally not involved citizenship of the cosmos—nor was it an ethical stance, like the original position, whence to view one's obligations to all humans behind some veil of ignorance.[17] Rather, "universal citizenship" has generally meant

---

13. Ando 2000: 336–62.

14. Ando 2010.

15. Pagden 2000; see also Pagden 2003, Pagden 2005, and Dallmayr 2013: esp. 30–46. Pagden's primary target was Nussbaum 1997, but it seems to me that his critique applies quite cogently to subsequent theorists of cosmopolitanism and assorted universalisms in a liberal vein, including Appiah 2006, Held 2010, Ingram 2013, and to a point Benhabib 2006, who would have done better to heed her own anxieties about Kantian universalism. I bracket from this list Godrej 2011.

16. The Introduction provides further discussion of the relationship of cosmopolitanism to hegemonic ideologies (Lavan, Payne, and Weisweiler, this volume).

17. To a point, this distinguishes earlier cosmopolitanisms from post-Kantian ones, some of which are grounded instead in appeals to moral individualism.

citizenship of a particular state, which might or might not have pretensions to world rule, and its citizenship is deemed universal because it embraces polities once autonomous and now subordinate. Cosmopolitanism emerges from power relations. We must therefore always ask, who speaks of cosmopolitanism, metropolitans or subalterns, and to what end? What in any given context is the correlate to imperial citizenship: Remaining local? Radical alienism? Or voluntary exile? The answer to this latter question might serve as a useful index of the hegemonic power achieved by specific discourses of imperial belonging, and of their ability to capture potential alternative foci for patriotic affection and political aspiration.

III

With these considerations in mind, one should perhaps open at the end. In the high and late Roman empire, once the universalization of citizenship had occurred in actual fact, it was retroactively celebrated not simply for its emancipatory effects but as if these had been central to its motivation and its realization had been planned, indeed foreordained. In a speech of the 380s, for example, the Greek orator Libanius, from Antioch in the eastern Mediterranean, spoke as follows:

> Going forth in alliance with these gods and fighting with their foes, the Romans used to fight against their foes, conquer them and, having conquered, creating for the defeated a better life than the one they had before, taking away their fears and given them a share in their *politeia*, their citizenship and civic government. [My phrase "citizenship and civic government" translates Greek *politeia*, which is, of course, an abstraction from *polis/politês*.][18]

As it happens, Roman policy on citizenship had proved an object of fascination to non-Roman peoples, particularly the Greeks, well before the consolidation of topoi in the flowering of the praises-of-empire tradition.[19] But even a glance at this earlier literature will reveal important points of difference with the themes of Libanius's account. For example, already in 215 BCE, the Macedonian King Philip V famously wrote to the Greek city Larisa in Thrace, advising it not to be typically Greek and chary with the franchise. Rather emulate the Romans, who by granting citizenship to their manumitted slaves have so flourished in numbers that they have sent colonies to over seventy places.[20] The notion that colonization is conquest by another name—that colonization is simply

---

18. Libanius *Or.* 30.5.
19. For a survey, see Sherwin-White 1973: 397–444.
20. *SIG* 543.27–40.

imperialism through sheer fertility—is likewise a major theme in Appian's history of the Roman conquest of Italy, which combines in a most fascinating way a Greek vocabulary and political sensibility while drawing on Latinate sources otherwise lost.

Roman policy on citizenship was also a major theme in the *Antiquities* of the Augustan Greek polymath Dionysius of Halicarnassus: he makes it a theme of his preface; he observes those occasions when, on his reconstruction, Roman policy changed (e.g., the moment when they began granting citizenship to manumitted slaves); he frequently digresses, sometimes at length, to contrast Roman policy with that of named Greek polities;[21] and he allows characters in the history to comment on the patriotic affection that Roman policy wins. Three themes in these remarks deserve our attention: (1) Dionysius, too, remarks and approves that Rome granted citizenship to manumitted slaves and conquered persons (as opposed to slaughtering or enslaving all adult males and leaving their cities in ruin, which are the alternatives he envisages) (2.16.1); (2) although he imagines blanket grants of citizenship to whole populations, he also speaks of grants to specific individuals, to wit, "those from whom the *res publica* [τὸ κοινόν] might derive some benefit" (1.9.4); and (3) Dionysius quite specifically connects Roman policy on citizenship with the recruitment of bodies for its colonial project, and colonialism he understands as a form of power: in his text, it is Roman settlers at Capua who describe their countrymen as "planning to rule all Italy through their colonies" (15.3.9).

The profound distance in political consciousness in respect to Roman citizenship and the Roman imperial project that separates Dionysius and Libanius testifies to the massively discontinuous nature of the history of Roman citizenship.[22] To the history of imperial citizenship in the context of republican empire, I now turn.

IV

In regard to the early history of Rome, we are, of course, nearly wholly at the mercy of sources of a much later period, and so we cannot say anything with certainty about the languages of contemporary politics and therefore little of precision in respect to ideologies of empire and political belonging. But this much at least seems clear: citizenship in the early Republic was one of two primary means for the extension of state power, the other being the confiscation of alien land as *ager publicus*, property of the Roman state. In this period, if something—a body, a field—was not Roman, it was not governed.

---

21. Dion. Hal. *Ant.* 2.17.

22. One index of just how discontinuous that history is might be the lack of either Introduction or Conclusion to Sherwin-White's *Roman Citizenship* (1973), although it might also testify to his confidence that the nature of his project is self-evident.

Given the problematic nature of the evidence, allow me to focus your attention on three themes in this material, which I think can be discussed as features of Roman history in the sixth to fourth centuries BCE, which is to say, the early years of the Roman Republic, without the obligation to posit any developmental schema that could not be defended in a chapter of this scope. The themes are, first, the use of citizenship as a means to incorporate conquered populations within the structures of the state; second, the non-voluntarist nature of such grants; and third, the essential functioning of the people as sovereign in receiving any persons into citizenship and the state.

Two decades or so ago, thanks in large measure to Tim Cornell, scholars paid great attention to the horizontal mobility of elite families in archaic Italy.[23] Such movements were, of course, voluntary on the parts of both immigrant group and Roman state. Scarcely any attention has been paid to the forcible imposition of citizenship on defeated enemies, but it emerges as a pattern already in Cicero and Livy's narratives of the regal period.[24] According to Cicero, for example, "after Ancus conquered the Latins in war, he adopted them into citizenship and the state."[25] Livy writes similarly of Ancus on the sack of Politorium: *hostibus in civitatem accipiendis, multitudinem omnem Romam traduxit*, "the enemies having been accepted into citizenship and the state, Ancus transferred the entire multitude to Rome."[26] The same language, *in civitatem acceptis*, is likewise used at the defeat of Tellenae and Ficana. The purpose of this practice (at least in later understandings) is made clear in the speech ascribed to Lucius Furius Camillus before the settlement of Latium: "The gods have given you the power to decide whether Latium will exist or not. You could kill them all and create an empty solitude, or you could follow the example of your ancestors and increase the Roman commonwealth by accepting the conquered into citizenship and the state."[27]

The immense consequence of the imposition of citizenship, which is to say, the absolute elision of one's polity from public memory, is made clear in those moments when different outcomes are imagined for discrepant participants to some military engagement.[28] In the aftermath of Rome's defeat of the Hernici, for example, citizenship was imposed on all defeated parties. To three constituent communities who had sided with Rome in the war, however, citizenship was merely offered: they preferred that their laws and rights of intermarriage should be returned, an ancient shorthand for retaining their status as autonomous

---

23. Cornell 1995: 157–9.
24. Coskun 2009: 31–155 likewise expresses skepticism about the intentions of Rome in respect to those on whom it bestowed/imposed citizenship in the early Republic. See also Ando 2011: 86–8.
25. Cicero *Rep.* 2.33.
26. Livy 1.33.
27. Livy 8.13.
28. On public memory and change of citizenship, see Ando 2015b.

polities.[29] Not long thereafter, their example was cited by the Aequi, who were threatened with war:

> They responded that the Roman demands were merely an attempt to force them, under threat of war, to suffer themselves to become Romans. The Hernici had shown how greatly this was to be desired, when it was given to them to choose and they had preferred their own laws to Roman citizenship. To those to whom the opportunity of choosing was not given, citizenship would necessarily be *pro poena*, a form of punishment.[30]

And indeed, populations are on record declining Roman citizenship down to the Hannibalic War.[31] It is only with such politics in focus that we can appreciate the dilemma posed by the Social War, in which all possible outcomes, including integration on either side's terms, were understood to bring profound negative entailments. Not for naught does the last, contemporaneous celebration of the imposition of citizenship on the defeated derive from historiography on the outcome of that war.[32]

Finally, commencing in Livy's narrative of the later fourth century, the point is emphatically made that grants of citizenship are sovereign acts of the Roman people.[33] Proposals may be brought before the Senate and referred to the People *ex auctoritate patrum*, but the grant itself is made by statute.[34] The constitutional point is established in Livy's narrative for 188 BCE (as so often, by means of the ex post citation of an earlier pattern as though it had had a rational basis, which acquires precedential value at the moment when it carries the day). In that year, we are told, a tribune proposed a plebiscite granting full citizenship to three cities but his motion was vetoed by other tribunes because he had not put it first to the Senate. "Having been told that the *ius suffragium impertire* belonged to the people, not the Senate, they withdrew their veto."[35] The motion was therefore carried *ex Valerio plebiscito*.[36] This may seem a simple and unsurprising point; its importance will become clear shortly.

If I might digress momentarily on the language attributed here to the Aequi, *Romanos fieri*, "to become Roman": this appears to be a *termus technicus* in Roman public law, being used already in this form by Ennius.[37] Although the

---

29. Livy 9.43.22–4.
30. Livy 9.45.6–8.
31. Livy 23.20.2.
32. Granius Licinianus 35.27–34 Criniti: the Samnites said that they would enter into peace only on the conditions that citizenship be given to them and all who had fled and their property be restored. Later, *dediticiis omnibus civitas data est*, "citizenship was granted to all those who formally surrendered."
33. For an attempt to historicize this theme in Roman historiography, see Millar 2002: 122, 151–2.
34. See Livy 8.21.
35. Livy 38.36.5–8.
36. Livy 38.36.
37. Ennius *Ann.* l. 157 Skutsch = l. 169 Vahlen³ = Warmington Spuria no. 2, from [Censorinus], *De metris* in H. Keil, ed., *Grammatici Latini*, vol. VI, *Scriptores artis metricae* (Leipzig, 1874), 612: *Cives Romani tunc facti sunt Campani.* See also Livy 8.17.12 and 21.9. On the term and its importance, see Ando 2015c: 87–97.

phrase is most often used of people becoming Roman, it can also be used of Romans resigning their citizenship to enroll in a Latin colony. The term "Latin colony" refers to colonial foundations in which the population had the legal status of Latin, which in Roman law was alien in respect to the metropole but possessed certain privileges not granted to aliens. Romans who enrolled in those colonies could be described as having "become Latin." The phrases *Romanos fieri* and *Romani facti* should therefore be understood as grammatical middles, kindred to the classical term *hellênizesthai*, which only starts to be used as a transitive, with the meaning "to forcibly make someone Greek," in the Hellenistic period in the context of empire. That said, another feature of the term's usage is worth noting: one becomes Roman by becoming juridically Roman. Nowhere in any classical Roman text that I can think of does one make oneself Roman—self-fashion as Roman in language or dress or cuisine—in order to appear worthy of citizenship. (Playing at being Greek when one should act Roman is a theme of some high imperial literature, and it is in that context that the term "Romanness," *Romanitas*, to discuss matters of cultural performance is first attested, around the year 200 CE.[38]) This, too, is a point to which I shall return.

V

It is at this point, within two or three generations of Ennius and the so-called Valerian plebiscite, which is to say, in the middle and late second century BCE, that an altogether new system starts to come into view. I refer to the so-called *ius civitatis per magistratum adipiscendae*, the right of obtaining Roman citizenship through holding a local magistracy. The fullest evidence for its functioning derives from the Flavian municipal charter known principally from Roman Spain of the late first century CE, where its functioning also received abundant epigraphic attestation.[39] Copies of the charter are known from a number of cities; the text was adjusted in the most minimal way to particular localities; but the staggering majority of its content was standardized and, indeed, written in Rome.[40]

Three chapters of the statute deal with the granting of citizenship to magistrates, one specifying the right involved, the others dealing with its consequences

38. On the first surviving appearance of the term *Romanitas* ca. 200 CE in Tertullian's *De pallio*, see Ando 2015c: 46, 88.

39. See, e.g., *CIL* II 1945: L(ucius) Munnius Quir(ina) Novatus et/L(ucius) Munnius Quir(ina) Aurelianus/ c(ivitatem) R(omanam) per h[ono]rem IIvir(atus) consecuti ("Lucius Munnius Novatus of the voting tribe Quirina and Lucius Munnius Aurelianus of the voting tribe Qurina, having obtained Roman citizenship through holding the office of *duumvir*"). See also II² 5.291, 292, 308 (where the text explicitly allows that the office-holder obtain citizenship "along with his own [family members]"), 401, and 615.

40. González 1986.

for private legal relations in the aftermath of the grant. (The problem, as I have said, was that certain relations, particularly with social dependents both within the family and with ex-slaves were understood to rest upon one's juridical status; there was therefore a risk that the acquisition of Roman citizenship would have significant negative entailments, if these were not estopped.) I quote only the first clause:

> Rubric. How they may acquire Roman citizenship in that *municipium*.
>
> Those among the senators, decuriones or *conscripti* of the Municipium Flavium Irnitanum who have been or are appointed magistrates, as is laid down in this statute, when they have left that office, are to be Roman citizens, along with their parents and wives and any children who are born in legal marriages and have been in the power of their parents, likewise their grandsons and granddaughters born to a son who have been in the power of their parents, provided that no more may become Roman citizens than the number of magistrates it is appropriate to appoint under this statute. [41]

It lies in the nature of Roman history as a scholarly enterprise that nothing—or nearly nothing—is ever new under the sun. Indeed, once an institution is named (very often using labels unattested in antiquity, as is the case with the phrase *ius civitatis per magistratum adipiscendae*), it rapidly becomes part of the landscape. So it seems to me in this case. So let me stress what it enacts: Romans are henceforth made not by sovereign act of the Roman people, but through election in localities that are legally alien in respect to the metropole. In this world it is not the conqueror who selects aliens and accepts them into citizenship and the state, but those once conquered, who select candidates for citizenship according to their lights and priorities.

Of course, there is a great deal that one might say about this institution in the perspective of empire studies: it was a principal mechanism by which elites, chosen as elites through local processes of legitimation, were co-opted in service of the metropole, the grant of citizenship being understood to conduce an alignment between personal and Roman interest. And there is much, too, that one might say about the context in which the institution was probably first developed, and about the massive historical developments that enabled its export beyond the Italian peninsula. But let me focus your attention on two issues only: the politics of imperial citizenship at the time of its invention and the importance of democratic politics to its operation.

The earliest secure attestation of the *ius civitatis adipiscendae* concerns a law passed in 89 conferring Latin status on the communities of Gaul north of the

---

41. *Lex Flavia municipalis* ch. 21; translation by Michael Crawford from González 1986: 182.

Po.[42] But it has been conjectured that its existence was presumed in a law on magisterial malfeasance from the 120s BCE.[43] Alas, the text of that inscription is nearly wholly defective, and the two most plausible restorations differ crucially on the question of whether the relevant clause concerns merely those of Latin status, or those of Latin status who, despite having held office, have nonetheless chosen not to become Roman. But it does seem worth mentioning, in light of my remarks earlier, that in either restoration, the possibility appears to have been imagined at Rome that someone might decline Roman citizenship in favor of his local one, thus remaining alien in respect to the metropole. In the latter case, what was envisioned was rewarding the person declining Roman citizenship with various legal rights as if he were a citizen. There comes a time when declining Roman status is simply no longer imagined—when local identity as an alternative to Romanness is first subsumed, and later effaced—but not yet.

As regards democratic politics, it seems crucial to emphasize that the operation of the institution rested fundamentally upon the organization of local politics along democratic lines.[44] We possess from the middle and later second century BCE considerable evidence for the imposition by Rome of democratic constitutions on the cities of Greece and Macedonia, and, of course, one should probably say of many places, that Rome simply reorganized such democratic institutions as preexisted Roman hegemony. The same is true in the western Mediterranean, though the evidence there is not so chronologically concentrated. Now on one level this is not surprising: it had been a truism of empire as early as the Achaemenid hegemony in Ionia that democratic polities are the easiest for an empire to rule.[45] To invoke such comparisons, however, will only highlight the very different use to which Rome put local democratic government: under Rome, local non-elites were invited to select their own leaders not simply by way of creating a local elite; they also elected them *de iure* into imperial citizenship, and so create an imperial one.

We can thus appreciate both accuracies and inaccuracies in the praise of Rome delivered by the second-century CE Greek orator Aelius Aristides. He wrote of Roman citizenship that it deserved as much attention and admiration as all other aspects of Rome's achievement put together:

> because there is nothing like it in the records of all mankind. Dividing into two groups all those in your empire—and with this word I have indicated the entire civilized world—you have everywhere appointed to your citizenship, or even to kinship with you, the better part of the

---

42. *Lex Flavia municipalis* ch. 21; translation by Michael Crawford from González 1986: 182.

43. *Lex repetundarum = Roman Statutes* no. 1 = Girard-Senn no. 7 [Claude Nicolet], lines 78–79, on which see Ando 2015d.

44. Ando 2006: 181–2.

45. Herodotus 6.42.

world's talent, courage, and leadership, while the rest you recognized as
a league under your hegemony.[46]

But, of course, as we have seen, in many places it was not Rome, which is to say, it was not the Romans as sovereign who appointed people to citizenship. It was local politics as conducted among aliens that did that.

Roman investment in the legitimating powers of democratic institutions might be usefully contrasted with the baroque decay of democratic politics in the Greek cities of the Hellenistic period, with their fairly naked reliance on raw materialism as the basis for social prestige.[47] The elevation of women, children, and infants to local honors throughout the Hellenistic world is an important index of this: when push came to shove, it was apparently possible, even desirable, to upend gender norms rather than threaten the preeminence of wealth as the basis of social prestige. The comparative poverty of public institutions in those cities—or, one might say, the need of those communities to rely on private wealth to fund public goods in expressions of euergetism—is, of course, an essential feature of this story, even if its political import has rarely been nakedly exposed. In those places, the monopolization of both landed wealth and the means of production by elite families effectively robbed democratic politics of any real meaning. To adopt the language of John Weisweiler, one might therefore say that Greek democratic politics served to create and sustain an aristocracy of wealth, which fact its democratic and poliadic ideologies served to occlude, where Roman democratic politics of the same period, including its explicit wealth qualifications for magistracy, served to create an aristocracy of office.

VI

Let me offer now some preliminary conclusions about Roman citizenship in colonial contexts.

First, the transformation of local elites into an imperial elite, and the creation of select individuals as Romans, thus rested upon and indeed calqued local systems of social differentiation and social prestige. After all, individuals were elected locally and acquired citizenship from that fact alone. They therefore "became Roman" by virtue of having been endowed with Romanness as a juridical fact, not through any instrumentalist cultural performance or act of self-fashioning. In that sense the one-time and perhaps continuing focus of historians of colonial cultures upon questions of agency in processes of

---

46. Aristides *Or.* 26.59; translation J. H. Oliver.
47. Ando, forthcoming a.

Romanization—summarized in claims that provincials "Romanized themselves"—may have put the cart before the horse.[48]

Second, the histories of imperial government, imperial citizenship and local
government are inseparably intertwined. In this unified history, Rome played
a crucial role in the spread of democratic institutions and, consequently, in the
stabilizing of local elites—which is to say, that under Rome local elites were
elites not of birth but of office, and, I might add, one held local office by virtue
of election.

Of course, the hiving off of the governing class as an elite, and its potential
assimilation to an imperial elite, rested as a secondary matter upon its control
over the public sphere (in an ancient sense of the term): it was municipal coun-
cils that controlled the mechanisms of self-display that advertised the unique
capabilities of the elite to office, above all the use of public spaces for honorific
commemoration and institutions of public speech for thanksgiving.

To return to the point on which I opened: it might seem that I have colluded
with empire, in proposing a model of imperial belonging that effaces various
structural tensions between the local and the imperial, or the local and the
cosmopolitan, in respect to language, dress, culture, and cuisine. The varied
populations of the empire no doubt differed greatly along these axes, and many
others one might name. Furthermore, the system might also be said to have
contained the seeds of its own undoing, as the spread of Roman citizenship
gradually diluted its utility as a marker of social differentiation. A history of
cosmopolitanism must therefore pose the question, how difference might be,
could be, and was in fact both asserted and contained within a framework of
nominal ecumenism, even as one asks how claims to ecumenism were vindicated, in light of the fact of massive difference.[49] Here, Aristides is crucial
in reminding us that cosmopolitanism was ideally an ecumenism of an elite,
which functioned in part because actual unity of the elite never had to be cashed
out. Our ability to see this is diminished by our focus on formal and material
markers of elite status (e.g., exactly the sort of epigraphic evidence with which
I began) over against aspects of performance: any faith we might have in the
unity of the imperial elite should be tempered by the disdain often expressed for
local accents, for example. But, in the end, that is the nature of imperial elites,
which is to say, it lies in the nature of premodern empires that the practice of

48. For the phrase, "Provincials Romanized themselves," see Brunt 1976, 1990: 268. Brunt focuses on indigenous agency in the first instance because, in his view, Rome lacked the institutions to promote cultural
change. His language has been taken by many. A famous restatement of the problematic is Millett 1990. For an
effort to grapple with but also surmount simplistic inquiries into agency in colonial and postcolonial histories
of Rome, see Ando 2016a.

49. For readings of later edicts of Caracalla as allowing for the enforcement of particular forms of social
difference, the salience of citizenship have been diminished, see Bryen 2016 and Ando 2016b. For modern bibliography on the politics of exclusion in modern democracies, see Ando (forthcoming b).

politics never brought local elites face to face, as they did not so much govern each other (being governed and governing in turn) as govern themselves (and their subalterns) on behalf of the empire.

VII

Let me close with a few remarks about *denaturalization*, a topic connected tightly both logically and politically to those that I have discussed so far. These remarks are in large measure provoked by the splendid recent work of Patrick Weil.[50]

Cicero discussed the topic of denaturalization several times in forensic speeches, first in his defense of Caecina in 69 BCE and again in the mid-50s. His argument on all occasions is the same: it is not possible for citizenship to be taken away from a citizen, only for a citizen to relinquish it. Consider, for example, the following passage from Cicero's speech *pro Caecina*:

> [99] But if liberty or citizenship can be taken away under these most particular circumstances, do those who recall these things not understand that our ancestors desired that it should be possible for it be taken away for these reasons, but they did not want this to be possible under any other circumstances? [100] As they offer these instances from our law, so I would like them to explain by what statute or legislative act citizenship or liberty has been taken away. As far as exile is concerned, the situation can be clearly understood. Exile is not a punishment, but an escape or outlet from punishment. For those who want to escape some punishment or disaster "turn over the soil," that is, they change their seat and home. In no law of ours is it found, as it is in other communities, that any misdeed is punished with exile. On the contrary, when men avoid chains, death or disgrace, which are established (as punishments) in our laws, they flee into exile as if to an altar. If someone were willing to undergo the force of law in citizenship among his fellow citizens, he would lose citizenship only with loss of life. Because they are not willing to do this, citizenship is not taken from them; rather, it is abandoned and set aside by them. For just as in our law no one can be a member of two citizen bodies, so this citizenship is lost at that moment when he who flees is received into exile, that is, into another citizen body.

Cicero's language and argument inspires a number of reflections. First, Cicero (and other Roman authors) situate citizenship and liberty in tight correlation not because they viewed liberty as an essential quality of citizenship writ

---

50. Weil 2012.

large—the identity of one's polity being irrelevant to the question whether its citizens were free—but because the Romans as holders of empire were uniquely free. To give up Roman citizenship was to give up freedom because the freedom of all other polities—the freedom attached to all other citizenships—was defective. To quote the language of instruments of Roman international law, their freedom existed on the sufferance of Rome, which conceived itself to grant freedom and autonomy to subordinate and subjugated polities "so long as the People and Senate shall wish." They were free, they existed, because Rome had declined to enslave or destroy. We exist now under the cloud of Hobbesian sovereignty by acquisition.[51] The meaning of Scipio's claim, that freedom depends on power of command, *ex imperio libertas*, is at last clear.

Second, Cicero does not, alas, explain why one cannot denaturalize a citizen. One might gesture to the tight correlation established between citizen and citizen body through the metonymic reach of the term *civitas*. That is to say, the term *civitas* described the juridical quality of each citizen that made him a member of the polity, and it also described the membership of the polity as a collective (*civis:civitas::civitas:populus*).[52] Perhaps the ontological integrity of the unitary *civitas* depended crucially in its ongoing existence in each *civis*, out of whom it was extracted and in each of whom it was lodged synechdochically? If so, we are very close to the doctrine of the sovereign citizen as elucidated by Weil, but we have arrived there by very different means.

But if that is so, it is difficult to build a larger narrative upon this observation. Among other things, as we have already seen, the practice of granting alien communities the power of creating Roman citizens had begun several decades before any of Cicero's reflections on the topic. In other words, no simple or single developmental schema connects the separate histories of citizenship, popular sovereignty, and the sovereign citizen in the late Roman Republic.

A similar difficulty attends the history of republican citizenship in the monarchic republic. As we have seen, newly enfranchised citizens around the empire advertised their status using language, genres, and media tightly connected with Roman cultural forms writ large. They claimed a specifically republican form of citizenship: hence the proud declaration of one's voting tribe. But citizens abroad, like citizens at Rome, had long since lost any meaningful opportunity to vote for anything. Indeed, under the monarchy, as sovereignty was lodged more and more fully in the person of the emperor, it became possible on more and more pretexts to deprive citizens of citizenship. Republican citizenship is thus most visible to us, its discourse most dominant in the public sphere, when those values most esteemed in modern normative theory were wholly vitiated, if indeed, they had ever existed.

---

51. Ando 2012b: 33–6, Ando 2014: 21.
52. Ando 2015c: esp. ch. 2, Conclusion.

9

From Empire to World-State

Ecumenical Language and Cosmopolitan Consciousness in the Later Roman Aristocracy

John Weisweiler

Weisweiler's paper illustrates the radical reconfiguration of relations between imperial and local elites under a regime of 'assimilation'. More specifically, he looks at the role played by cosmopolitan ideology in the Later Roman Empire (mid-third to fifth centuries CE). Honorific inscriptions of this period enable us to trace a far-reaching shift in the public image of the emperor. Commissioners of epigraphic texts depicted him no longer as Roman magistrate, delegate of the Roman senate and the Roman people, but as global ruler, whose care extended to the whole human species. The spread of the idea of the monarch as caretaker of the entire world had material consequences. It enabled the military emperors of the third and early fourth centuries to curtail the economic and social privileges of imperial and local aristocracies, in ways which would have been unthinkable in earlier periods of Roman history. But it also reshaped the self-understandings of aristocrats. In the fourth century, some senior officials (both scions of ancient nobilis families and new men) began to present themselves as a global class, whose membership transcended divisions of ethnicity, geography and culture. The texts produced in this exalted milieu highlight the potential of Roman assimilative ideology. It had now become possible to conceive of the Later Roman Empire as a world in which local elites were no longer the subjects of universal rulers, but members of the same class.

INTRODUCTION

In a previous chapter, Myles Lavan has explored the role played by universalist ideas in the political language of the early Roman empire (first to mid-third century CE). Lavan pointed to the scarcity of cosmopolitan language in texts produced by the governing elite of the Roman empire of this period. While among Greek-speaking elites in the eastern half of the Mediterranean, the idea of the Roman empire as a unified world-state was widespread, the top strata of the imperial aristocracy in Rome for a remarkably long period of time adhered to a more exclusivist image of the political world in which they lived. In inscriptions and literary texts, senators and equestrians stubbornly insisted on the importance of the dividing lines which separated citizens from noncitizens, Italians from provincials, and members of the imperial aristocracy from all other inhabitants of the Roman empire.[1]

In this chapter, I continue the story into the later Roman empire (roughly the period from the mid-third to the fifth century CE). I will explore how the self-understandings of the governing elites of the Mediterranean world changed in the wake of the political and military crises of the third century. For this purpose, I will draw on two bodies of evidence. I begin by looking at what honorific inscriptions for emperors reveal about the ways in which the Roman political order was conceptualized by propertied classes in the Roman empire. Thousands of such texts have survived. As Carlos Noreña has shown in his groundbreaking monograph on imperial ideals in the early Roman empire, these materials offer the rare opportunity to apply a quantitative approach to the study of imperial ideology.[2] I will apply Noreña's approach to third-century inscriptions. By looking at the terminology employed in honorific epigraphy, I will trace the imperceptibly slow process by which the worldview of propertied classes in the Mediterranean world changed in late antiquity. I will then calibrate the findings derived from inscriptions through close readings of select literary texts. I focus on the evidence from imperial panegyrics. These complex texts, created by highly trained experts, offer a useful point of comparison to the more standardized rhetoric deployed by the commissioners of honorific monuments.

I will argue that both types of evidence enable us to trace a shift in the public image of emperor and imperial aristocracy. The age of globalization has witnessed the development of a new cosmopolitan ethics of recognition, which does not deplore but celebrates differences in ethical outlook between culturally, ethnically, and religiously diverse populations. In the words of Craig Calhoun, cosmopolitanism has become the "class consciousness of frequent travelers."[3] In this chapter, I suggest that among the top stratum of the ruling élite of the later Roman empire, we can discern traces of the emergence of such a new cosmopolitan consciousness. In texts written by and for leading members of the imperial aristocracy, it was claimed that the transformation of the governing elite of the empire into a global class had unlocked access to forms of virtue which had been unavailable to the ethnically exclusive rulers of Republican and early imperial Rome. For the first time in the history of the Mediterranean and the

---

1. See Lavan, this volume. On the exclusivist self-image of the Roman elite, see further Lavan 2013b.
2. Noreña 2011.
3. Calhoun 2002.

Near East, an imperial elite presented itself as a truly global class, whose members transcended divisions of ethnicity, geography, and culture. Of course, only a small group of inhabitants of the later Roman empire endorsed this idea of the senate as a world aristocracy. Still, the ideological claims advanced by the top stratum of the imperial elite expose the potential of Roman assimilative ideology. It had become possible to conceive of the later Roman empire as a world in which local elites were no longer the subjects of universal rulers, but members of the same class.

Reversing Imperial Crisis

In order to understand the parameters which shaped the relationship between state and landowning elites in the later Roman empire, it is useful to look more closely at the ways in which this constellation of authority came into being. After Augustus in 30 BCE defeated his last rival to sole power in the Roman empire, and after his lieutenants concluded wars of expansion in Illyricum and Spain, the empire entered a prolonged period of imperial peace. For the next two centuries, warfare was mostly restricted to occasional skirmishes in the frontier regions of the empire. As a result, Augustus was able to halve the size of the imperial army. The end of military conflicts enabled the imperial government to reap a significant "peace dividend." As Andrew Monson has shown, in the provinces of the early Roman empire, taxes were much lower as they had been in the competitive interstate system of the Hellenistic period.[4] Under the carapace of the imperial peace, the senatorial aristocracy in Rome and local elites dispersed over thousands of small towns of the empire were able to accumulate vast wealth. In the words of Peter Bang, a "privileged cocktail of protection, land and tax benefits was offered to those in powerful positions, who were willing to co-operate, around the provinces of the empire."[5] By sharing the profits of empire with property-owning aristocracies, Augustus and his successors bought their cooperation with the system of imperial rule. This splendid coalition with landed elites enabled emperors to maintain control over conquered territories with a staggeringly small imperial administration.[6]

But in the late second and early third century CE, the geopolitical situation of the Roman empire began to deteriorate. Prolonged contact with Roman economic and political networks increased levels of social stratification in Central European societies and led to the formation of larger political units. Already in 168 CE, a group of invaders had reached the gates of Aquileia in northern

---

4. Monson 2012.

5. Bang 2008: 93–115, cited at 104.

6. Classics accounts of the minimalist state of the early Roman empire are offered by Garnsey and Saller 1987 and Lendon 1997.

Italy. In the early third century CE, the pace of incursions accelerated. Rhine and Danube frontiers became porous, and Gaul and Balkans were ravaged by foreign armies. Meanwhile, in the east, the formation of the Iranian empire threatened the Euphrates frontier. In 238 CE, Antioch, the third-largest city in the empire, was plundered by an army under the leadership of the Great King Ardashir I. In 260 CE, Ardashir's successor Shapur I captured the Roman emperor Valerian. For the next one-and-half centuries, Roman emperors would frequently be involved in wars on two fronts against Central European and Iranian enemies.[7]

At the same time, the recurrent defeats against foreign enemies undermined the legitimacy of rulers. Since the end of the Severan dynasty in 235 CE, usurpations became frequent events. Most strikingly, after the emperor Valerian fell into Persian captivity, armies in different regions of the empire proclaimed four different emperors. For a short period of time, it seemed as if the empire might disintegrate under the weight of civil war and external invasions. But then, emperors slowly were able to reassert their authority over the Mediterranean world.[8] The reign of the emperor Aurelian (270–275 CE) was the turning point. Invading groups now began to be decisively repelled and the most dangerous usurpers defeated. Under the reign of Diocletian and his co-rulers (284–305 CE), new administrative, fiscal, and economic structures were established which would shape the course of Roman history for the next centuries.[9] Diocletian's reforms were consolidated and deepened by the emperor Constantine, the first Christian ruler in the Roman empire. By the time of his death in 337 CE, the onset of crisis had been reversed. Not only did emperors succeed in preventing the disintegration of the empire as a unified political structure. They managed to create a new "strong state" which appropriated a larger size of the surplus generated by the population of the empire than the "minimalist state" of the Principate. Christopher Kelly points to the remarkable achievements of the new empire created by the Tetrarchs and Constantine: "In the fourth century alone the Roman state raised enough revenue to enable it (among many other expenses and obligations) to pay for a professional standing army larger than that maintained in the first two centuries CE, to finance a new religion, and to found a second imperial capital at Constantinople." The Roman empire was not only again the unrivalled master over the Mediterranean world. It was also present in the lives of its subjects as never before.[10]

---

7. Excellent recent accounts of the sociopolitical history of the third century are provided by Carrié and Rousselle 1999 and Ando 2012a. On the dynamics of the Roman frontier, see Whittaker 1994 and Heather 2009.

8. The ground-breaking study Peachin 1990 establishes a firm basis for the chronology of the period. Imperial self-presentation in the third century is mapped Potter 2004: 215–98 and Manders 2012.

9. Kolb 1987, Carrié 1994, Rees 2004.

10. Matthews 1989, Brown 1992, Kelly 2004, cited at 110, outstandingly map the sociocultural shape of the strong state of late antiquity.

What made possible the impressive speed of imperial recovery? Institutional reforms certainly played a role. As Peter Eich and Christopher Kelly have shown, late antique emperors built up a centralized imperial bureaucracy which was not only much larger but also much more impervious to the pressures of local power-wielders than the patrimonial administration of the early empire.[11] Even more crucial were the fiscal transformations undertaken by the imperial government of the late third and early fourth centuries CE. Jairus Banaji, Gilles Bransbourg, and Cam Grey have elucidated the functioning of the new taxation system through which Diocletian and his successors managed to appropriate a greater share of the resources produced by their subjects.[12] But I would like to suggest that at least as important as these institutional and fiscal transformation was a shift in the *cultural* image of the Roman monarchy. If late antique emperors managed to remove privileges which had been enjoyed by landowning elites of the empire for centuries, this was only possible because the ways in which the inhabitants of the empire *thought about* the role played by the empire's aristocracies had changed. In order to understand the factors which made possible the restoration of Roman power, we need to obtain a better understanding of the subjective ways in which contemporaries made sense of the political world in which they lived.

REPUBLICAN MONARCHY

The language employed in Latin honorific inscriptions put up for Roman emperors by their subjects serves as a useful thermometer through which the change in ideological climate can be measured. By the term "honorific inscriptions," I refer to texts carved on statues, public buildings, and other monuments. From the reign of Augustus until the disintegration of the western half of the Roman empire, thousands of such inscriptions are extant. Paid for by local commissioners and often carved on expensive materials, they were designed as permanent memorials of the close relationship of the emperor with propertied elites in the Roman empire. At the same time, the material and symbolic investment made by commissioners in these texts makes them tremendously useful as markers of the ways in which the person of the emperor was perceived by Latin-speaking elites across the Mediterranean world.[13]

During the first two centuries CE, the language employed in Latin inscriptions to describe the power of the emperor was tediously uniform. The great majority of imperial epigraphy employs what we call the "official titulature"

---

11. Kelly 2004: esp. 138–84 and Eich 2005.
12. Banaji 2007, Bransbourg 2009, and Grey 2011: 178–225.
13. Pioneering studies of the ideological content of this genre of texts were undertaken by Alföldy 1984, Noreña 2011, and Witschel 2011.

of the emperor. This "official titulature" begins with his full name, followed
by the public offices and honorific titles conferred upon him by the Roman
people and the Roman senate. An inscription carved on the base of a statue
put up in Carthago Nova (modern Cartagena on the coast of southeast Spain)
in the middle of the second century CE exemplifies the genre. The text originally belonged to an honorific monument of the emperor Antoninus Pius
(138–161 CE), which had been commissioned by the local notables of the district
Carthaginiensis. In charge of the erection of the monument was a *flamen,* high
priest of the imperial cult, with the name Postumius Claranus:

> To Imperator Caesar
> Titus Aelius
> Hadrianus
> Antoninus Augustus
> Pius, father of the fatherland, four times consul,
> supreme pontiff, with tribunician powers,
> the region of Carthaginensis (put up this statue). Executed
> by Postumius Claranus, *flamen.*[14]

The text begins with the full name of the emperor (Imperatori Caesari Tito
Aelio Hadriano Antonino Augusto Pio). This is followed by the honorific title
"father of the fatherland" (PP, the abbreviation for *patri patriae*), conferred
upon Antoninus Pius in a motion of the Roman senate in the year 139 CE. Next,
readers are informed that the Roman people had elected him four times to the
consulate (*consuli* IIII), made him supreme priest of the state cult (*pontifici
maximo*), and gave him the legal authorities of the ancient Republican magistracy of tribune of the plebs (*tribunicia potestate*). From the first two-and-half
centuries CE, thousands of similar inscriptions have survived. To us, these texts
appear dull and monotonous. However, the circumstantial detail in which the
public offices of the emperor are described communicated an important ideological message. By recording the precise legal authorities of the emperor, commissioners of inscriptions such as Antoninus's statue in Carthago Nova staked
out a claim that emperors were not Oriental despots, who ruled over their subjects like a master over his slaves, but Republican magistrates, whose authority
derived from juridical acts by the senate and people of Rome.[15]

At first sight, this form of representation may appear as a meaningless survival of an outdated political tradition. As a local notable such as Postumius

14. *CIL* II 3412 = *CartNova* 43 *Imp(eratori) Caesar(i) / T(ito) Aeli[o] / [H]adriano / Antonino Aug(usto) /
Pio p(atri) p(atriae) co(n)s(uli) IIII / pontif(ici) max(imo) trib(unicia) / potest(ate) conventus / Carthag(inensis)
curante / Postumio Clarano / flamine.*
15. In taking seriously the Republican aspects of early imperial ideology, I am inspired by the innovative
recent studies by Winterling 1999, 2005, 2009. On mastery, fatherhood and other metaphors for monarchical
rule, see Roller 2001.

Claranus no doubt was well aware, Antoninus Pius owed his power not to an election by the institutions of the Roman city state, but to a dynastic adoption by his predecessor Hadrian. Nor did the senate and people of Rome impose legal limits on the emperor's authority; both in juristic theory and in social practice, the power of the emperor was unconstrained by any legal boundaries.[16] But although the ideal of Republicanism was a fiction, this fiction had real consequences. It expressed and shaped the ways in which material resources were distributed in the Roman empire.

On the one hand, the public image of the emperor as first citizen of a restored Republic reflects the special role played by senators in the structures of the early Roman monarchy. The senate consisted of the six-hundred current and former senior office-holders of the Roman state who assembled each month in the curia in Rome. By fashioning themselves as restorers of the traditional form of government, emperors staked out a claim that this tiny group of men would continue to receive an outsize share of the proceeds of empire. This promise was largely fulfilled by Augustus and his successors. Most emperors went out of their way to treat senators as their friends and to provide them with privileged access to their presence and to their patronage. This intimate relationship to the ruler of the world was highly lucrative. In the first two centuries CE, senators remained the wealthiest landowners, most powerful office-holders, and most influential brokers of imperial patronage in the Roman empire.[17]

On the other hand, the image of the emperor as Republican magistrate articulated the nature of his relationship to men such as Postumius Claranus—the ten-thousands of small-town notables who dominated economic, political, and cultural life in the provinces of the Roman empire.[18] Most cities in the western half of the Roman empire replicated Roman political institutions. They were mini-Republics, run by elected office-holding aristocracies with Roman citizenship.[19] The close resemblance between metropolitan and colonial political institutions gave the Roman political idiom potent resonance in local societies. If the emperor was a Republican magistrate, whose power was based on Republican magistracies and the supreme priesthood of the state cult, this implied that their own local authority, also based on public offices and priesthoods, was equally just and legitimate. A parallel process has been traced by Noreña in his analysis of the ethical values employed by commissioners of honorific inscriptions for emperors. He shows that town notables ascribed to themselves the same virtues as were advertised on monuments for the imperial monarch: "In this way,

16. Brunt 1977 convincingly demonstrates that the emperor's powers were also legally unlimited.
17. On economic profits, see the evidence assembled by Duncan-Jones 1982: 143; on office-holding, Eck 2000; and on patronage, Saller 1994.
18. On the social world of small-town aristocracies in the Roman empire, see most recently Zuiderhoek 2009.
19. Ando, this volume.

these local aristocrats could claim some share in the authority and legitimacy of the emperor himself."[20] I would like to suggest that by presenting themselves as priests and magistrates, local elites pursued the same purpose as through their self-fashioning as virtuous benefactors. They claimed that they were mini-emperors, whose power rested on the same juridical foundations as that of the imperial monarch in Rome. On this reading, by commissioning thousands of inscriptions and public monuments in honor of the emperor, civic elites not only expressed their loyalty to the imperial system but also justified their own preeminence in provincial societies.

From this perspective, the Republican image of early Roman emperors was not a meaningless remnant of long irrelevant constitutional forms. Rather, by depicting the ruler of the ruler of the world as a civic magistrate, senatorial aristocracy and civic elites advanced their own interests. In this sense, the careful maintenance of the idea of the emperor as a Republican office-holder aptly encapsulates the shape of the social coalition whose material interests the minimalist state of the Principate served.

From Republican Magistrate to Divine King

But in the late second and early third century CE, the traditional imperial image imperceptibly began to lose its attractiveness. Commissioners of honorific inscriptions started to experiment with new modes of representing monarchical power. To be sure, throughout this period, the traditional titulature remained (by far) the most popular way to depict the place of the emperor in Roman society. But as Noreña shows, in the reign of Commodus (180–192 CE) and under the emperors of the Severan dynasty (193–235 CE), some dedicators of honorific statues and public buildings began to use new forms of honorific terminology. The emperor's military achievements were celebrated in more extravagant fashion, and his links to the divine sphere were more explicitly articulated. A new honorific epithet appears, which had previously been carefully avoided by commissioners of honorific inscriptions: *dominus*, "master," denoting the absolute authority of a slave-owner over his human cattle. The new style of imperial representation is first found in texts commissioned by middling social strata, such as military officers, freed slaves, and mid-ranking civilian officials, then percolated upward to the higher echelons of the imperial aristocracy.[21]

In the middle decades of the third century CE, the pace of ideological change accelerated. Now the new titulatures were employed with increasing

---

20. Noreña 2011: esp. at 272–6 and at 318–20, cited at 319.
21. Noreña 2011: 225–7 and 283–97 carefully traces the gradual emergence of a new imperial image in the reigns of Commodus and the Severans. The shift in the social composition of dedicators of honorific monuments clearly emerges from the collection of evidence in his appendix at 364–415.

frequency in honorific inscriptions. They were also given official sanction by the imperial court. Since the reign of Aurelian (270–275 CE), the title *dominus* was used in imperial coinage.[22] At the same time, officially produced portraits showed the emperor no longer as clean-shaved civilian magistrate, nor as full-bearded philosopher king, but as a soldier with a rough military stubble.[23] The new trends were radicalized in the late third and early fourth centuries, during the long reigns of Diocletian and his co-rulers (284-305 CE) and of Constantine (306-337 CE). Emperors were now shown with unnaturally large eyes—as contemporary panegyrists make clear, this was an allusion to their panoptic gaze and divine omniscience. Since Constantine, the emperor appeared again clean-shaved, as a divine youth. Another shift is even more striking. Since the latter half of Constantine's reign, rulers regularly wore a diadem—a symbol of monarchical power, which had been pioneered by Hellenistic kings, but was carefully avoided by earlier Roman emperors.[24]

Titulatures change accordingly. The text carved on the base of a statue of Constantine, displayed in Trajan's Forum in Rome, exemplifies the new style of imperial representation:[25]

> To our master, renewer of the human species,
> enlarger of the empire and of Roman power,
> also the founder of eternal security,
> Flavius Valerius Constantinus, blessed,
> the greatest, pious, always Augustus, son of the
> divine Constantius, always and everywhere revered,
> Gaius Caeionius Rufius Volusianus, of senatorial rank,
> ordinary consul, prefect of the city, appellate judge of the sacred emperor,
> most devoted to his divine energy and majesty (dedicated this statue).[26]

This inscription was dedicated by one of the highest-ranking office-holders in the Roman empire. As urban prefect, Caeionius Rufius Volusianus was the chair of the senate and the senior imperial official in Rome. But although Volusianus was a member of the highest stratum of the imperial aristocracy, the inscription records none of the emperor's formal legal titles. Instead, the text squarely

---

22. *RIC* V.1 299, no. 306 *imp(eratori) deo et domino Aureliano Aug(usto)* and V.2 109, no. 841 *imp(eratori) deo et domino Probo Aug(usto)* with Alföldi 1970: 211.

23. Wegner 1979 collects the evidence.

24. On Tetrarchic portraiture and ideology, see L'Orange et al. 1984, R. R. R. Smith 1985: 180–3, Kolb 1987, and Rees 2004; on Constantine, see R. R. R. Smith 1985: 215–21, 1997, and Bardill 2011.

25. Rösch 1978 and Chastagnol 1988 excellently survey late antique honorific epithets.

26. *CIL* VI 1140 = *ILS* 692 *D(omino) n(ostro) restitutori humani generis / propagatori imperii dicionisq(ue) Romanae / fundatori etiam securitatis aeternae / Fl(avio) Val(erio) Constantino Felici / Maximo Pio semper Augusto filio divi / Constanti semper et ubique venerabilis / C(aius) Caeionius Rufius Volusianus v(ir) c(larissimus) / consul ordinarius praef(ectus) urbi vice sacra iudicans / numini maiestatiq(ue) eius dicatissimus.*

focuses on the emperor's absolute power (DN, *domino nostro*, "our master"), his military achievements (*propagatori imperii dicionisque Romanae fundatori etiam securitatis aeternae*, "enlarger of the empire and of Roman power, also the founder of eternal security") and on his larger cosmic role (*restitutori humani generis* ... *Maximo Pio semper Augusto*, "renewer of the human species ... blessed, the greatest, pious," values reinforced by the dedication *numini maiestatique eius*, to Constantine's "divine energy and majesty"). Even in the capital of the empire, and among senior members of its ruling elite, the honorific titulature of the emperors emphasized not the legal authorities conferred upon him by Republican traditions, but his divine charisma.[27]

The inscription from Trajan's Forum is typical. From the 320s onward, inscriptions containing the full array of Republican offices held by the emperor became exceedingly rare. From Constantine's death until the end of the century, only two more epigraphic texts survive which contain the traditional titulature. Commissioners of Latin honorific texts depicted the emperor no longer as a Republican magistrate, whose power was defined by the legal authorities conferred upon him by the senate and people of Rome, but as a charismatic ruler, who had been selected by divine powers to defend human civilization against barbarian enemies.[28]

FROM ROMAN MAGISTRATE TO GLOBAL RULER

The new honorific language not only expressed a new vision of the place of the emperor in the cosmos. It also articulated a new vision of the shape of the Roman political community. By representing the emperor as a Republican magistrate, early imperial inscriptions highlighted his *Roman* identity. They depicted him as representative of the *Roman* senate and the *Roman* people. In this way, early imperial inscriptions call attention to the institutions of empire. They make unambiguously clear that Rome was not a nation-state, in which all citizens are equal, but an empire, in which a Roman imperial people and a Roman imperial aristocracy ruled over a heterogeneous variety of subject communities. In this sense, the political language of Republican monarchy expressed the commitment of emperors to defend the power of senators in Rome and enfranchised local notables in the provinces. Late antique inscriptions present a stark contrast. By situating the power of the emperor in a cosmic context, they efface earthly inequalities. From the religious perspective taken by the commissioners of these texts, mundane political distinctions such as those between citizens

27. Modern scholarship tends to emphasize the resistance by the oldest Roman families to the new forms of imperial ideology developed at the imperial court—mistakenly, in my view. On the enthusiastic adoption by *nobiles* of monarchical ideology, and the symbolic and material benefits obtained by them see from the new constellation, see Weisweiler 2012 (epigraphy) and Weisweiler 2014 (literary texts).

28. On the new epigraphic protocol, see Chastagnol 1988 and Cameron 2011: 52–4.

over noncitizens, Italians over provincials, and members of the imperial aristocracy and the rest, lost in importance. As mediator between heaven and earth, the emperor extended his care not merely to the senate and people of Rome, but to all inhabitants of the world.

The transformation of the emperor from a Roman magistrate into a universal monarch emerges most clearly if we look more closely at the meaning of the new unofficial titulatures deployed by late antique rulers. I collected all Latin inscriptions in which the emperor is described as a global ruler—a monarch whose care extends indiscriminately to the "entire earth" (*orbis, orbis terrarum*, or *mundus*) or "mankind" (*genus humanum*). In total, there are 173 such inscriptions. I have allocated them to six chronological periods of roughly equal length: the Julio-Claudian dynasty (14-68), the Flavians, Nerva, and Trajan (69-117), the Antonine period (117-180), Commodus and the Severans (180-235), the third-century crisis (235-284), the Tetrarchy and Constantine (284-337), and the Constantinian and Valentinianic dynasties (337-395). Figure 9.1 traces the absolute number of Latin honorific inscriptions containing descriptions of the emperor as universal monarch. Until the end of the reign of Marcus Aurelius (161-180), ecumenical rhetoric is almost entirely absent. Only from the reigns of Commodus and the Severans do such texts become more frequent. The incidence of ecumenical language then steadily rises through the third and fourth centuries.

But absolute numbers only tell part of the story. In order to understand the role played by ecumenical language in the overall system of imperial ideology, we need to gauge the relative importance of these texts compared to the overall output of imperial epigraphy. From the mid-third century CE onward the production of honorific inscriptions drastically declined. This means that ecumenical language played a markedly more important role in late antique epigraphy than the numbers shown in figure 9.1 suggest. It is difficult to quantify this

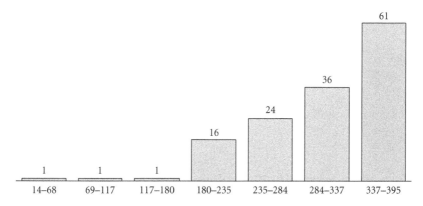

FIGURE 9.1. Imperial inscriptions containing ecumenical rhetoric from the time of Augustus until the end of the fourth century (count) © Author.

Cosmopolitanism and Empire

development precisely, as there is no corpus of dated imperial inscriptions. Still, it is possible to obtain a rough idea of the changing significance of ecumenical language. The Epigraphic Database Heidelberg (EDH) currently includes 71,000 Latin inscriptions. Although the coverage of the database is geographically uneven, it contains a majority of the inscriptions produced in the provinces of the empire, and a large proportion of Italian epigraphy. The database can be searched according to criteria such as date, genre, and persons mentioned in the text. Figure 9.2 shows what proportion of the overall number of inscriptions recording the name of an emperor and included in the EDH contains ecumenical language.

This chart enables us to nuance our understanding of the role played by ecumenical language in monarchical ideology. It becomes clear that even in the mid-third century, the idea of the emperor as a global ruler had only very limited importance. Not much more than 1% of imperial inscription included in EDH (7 out of 581) present the emperor as caretaker of the human species. It was only under the Tetrarchy and in the fourth century that the idea of the emperor as a global ruler became a significant aspect of his public persona. By now, 5% (15 out of 287) of all imperial inscriptions include ecumenical rhetoric. In the later fourth century, this proportion rises to 10% (16 out of 166). Of course, even now, most inscriptions did not include honorific terminology at all. They contained the mere name of the emperor, supplemented with the title *dominus*, "master" (which now had become an obligatory part of monarchical titulature). Even among those texts which include honorific terminology, military epithets such as *victor* or *triumphator perpetuus* predominate. Still, ecumenical language has become a recurrent feature of this genre of texts. The fact that around one-tenth of all inscriptions produced from Constantine to Theodosius

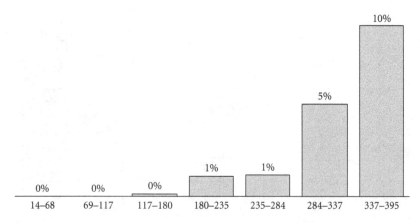

FIGURE 9.2. Imperial inscriptions containing ecumenical rhetoric from the time of Augustus until the end of the fourth century (proportion) © Author.

celebrate the emperor as a protector not merely of the Roman people, but of the entire human species, marks a significant shift in the ways in which the nature of his rulership was perceived. The care of the imperial monarch for the world became an important part of his image, in ways in which had been purposely avoided in earlier centuries of Roman history.

The rise in universalist rhetoric brings out the political significance of the new language of power. The replacement of the traditional Republican vocabulary by a new explicitly monarchical political idiom entailed a new conception of the structure of the Roman state as a political community. Rome was seen no longer as a Republican empire, in which an imperial people and an imperial aristocracy lorded it over a mosaic of conquered populations, but as a world-state, in which one divine emperor governed one unified community of monarchical subjects.

THE DOMESTICATION OF ARISTOCRACY

This new ideology provides an important context in which the fiscal and institutional reforms undertaken by emperors of the late third and early fourth centuries need to be situated. By fashioning themselves as Republican magistrates, the first emperors implicitly promised to preserve the place of the Roman senate and the Roman people as the rulers of the empire. By contrast, the idea of the emperor as a global ruler reconfigured the position of these groups in the structures of imperial rule. If the emperor was not a representative of the traditional institutions of the Roman city state, but a universal ruler who was divinely ordained to defend the entire human species against barbarian enemies, it became more difficult for the Roman senatorial aristocracy and enfranchised local notables to justify their inherited privileges. Could it not be expected that senators and civic elites should contribute to the preservation of imperial culture in the same way as less advantaged subjects of the emperor? In this sense, it is no coincidence that the elaboration of new ideologies of universal rulership was accompanied by the dissolution of several of the privileges of the traditional governing elites of the Roman empire.

On the one hand, during the permanent warfare of the third century CE, the power of local notables was curtailed. In order to raise sufficient revenues to pay the imperial army, imperial officials began to intervene more frequently and more aggressively into municipal finances.[29] The fiscal autonomy of Roman cities became increasingly precarious. Under the emperor Diocletian, a more centralized system of taxation was regularized. In line with new universalist ideology, all lands in the empire, including municipal properties, were subjected

---

29. Jacques 1984 traces the early stages of this process.

to a unified system of assessment. As Gilles Bransbourg has shown, this entailed considerable financial losses for local notables. Previously, civic lands had been tax-exempt. This enabled local elites to lease them at artificially low rents. Now this source of profit was removed by the imperial government.[30] Concomitantly, the political power of local notables was curbed. The formation of a much-expanded and salaried imperial administration, whose members claimed to derive their authority directly from the emperor, made it more difficult for municipal elites to resist the wishes of the central government. Of course, the impact of these transformations should not be exaggerated. There was no radical shift in the social composition of provincial aristocracies. As Peter Heather has pointed out, most members of the newly expanded imperial administration were recruited from former city councilors.[31] Nor did the fiscal reforms undertaken by Diocletian in any way lead to the financial ruin of municipal elites. City councilors not only maintained their private properties but also remained responsible for local tax collection.[32] This meant that they retained many opportunities for profit-making. Still, the introduction of a more unified fiscal system and the strengthening of the imperial administration had the consequence that local notables no longer exercised quite the same suffocating control over local politics, as they had in previous centuries of Roman history.[33]

On the other hand, the new ideologies of rulership made it possible to reduce the power of the senate. In the first two centuries CE, senators enjoyed a near monopoly of senior government posts in the empire; almost all of the most prestigious and remunerative executive positions—among them governorships of all provinces in which armies were stationed—were exercised by the old ruling elite of the empire.[34] However, since the early third century CE, emperors increasingly employed equestrians (members of the second-highest status group in the Roman empire) in key executive positions. The emperor Gallienus (r. 260-268 CE) prohibited senators from governorships of provinces in which armies were stationed.[35] Later emperors continued these policies. They further reduced the participation of senators in high office and increased the fiscal burden of senators. In 291 CE, Diocletian and his co-rulers divided Italy into provinces. For the first time since the Middle Republic, the homeland of empire was subjected to direct taxation.[36] Senators suffered especially from this measure, since their

---

30. Bransbourg 2008.

31. Heather 1994, 1998.

32. Schmidt-Hofner 2006 refutes the myth of a confiscation of municipal properties by the imperial state and analyzes the workings of the new system based on the distribution of tax-allotments by the central government.

33. On the transformation of civic government in late antiquity, see Whittow 1990, Laniado 2002, and Schmidt-Hofner 2014.

34. Hopkins 1985 and Alföldy 1977 map the social history of this office-holding aristocracy.

35. Christol 1986.

36. Giardina 1986.

lands were disproportionately concentrated in Italy. The emperor Constantine (r. 306-337 CE) further increased the taxes of senators. Just as every province in the empire on the imperial birthday had to pay a special tax—the *aurum coronarium*—to celebrate this happy event, so senators on these occasions had to pay a new levy, euphemistically called *aurum oblaticium*, "voluntary gold." At the same time the emperor subjected them to a new land tax, the so-called *gleba*.[37]

Of course, these reforms did not mean that the later Roman empire had a progressive taxation system. Also after Diocletian's and Constantine's reforms, municipal councilors and senators enjoyed a variety of formal exemptions and informal privileges which allowed them to pay tax rates which were proportionally lower than those of other taxpayers. Nevertheless, the fact that these groups were subjected to a variety of new levies shows that the new ideologies of rulership had shifted the horizon of the politically possible. Senators and local notables were seen no longer as imperial aristocracies, who justly could lay claim to an outsize portion of the profits of empire, but as two of several groups of monarchical subjects, each of which had to make an appropriate contribution to the maintenance of the imperial state. By endorsing the idea of the empire as an integrated world monarchy, emperors managed to contain the power of their wealthiest and most powerful subjects.

THE GEOGRAPHY OF VIRTUE

But did the development at late antique courts of new forms of universalist ideology have a larger effect on the self-understandings of Roman elites? Did the late third and early fourth centuries CE witness the emergence of some kind of cosmopolitan consciousness among the propertied classes of the empire? At first sight, there seems little reason to overestimate the impact of the integrative ideals asserted in late antique imperial inscriptions. As Benjamin Isaac has shown, Roman understandings of ethnic difference were deeply shaped by environmental theory. According to this theory, the behaviors of different peoples were molded by the climatic zones in which they lived. The cold weather of northern Europe was believed to produce men and women who exhibited impressive courage and vast physical strength, but who lacked capacities for rational thought and self-control. By contrast, peoples who had their homelands in the tropics exhibited exceptional intellectual skills, but lacked the masculine virtue required for military success and political leadership. Only inhabitants of the temperate zone exhibited the right mix between rationality and valor. In particular, the Apennine Peninsula (or so it was claimed by Roman authors)

---

37. Gera and Giglio 1984 and Giglio 2007 survey senatorial taxation in late antiquity.

featured optimal climatic conditions for developing the exalted forms of virtue which were necessary for ruling the world.[38]

This environmental theory of ethnic difference retained its popularity in late antiquity. For example, when the historian Ammianus Marcellinus included in his work (written around the year 390 CE) an excursus of the lifestyle of the inhabitants of Gaul (modern France), he proudly advertised that his account was based on Timagenes, who had written in the reign of Augustus.[39] In Ammianus's view, four centuries of Roman rule had done nothing to change the fundamental character of the Gauls, shaped as it was by the environment in which they lived: "Almost all Gauls are of imposing stature, fair-skinned, with reddish hair, fearsome because of their savage eyes, eager to quarrel and excessively insolent."[40] Ammianus is not exceptional. Depictions of foreign peoples by late antique authors follow the same stereotypes as had been deployed by their predecessors in the late Republic and early empire. Since it was not nature, not history, which defined the *Volksgeist* of an ethnic group, Roman elite writers felt no compunctions to reproduce ethnographic accounts which had been written half a millennium earlier. The unshaken faith in the tenets of environmental theory, displayed in a variety of late antique writers, might suggest that the formation of a new ecumenical political culture had only limited effects on the ethnic self-understandings of Roman elites.[41]

And yet, there are subtle signs of change. For example, in the written version of the speech of praise given by the north Italian senator Pliny the Younger on the Trajan in the year 100 CE, any mention of the emperor's place of birth is conspicuously avoided. Trajan was born in Italica (near modern Seville) in Spain and was the first provincial Roman to become emperor. Clearly, for a Roman senator of the early empire, the potential implications of his extra-Italian origins were best left unexplored in an official speech. By contrast, late antique panegyrists felt no such hesitations. When Quintus Aurelius Symmachus, scion of a prominent senatorial family, in 368 or 369 CE gave a panegyric on the Pannonian emperor Valentinian I, he made the striking claim that his northern origins made him not only equal, but superior to the Italian rulers of old.[42] Born in the snows of Illyria, the future emperor as a young man used to drink water, melted from blocks of glacier ice. Valentinian's knowledge of the harsh

---

38. Isaac 2004.

39. Amm. 15.9.2.

40. Amm. 15.12.1 *Celsioris staturae et candidi paene Galli sunt omnes et rutili luminumque toruitate terribiles, auidi iurgiorum et sublatius insolentes.* Ammianus's depiction of Gaul is incisively analyzed by Barnes 1998: 98–100 (whose excellent translation of the passage I adopt here) and Woolf 2011: 105–11.

41. The reasons for the remarkable stability of ethnographic stereotypes are explored by Woolf 2011: 32–58 and 112–17.

42. *Or.* 1. On the context of Symmachus's speeches, see the excellent accounts by Pabst 1989 and Sogno 2006: 1–30.

border regions of the empire would enable him to defeat the empire's barbarian enemies and expand the empire to the border regions of the inhabitable earth:

> Or if you decide to move forward the borders of (the province of) Pontus to the ice kingdoms of Scythia and to the frozen Tanais, there too you will pursue the fleeing enemies over all rivers, recognizing the nature of your homeland.[43]

On Symmachus's remarkable reading, the climatic (and social) conditions in the "homeland" of the Roman emperor are similar to those prevalent in what, since Herodotus, had been considered the border regions of the inhabited world: the "Scythian kingdoms" extending from the Crimea down the River Don in modern Ukraine. But precisely because of this close resemblance of his own *patria* and the lands inhabited by the wildest barbarians Valentinian is so well-suited as a ruler. It ensures that he has the manliness required to defeat the empire's most dangerous enemies.

Symmachus suggests that Valentinian established an entirely new standard of masculinity among emperors: "You established an example for future rulers of how a man needs to act."[44] None of the great Romans of previous generations can rival Valentinian's virtue. Scipio Africanus (d. 183 BCE) may have defeated Hannibal, but as a young man indulged in debaucheries in Sicily. Lucullus (d. 57 BCE) may have defeated King Mithridates of Pontus, but soon afterwards wasted the fruits of his victory by living a life of dissolute luxury on the Black Sea Coast. And although Mark Antony (l. 83–30 BCE) received victory monuments all over the Orient, after his marriage to Cleopatra his strength withered away. "These are men who triumphed? Busy with effeminate occupations, looking out for swanky beaches and fancy food?" Nor were emperors any better than these Republican leaders. Augustus ruined state finances by building new oyster banks at the Lago di Lucrino in Campania, Tiberius (r. 14-37 CE) led a life of sexual depravity in the grottos of Capri, and Marcus Aurelius (r. 161-180 CE) relaxed from the hard business of government in philosophical debates. Seen against the background of the effeminate decadence of these previous rulers, Valentinian's manly virtue stands out all the more brilliantly: "You never take a break from incessant warfare, and what you like most about Gaul is that it offers no opportunity to lead a leisured life [*otiari*]."[45] "Leisured life" (*otium*), denoting the literary and philosophical interests pursued by senators when not engaged in state business, had always been a central value in senatorial society.[46] But on Symmachus's reading, Valentinian was precisely so successful as a ruler because

43. *Or.* 1.2.
44. 1.14 *docuisti . . . fortunam regiam, quid uirum facere conueniret.*
45. *Or.* 1.16 *tibi nullae sunt feriae proeliorum, maximeque hoc in Galliis delegisti, quod hic non licet otiari.*
46. André 1962, Matthews 1990: 1–12, and Dewar 2014.

he rejected the enjoyments in which earlier leaders of the imperial state had indulged. The speech highlights not the similarities, but the differences between the current emperor and previous leaders of the imperial state. An unbridgeable gap separates this hyper-masculine emperor from Pannonia from men coming from the civilized center of the world. By celebrating Valentinian's origins in the remote border regions of the world, Symmachus turns upside-down the conventional tropes of environmental theory. In his vision of human geography, political virtue was no longer tied to one geographical space, the region of Italy in the center of the known world. Instead, different regions were able to generate their own distinctive forms of moral excellence, some of which excelled those produced in the center of the empire.

Symmachus's vision of imperial geography is not unique. For example, when in 392 CE the Gallic orator Pacatus gave a speech of praise on another Spanish ruler, Theodosius I (r. 378-392 CE), the emperor's masculine virtue is claimed to be the product of Hispania's rich nature and temperate climate (ironically, the emperor Trajan, whose geographical origins Pliny had conspicuously not mentioned, is now invoked as an example of a distinctively Spanish capacity for rulership).[47] Similarly, the North African senator Aurelius Victor, who under the reigns of Constantius II (r. 337-361 CE) and Julian (r. 361-363 CE) wrote a history of Rome under the emperors, claimed that the tough endurance which was a hallmark of the Pannonian national character made Diocletian and his co-rulers at least as well qualified for rulership as their senatorial predecessors.[48] These texts enable us to glimpse the outlines of a new cosmopolitan ethics of recognition, which does not lament but celebrate ethnic diversity among the rulers of the imperial state.[49] On this new understanding of ethnic difference, there was no longer a clear hierarchy of peoples, but different regions of the empire produced their own forms of virtue, each of which might usefully contribute to successful imperial governance.

GLOBAL ARISTOCRACY

These new cosmopolitan ideals also reshaped the public image of the imperial aristocracy. Of course, already in the early empire, aristocrats from outside Italy had regularly been admitted to the senate. By the year 200, senators of provincial origin may for the first time have outnumbered Italians.[50] However, in line with the exclusivist vision of the world adumbrated in the literature produced by

---

47. *Pan.Lat.* 2(12).4-5.
48. Aur. Vict. *Caes.* 39.16 *qui, quamquam humanitatis parum, ruris tamen ac militia miseriis imbui satis optimi reipublicae fuere.*
49. Classic formulations of such cosmopolitan ethics are offered by Appiah 2006 and Beck 2006.
50. Hammond 1957.

the Roman aristocracy,[51] the integration of provincial grandees into the ruling elite of the empire was not justified by cosmopolitan arguments. In the year 48 CE, the emperor Claudius gave a speech before the senate in which he advocated for allowing a select group of Gallic aristocrats to run for senatorial offices. This text has survived in a fragmentary epigraphic copy, discovered in Lyon, and in a literary version, created by the early second-century historian Tacitus.[52] In neither of these two texts, did the emperor justify his proposal by claiming that the Gauls possessed some unique form of virtue which should be harnessed for the benefit of the imperial state. Rather, Claudius offers two reasons for admitting local grandees into the Roman elite. On the one hand, the emperor argued that once these foreign aristocrats were transplanted into their new environment, they would soon resemble their Italian peers. To cite the version of the speech included in the work of Tacitus: "Do we regret that the family of the Balbi relocated from Spain or that some no less illustrious men came here from southern Gaul? Their descendants remain with us, and they love this home-country as much as we do."[53] On the other hand, the admission of Gallic senators would bring economic benefits: "We share already lifestyle, culture and ties of marriage with them. Let them now also bring their gold and wealth here, rather than keep it separate."[54] By invoking cultural and economic reasons to justify the integration of regional aristocracies into the senate, Claudius did not put forward an idiosyncratic view. Significantly, the legal rules to which senators were subjected in the early empire expressed precisely the same expectations. Every senator was required by law to relocate to Rome,[55] and to hold one-third of his property in Italian land.[56] The image was carefully maintained that senators were an ethnically Roman aristocracy, the rightful successors of the ruling elite of the Roman city state.

By contrast, in the fourth century CE, the senate was transformed into an explicitly trans-regional group. In the early 320s, the emperor Constantine carried out the most radical reform that the governing elite of the Roman empire ever attempted. He conferred membership in the senate on hundreds of senior office-holders and wealthy local elites, who previously only had been members of the equestrian order (the second-highest status group in the Roman empire). Many of them had never lived in Rome, nor would they live there after their admission into the imperial aristocracy. Constantine's successors continued to further expand

---

51. See the literature cited in nn. 1 and 40 above.

52. *CIL* XIII 1668 = *ILS* 212 and Tac. *Ann.* 11.24.

53. Tac. *Ann.* 11.24.3 *num paenitet Balbos ex Hispania nec minus insignes uiros e Gallia Narbonensi trasiuisse? Manent posteri eorum nec in hanc patriam nobis concedunt.*

54. Tac. *Ann.* 11.24.6 *iam moribus artibus adfinitatibus nostris mixti aurum et opes suas inferant potius quam separati habeant.*

55. Chastagnol 1977.

56. Plin. *Ep.* 6.19. According to Hist. Aug. *Marc.* 11.8, the proportion of Italian property was later reduced to one-quarter.

the senate. By the latter half of the fourth century, total membership had risen from six hundred to more than four thousand. The massive expansion of the imperial aristocracy marks a turning point in Roman social history. The senate was no longer a face-to-face society, concentrated in Rome, but a trans-regional group, whose members were dispersed across the Mediterranean world.[57] At stake in this widening of membership was not merely a reorganization of administrative structures. Rather, the expansion of the senate expressed a new cultural understanding of what it meant to be a member of the ruling elite of the Roman empire.

When in March 321 CE (some months after the beginning of Constantine's reform program) the Gallic orator Nazarius gave a speech in the Roman senate, he used this occasion to praise the emperor for the widening of senatorial membership:

> You experienced, Roma, that at last you were the citadel of all nations and of all lands the queen, now that you were promised the best men from all the provinces for your city-council, so that the dignity of the senate was no more illustrious in name than in fact, since it consisted of the flower of the entire world.[58]

Nazarius's panegyric is the first text in which the senate is a characterized not merely as the aristocracy of the city of Rome, but as an explicitly trans-regional group: "the best men from all the provinces" (*ex omnibus prouinciis optimates uiros*) and "the flower of the entire world" (*ex totius orbis flore*). As I have shown elsewhere, the same idea of the senate as a global aristocracy repeatedly recurs in the literature of the fourth century.[59] For example, when the Alexandrian poet Claudian on January 1, 399 CE in the imperial palace in Milan declaimed a speech of praise on Mallius Theodorus (an Italian small-town notable who in 399 CE was appointed to the highest office of the Roman state), he celebrated the varied origins of the high officials assembled in his audience: "Through this assembly I calculate the magnitude of the globe, here I see gathered what shines everywhere."[60] And in a speech in support of an application for senatorial membership put forward by a medium-ranking provincial notable, Symmachus depicts the senate as the aristocracy not merely of the Roman people but of the entire world: "the most noble men of the entire human species."[61]

---

57. The administrative reforms which transformed the senate into a trans-regional elite are traced by Jones 1964: 2:552–4, Löhken 1982: 103–7, Chastagnol 1992: 312–14.

58. *Pan. Lat.* 4(10).35.1–2. This translation is a modified version of the excellent rendering by B. S. Rodgers in Nixon and Rodgers 1994: 380.

59. Weisweiler 2014: 29–34.

60. *Panegyricus dictus Manlio Theodoro consuli*, Praefatio, quoted at 17–20.

61. *Or.* 6.1 *nobilissimos humani generis.* This passage is usually taken as expressing the exclusivist self-understandings of leading Roman families but this interpretation neglects that the speech was given in favor of a Spanish *curialis*. Similarly, when in *Ep.* 1.64, Symmachus calls the senate *pars melior humani generis*, it is important to keep in mind that he refers to an institution most of whose members were provincial aristocrats.

These texts depict the senate no longer as the aristocracy of the city of Rome, who ruled a variety of conquered subject territories, but as a global elite, which was composed of the best men from all regions of the empire. Like the celebration of the diverse ethnic origins of emperors, so also the praise of the transregional composition of the senate marks the emergence of a new understanding of what it meant to be a member of the ruling elite of the empire. Admission to the imperial aristocracy was claimed to depend no longer on Roman descent, nor on complete assimilation of Roman culture, but solely on the possession of superior virtue. Diversity among the imperial aristocracy was no longer lamented but celebrated.

Conclusion

It may be no coincidence that a developed cosmopolitan ethics which recognizably resembles those advocated by contemporary theorists of globalization emerged in the most fiscally and institutionally integrated empire of ancient western Eurasia. As I argued in the first part of this chapter, the development of a universalist theory of empire was a crucial prerequisite for the strengthening of state structures undertaken in the later third and early fourth century. Only by laying claim to forms of legitimacy which transcended class, ethnicity, and geography were rulers able to justify the curtailing of the privileges traditionally enjoyed by the dominant classes of the Mediterranean world and extract from them the resources necessary to defend imperial civilization against barbarian invasions. But the new ideologies not only advanced the interests of the imperial state but also created new solidarities among members of the imperial aristocracy. The fourth century was a period of unprecedented geographical and social mobility among ruling elites of the empire. The formation of a centralized and much expanded imperial administration motivated thousands of young aristocrats to leave the small towns in which they were born and to relocate to larger provincial capitals. Peter Brown describes the social consequences of this development: "Young men had to sit at the feet of males other than their fathers. Furthermore, they often did so in a city distant from their own."[62] The expansion of the senatorial order had similarly dislocating effects. While some new senators remained in the provinces from which they stemmed, many relocated to imperial courts, to the old imperial Rome or the new imperial center of Constantinople. In this situation of social dislocation, cosmopolitan culture served as a crucial (to quote Seth Richardson, this volume) "bridging device." It created new forms of commonality among a group which was more geographically, ethnically, and culturally diverse than ever before.

62. Brown 2000: 332.

At the same time, it is important not to overestimate the reach of this cosmopolitan culture. The historian Ammianus Marcellinus was in some sense the archetypal imperial cosmopolitan. He stemmed from the Greek-speaking eastern Mediterranean (probably from Antioch near modern Antakya in southeast Turkey), but wrote his monumental history of the Roman empire in Latin. By choosing to write in the imperial language, he neatly encapsulates the complex patterns of literary circulation which are often created by empires and which have been brilliantly analyzed by Alexander Beecroft.[63] And yet, as has been seen above, Ammianus's description of foreign peoples evinces few traces of a cosmopolitan consciousness. On the contrary, he closely followed theories of ethnic superiority acquired by Roman intellectuals in the age of imperial conquest. Nor is there any sign that he welcomed the integration of unprecedented number of provincial aristocrats in the senate with the same warm enthusiasm as the imperial panegyrists Nazarius and Claudian, or the Roman *nobilis* Symmachus, whose deep connections to the imperial court had procured him appointments to the highest ranks of the imperial hierarchy. At least, in his account of the imperial visit to Rome by Constantius II in 357, Ammianus reports that the emperor was dismayed to find that the senate had transformed from an "assembly of kings" into an "asylum of the whole world."[64] On this interpretation of the Constantinian reforms, the senate encompassed not the best men of the world but an international group of refugees and convicts. Whether the *bon mot* is Constantius's or Ammianus's, it shows that outside the top stratum of the imperial aristocracy, the reach of the distinctive brand of imperial cosmopolitanism developed in the later Roman empire remained limited.

63. Beecroft 2008 and 2015.
64. Amm. Marc. 16.10.5 *cumque urbi propinquaret, senatus officia reuerendasque patriciae stirpis effigies ore sereno contemplans non ut Cineas ille Pyrrhi legatus in unum coactam multitudinem regum, sed asylum mundi totius adesse existimabat.*

10

Iranian Cosmopolitanism

World Religions at the Sasanian Court

Richard E. Payne

Payne examines how the Iranian empire developed cosmopolitan techniques through which to overcome the religious contradictions of its elite. The imperial elite of Iranians cohered through Zoroastrian institutions that provided its shared self-conception and normative framework, while the local elites they subordinated frequently practiced other religions—notably Christianity— whose cosmologies were incompatible with the ruling religion. Imagining their mythical-historical lineage as the source of all human knowledge, however, the Iranians considered themselves capable of integrating—by means of subordination—even potentially contradictory cultures. The late Sasanian court adopted the cosmopolitan practice of the dialectical disputation from the Roman empire to manage difference, showcasing the banal commonalities of all religious and philosophical traditions without jeopardizing the superior position of Zoroastrianism. In acting as the authorities in intra-Christian disputations, the Iranians even became the arbiters for competing Christian claims to doctrinal truths. Iranian cosmopolitanism thus reveals the subordinating mode in action, as Christian sub-elites acknowledged their superiors as the source of their cultural legitimacy and authority as well as of imperial perquisites and privileges.

THE Iranian empire (226-636 CE) integrated the various cultures of the Near East from the Euphrates to the Oxus in a cosmopolitan political culture in late antiquity.* More than simply an effect of the diversity of Iranian territories, cosmopolitanism served as an instrument of rule, a complex of practices that enabled the imperial elite to establish its cultural superiority and universalist authority in an era of the heightened flow of texts, ideas, and objects between Eurasian regions. The ruling Iranians constituted the masters of the world, a restricted class, and granted membership in the

* I would like to thank Joan Cocks for inspired conversations that formed a backdrop for this article and Jack Tannous for a critical reading that tightened its argument.

ranks of their sub-elite only to those who accepted subordinate positions in a hierarchical ordering of persons and communities, each with their own identity in an Iranian taxonomy. From the Neo-Assyrians onward, Near Eastern empires had sought to balance distinction and commonality with the provincial elites on whose cooperation their rulers depended. In late antiquity, the proliferation of religious communities with clearly defined doctrines, boundaries, and identities—such as Manichaeism, Christianity, and Rabbinic Judaism—compounded the problem of difference.[1] The Iranian court derived its ideological and, in part, infrastructural power from such a distinct religion: Zoroastrianism. It nevertheless incorporated into its networks elites who practiced religions that actively opposed Zoroastrian doctrines, rituals, and religious specialists. Of the various religious leaders who challenged Zoroastrian supremacy, Christian bishops and monks most articulately antagonized the imperial religion and most effectively organized communities in strategic regions, such as Armenia, northern Mesopotamia, and northeastern Arabia. Christian aristocrats in these regions had become indispensable to the fiscal and military administration of the empire by the late Sasanian period (488-636 CE).[2] But their religious leaders advocated militantly monotheistic beliefs and often adopted uncompromising positions vis-à-vis religious others. In the process of integrating its provincial elites, the Iranian court thus confronted the irreconcilable worldviews, rooted in distinct cosmologies and rationalities, of two world religions.[3]

The Iranian approach to difference derived from Zoroastrianism, known to its ancient adherents as the Good Religion. According to their cosmology, the Iranian ruling elite descended from mythical universal sovereigns, the *ēr* in Middle Persian, and their lineages authorized them to reunify humanity politically in order to accelerate the cosmic restoration of the world to its primordial state of perfection.[4] As part of this process, the various populations of the world were to become subjects of the Iranian kings of kings, directly or indirectly. But the "varieties" (*sardag*) of human remained distinct. In Zoroastrian accounts, hierarchical taxonomies placed the Iranians (*ēr*) at the apex of the

---

1. Morony 1974. More recent studies emphasize the fluid, malleable nature of these evolving religious identities and structures and their engagement with Iranian society and political culture, even as Christian and Jewish leaders created distinct communities (Mokhtarian 2015, Smith 2015, Payne 2015). Debié 2010 and Walker 2014 provide current overviews of the historiography of Christianity in the Iranian empire.

2. Garsoïan 2009, Toral-Niehoff 2014, Payne 2015: 133–9.

3. The term "world religion" is used to designate a belief system that aspired either to persuade all human populations of its truth, or to subordinate all human populations to its specialists or practitioners. The relation of ancient conceptions of religion and their intercultural comparison to the nineteenth-century concept of "world religion" will be discussed below. Woolf 2009b: 32–34 suggests the rise of world religions across Eurasia was intimately connected with the development of world empires from the middle of the first millennium BCE through the first millennium CE.

4. On the origins and semantic range of the term *ēr* and the Zoroastrian ordering of human populations, see Gnoli 1989, Shaked 2008, and Shaked 2010.

discrete peoples scattered throughout the seven climes.[5] If they subordinated themselves to Iran, the Arabs, Romans, Turks, and Chinese could occupy legitimate positions as rulers of their respective populations. The traits that distinguished them ethnically were the results of the mythical-historical scattering of humanity and geography.[6] Despite their inferiority to the Iranians, they shared an origin in the creation of the benevolent deity, Ohrmazd, and a destiny in the eschatological cosmic restoration.[7] This Zoroastrian vision of a hierarchical ordering of peoples and cultures on a global scale under Iranian supremacy stimulated the innovation of practices through which human groupings could be defined, located, and included within the Iranian empire. Iranian cosmopolitanism entailed the recognition, subordination, and granting of comparative status to the various human communities within and beyond the empire that its ruling elites encountered. What we might call the Zoroastrian anthropology failed to envision was the organization of groups along doctrinal lines that cut across their ethnographic boundaries, resisted subordination, and challenged Iranian supremacy. The cosmological framework of hierarchical, differential inclusion, however, proved flexible in the face of irreconcilable cultures. The openness of the Iranian elite to institutional innovations from beyond Iran, the present chapter argues, enabled them to adapt a Roman cosmopolitan technology, the public disputation, to the task of integrating and subordinating Christian communities.

ĒRĀNŠAHR AND ITS EURASIAN CONTEXT

The name of the empire announced a cosmopolitan project: Ērānšahr, the "territory of the *ēr*," or the "Iranian empire." In claiming succession to the mythical-historical kings and warriors of the Avesta, the *ēr*, the kings of kings of the Sasanian dynasty and their aristocratic allies—largely of Parthian descent—designated themselves the supreme rulers of humanity.[8] United in their Zoroastrianism, the various aristocratic houses of the Iranian plateau formed an ethno-class of "Iranians" (*ēr*) that conceived of itself as genealogically intertwined and constituted the dominant ruling elite throughout the empire.[9] They ruled as the highest ranks of the aristocracy, the *wispuhrān* and *wuzurgān*, over a sub-elite of local landowners known as *āzādān*, as well as the

---

5. *Bundahišn*, ed. and trans. Anklesaria: 134–5.
6. Lincoln 2010: 9–10.
7. De Jong 2005.
8. Gnoli 1989.
9. The concept of the "ethno-class" is derived from the work of Pierre Briant on the Achaemenian elite that carefully preserved its exclusive, superior position in dealings with the sub-elites on which the court depended (Briant 1987: 12–15). Histories of the Iranian aristocracy tend to overemphasize its internal conflicts rather than

dependent laborers that formed the great bulk of the population.[10] But they did not only rule the empire they named after themselves. Within two decades of the inauguration of the empire in 226 CE, the second Sasanian ruler, Shapur I (r. 242–272), made the claim explicit on his coinage: "king of kings of the Iranians [*ērān*] and the non-Iranians [*an-ērān*]."[11] He adopted this title in recognition of the victories he and his predecessor, Ardashir I (r. 226–242), had achieved over the Romans, whom they had placed in an appropriate relation of subordination. It was a sign of the importance of inter-imperial relations to the self-conception of the Iranian elite. The increasingly intimate interactions between the societies of the Near East, the Mediterranean, South Asia, Central Asia, and East Asia from the fourth century BCE through late antiquity made elites aware of their near and distant neighbors.[12] Inter-imperial networks of merchants and religious specialists established institutional channels through which objects, texts, and ideas circulated, via the caravan routes of the so-called Silk Road and the Arabian desert, the sea lanes of the Indian ocean, or the roads across Iran's Roman frontiers.[13] Late antiquity was a heyday of trans-Eurasian exchange, and Iran occupied the central position in its networks. Among elites knowledgeable of Roman, Chinese, and South Asian rivals, the claim to universal sovereignty Near Eastern rulers had espoused since the third millennium BCE had become implausible.

But the early Sasanians assumed the mantle of the universal sovereign with enthusiasm. Representing the political and cultural circumstances the empire encountered, and itself precipitated, in terms that underpinned rather than undermined the ideology of Ērānšahr was the primary concern of the literary and artistic production of the court. Royal historiography, rock reliefs, and other media portrayed the kings of kings as universal rulers, to whom Roman, Indian, and even Chinese rulers were subject. As Matthew Canepa has shown, early Sasanian art carefully delineated the relationship between the kings of kings and the Roman emperors, their primary rivals, while commemorating the victories that proved their claims.[14] Not merely the enemies of Iran, the so-called caesars were granted a distinguished status in relation to their Iranian sovereigns, as partners in universal rule. The theory of a collective sovereignty of rulers across the globe acting at the behest of the kings of kings found explicit

---

its remarkable unity across the four centuries of Iranian rule (Pourshariati 2008). Wiesehöfer 2010 nevertheless offers a more balanced account.

10. On the hierarchical taxonomy of the elite and its dependents, see Colditz 2000.

11. Alram, Blet-Lemarquand, and Skjaervø 2007.

12. The material culture suggests antecedents to the well-documented, institutionalized networks of late antiquity, such as those of the Sogdians, were already in operation in the Achaemenian, Hellenistic, and Parthian periods. For examples of recent work, see Zhaoming 2014 and Nickel 2013. Chin 2014 situates the rethinking of the Han political economy in the context of heightened Eurasian interaction.

13. De la Vaissière 2005, Bukharin 2009, Banaji 2015.

14. Canepa 2009: 53–78.

expression in the historiography of the court, the so-called *Book of Kings*, from the fifth century onward. Fictive genealogies were constructed on the basis of Avestan myths that rendered the Roman emperors as well as the various nomadic rulers of Central Asia the descendants of the *ēr*.[15] Through acts of treachery in the mythical past, they had disassociated themselves from the authoritative lineage of the kings of kings, but nevertheless remained genealogically bound to the Sasanian dynasty. If willing to cooperate, they could legitimately wield power on behalf of the kings of kings within their respective domains. And there were numerous historical occasions of such cooperation—especially between the Romans and the Sasanians throughout the fifth century, and between the Turks and the Sasanians in the sixth—that appeared to put the theory of indirect global rule into practice. Recognition of Iranian sovereignty was nevertheless required of the subordinate powers. The payment of diplomatic subsidies in gold on the part of the Romans and the flow of high-value commodities from Central Asia were presented as signs of the tributary status of polities beyond Iran, in a grammar of sovereignty as readily comprehensible in China or Rome as in Iran.[16] Such symbols became particularly important in the course of the fifth and sixth centuries, when the Iranian court was compelled to submit tribute to the Huns and Turks. Behind the illusions of Ērānšahr stood a highly flexible conception of universal sovereignty well-suited to the inter-imperial dynamics of the age.

REASSEMBLING THE WORLD'S KNOWLEDGE

Universal rule required, theoretically if not in practice, the integration of all known cultures, and the Iranian court from its inception engaged in the selective appropriation of objects and ideas from non-Iran. Deriving ultimately from the mythical Iranian kingdom that had unified humanity, Roman, Chinese, and Indian civilizations possessed goods of their own, unlike the nomadic Huns, Turks, and Arabs devoid of civilization, according to the historiographical tradition of the court.[17] Iranian aristocrats reclined over Roman mosaics, donned Chinese silks, and even patronized Christian churches, all of which were prized not merely for their exoticism, but as emblems of the global reach of the elite.[18] The fiction that the accoutrements of civilization originated in Ērānšahr's mythical predecessor authorized Iranian elites to acknowledge the merits—and

---

15. Daryaee 2006, Shayegan 2011: 21–9. See Yarshater 1983, for an unsurpassed exposition of the narratives and their evolution.

16. Börm 2008, Payne 2013.

17. Firdawsī, *Šāhnāme*, v. 6, 544–5, v. 7, 139, 266–82, 304–83.

18. Ritter 2005, Canepa 2009: 75–8, Canepa 2010c: 136–40, Canepa 2014. For the church building of Yazdgird I (r. 399–420), see Payne 2011: 95–6, and for its trans-imperial political context, Fowden 1999: 52–6. Early aristocratic patrons of churches were not necessarily committed Christians (Payne 2015: 50).

sometimes even the superiority—of foreign cultures. Iranian historiography thus juxtaposed accounts of the virtues of Roman and Indian civilizations with narratives of the political history of a court often at war with those same polities. The common function of such accounts was to bolster the idea of Iran in the face of the aforementioned political and cultural challenges. The reassemblage of civilizational goods in Iran was a sign, alongside the collection of tribute, of the effective exercise of universal sovereignty. In the domain of ideas, Alexander was reported to have scattered Iranian texts and knowledge across the world after destroying a mythical library of the Achaemenians.[19] According to the fourth book of the *Dēnkard*, a ninth-century compendium of Zoroastrian cosmological texts, the second king of kings, Shapur I (r. 241-271), began the process of returning the world's knowledge to Iran:

> [Shapur I] collected the nonreligious [*ī az dēn bē*] writings on medicine, astronomy, movement, time, space, substance, accident, becoming, decay, transformation, logic and other crafts and skills which were dispersed throughout India, Rome, and other lands, and collated them with the Avesta, and commanded that a copy be made of all those (writings) which were flawless and be deposited in the royal treasury.[20]

The passage, like much of Middle Persian literature, reflects the circumstances of the late Sasanian court rather than either the third or ninth centuries.[21] What merits emphasis is the idea that Roman and Indian sciences could be "collated with the Avesta," that is, married with Zoroastrian religious thought. Because Ohrmazd, the supreme benevolent deity, was the source of all knowledge and the Avesta its primary vehicle for dissemination, Zoroastrianism necessarily encompassed all truths—scientific, philosophical, artistic, and religious—even if they were found far from Iran.[22] As the representatives of Ohrmazd, the kings of kings presided over the reunification of knowledge and its collation with the existing body of Zoroastrian thought.

It was a sixth-century empire that regularly exchanged diplomats with Rome and China, dominated the Indian Ocean trade, and expanded in the four cardinal directions simultaneously that sought to realize the unification envisioned in the *Dēnkard*. The court of Husraw I (r. 531-579) actively worked to return the sciences of India and Rome to Iran.[23] Under his patronage, the physician Burzōy translated the *Pañchatantra* from Sanskrit into Middle Persian, from which the

19. Van Bladel 2009: 32–6.

20. *Dēnkard IV*, ed. Madan, 412–13, and trans. Shaki, 119; Gutas 1998: 36.

21. Van Bladel 2009: 36–7, 41–7, nevertheless makes a strong case for the undertaking of translations from Greek into Middle Persian—for instance, of the Hermetic corpus—already during the reign of Shapur I.

22. Gutas 1998: 42–5.

23. Gutas 1998: 25–7.

Syriac and Arabic versions of the text were derived.[24] A collection of astronomical texts was also translated from Sanskrit at the court in 556, and these known instances of translation are likely only a fraction of the textual sharing between Iran and South Asia that took place—via Bactrian intermediaries as well as through direct contacts—in the sixth century.[25] Engagement with the Roman sciences was even more sustained and substantive. The Neoplatonist philosophers Damascius, Simplicius, and their associates fled a Roman empire increasingly inhospitable for non-Christian thinkers to the court of Husraw I in 531, on the strength of the reputation of the king of kings for sponsoring philosophical study.[26] Most often analyzed as a moment in the decline of traditional philosophical education in the Mediterranean, the event highlighted the awareness among Roman intellectuals that the Iranian court was receptive to their sciences. Although there were precedents for the Iranian incorporation of foreign knowledge, most notably under the Achaemenians, the scale of patronage for translation and scholarship was unprecedented in the ancient Near East. Only its direct heir, the Abbasid translation movement, would surpass the efforts of the Iranian court to collect and to comprehend the world's knowledge.

Imperial investment in scholarship foreshadows the cosmopolitan practices to which the universalist imperial ideology gave rise. The appropriation of outside learning is not in itself cosmopolitan, for the reception of Roman philosophers and the translation of Indian astronomical texts did not directly facilitate the participation of culturally distinct elites in a common political culture. Neither Romans nor Indians were integrated into Iranian political networks and institutions. The discrepancies of their worldviews could thus go unnoticed in quotidian elite interactions, and there was no political urgency to resolve their contradictions. The test of the viability of a cosmopolitanism is its capacity to facilitate the inclusion of persons with potentially contradictory worldviews in its framework.[27] Cosmopolitanism in this sense becomes an instrument through which imperial networks can be constructed and maintained, instead of a mere aesthetic. At this level, Roman philosophers and Sanskrit texts were, together with exotic commodities, merely emblems of the universalism of the court for an internal audience, rather than manifestations of an attempt to incorporate others into the empire. But the encounter with Roman and Indian philosophical schools suggests a capacity to investigate and to subordinate bodies of knowledge sharply divergent from Zoroastrianism that also enabled the court to manage cultural difference within its frontiers. A literate culture

24. Paykova 1968, De Blois 1990: 58–60, 81–7, Jany 2012.

25. Panaino 2010. Van Bladel 2011 underlines the role of Bactrian intermediaries in Sanskrit translation in the early Islamic period and the possibility of their role in Sasanian scholarship.

26. Hartmann 2002, Watts 2005, Watts 2006: 138–41. See Agathias, *Histories*, ed. Keydell, 77, recounts the ways in which some Roman intellectuals idealized the king of kings.

27. Latour 2004.

that emerged in Iran while extending beyond its boundaries in all directions, Christianity, tested the limits of Iranian cosmopolitanism, and the history of the encounter between two ideologies with apparently incompatible beliefs reveals the political efficacy of the cosmopolitan practice of the court.

Universalisms in Confrontation: Zoroastrianism and Christianity

For Zoroastrians claiming to encompass all bodies of knowledge, the presence of an articulate, highly literate class of religious specialists often well-versed in Greco-Roman philosophy and invariably hostile toward Zoroastrian beliefs within the empire, and even at court, posed an obvious challenge. The varieties of Christianity offered, moreover, a rival universalist vision of human community. The Syriac-writing representatives of the two major Christian sects, the East Syrians (inaccurately known as Nestorians) and the West Syrians (also known as Miaphysites), actively worked to bring the faith to every ethnic and/ or political community of humans, insisting that the religion could be combined with various cultures, all of which would benefit from the discipline of Christian teaching.[28] Their grandiose ambitions were at least partly fulfilled in the course of missions to South India, Central Asia, and China. By the middle of the seventh century, the patriarch of the Church of the East, based in the Iranian capital of Seleucia-Ctesiphon, could regard himself as the leader of a truly global community of Christians extending from Jerusalem to the Tang capital of Chang'an.[29] The structures of this community were nevertheless integral components of the Iranian empire. To ensure the cooperation of this potentially disruptive group, the early Sasanians—especially Shapur II (r. 309-370)—employed violence selectively against its religious leaders.[30] But they soon adopted another means of subordinating Christian bishops: patronage. In 410, the king of kings Yazdgird I established the Church of the East— whence the label East Syrian—on the model of its Roman imperial counterpart, granting ecclesiastical leaders patronage in exchange for loyally assisting the Iranian court in economic and diplomatic affairs.[31] Bishops became agents of Iran throughout the late Sasanian period, and the satellite Christian communities that appeared in China and India were perceived as Iranian institutions, so close was the link between the Church of the East and the court. However

---

28. Brock 1996 succinctly outlines the development of East Syrian doctrine in relation to its rivals. Christian universalism was often framed in terms of an ethno-religious community that subsumed all human groups into its ranks (Buell 2002).

29. On East Syrian Christianity in China and its distinctively Iranian face, see now Godwin 2015.

30. Payne 2015: 38–48.

31. McDonough 2008.

antagonistic toward Zoroastrianism, Christianity expanded institutionally in the Iranian world with the express sanction and support of a Zoroastrian elite.

When the Sasanians initially brought bishops into power, they seem to have been scarcely aware of the complexities of Christian doctrine or its hostility toward other religions. Heirs to what Jan Assmann has termed the monotheist distinction between wholly true and wholly false belief systems, Christians could find neither ethical good nor religious truth outside their own tradition.[32] To create a place for themselves in a Zoroastrian political system, Christians in the Iranian empire produced a literature that is largely anti-Zoroastrian in nature, a polemical literature designed to deconstruct the rituals and doctrines of the Good Religion in order to establish a clear, impenetrable boundary between truth and falsehood. East Syrian authors only rarely acquired detailed knowledge concerning Zoroastrian rituals and beliefs, preferring in the main to recycle Roman polemics against paganism that evinced little awareness of actual practices.[33] A substantive exchange of ideas and reformulation of one religion in light of the other of the kind Alexander Beecroft shows to have taken place nearly contemporaneously between Confucianism and Buddhism was unimaginable, at least from the perspective of ecclesiastical leaders.[34] The only known Christian to have attempted to find convergences, the East Syrian philosopher Paul the Persian, reportedly apostatized from Christianity.[35] In place of such an encounter, ecclesiastical leaders maintained the illusion that the Iranian court was a secular entity, or even partial to their beliefs.[36] This secularization of the state depended on biblical accounts of the beneficent Achaemenian rulers, as well as polemics that sought to disentangle the political from the religious. Represented as just rulers only occasionally prone to the malevolent interventions of Zoroastrian priests, neither the kings of kings nor their aristocratic associates would have recognized themselves in the accounts Christians produced. If mutual ignorance of one another's beliefs initially facilitated the integration of Christians into the network of Zoroastrian elites, the illusion of harmony could not endure indefinitely, especially as Christians and Zoroastrians became more intimate in the various institutions of the court and aristocratic sociability, ranging from fiscal offices to the royal banquet.

The first royal initiatives to investigate Christian beliefs came at the end of the fifth century. The immediate context for the inquiry was the controversy within Christian communities concerning the nature of Christ following the

32. Assmann 2008.

33. Bruns 2014 provides a survey of the material. For an exception, see Payne 2015: 75–91.

34. Beecroft 2010. The ecclesiastical elite's conception of orthodoxy could not preclude believers from participating in Zoroastrian rituals or espousing Zoroastrian beliefs (Payne 2015: 69–92).

35. Bruns 2009: 49–50, King 2013b: 63–4.

36. Becker 2014. Narratives of the clandestine conversions of Sasanian kings of kings to Christianity presented the court as only outwardly Zoroastrian, and inwardly Christian (Schilling 2008).

Council of Chalcedon in 451. By the end of the fifth century, there were advocates of the single nature doctrine (miaphysite), known as the West Syrians or Miaphysites, actively rivaling the East Syrians, advocates of the two nature doctrine (dyophysite), in Iranian territory.[37] A well-known West Syrian polemicist, Simeon of Beit Arsham, challenged the bishop of Seleucia-Ctesiphon, Babai, to a public debate ca. 500.[38] The questions under discussion were sufficiently unsettling for a *marzbān*, a frontier military commander, to have acted as the mediator of the debate.[39] The proliferation of controversies among Christians compelled the court to take an interest in their doctrines. In keeping with the scholarly tendencies that would characterize the reigns of his successors, Kawad I reportedly commanded that every religion in the empire produce a written statement (*kitāb*) of its beliefs (*i'tiqād*) for presentation to the king of kings in the last decade of the fifth century.[40] The resulting accounts of the Christian faith were translated into Middle Persian. According to this East Syrian account, in the *Chronicle of Seert*, the king of kings declared dyophysite doctrine superior to the accounts of all other religions, a topos of royal preference for a particular Christian sect that recurred in Christian narratives. At roughly the same time, however, the West Syrians reported that Kawad had granted permission to their well-known polemicist, Simeon of Beit Arsham, to travel throughout the known world in order to compile statements of the Christian faith and to determine the most universal Christian doctrine.[41] Despite their apparent distortion of events to their own purposes, these two accounts share the presumption that the court of Kawad solicited written statements of doctrine, with a view to making sense of the competing varieties of Christianity within their empire.[42] The rivalry of East and West Syrian ecclesiastical leaders brought the problem of Christian doctrine to the attention of the court from the late fifth century onward, beginning a process of investigation that would ultimately compel Iranian elites not only to adjudicate between rival Christian orthodoxies but also to address the contradictions between Christian and Zoroastrian forms of knowledge. The collection and translation of Christian texts gave the court access to the thought of East and West Syrians, but only heightened awareness of the ideological

---

37. The West Syrians organized themselves into a rival ecclesiastical community in the first decades of the sixth century, and soon thereafter introduced their doctrines to the Christian communities of Iran (Menze 2008, Saint-Laurent 2015: 80–95).

38. John of Ephesus, *Lives of the Eastern Saints*, ed. and trans. Brooks, 147–52.

39. Simeon predictably emerged the victor in the polemical account of John of Ephesus, earning the recognition of the *marzbān*—and thus of the Iranian court—for West Syrians who had lost Roman support (Saint-Laurent 2015: 90).

40. *Chronicle of Seert*, v. 2 (II), 126.

41. John of Ephesus, *Lives of the Eastern Saints*, ed. and trans. Brooks, 153–7; Hainthaler 2002: 264–5.

42. Statements of doctrine were translated from Syriac into Middle Persian at the disputation of 612, discussed below (Babai the Great, *History of George the Priest*, ed. Bedjan, 513–14). Talmudic references to the court possessing Jewish scrolls in the late Sasanian era suggests similar written documentation of beliefs was requested from Jewish communities (Secunda 2011: 364–6).

challenge this antagonistic religion posed to the Zoroastrianism on which imperial authority was predicated. Unlike Roman or Indian philosophies, Christian truths could not be as easily collated with Zoroastrian doctrine.

THE DISPUTATION: A COSMOPOLITAN PRACTICE

The encounter with universalist monotheism led the court to adopt an alternative cosmopolitan technique: the disputation. From Shapur I's encounter with the profit Mani onward, the Sasanians had sought to monitor the religious beliefs of their subjects.[43] Kawad's successor, Husraw I, went beyond the mere compiling of religious doctrines to organize debates of their contents, in an entirely novel way. The early Sasanians had established religious truths through ordeals—of fire, water, and molten metals—supernatural prophecies in which the deities inhering in sacred elements determined the truth value of human statements. The sixth century, by contrast, witnessed the enthusiastic adaptation of Greco-Roman practice of disputation that began with Husraw I. In the *Sīrat Ānūširwān*, an autobiographical account of his reign, the king of kings learned of certain nobles "whose religion was opposed to what we inherited from our prophet."[44] Instead of violently repressing the deviants, something Husraw I did not hesitate to do in other contexts, he invited them to a hearing at court: "I had those of contrary opinions brought into my presence [and commanded that they] dispute until they arrived at the truth."[45] He organized, in other words, a contest according to the Hellenistic model, in which religious or philosophical rivals verbally competed to prove the truth of their respective ideologies. The account of the *Sīrat Ānūširwān* finds confirmation in narratives of disputations between Christians and Zoroastrians and between East and West Syrian Christians that took place at the court of Husraw I. The East Syrian patriarch, Mar Aba, participated in a disputation with Zoroastrian authorities that began, in traditional fashion, with an ordeal of fire.[46] But after his triumphant march through the flames, a *mowbedān mowbed* (chief religious authority) initiated a disputation in the form of question-and-answer in the tradition of Greco-Roman philosophers. According to the Roman West Syrian historian John of Ephesus, moreover, the king of kings invited bishops from the two Christian sects, "to come and debate with one another before him about their faith, that he also might understand and personally examine those things that were being said by them . . . that he might judge their words and decide which were most

43. Shapur I's investigation into Mani's beliefs resulted in the *Šāpuhragān*, a defense of Manichaean doctrine in the form of a dialogue between prophet and king of kings at court (MacKenzie 1979).

44. *Sīrat Ānūširwān*, ed. Imāmi, 191–2, and trans. Grignaschi, 18–19.

45. *Sīrat Ānūširwān*, ed. Imāmi, 191, and trans. Grignaschi, 19.

46. *Chronicle of Seert*, v. 2 (II), 164–6.

according to reason."[47] However idealized a portrayal of the king of kings he composed, the West Syrian author was right to stress the importance Husraw I ascribed to rational argumentation as an instrument through which the adherents of seemingly incompatible schools of thought could collaboratively seek the truth. The best documented late Sasanian disputation was held in 612, when Husraw II (r. 590–628) invited East and West Syrian leaders to a debate held in the presence of Zoroastrian authorities.[48]

The practice of disputation was among the cultural goods imported from the Mediterranean. Once thought to have declined with the rise of Christian orthodoxies the Roman state enforced, disputations proliferated throughout the fifth-, sixth-, and seventh-century Christian Roman empire, albeit in a form that took the fundamentals of Nicaea as its starting point.[49] The Chalcedonian controversies gave rise to a culture of public disputation between representatives of dyophysite and miaphysite orthodoxies that spanned imperial frontiers, and the Iranian court likely became familiar with the practice through Christian intermediaries. To appropriate the practice for their own purposes, however, the late Sasanians sought out specialized knowledge of its workings. The above-mentioned philosopher Paul the Persian composed a work on dialectics, known as the *Treatise on the Logic of Aristotle*, on behalf of Husraw I.[50] As an introduction to rational, dialectical argumentation, the treatise provided a template for arriving at mutually acceptable truths on the basis of shared premises, a technique readily applicable in the politics of a culturally diverse elite. An East Syrian Christian able to draw on Syriac, Greek, and Middle Persian languages, literatures, and scholarly traditions, Paul the Persian was well-placed to instruct the court in techniques that could facilitate substantive communication between representatives of religious cultures adversarial to one another. If the rudiments of Aristotelian dialectic were undoubtedly already known to Iranian elites, patronage for further study of Greek logic on the part of the court suggests the arts of argument were considered as important as the politically indispensable sciences of astrology, cosmology, and philology. Transcripts of disputations undertaken at court according to Aristotelian principles of dialectic have not survived, unlike the Abbasid debates of scholars and religious specialists that were expressly modeled on pre-Islamic Iranian precedents. Nevertheless, a profound shift in the polemical strategies of East Syrian Christians in the sixth century reflected the evolving intellectual

---

47. John of Ephesus, *Ecclesiastical History*, 39; Walker 2006: 178–9.

48. Babai the Great, *History of George the Priest*, ed. Bedjan, 513–14; Walker 2006: 179–80, Payne 2015: 187.

49. Lim 1995, Walker 2006: 165–80, Tannous 2013: 92–3, King 2013b: 68–70, Cameron 2014, Van Nuffelen 2014.

50. For the philosophical context of Paul the Persian's work, see Hugonnard-Roche 2004: 233–54 and King 2013a: 112–14. King 2013b argues East and West Syrian polemicists used Aristotelian logic only superficially, implying that only external political authorities—such as Husraw I or the Abbasid caliph al-Mahdi—could compel them to adhere to the principles of logic in their disputations.

circumstances of the court, even at the provincial level. The bulk of East Syrian writings on Zoroastrianism constituted straightforward polemics, often framed in terms of miraculous events.[51] The *History of Mar Qardagh*, by contrast, presented its saint's polemic against Zoroastrianism in the form of an Aristotelian disputation, while drawing on the philosophy of the Alexandrian intellectual John Philoponus.[52]

Composed in the aristocratic Christian milieu of northern Mesopotamia, the hagiographical work included a debate that resembled—in a distorted form—the dialectical disputations that took place at court.[53] It occurred, however, not in the presence of a king of kings or a *mowbed*, but on the polo field—the site of aristocratic *otium*—in the presence of the noble Qardagh.[54] A monk interrupted a match of polo to challenge the Zoroastrianism the aristocratic processed through dialectical argumentation. Beginning from the shared premises that eternal entities are divine and that mortal entities are created, the monk deduced that Zoroastrians worshiped creatures rather than the creator, before turning to the question of whether the stars were divine.[55] Using the argument of John Philoponus that the luminaries were in motion and therefore perishable, the monk successfully rendered the Zoroastrian doctrine of their divinity untenable. The inclusion of such a disputation in a provincial hagiographical work shows how common dialectics had become in the late Sasanian period as a means of framing inter-religious encounters. Even the aristocratic audience of the comparatively humble city of Arbela, distant from the intellectual life of the court, could recognize the rules of disputation and its authoritative status.[56] The recourse the hagiographer made to Alexandrian philosophy, moreover, constituted a critique of Iranian cosmopolitan claims: How could Zoroastrians encompass Roman thought within their purview if the cutting edge of Roman cosmology undercut their fundamental doctrines? By foregrounding the contradictions between Roman philosophy and Zoroastrianism, *The History of Mar Qardagh* offered a response—otherwise unprecedented in East Syrian literature—to the efforts of the court to incorporate the sciences of the world. What the text nevertheless shared with the court was the presumption that religious antagonists could compare their systems of belief and regard their religions as intellectually commensurable, different varieties of the same genre

---

51. For examples of the role of miracles in demonstrating Christian truth vis-à-vis Zoroastrians, see Gignoux 2000 and Payne 2015: 87–91. The *History of Mar Qardagh* is scarcely devoid of the miraculous, even if its disputation is conducted in rational terms.

52. Walker 2004: 522–34, 2006: 189–205.

53. Walker 2004: 512–13.

54. *History of Mar Qardagh*, ed. Abbeloos, 18–21, and trans. Walker, 25–6.

55. *History of Mar Qardagh*, ed. Abbeloos, 22–31, and trans. Walker, 28–32.

56. For the aristocratic context of the text, see Payne 2015: 127–63.

of human thought and experience. This was a possibility the Roman state had foreclosed in the course of its Christianization.[57]

From the Roman perspective, disputations critical of religious truths became a signature of Iranian political culture. According to an account known as the *Religious Controversy at the Sasanian Court*, a Greek text composed in Roman Syria in the sixth century, the Iranian court hosted a freewheeling disputation between Christians, Jews, and polytheists that involved a wide range of texts and ideas the contemporary Roman court would have regarded as heretical and therefore illicit.[58] As Hubert Cancik has recently observed, the account is unprecedented in Roman literature.[59] One of its characters, Aphroditian, adopted a rational, skeptical middle path, transcending the peculiarities of Greco-Roman polytheism and Christianity, and the disputation aimed at the mutual recognition of shared truths rather than the vindication of a single orthodoxy.[60] Even if he were a Roman Christian, the anonymous author recognized the greater openness of Iranian disputational and intellectual culture in locating this imagined debate at the court of the Sasanians.[61] Such a portrayal of Husraw I's court was not without foundation. There are at least two known leading intellectuals at the sixth-century who abrogated religion in favor of philosophical skepticism, not unlike Aphroditian in the *Religious Controversy at the Sasanian Court*: Borzoy, the translator of the *Pañchatantra*, and Paul the Persian, the interpreter of Aristotle's logic.[62] Their responses were nevertheless exceptional. The disputations tended, on the contrary, to reinforce the position of existing religions by means of conclusions that emphasized shared beliefs of the kind the Roman observer of Iranian disputational culture described. The aforementioned Christian narratives of the disputations uniformly presented their own parties—whether East or West Syrian—as the victors in what were willful misrepresentations of the events. They could claim victory because Iranian disputations were left open-ended. If Greco-Roman debates concluded with clear winners and losers, controversies at the Iranian court came to a close with the word of the king of kings, or another political authority. The Abbasid debates

57. Lim 1995: 217–29.
58. Bratke 1899: 249–56, Cancik 2008: 21–3.
59. "Ich kenne keinen anderen antiken Text, in dem so viele Religionsparteien—Christianer, Judenchristen und Juden, Hellenen, Magier—miteinander kommunizieren und agieren wie in diesem Religionsgespräch am Hofe der Sasaniden" (Cancik 2008: 23).
60. *Religious Controversy at the Sasanian Court*, ed. Bratke, 41–3; Cancik 2008: 22, Heyden 2009: 124, 139–43.
61. Bratke 1899: 251 insisted on the orthodox identity of the author, while Heyden 2009: 118 considers the work "der literarische Widerstand eines liberal denkenden Christen" critical of the repressive religious policies of Justinian.
62. Shaked 1999: 69–70, Bruns 2009: 49–53. Paul the Persian—a well-known figure in the Roman Near East and, like Aphroditian, an intimate of the king of kings—could have been a model for the author. Bratke 1899: 263 and Cancik 2008: 22 both suggested the possibility of a historical figure behind this fictional character, without considering Paul.

that were based on Iranian models evinced a characteristic ambiguity: in cases where accounts from the different religious groups party to a debate have survived, each claimed victory for itself.[63] The Iranian court adopted the disputation from the Romans, but innovated a novel structure that allowed competing parties to present and to debate their beliefs without resolving their contradictions. This reworked disputation came to showcase the universal knowledge of the court. If the original function of religious disputation was, in the words of John of Ephesus, to gain understanding of different beliefs, this gave way to another priority: demonstrating the capacity of the king of kings to comprehend the views of the various schools of thought within the empire and to select the components of their ideologies he deemed meritorious and/or compatible with the imperial religion. The artfully orchestrated ambiguity of the disputation allowed ecclesiastical leaders to depart from the court claiming the king of kings had recognized the truth of their religion, while the supremacy of Zoroastrianism remained unchallenged. In pursuing shared truths in the manner the *Religious Controversy at the Sasanian Court* envisaged, the disputation functioned to maintain the superior position of a Zoroastrianism that now faced an articulate opposition within the ranks of the imperial elite.

The court accordingly placed an emphasis on the banal essentials of religions without any intention of reconciling incompatible systems of belief. The only surviving Middle Persian record of the disputation shows how Zoroastrians regarded the institution as another means of communicating their own unimpeachable intellectual superiority. In this account, the intellectual tendencies of the sixth-century court were projected into the fourth, the era of a legendary *mowbed* and scholar Ādurbad ī Mahraspandān.[64] Better known in Zoroastrian literature for his participation in the miraculous ordeals traditionally used to conduct religious controversies before the introduction of the disputation, he appears here as the impresario of the debate between himself and scholars from Rome and India concerning the nature of good and evil.[65] The questions and answers recorded were, according to the editor Jes Asmussen, entirely lacking in originality. The good constituted unchallenged rulership for the Roman, wealth for the Indian, and the state of being without fear for the *mowbed*.[66] The disputation resulted in a collection of gnomic banalities nearly any ancient person could have pronounced. With an insistence on the parties professing to shared truths, the text is diametrically opposed to Christian narratives of

---

63. See, for instance, the East and West Syrian accounts that have survived (Griffith 1992).

64. Numerous *andarz*, "wisdom-literature," texts were ascribed to this legendary *mowbed*, who became paradigmatic for the late Sasanian religious elite (Macuch 2009: 161–2).

65. Asmussen 1971: 275–6. In the early and middle Sasanian periods, the ordeal was the primary public means of evaluating competing religious specialists and truths. It retained a juridical function throughout the history of the empire (Perikhanian 1979).

66. Asmussen 1971: 276.

disputational triumph. The scholars who composed and preserved this account regarded superficial commonalities as evidence of Zoroastrian universalism, of the religion's capacity to integrate the true elements of foreign ideologies. A collection of ethical truisms was used to demonstrate that Romans and Indians acknowledged the supremacy of the integrative truth of Zoroastrianism. Beyond the substantive knowledge of religions and sciences the late Sasanian court acquired through the institution, the disputation served to safeguard the Good Religion from the omnipresent intellectual challenges that the heightened trans-regional traffic in texts and ideas posed to its standing and, perhaps more important, to subordinate the rival systems of belief proliferating in the empire. Iranian cosmopolitanism depended on the illusion that Zoroastrianism could encompass all bodies of knowledge, and the disputation provided the underpinnings of such an illusion through the securing of assent to the superior position of Zoroastrian rulers as adjudicators and through the production of banalities as stable points of commonality.

A similar reassertion of Zoroastrian supremacy within the framework of rational disputation took place in contemporary discussions of Christians and Zoroastrians on the nature of religion as a category. In the late Sasanian period, East Syrian Christians and Zoroastrians developed existing concepts of religion in ways that allowed them to categorize even rival belief systems as fellow "religions," a necessary prerequisite for, and possible byproduct of, religious disputation, as opposed to philosophical disputation of the kind Ādurbad ī Mahraspandān was supposed to have undertaken. Disputants had to recognize an opposing party possessed something called religion comparable to one's own before debating which religion was true. As Adam Becker has recently demonstrated, in sixth-century East Syrian texts a term for religion with roots in the Peshitta, the Syriac version of the Hebrew Bible, gained newfound prominence: *deḥlta*, "fear," or *deḥlta d-alaha*, "fear of God." Only Christians could fear God, while the adherents of other religions were held hostage to false fears. Fear, according to Becker, denoted the affective relationship between persons and the supernatural powers or power to which they were subject. All humans, in this emergent understanding of the religious self, feared, and what distinguished Christians was that their fear was well-placed, their religion the true fear. The discourse of fear represents the development of a framework for understanding human interactions with the supernatural as essentially comparable phenomena, as *deḥlata* "religions" cognate with our modern conception of religion even if their intellectual trajectories never merged.[67] A corresponding Zoroastrian discourse of comparative religion had roots at least in the early Sasanian period. Zoroastrian scholars spoke of religions as *dēn: wehdēnīh*, "Good Religion,"

67. Becker 2009: 303–4.

which designated their own perfect system of ritual, action, and belief, while *agdēnīh*, "Bad Religion," described the other irredeemably deficient religions.[68] Unlike other terms available to Zoroastrians, such as *kēš*, "sect," *dēn* presumed the theoretical comparability of religions. These two Sasanian discourses converged at the court, which insisted that the representatives of both religions employ their terms of comparative religion rather than the available alternatives. The symmetrical development of *deḥlata* and *dēn* even suggests a common origin in the intellectual culture of the court.

The significance the court ascribed to the terminology of religion emerges from a work of an East Syrian leader, Babai the Great (ca. 551-628 CE). The *History of George the Priest* related the interrogation of an East Syrian monk for apostasy from Zoroastrianism, a criminal offense in Iranian law. In the course of the interrogation, George was submitted an account of his beliefs, in which he referred to the Zoroastrianism of his youth as *pōryōtkēšīh*, "the sect of one's ancestors."[69] The accused was chastised for using a term apparently forbidden at court and required to refer to the religion as *wehdēnīh*, "Good Religion." *Pōryōtkēšīh* implied that tradition trumped reason, and it was only on the basis of rational argumentation that Zoroastrianism and Christianity could be compared as *deḥlata* and *dēn*. *Pōryōtkēšīh* was, however, a current, common description of the religion in Middle Persian texts emerging from the same milieu.[70] Within their own discourse, the term was an unproblematic characterization of a religion frequently conceived as an ancestral inheritance. Indeed, Armenian Christians employed a similar concept to describe their faith as *awrenk'*, "ancestral custom."[71] But in the public venue of the court the term was suppressed in favor of the terminology of *dēn*, which was amenable to comparison and to rational debate. The maintenance of such a linguistic code at court suggests its effort to present the Zoroastrianism as a rational religion amenable to comparisons through which its superiority would remain undiminished. It also suggests that Zoroastrianism was only partly comparable; only one facet of the religion was to be revealed, debated, and compared in public. The ancestral inheritance, *pōryōtkēšīh*, was to remain unquestioned throughout the disputations of the court, and hence had to remain concealed to allow them to take place.

The notion of a multilayered, multifaceted religion was well rooted in Zoroastrian thought. As a complete body of cosmological and ritual knowledge, the Good Religion was beyond debate, beyond words, and beyond the

---

68. Shaked 2008.

69. Babai the Great, *History of George the Priest*, ed. Bedjan, 526-7.

70. *Mēnōg ī Xrad*, ed. and trans. Chunakova, 66/111; *Ardā Wirāz Nāmag*, ed. and trans. Vahman, 105/ 219; *Widēwdād*, ed. and trans. Moazami, 96-7. The teachers of correct doctrine were routinely known as the *pōryōtkēš*: *Widēwdād*, ed. and trans. Moazami, 126-7, 172-3, and *Dēnkard VI*, ed. and trans. Shaked, 2-3, 154-5, 212-13, to cite only a handful of examples.

71. Thomson 2004: 384.

particularities of individual religions. Its solid core, the Avesta, stood within a seven walled fortress that even Zoroastrians could not penetrate, in scholarly discussions of the nature of religion.[72] Zoroastrianism in its entirety was the preserve of the scholars, members of the major ruling aristocratic houses, who had studied the Avesta and its exegesis.[73] The great bulk of Zoroastrians were discouraged from acquiring knowledge of the core of religion that resided beyond rational inquiry. According to one scholar, the intelligence of humanity consisted of thirty seeds: "This one seed is at least consequence, that by which one ought to learn the Avesta."[74] The metaphor of the seeds simultaneously underlined the diffuse state of knowledge that had been scattered among humanity as well as the singular importance of the select few, the Iranian elite, who were in possession of the Avestan seed as well as the other twenty-nine. The foundation of true religion was located in an impenetrable domain—a seven walled fortress—humans could not access through reason, a theory that allowed Zoroastrians to compare various aspects of their religion without subjecting its essentials to criticism.[75] The Sasanian disputations therefore entailed the concealing of beliefs as well as their unveiling. If the court fostered inter-religious debates on the basis of logical reasoning, its efforts were ultimately directed at bolstering the position of Zoroastrianism rather than acknowledging the truth of *agdēnīh* or producing a synthesis of philosophical truths that transcended individual religions. The disputations had to respect the limits that kept the core of the religion intact. One of those limits was linguistic: the use of *dēn* rather than *pōryōtkēšīh* to describe religion at court. The Good Religion nevertheless remained a *pōryōtkēšīh* in the minds of its representatives even while they engaged in comparative discussions of rival *dēn*.

The Zoroastrian approach to Christianity thus prefigures modern constructions of "world religions," in which nineteenth- and early twentieth-century scholars selectively compared aspects of Christianity, Judaism, Hinduism, Buddhism, and other religions to rearticulate the superior standing of Western Christianity—however secularized its form—in the guise of a cosmopolitan pluralism.[76] At the Iranian court, Christian sects—and perhaps other religions— were examined, debated, and evaluated in pursuit of aspects that were compatible with Zoroastrianism. These were likely as banal as the verities Ādurbad ī Mahraspandān was believed to have extracted from the Indian and Roman philosophers, or as the nineteenth-century tropes of Eastern religious wisdom, but their potency may have derived precisely from their banality, the readiness of

---

72. *Dēnkard VI*, ed. and trans. Shaked, 84–5.
73. Shaked 1969.
74. *Dēnkard VI*, ed. and trans. Shaked, 84–5.
75. *Dēnkard VI*, 84–5.
76. Masuzawa 2005.

Zoroastrian and Christian elites to profess commonalities that posed no threat to the core of their beliefs. The kings of kings Kawad I, Husraw I, and Husraw II could affirm the merits of Christian doctrine in such a way that East and West Syrian Christians alike could claim royal sanction for their creeds, without compromising a Good Religion concealed within its seven walled fortress. The collection of statements of Christian doctrine, moreover, served to place the court in a position of authority over Christians' own bodies of knowledge, and the different Christian sects continued to compete for royal recognition as the widely recognized validation of truth, even among the Christians of the empire. In the early seventh century, after the conquest of the Roman Near East, the king of kings came to occupy the role of arbiter of Christian truth that the Roman emperor had once occupied, and East and West Syrians alike readily acknowledged Husraw II as a guardian not only of their churches, but of their doctrines.[77] Defined as a discrete entity subordinate to the court, the rival universalism of Christianity came to complement, rather than undermine, the universalist project of Ērānšahr. East and West Syrian churches became religions of the empire, in positions subordinate to the Good Religion.

As a consequence, the institutions and symbols of Christianity became vehicles for cosmopolitan claims to integrate all cultures under the carapace of the Iranian empire. The court began to support the expansion of Christianity in the sixth century. In the 550s, Husraw I commissioned the patriarch of the Church of the East, Mar Aba, to send a bishop to the Hephthalite Hun kingdom in Bactria, Iran's frequent adversary, effectively employing an East Syrian leader as a representative of the empire in Central Asia.[78] Only a few decades later, the king of the Lakhmid Arabs, an Iranian satellite, converted to East Syrian Christianity in the 590s with Sasanian support.[79] In each of these cases, the ideology and institutions of the Christian religion served as extensions of the Iranian court that regarded the contradictions between Christianity and Zoroastrianism to have been successfully contained. Unlike the fifth-century kings of kings who sought to keep the religion's political influence in check, for example, in the Caucasus, Husraw I and Husraw II expressly identified themselves as agents of the Christian god and, vice versa, Christian supernatural powers as agents of their empire.[80] The Sasanians even became rivals to a Rome seeking to create a global commonwealth of Christian kingdoms.[81] Husraw II sent gifts to the shrine of the Near East's most powerful saint, Sergius, displayed crosses at court, and, after conquering Jerusalem from the Romans in 619,

77. Payne 2015: 185–8.
78. *History of Mar Aba*, ed. Bedjan, 267–9.
79. Toral-Niehoff 2014: 199–208.
80. Payne 2015: 171–4.
81. Payne 2015: 174–92.

brought the True Cross—the most potent symbol of the Christian faith—to the imperial treasury in Seleucia-Ctesiphon. Employing the knowledge of Christian doctrine the Iranian court had accumulated, he drew attention to the heretical status of the Christianities of Arabia, the Caucasus, and much of the Fertile Crescent vis-à-vis Rome, to position Iran as the center of a global Christianity. It is well to recall that Simeon of Beit Arsham had purposefully presented his Christian orthodoxy as the faith of not only of the Roman and Iranian empires but also of lands beyond, reportedly traveling widely to collect material for his case. The Iranian court aimed at an alternative Christian universalism that differed in two important respects from what developed in the Christian Roman empire: its orthodoxies were multiple, united around a shared loyalty to an unbelieving king of kings, and were subordinated to a Zoroastrian political elite regarding itself as transcending the cultural peculiarities of its subjects. Christian universalism became ancillary to Iranian cosmopolitanism.

CONCLUSION

The Iranian court sought to realize its cosmopolitan claims in the face of strident literary cultures that contested its maintenance of superior, all-encompassing knowledge. Encounters with Roman, Indian, and Christian intellectual cultures resulted in efforts to translate their literatures, to draw insights from their learning, and ultimately to reunite human knowledge. Christianity posed a special challenge, with its own cosmopolitan aspirations and inveterate hostility toward rival systems of belief, and yet the court successfully gathered knowledge of its doctrines and, in the process, disciplined its representatives, placing them and their sciences in subordinate positions in relation to an incommensurable superior Zoroastrianism. Iranian cosmopolitan elites stood above the peculiarities of Christianity as well as the Roman and Indian sciences, as the organizers and superintendents of civilization, including human knowledge. Their interest in other cultures was not a benign proto-multiculturalism, but an instrument of power. Only an Iranian could look down on to the world's cultures, pick and choose among them, and assemble a new mosaic appropriate for their political circumstances. As their superiority resided in religious knowledge beyond the reach of non-Iranians, even such a contradictory body of knowledge such as Christianity could be placed within the imperial order without challenging Zoroastrian dominance. The religious disputation was an institution primarily designed to facilitate not the exchange of ideas, but the recognition of difference, of a bounded cultural entity. The cosmopolitan *mowbed, marzbān,* or king of kings standing above and beyond human particularities could call into being clearly defined groups subordinate to himself. The king of kings and his associates, in inviting and attending Christian declarations of belief, made themselves the authorities behind the definition of Christian identities. This was pointedly communicated through the preservation of field statements of belief in the royal archives. Through such cosmopolitan acts, Christians and other groups came to imagine highly contradictory, rationally incommensurable cultures as interdependent, and themselves as dependent on the authority of a thoroughly Zoroastrian imperial apparatus. The power of Iranian cosmopolitanism resided in its ability to have Christians accept subordinate positions for themselves in the very act of articulating their beliefs, in its ability to place groups in a hierarchical ordering that underpinned the authority of the court.

The successful practice of cosmopolitanism, the present chapter argues, was necessary for the maintenance of the position of the ruling elite that crisscrossed religions, languages, and ethical orders as well as territorial regions. The Zoroastrian ethno-class that took shape in the third century initially regarded its position of universal rulership as self-evident. The Iranians had, after all, definitively subjugated the Romans and established their hegemony across the Near East. Although the occasional religious deviant, such as the prophet Mani, challenged Zoroastrian doctrines, no movement jeopardized the authority or integrity of the early Sasanian ruling elite. The rise of Christianity in the fourth through seventh centuries, however, confronted the Iranian court and aristocracy with an ever more pressing provocation. It was not only the polemical practices of ecclesiastical leaders but also the political indispensability of the Christian secular elite that made the religion potentially corrosive to the aristocratic networks through which the court governed. As *ēr* sought to rule regions—especially northern Mesopotamia and the Caucasus—whose landowning aristocracies were largely Christian before the end of the fourth century, the necessity of defining the relationship of the Zoroastrian Iranians to Christian local elites became plain. The initial use of violence gave way to patronage in the early fifth century as a means of ensuring Christian discipline. But the inherent irreconcilability of Zoroastrian and Christian cosmologies remained. The growing importance of Christian aristocrats as provincial officials, military commanders, and cavalrymen stimulated the court to innovate cosmopolitan practices that preserved its universal political order while overcoming the differences that threatened to break the ties binding its religiously disparate elites. One such practice was the continued patronage of bishops, monks, and saints as well as the use of relics symbolically to represent the kings of kings as Christian rulers, even as they remained Zoroastrian. The practice of the disputation crucially made these gestures resonate within their Christian audience, by means of its creation of apparent equivalencies between religions and its recognition of Christian truth. The polemical assaults of ecclesiastical leaders against Zoroastrianism were thereby deprived of their potency. Even as bishops and monks continued to rail against the Good Religion, Christian aristocrats—and even the majority of ecclesiastical leaders—could view the Iranians as a benevolent ethno-class that recognized their religious legitimacy without denying its own religion. The disputation thus served, in conjunction with the other institutions of Iranian political culture, to bind Christian local elites into a trans-regional network offering them access to a share in the rents of empire while reinforcing the position of the Iranians, the upper stratum of a hierarchically differentiated elite that had created Iran in its own service.

Ancient Sources

Agathias, *Histories*, ed. R. Keydell, *Agathiae myrinaei historiarum libri quinque* (Berlin, 1967).

Ardā Wirāz Nāmag, ed. and trans. F. Vahman, *Ardā Wirāz Nāmag: The Iranian "Divina Commedia"* (London, 1986).

Babai the Great, *History of George the Priest*, ed. P. Bedjan, *Histoire de Mar Jabalaha, de trois autres patriaches, d'un prêtre et de deux laïques nestoriens* (Paris and Leipzig, 1895), 416–571.

Chronicle of Seert, ed. and trans. A. Scher, *Histoire nestorienne (Chronique de Séert)*, vols. 1–2 (Paris, 1908–19).

Dēnkard IV, ed. D. M. Madan, *The Complete Text of the Pahlavi Dinkard* (Bombay, 1911), 409–31, and partial trans. M. Shaki, "The Dēnkard Account of the History of the Zoroastrian Scriptures," *Archív Orientální* 49 (1981): 114–25.

Dēnkard VI, ed. and trans. S. Shaked, *The Wisdom of the Sasanian Sages* (Boulder, 1979).

History of Mar Aba, ed. P. Bedjan, *Histoire de Mar Jabalaha, de trois autres patriaches, d'un prêtre et de deux laïques nestoriens* (Paris and Leipzig, 1895), 206–87.

History of Mar Qardagh, ed. J. B. Abbeloos, "Acta Mar Kardaghi," *Analecta Bollandiana* 9 (1890): 5–106, and trans. J. T. Walker, *The Legend of Mar Qardagh: Narrative and Christian Heroism in Late Antique Iraq* (Berkeley, 2006), 19–61.

John of Ephesus, *Ecclesiastical History*, ed. E. W. Brooks, *Iohannis Ephesini Historiae Ecclesiasticae pars tertia* (Louvain, 1935).

Mēnōg ī Xrad, ed. and trans. O. M. Chunakova, *Zoroastriiskie Teksti: Suzhdeniya Dukha Razuma (Dadestan-i Menog-i Khrad)—Sotvorenie Osnovi (Bundahishn) i Drugie Teksti* (Moscow, 1997).

Religious Controversy at the Sasanian Court, ed. E. Bratke, *Das sogennante Religionsgespräch am Hof der Sasaniden* (Leipzig, 1899), 1–45.

Sīrat Ānūširwān, ed. Abū al-Qāsim Imāmi, *Tajārib al-umam* (Tehran, Dār Surūsh, 1987), 188–209, and trans. M. Grignaschi, "Quelques spécimens de la literature sassanide conserves dans les bibliothèques d'Istanbul," *Journal Asiatique* 254 (1966): 1–142.

Widēwdād, ed. and trans. M. Moazami, *Wrestling with the Demons of the Pahlavi Widēwdād: Transcription, Translation, and Commentary* (Leiden, 2014).

11

"Zum ewigen Frieden"

Cosmopolitanism, Comparison, and Empire

Peter Fibiger Bang

An afterword by Peter Bang situates the themes of the volume in the context of the modern debate on empire in Europe and North America. Taking his start-ing point from Kant's 1795 essay 'on eternal peace', Bang traces the ways in which the history of the nineteenth and twentieth centuries contributed to dis-credit universalist ideals. All the more surprising is the revival of empire and cosmopolitan thought in the twenty-first century. He suggests that the papers assembled in our volume contribute to a better understanding of this current historical juncture. By highlighting the contradictions in ancient imperial ideals, they both bring out the limits faced by all universalist projects, and are suggestive of the compromises the development of new forms of trans-regional organization will require.

Appearing in the outward shape of a formal treaty, Kant's essay from 1795 "on eternal peace" has become a charter text of modern civilization.[1] Calm and composed, his idea of a global federation rationally to regulate rela-tions between sovereign states and prevent war provided the ideological basis for the United Nations. It has also become a classic of cosmopolitan thought, bedrock for most current attempts to reflect on the prospect, possibility, even necessity of "world community" and citizenship.[2] Within "the supplements" to his cosmopolitan treaty, the philosopher from what was once Königsberg on the Baltic rim, left the following sting, a remark which could still be taken to voice a serious challenge and objection to the purpose of a volume such as this one:

The idea of international law presupposes the separate existence of many independent but neighbouring states. Although this condition is itself a state of war (unless a federative union prevents the outbreak of

---

1. I am deeply grateful to John Hall who generously commented on a first draft of this piece and, not least, to Elaine Yuan for many thoughtful discussions and, in particular, for introducing me to the work of Wang Hui.
2. To the titles quoted in other chapters of this volume, I add Bartelson 2009. Further Hurrell 2007: 69–70.

hostilities), it is still nonetheless, from a rational perspective, preferable to the amalgamation of states under one superior power, as this would end in one universal monarchy, and laws always lose in vigour what government gains in extent; hence a soulless despotism falls into anarchy after stifling the seeds of the good. However, every state, or its ruler, desires to establish lasting peace in this way, aspiring if possible to rule the whole world. But nature wills it otherwise.[3]

Between Kantian universalism and the ancient world monarchies, the object of this book, lies an unbridgeable gulf. Both reason and nature are ranged against us, or so it would seem. As Tamara Chin observes in her contribution, it is far from straightforward to harness the philosophical concept of the cosmopolitan, an ideal often articulated in rejection of mundane politics, to the study of imperial elites. But, perhaps in this case, it would be even more problematical not to make the attempt. Pragmatism alone, of course, would counsel use of the word to examine the formation of trans-regional elites within empires proclaiming their universal reach. No better conceptual coinage is readily on offer. But, far more important, Kantian universalism has itself run up against its limits. Like most of the other grand utopias of the enlightenment, the Kantian world republic has turned out to be an elusive quest, in practice anything but rational and ordered. Recently Mark Mazower concluded his history of the idea of world government in dismay: "Our representatives continue to hand over power to experts and self-interested self-regulators in the name of global governance while a sceptical and alienated public looks on. The idea of governing the world is becoming yesterday's dream."[4] To be sure, one may simply note in disappointment that reality falls far short of ideals. But the problem lies deeper. Never before has the world possessed such a densely textured web of transnational organizations, yet the arena of world government is far from even and coherent; everywhere is compromise, coexistence of seemingly contradictory arrangements and hypocrisy, not as systemic flaws, but as a necessity. The field of cosmopolitan politics, Bruno Latour has remarked in debate with the late Ulrich Beck, must be approached as a "pluriverse," not a logically coherent system.[5] As individuals we may take different political views of this situation, but as historians we would be failing if we did not know how

---

3. Kant, translation modified from the version (no translator stated) provided at http://www.constitution.org/kant/1stsup.htm. German version: *Zum Ewigen Frieden*, Erster Zusats (1917: 45–6).

4. Mazower 2012: 427. Discussion, on pp. 15-18, of Kant and his enlightenment faith in reason eventually producing the conditions of a perpetual peace. The connoisseur may object to the choice of words here that strictly speaking Kant's text advocated a voluntary federation of states, not a world republic. True, but only up to a point. The underlying ideal informing Kant's analysis, and many of his followers in succeeding generations one might add, was that of a world republic to which the federation could eventually approach. So, conclusively, Kleingeld 2011, chap. 2.

5. Latour 2004: 454.

to illuminate the problems and contradictions of contemporary universalism with the experience of the past. For few phenomena could prepare us better to understand and realistically assess the challenges of modern cosmopolitanism than the universalisms of old. They never labored under the illusion of uniformity and logical coherence. Universal rulers normally had to embrace and perform contradictory roles, combining incompatibles. The Ottoman sultan would pose as a warrior of Islam while patronizing the Christian, ecumenical patriarch of Constantinople.[6] In this volume, Richard Payne details how the Sasanian monarchs saw themselves as Zoroastrian rulers, yet carefully staged demonstrations of respect for the Christian church under their tutelage. Religious disputations were set up at court between members of different faith communities, but no final judgement was passed. Participants could walk away, each with a feeling of having carried the day. Withholding their verdict, the Sasanian monarchs rose above petty conflict and doctrinal antagonisms, truly to make manifest their world rule. "We need the weak exclusivity of premodern or early modern histories," to quote Prasenjit Duara, better to guide our appraisal of the multifarious, often contradictory character of cosmopolitan modes of organization in the present world and prepare us for their inner tensions, limitations, and implicit hierarchies.[7]

Alexander has often served as an icon of modern cosmopolitanism; but the lasting interest of his example lies precisely in its capacity to serve as a prism refracting the manifold components of ancient universalisms, to lay bare their conflicts and inconsistencies. His reign became a site for debating imperial lordship among later generations. Emblematic, for instance, is his attempt to promote marriages between the Macedonian conquest elite and daughters of the Persian nobility, "that by this sacred bond I might prevent every distinction between defeated and victor," in the high-sounding words of the Roman historian Quintus Curtius, and forge a new common elite for his empire.[8] Harmony, however, would not necessarily issue from such gestures to overcome division. The histories of Alexander's conquests overflow with critique and admonitions not to forget his Macedonian background and not to let down his old comrades in arms in his attempt to woo the Persian aristocracy. Ancient universalism, Myles Lavan shows in his chapter, was thin and limited. Master-slave, ruling people-subject ethnicities, citizen-foreigner, civilized-barbarian, a range of unequal oppositions continued to maintain barriers and create distinctions as the process of imperial, cosmopolitan integration set in motion. In fact, as the editors point out, hierarchical subordination was a crucial mode of government to keep the gaudy patchwork of imperial societies together.

---

6. Kolodziejczyk 2012, Bang 2011.
7. Duara 2014: 90.
8. Quintus Curtius, *History of Alexander*, book X, iii, 12 (this and the following passage translated by this author).

So, too, was the capacity to paper over inconsistencies and live with internal contradiction. At the end of the first book of Strabo's *Geography,* written during the reigns of Augustus and Tiberius, is a curious, but illuminating discussion defending the advisors of Alexander against a critique from a certain Eratosthenes. The latter had praised Alexander for ignoring the counsel of the former to favor the Greeks and having chosen instead to look for men of distinction and excellence from across his realm. But, Strabo argued against Eratosthenes, surely that was what the advisors had implied in the first place by their recommendation to give preference to Greeks, that the empire should be governed by men of only true nobility: "And so Alexander, not disregarding his advisers, but rather accepting their opinion, did what was consistent with, not contrary to, their advice; for he had regard to the real intent of those who gave him counsel." Admittedly, the syllogism is a bit shaky; it might look as if Strabo was trying to have his cake and eat it at the same time.[9] But ancient cosmopolitanism was more Burkean than Kantian; it was capable of just such violations of logic—of paradox and self-contradiction; ethnicity and "virtue" could both, in unresolved tension, serve as vehicles of aristocratic distinction. This was sufficient to form a lose amalgam for linking different elite groups with each other. From the courts emanated networks of patronage, letter writing, and religious ritual, a theme of both Richardson and Fischer-Bovet's chapters, to form an economy of command and prestige. Fractures normally continued to run through these thinly connected groups and the ruler had to be able to communicate in different registers to address the concerns of each and honor their position. To return to Curtius's portrayal of Alexander: "the letters which he sent to Europe, he stamped with his old signet ring while those he wrote to Asia, were impressed with the ring of Dareius."[10] One might see the same language of mixed symbolisms reflected in the Ptolemaic trilingual inscriptions discussed above in chapter 7. Articulating a complex hierarchy, ancient royal universalisms were both composite and compromised.

They were also severely hedged about by localism. Clifford Ando, for instance, notes how the gradual dissemination of Roman citizenship to provincial elites created a need for them also to preserve their local rights and privileges as members of a different people. Among many members of such elites, the home community would have dominated their horizons and the formation of identities. Both Kathryn Stevens and Johannes Haubold point to the prevalence and force of local political identities. As both Mesopotamian and Greek city states were spun into the wider networks of the Hellenistic age, they attempted to

---

9. Strabo, *Geography* I 4.9 (trans. H. L. Jones in The Loeb Classical Library). Isaac 2004: 299–300 rightly points out the inconsistency of Strabo, but fails to see that it reflects an unresolved tension in this form of universalist ideology, a symptom as much as a flaw.

10. Curtius, *History of Alexander*, VI, vi, 6 (given a hostile interpretation by Curtius).

assert their local identities and institutions. Temple priests would inscribe the reigning monarchs into a much deeper history of the local patron deity, a story that preceded the imposition of Hellenistic rule and which would presumably outlast it as well. In cuneiform temple inscriptions, lists of kings and sages, and chronicles from cities such as Uruk, Borsippa, and Babylon, the Seleucid king would be presented in a local context of timeless Mesopotamian kingship. If rulers attempted to forge a universalism which reached out to subject elites by recognizing difference and embracing their "traditions," the other side of the resulting dialogue might respond simply by appropriating royal authority to cement the edifice and legitimacy of local and regional communities. A stock theme of Roman imperial history is the habit of Hellenic elites conspicuously to ignore most of what was Roman about the Caesars and instead cast them in the role of an Alexander-like monarch or a Greek philosopher king.[11] Imperial power was constantly subject to erosion by the attempts of provincial elites to arrogate as much to themselves as possible and take it over.

Recently Garry Runciman likened empire to a volatile state maintained only by keeping the right balance between absorption and disengagement.[12] With the coming of the third century, for instance, Roman cosmopolitanism moves into a higher gear. This is a theme of both the chapters of Ando and, in particular, of Weisweiler. The scene is set by the grand extension of the Roman citizenship to the majority of the provincial population under Caracalla; and the tetrarchs, from Diocletian to Constantine, followed suit by fostering a much extended and truly cosmopolitan aristocracy, subject to the same system of ranks across the empire. To these developments should be added the adoption of Christianity by the rulers and large swaths of the population and elites during the fourth century. But, just as Runciman leads us to expect, these intensified forces of absorption and unification sparked off increasing pressures of disengagement and fragmentation. It was a long time since emperors had had to hail from Italy. Now, however, with the greater inclusion of provincials in the imperial state apparatus, governmental power gravitated inexorably toward the provinces. Rome ceased to be the seat of the emperors while regional courts sprouted. Trier, Sirmium, Nicomedia, Milan, Constantinople, the list is far from exhaustive. It was only for short periods that any single emperor would prove capable of holding the reigns of the realm together. More often than not, power had to be shared between co-rulers and sometimes rivals. Not even, or perhaps especially not, the Church could avoid these centrifugal tendencies. Monotheist, based on a set of common scriptures and with a network of bishops, the Church constituted a highly articulated form of ecumenical or cosmopolitan organization.

11. Millar 1977, Woolf 1994, Swain 1996, Whitmarsh 2001a.
12. Runciman 2011.

But doctrinal differences tended to be fused with regional interests to exacerbate strife. No sooner had the Church won the support of the rulers, than schism and regional division began haunting the specter of Christianity. Cosmopolitan integration remained thin.[13]

One of the key questions posed by the volume is what sort of elite subjectivities were fostered by this kind of integration. Dealing with the Assyrians, Richardson, for instance, finds little in the way of Foucauldian governmentality and subjectivation. But there are alternatives to the postcolonial language of subjectivity and empowerment striving to allow hidden, but more authentic voices to emerge. Trans-regional identities, forming around royal grants and shared courtly rituals of social distinction, can be studied through other means. The lasting greatness of Droysen, not merely as the student of the Hellenistic, but as a historian *tout court*, was to recognize the significance and value of the more generalized idioms of Greek culture which can be seen spreading ever wider in the wake of the conquests of Alexander.[14] Hailing Attic Greek and its literature as canonical, this culture was and has often enough continued to be perceived as lacking in genuineness, a studied and decontextualized expression, rather than a spontaneous, authentic growth. But it is exactly the capacity to wear artful social masks effortlessly which is the defining trait of cosmopolitan and civilized behavior.[15] This sets it in express opposition to nationalism and its recent offshoot in the shape of modern identity politics. It is not by coincidence that it would be Ernest Gellner, the great theorist of nationalism, who perhaps better than any other came to frame the question of premodern elites in terms of their deracination. As slave soldiers and office-holders, the Mamelukes and Ottoman janissaries constituted in his book the ideal-typical and therefore extreme example of the tendency for preindustrial elites to form a segment severed from the rest of society.[16] With this in mind, one might note in passing that both imperial militaries and the eunuchs and slaves employed at ancient courts and in royal offices could perhaps in future work warrant greater attention than they receive here. About the latter group, however, already Aristotle had objected to Plato's attempt to deny family and private property to the rulers of his ideal polis.[17] Education and public service, polished speech and manners, office-holding, and a splendid lifestyle, these would more often be among the means through which aristocratic, landowning elites in the ancient world marked

13. Sarris 2011: 160–8 is very strong on the tendency for theological disputes to overlap with geographical divisions.

14. Droysen [1843] 2008: xxi: "Ich will von Rom nicht sprechen; es liegt mir hier näher, den Blick auf Griechenland zu wenden; gemeinsam ist beiden, sich je länger je mehr zu denationalisieren, sich endlich völlig man möchte sagen aufzulösen zu Allgemeinheiten, Prinzipien, Potenzen."

15. Hall 2013, chapter 6 in particular.

16. Gellner 1983, 1981.

17. Aristotle, *Politics* II, i–ii. For a detailed and more nuanced discussion of Plato versus Aristotle on property and family, see Garnsey 2007: ch. 1.

themselves off from the commoners and engaged in wider trans-regional, or to use the concepts of this volume, cosmopolitan networks.[18]

Gellner, however, was not only the great student of nationalism. His anthropological work on sainthood within Islam, monotheist and universal, was of no less high-grade caliber.[19] It would be one of the inspirations for the work of Peter Brown on late antique saints. As god became increasingly elevated and transcendental, people needed local, personified representatives to mediate between human and divine; the power of ancient cult, polytheistic and local, reasserted itself through the worship of saints and other attempts to make concrete and accessible the force from above, god or king. High culture, in other words, was characterized not simply by trans-regional integration, but by a tension between cosmopolitan and local. Taken as a whole, it is exactly that tension, captured so well by Gellner's sociology, which the different chapters of this volume seem to circumscribe, some emphasizing either one or the other pole. But for elites of our kind, it was rarely a stark choice of either/or, but a question of balancing in various gradations local loyalties with an ability to opt into a wider world. Think, for instance, of the many people documented from Ptolemaic Egypt sporting both a Hellenic and an Egyptian identity. Gellner analyzed this phenomenon through the famous identification by David Hume of "a flux and reflux in the human mind . . . a tendency to rise from idolatry to theism, and to sink again from theism into idolatry."[20] The relationship between local identity and cosmopolitan transcendence is best described as an oscillating movement; and this brings me full circle.

For as Page duBois argues, Hume's principle of an oscillating flux and reflux is still highly relevant to put into focus the continuing significance of polytheism in the modern world.[21] By the same token, the study of the connection between ancient empire and cosmopolitan integration ought to add both historical depth and perspective to the challenges of a globalizing age such as our own. Then and now, the formation and growth of trans-regional networks went in tandem with steeper hierarchies, an argument made with elegance and sophistication by Harold James in *The Imperial Predicament.* It is one of the great unexpected turns of our times that the question of empire has come back so forcefully on the agenda. A generation ago, it looked as if decolonization and the end of the Cold War had once and for all swept empire off the map. Three decades on, matters are less neat. The United States promoted an international order, seemingly based on Kantian principles, but now we must ask whether it is perhaps better understood as a form of empire.[22] Europe is torn between

18. Bang 2015: 65–66.
19. Gellner 1969. See Hall 2010, chap. 9 for an introduction.
20. Hume 1998: 158–9 (*The Natural History of Religion*, ch. 8). Further discussion and analysis in Bang 2015.
21. duBois 2014: ch. 3.
22. Go 2011.

the nation and a super-state; the outcome looks nothing so much as that of a weak form of empire.[23] Rising China, finally, is challenged with the task of transcending our opening Kantian dichotomy between universal empire and sovereign states, "by merging together nation and state on the foundation of the old Qing dynasty" multiethnic dominion.[24] The United States, Europe, and China, each in their own way, struggle to find a formula for combining the nation with more universalist and imperial forms of organization. This has become a pressing question and knowing about the ancient past may prepare us better for the composite and messy solutions that an answer will require. Perhaps, in the end, Virgil, the bard of Roman universalism, may still be as illuminating of cosmopolitan conditions as Kant: "You, Roman, remember to govern the peoples with might . . . and impose morals on peace."[25]

23. Zielonka 2006.
24. Wang Hui 2014: 137.
25. Virgil, *Aeneid*, VI, 851–2 (my translation). The Latin word *mos* denotes the customary ways, often in the sense of good morals; in the Kantian context of this essay, I have chosen in translating to emphasize the latter.

Works Cited

Abd el-Fattah, A., Abd el-Maksoud, M., and Carrez-Maratray, J.-Y. (2014). "Deux in-scriptions grecques du Boubasteion d'Alexandrie." *Ancient Society* 44: 149–177.

Agut-Labordère, D. (2016). "From Cultural to Political Persianism: The Use and Abuse of the Memory Concerning the Looting of the Egyptian Temples during the Ptolemaic Period," in M. J. Verslyus and R. Strootman, eds., *Persianism in Antiquity*. Leiden.

Alcock, S. E., J. Bodel, and R. J. A. Talbert, eds. (2012). *Highways, Byways, and Road Systems in the Pre-modern World*. Chichester and Malden.

Alcock, S. E., T. N. D'Altroy, K. D. Morrison, and C. M. Sinopoli, eds. (2001). *Empires: Perspectives from Archaeology and History*. Cambridge.

Alföldi, A. (1970). *Die monarchische Repräsentation im römischen Kaiserreiche*. Darmstadt.

Alföldy, G. (1977). *Konsulat und Senatorenstand unter den Antoninen: prosopogra-phische Untersuchungen zur senatorischen Führungsschicht*. Bonn.

Alföldy, G. (1984). *Römische Statuen in Venetia et Histria: Epigraphische Quellen*. Heidelberg.

Alram, M., M. Blet-Lemarquand, and P. O. Skjaervø. (2007). "Shapur, King of Kings of Iranians and Non-Iranians," in R. Gyselen, ed., *Des Indo-Grecs aux Sassanides: Données pour l'histoire et la géographie historique*. Bures-sur-Yvette: 11–40.

Anastasiadis, V. I., and G. A. Souris. (2000). *An Index to Roman Imperial Constitutions from Greek Inscriptions and Papyri: 27 BC to 284 AD*. Berlin.

Anderson, A. (1998). "Cosmopolitanism, Universalism, and the Divided Legacies of Modernity," in P. Cheah and B. Robbins, eds., *Cosmopolitics: Thinking and Feeling beyond the Nation*. Minneapolis: 265–89.

Ando, C. (2000). *Imperial Ideology and Provincial Loyalty in the Roman Empire*. Berkeley.

Ando, C. (2006). "The Administration of the Provinces," in D. S. Potter, ed., *A Companion to the Roman Empire*. Oxford: 177–92.

Ando, C. (2007). "Exporting Roman Religion," in J. Rüpke, ed., *A Companion to Roman Religion*. Malden: 429–45.

Ando, C. (2008). *The Matter of the Gods: Religion and the Roman Empire*. Berkeley.

Ando, C. (2010). "Imperial Identities," in T. Whitmarsh, ed., *Local Knowledge and Microidentities in the Imperial Greek World*. Cambridge: 17–45.

Ando, C. (2011). *Law, Language and Empire in the Roman Tradition*. Philadelphia.

Ando, C. (2012a). *Imperial Rome AD 193 to 284: The Critical Century*. Edinburgh.

Ando, C. (2012b). "Die Riten der Anderen." Translated by G. F. Chiai, R. Häussler, and C. Kunst. *Mediterraneo Antico* 15: 31–50.

Ando, C. (2014). "Pluralism and Empire, from Rome to Robert Cover." *Critical Analysis of Law: An International & Interdisciplinary Law Review* 1: 1–22.

Ando, C. (2015a). "Fact, Fiction and Social Reality in Roman Law," in M. del Mar and W. Twining, eds., *Legal Fictions in Theory and Practice*. Boston: 295–323.

Ando, C. (2015b). "Mythistory: The Pre-Roman Past in Latin Late Antiquity," in H. Leppin, ed., *Antike Mythologie in christlichen Kontexten der Spätantike*. Berlin: 205–18.

Ando, C. (2015c). *Roman Social Imaginaries: Language and Thought in Contexts of Empire*. Toronto.

Ando, C. (2016a). "Colonialism, Colonization: Roman Perspectives," in D. L. Selden and P. Vasunia, eds., *The Oxford Handbook of Literatures of the Roman Empire*. Oxford.

Ando, C. (2016b). "Three Revolutions in Government," in L. Reinfandt, S. Prochazka, and S. Tost, eds., *Official Epistolography and the Languages of Power*. Vienna.

Ando, C. (forthcoming a-). "The Political Economy of the Hellenistic Polis: Comparative and Modern Perspectives," in Henning Börm and Nino Luraghi, eds., *The Polis in the Hellenistic World*. Steiner.

Ando, C. (forthcoming b). "City, Village, Sacrifice: The Political Economy of Religion in the Early Roman Empire," in Richard Evans, ed., *Mass and Elite in the Greek and Roman World*. Ashgate.

André, J. M. (1962). *Recherches sur l'otium romain*. Paris.

Annus, A. (2002). *The God Ninurta in the Mythology and Royal Ideology of Ancient Mesopotamia*. Helsinki.

Appiah, K. A. (2006). *Cosmopolitanism: Ethics in a World of Strangers*. New York.

Asmussen, J. (1971). "Einige Bemerkungen zur sasanidischen Handarz—Literatur," in E. Cerulli, ed., *La Persia nel Medioevo*. Rome: 269–76.

Assmann, J. (2008). *Of God and Gods: Egypt, Israel, and the Rise of Monotheism*. Madison.

Assmann, J. (2010). "Globalization, Universalism, and the Erosion of Cultural Memory," in A. Assmann and S. Conrad, eds., *Memory in a Global Age: Discourses, Practices and Trajectories*. New York: 121–37.

Ataç, Mehmet Ali (forthcoming). "The Historical Memory of the Late Bronze Age in the Neo-Assyrian Palace Reliefs," paper given November 23, 2013, Sapienza Università di Roma.

Attridge, H. (1976). *First-Century Cynicism in the Epistles of Heraclitus*. Missoula.

Bach, J. (2013). "Berossos, Antiochos und die Babyloniaka." *Ancient West and East* 12: 157–80.

Bagg, A. (2013). "Palestine under Assyrian Rule: A New Look at the Assyrian Imperial Policy in the West." *Journal of the American Oriental Society* 133/1: 119–43.

Bagnall, R. S. (1976). *The Administration of the Ptolemaic Possessions outside Egypt*. Leiden.

Baker, H. (2013). "The Image of the City in Hellenistic Babylonia," in E. Stavrianopoulou, ed., *Shifting Social Imaginaries in the Hellenistic Period: Narrations, Practices, and Images*. Leiden: 51–65.

Baker, H. D. and M. Groß (2015). "Doing the King's Work: Perceptions of Service in the Assyrian Royal Correspondence," in S. Procházka, L. Reinfandt, and S. Tost, eds., *Official Epistolography and the Language(s) of Power*. Vienna: 73–90

Banaji, J. (2001/2007). *Agrarian Change in Late Antiquity: Gold, Labour, and Aristocratic Dominance*. Oxford.

Banaji, J. (2015). "'Regions that Look Seaward': Changing Fortunes, Submerged Histories, and the Slow Capitalism of the Sea," in F. De Romanis and M. Maiuro, eds., *Across the Ocean: Nine Essays on Indo-Mediterranean Trade*. Leiden: 114–26.

Bang, P. F. (2008). *The Roman Bazaar: A Comparative Study of Trade and Markets in a Tributary Empire*. Cambridge.

Bang, P. F. (2011). "Lord of All the World—The State, Heterogeneous Power and Hegemony in the Roman and Mughal Empires," in P. F. Bang and C.A. Bayly eds., *Tributary Empires in History*. Basingstoke: 171–92.

Bang, P. F. (2012). "Between Aśoka and Antiochos: An Essay in World History on Universal Kingship and Cosmopolitan Culture in the Hellenistic Ecumene," in P. F. Bang and D. Kołodziejczyk, eds., *Universal Empire: A Comparative Approach to Imperial Culture and Representation in Eurasian History*. Cambridge: 60–75.

Bang, P. F. (2015). "Platonism: Ernest Gellner, Greco-Roman Society and the Comparative Study of the Premodern World." *Thesis 11* 128: 56–71.

Bang, P. F., and C. A. Bayly, eds. (2003). *Tributary Empires in History: Comparative Perspectives from Antiquity to the late Medieval*. Special issue of *The Medieval History Journal* 6.2.

Bang, P. F. and C. A. Bayly, eds. (2011). *Tributary Empires in Global History*. Basingstoke and New York.

Bang, P. F., and D. Kołodziejczyk, eds. (2012). *Universal Empire: A Comparative Approach to Imperial Culture and Representation in Eurasian History*. Cambridge.

Bang, P. F., and K. Turner (2015). "Kingship and Elite Formation," in W. Scheidel, ed., *State Power in Ancient China and Rome*. New York: 11–38.

Bang, P. F., and W. Scheidel (2013). *The Oxford Handbook of the State in the Ancient Near East and Mediterranean*. Oxford.

Barbantani, S. (2005). "Goddess of Love and Mistress of the Sea: Notes on a Hellenistic Hymn to Arsinoe-Aphrodite (P. Lit. Goodspeed 2, I–IV)." *AncSoc* 35: 135–65.

Barbieri, G. (1952). *L'albo senatorio da Settimio Severo a Carino (193-285)*. Rome.

Bardill, J. (2011). *Constantine, Divine Emperor of the Christian Golden Age*. Cambridge.

Barfield, T. J. (2001). "The Shadow Empires: Imperial State Formation along the Chinese-Nomad Frontier," in S. E. Alcock, T. N. D'Altroy, K. D. Morrison, and C. M. Sinopoli, eds., *Empires: Perspectives from Archaeology and History*. Cambridge: 10–41.

Barjamovic, G. (2012). "Propaganda and Practice in Assyrian and Persian Imperial Culture," in P. F. Bang and D. Kołodziejczyk, eds., *Universal Empire: A Comparative Approach to Imperial Culture and Representation in Eurasian History*. Cambridge: 43–59.

Barnes, T. D. (1998). *Ammianus Marcellinus and the Representation of Historical Reality.* Ithaca and London.

Bartelson, J. (2009). *Visions of World Community.* Cambridge.

Beaulieu, P.-A. (1992). "Antiquarian Theology in Seleucid Uruk." *Acta Sumerologica* 14: 47–75.

Beaulieu, P.-A. (1993). "The Historical Background of the Uruk Prophecy," in N. E. Cohen, D. C. Snell, and D. B. Weisberg, eds., *The Tablet and the Scroll: Near Eastern Studies in Honor of William W. Hallo.* Bethesda: 41–52.

Beaulieu, P.-A. (1995a). "The Brewers of Nippur." *Journal of Cuneiform Studies* 47: 85–96.

Beaulieu, P.-A. (1995b). "Theological and Philosophical Speculations on the Name of the Goddess Antu." *Orientalia* 64: 187–213.

Beaulieu, P.-A. (2000). "The Descendants of Sîn-lēqi-unninni," in J. Marzahn and H. Neumann, eds., *Assyriologica et Semitica: Festschrift für Joachim Oelsner anläßlich seines 65. Geburtstages am 18. Februar 1997.* Münster: 1–16.

Beaulieu, P.-A. (2003). *The Pantheon of Uruk during the Neo-Babylonian Period.* Leiden.

Beaulieu, P.-A. (2005). "World Hegemony, 900-300 BCE," in D. C. Snell, ed., *A Companion to the Ancient Near East.* Blackwell: 48–69.

Beaulieu, P.-A. (2006a). "Official and Vernacular Languages: The Shifting Sands of Imperial and Cultural Identities in First-Millennium B.C. Mesopotamia," in S. L. Sanders, ed., *Margins of Writing, Origins of Culture.* Chicago: 191–220.

Beaulieu, P.-A. (2006b). "Berossus on Late Babylonian History." *Oriental Studies*, Special Issue: 116–49.

Beaulieu, P.-A. (2014). "Nabû and Apollo: The Two Faces of Seleucid Religious Policy," in F. Hoffmann and K. S. Schmidt, eds., *Orient und Okzident in hellenistischer Zeit.* Vaterstetten: 13–20.

Beck, U. (2006). *The Cosmopolitan Vision.* Cambridge.

Becker, A. (2009). "Martyrdom, Religious Difference, and 'Fear' as Religious Categories in the Sasanian Empire: The Case of the Martyrdom of Gregory and the Martyrdom of Yazdpaneh." *Journal of Late Antiquity* 2: 300–336.

Becker, A. (2014). "Political Theology and Religious Diversity in the Sasanian Empire," in G. Herman, ed., *Jews, Christians and Zoroastrians: Religious Dynamics in a Sasanian Context.* Piscataway: 7–25.

Bedford, P. R. (2009). "The Neo-Assyrian Empire," in I. Morris, and W. Scheidel, eds., *The Dynamics of Ancient Empires: State Power from Assyria to Byzantium.* Oxford: 30–65.

Beecroft, A. (2008). "World Literature without a Hyphen." *New Left Review* 54: 87–100.

Beecroft, A. (2010). "When Cosmopolitanisms Intersect: An Early Chinese Buddhist Apologetic and World Literature." *Comparative Literature Studies* 47: 266–89.

Beecroft, A. (2015). *An Ecology of World Literature: From Antiquity to the Present Day.* London.

Bencivenni, A. (2014). "The King's Words: Hellenistic Royal Letters in Inscriptions," in K. Radner, ed., *State Correspondence in the Ancient World: From New Kingdom Egypt to the Roman Empire.* Oxford: 141–71.

Benhabib, S. (2006). *Another Cosmopolitanism.* Oxford and New York.

Bennett, C. (2011). *Alexandria and the Moon: An Investigation into the Lunar Macedonian Calendar of Ptolemaic Egypt*. Leuven.

Benton, L., and R. J. Ross, eds. (2013). *Legal Pluralism and Empires, 1500–1850*. New York.

Bernard, P. (2005). "Hellenistic Arachosia: A Greek Melting Pot in Action." *East and West* 55: 13–34.

Bernbeck, R. (2010). "Imperialist Networks: Ancient Assyria and the United States." *Present Pasts* 2: 142–68.

Bertrand, J.-M. (1990). "Formes de discours politiques: Décrets des cités grecques et correspondance des rois hellénistiques," in C. Nicolet, ed., *Du pouvoir dans l'antiquité: Mots et realités*. Paris and Geneva: 101–15.

Bhabha, H. K. (1994). *The Location of Culture*. London.

Bianchi, R. S. (1978). "The Striding Draped Male Figure of Ptolemaic Egypt," in H. Maehler and V. M. Strocka, eds., *Das Ptolemäische Ägypten: Akten d. internat. Symposions, 27.-29. September 1976 in Berlin*. Mainz: 95–102 and fig. 152–69.

Bing, P. (2003). "Posidippus the Admiral: Kallikrates of Samos in the Milan Epigrams." *Greek, Roman, and Byzantine Studies* 43: 243–66.

Blasius, A. (2001). "Army and Society in Ptolemaic Egypt—a Question of Loyalty." *Archiv für Papyrusforschung* 47: 81–98.

Blinkenberg, C. (1912). *La Chronique du temple lindien*. Copenhagen.

Blinkenberg, C. (1915). *Die Lindische Tempelchronik*. Bonn.

Boffo, L. (1988). "Epigrafi di città greche: Un'espressione di storiografia locale," in L. Boffo, ed., *Studi di storia e storiografia antiche per Emilio Gabba*. Pavia: 9–48.

Börm, H. (2008). "'Es war allerdings nicht so, dass sie im Sinne eines Tributes erhielten, wie viele meinten . . .': Anlässe und Funktion der persischen Geldforderungen an die Römer (3. bis 6. Jh.)." *Historia* 57: 327–46.

Branham, R. B. (2007). "Exile on Main Street: Citizen Diogenes," in J. F. Gaertner, ed., *Writing Exile: The Discourse of Displacement in Greco-Roman Antiquity and Beyond*. Leiden: 71–86.

Branham, R. B., and M. Goulet-Cazé, eds. (1996). *The Cynics: The Cynic Movement in Antiquity and Its Legacy*. Berkeley.

Bransbourg, G. (2008). "Fiscalité impériale et finances municipales au IVe siècle." *Antiquité tardive* 16: 255–96.

Bransbourg, G. (2009). "Julien, l'*immunitas Christi*, les dieux et les cités." *Antiquité tardive* 17: 151–8.

Bratke, E. (1899). *Das sogennante Religionsgespräch am Hof der Sasaniden*. Leipzig.

Bremmer, J. (2009). "Zeus' Own Country: Cult and Myth in the Pride of Halicarnassus," in F. Graf, C. Walde and U. Dill, eds., *Antike Mythen: Medien, Transformation und Konstruktionen*. Berlin: 292–312.

Bremmer, J. (2012). "Local Mythography: The Pride of Halicarnassus," in S. M. Trzaskoma and R. S. Smith, eds., *Writing Myth: Mythography in the Ancient World*. Leuven: 55–73.

Brennan, T. (1989). "Cosmopolitans and Celebrities." *Race and Class* 31: 1–19.

Brennan, T. (1997). *At Home in the World: Cosmopolitanism Now*. Cambridge.

Bresson, A. (2006). 'Relire la Chronique du temple lindien', *Topoi* 14.2: 27–551

Briant, P. (1987). "Pouvoir central et polycentrisme culturel dans l'empire achémé-nide: Quelques réflexions et suggestions." *Achaemenid History* 1: 1–31.

Briant, P. (1988). "Ethno-classe dominante et populations soumises dans l'empire achéménide: Le Cas d'Egypte," in A. Kuhrt and H. Sancisi-Weerdenburg, eds., *Achaemenid History*. Vol. 3. Leiden: 137–73.

Briant, P. (1994). "Sources gréco-hellénistiques, institutions perses et institutions macé-doniennes: Continuités, changements et bricolages." *Achaemenid History* 7: 283–310.

Briant, P. (2002). *From Cyrus to Alexander: A History of the Persian Empire*. Winona Lake.

Briant, P. (2003). "Quand les rois écrivent l'histoire: La Domination achéménide vue à travers les inscriptions officielles lagides," in N. Grimal, ed., *Événement, récit, histoire officielle: L'Écriture de l'histoire dans les monarchies antique*. Paris: 173–86.

Briant, P. (2009). "Le Passé réutilisé dans les cours hellénistiques," in H. Barstad and P. Briant, eds., *The Past in the Past: Concepts of Past Reality in Ancient Near Eastern and Early Greek Thought*. Oslo: 21–36.

Bricault, L. (2006). *Isis, Dame des flots*. Liège.

Brisch, N. (2011). "Changing Images of Kingship in Sumerian Literature," in K. Radner and E. Robson, eds., *The Oxford Handbook of Cuneiform Culture*. Oxford: 706–24.

Brock, S. P. (1996). "The 'Nestorian' Church: A Lamentable Misnomer." *Bulletin of the John Rylands University Library* 78: 23–35.

Brown, B. (2014). "Culture on Display: Representations of Ethnicity in the Art of the Late Assyrian State," in B. Brown and M. Feldman, eds., *Critical Approaches to Ancient Near Eastern Art*. Berlin: 515–44.

Brown, D. (2000). *Mesopotamian Planetary Astronomy-Astrology*. Groningen.

Brown, E. (2006). "Hellenistic Cosmopolitanism," in M. L. Gill and P. Pellegrin, eds., *A Companion to Ancient Philosophy*. Oxford: 549–58.

Brown, P. R. L. (1992). *Power and Persuasion in Late Antiquity: Towards a Christian Empire*. Madison.

Brown, P. R. L. (2000). "The Study of Elites in Late Antiquity." *Arethusa* 33: 321–46.

Bruns, P. (2009). "Paul der Perser—Christ und Philosoph im spätantiken Sasanidenreich." *Römische Quartalschrift für christliche Altertumskunde und Kirchengeschichte* 104: 28–53.

Bruns, P. (2014). "Antizoroastrische Polemik in den Syro-Persischen Märtyrerakten," in G. Herman, ed., *Jews, Christians and Zoroastrians: Religious Dynamics in a Sasanian Context*. Piscataway: 47–65.

Brunschwig, J. (1994). "Remarks on the Stoic Theory of the Proper Noun" in J. Brunschwig, *Papers in Hellenistic Philosophy*. Cambridge: 39–56.

Brunt, P. A. (1976). "The Romanization of the Local Ruling Classes in the Roman Empire," in D. M. Pippidi, ed., *Assimilation et résistance à la culture gréco-romaine dans le monde ancient*. Paris: 161–73.

Brunt, P. A. (1977). "Lex de Imperio Vespasiani." *Journal of Roman Studies* 67: 95–116.

Brunt, P. A. (1981). "The Revenues of Rome." *Journal of Roman Studies* 71: 161–72.

Brunt, P. A. (1990). *Roman Imperial Themes*. Oxford.

Bryen, Ari Z. (2016). "Reading the Citizenship Papyrus. P. Giss. I 40," in Clifford Ando, ed., *Citizenship and Empire in Europe, 200-1900: The Antonine Constitution after 1800 Years*. Stuttgart: 29–43.

Buell, D. (2002). "Race and Universalism in Early Christianity." *Journal of Early Christian Studies* 10: 429–68.

Bukharin, M. D. (2009). *Araviya, Vostochnaya Afrika i Sredizemnomorye: Torgovie i Istoriko-Kulturnie Svyazi.* Moscow.

Burbank, J., and F. Cooper. (2010). *Empires in World History: Power and the Politics of Difference.* Princeton.

Burstein, S. M. (1978). *The Babyloniaca of Berossus.* Malibu.

Burton, M., and J. Higley (1987). "Elite Settlements." *American Sociological Review* 52/3: 295–307.

Calhoun, C. (2002). "The Class Consciousness of Frequent Travelers: Toward a Critique of Actually Existing Cosmopolitanism." *South Atlantic Quarterly* 101: 869–97.

Cameron, A. (2014). *Dialoguing in Late Antiquity.* Cambridge.

Cameron, A. D. E. (2011). *The Last Pagans of Rome.* Oxford.

Cancik, H. (2008). "Antike Religionsgespräche," in G. Schörner and D. Š. Erker, eds., *Medien religiöser Kommunikation im Imperium Romanum.* Stuttgart: 15–25.

Cancik, H., and J. Rüpke, eds. (1997). *Römische Reichsreligion und Provinzialreligion.* Tübingen.

Canepa, M. P. (2009). *The Two Eyes of the Earth: Art and Ritual of Kingship between Rome and Sasanian Iran.* Berkeley.

Canepa, M. P. (2010a). "Technologies of Memory in Early Sasanian Iran: Achaemenid Sites and Sasanian Identity." *American Journal of Archaeology* 114: 563–96.

Canepa, M. P. (2010b). "Achaemenid and Seleucid Royal Funerary Practices and Middle Iranian Kingship," in H. Börm and J. Wiesehöfer, eds., *Commutatio et contentio: Studies in the Late Roman, Sasanian, and Early Islamic Near East.* Düsseldorf: 1–21.

Canepa, M. P. (2010c). "Distant Displays of Power: Understanding Cross-Cultural Interaction among the Elites of Rome, Sasanian Iran, and Sui Tang China," in M. Canepa, ed., *Theorizing Cross-Cultural Interaction among the Ancient and Early Medieval Mediterranean, Near East and Asia.* Washington: 121–54.

Canepa, M. P. (2013). "Building a New Vision of the Past in the Sasanian Empire: The Sanctuaries of Kayānsīh and Great Fires of Iran." *Journal of Persianate Studies* 6: 64–90.

Canepa, M. P. (2014). "Textiles and Elite Tastes between the Mediterranean, Iran and Asia at the End of Antiquity," in M. L. Nosch, Z. Feng and L. Varadarajan, eds., *Global Textile Encounters.* Oxford: 1–14.

Canepa, M. P. (2015). "Seleukid Sacred Architecture, Royal Cult and the Transformation of Iranian Culture in the Middle Iranian Period." *Iranian Studies* 48: 71–97.

Caneva, S. (2014). "Courtly Love, Stars, and Power: The Queen in 3rd-Century Royal Couples, through Poetry and Epigraphic Texts," in A. M. Harder, R. F. Regtuit, and G. C. Wakker, eds., *Hellenistic Poetry in Context.* Leuven, Paris, and Walpole: 25–58.

Capdetrey, L. (2007). *Le Pouvoir séleucide: Territoire, administration, finances d'un royaume hellénistique (312–129 avant J.C.).* Rennes.

Carney, E. D. (2013). *Arsinoë of Egypt and Macedon: A Royal Life.* Oxford.

Carrié, J.-M. (1994). "Diocletien et la fiscalité." *Antiquité Tardive* 2: 33–64.

Carrié, J.-M., and A. Rousselle. (1999). *L'Empire romain en mutation.* Paris.

Carroll, M. (2006). *Spirits of the Dead: Roman Funerary Commemoration in Western Europe.* Oxford.

Cavigneaux, A. (2005). "Shulgi, Nabonide, et les Grecs," in Y. Sefati, P. Artzi, C. Cohen, B. L. Eichler, and V. A. Horowitz, eds., *An Experienced Scribe Who Neglects Nothing: Ancient Near Eastern Studies in Honor of Jacob Klein.* Bethesda: 63–72.

Chang, C. (2007). *The Rise of Chinese Empire.* Vol. 1: *Nation, State, and Imperialism in Early China, ca. 1600 B.C.–A.D. 8.* Ann Arbor.

Chaniotis, A. (1988). *Historie und Historiker in den griechischen Inschriften.* Stuttgart.

Chaniotis, A. (2011). "The Ithyphallic Hymn for Demetrios Poliorketes and Hellenistic Religious Mentality," in P. P. Iossif, A. S. Chankowski, and C. Lorber, eds., *More Than Men, Less Than Gods—Studies on Royal Cult and Imperial Worship.* Leuven, Paris, Walpole: 157–96.

Chastagnol, A. (1977). "Le Problème du domicile légale des sénateurs romains à l'époque impériale," in *Mélanges offerts à Leopold Sédar Senghor.* Dakar: 43–54.

Chastagnol, A. (1988). "Le Formulaire de l'epigraphie latine officielle dans l'antiquite tardive," in A. Donati, ed., *La terza età dell'epigrafia: Colloquio AIEGL-Borghesi 86 (Bologna, ottobre 1986).* Faenza: 11–65.

Chastagnol, A. (1992). *Le Sénat romain à l'époque impériale: Recherches sur la composition de l'Assemblée et le statut de ses membres.* Paris.

Cheah, P. (2006). "Cosmopolitanism." *Theory, Culture & Society* 23: 486–96.

Chin, T. (2014). *Savage Exchange: Han Imperialism, Chinese Literary Style, and the Economic Imagination.* Cambridge.

Christ, F. (1938). *Die römische Weltherrschaft in der antiken Dichtung.* Stuttgart.

Christol, M. (1986). *Essai sur l'évolution des carrières sénatoriales dans la seconde moitié du III s. ap. J.C.* Paris.

Ciffarelli, M. (1995). "Enmity, Alienation and Assyrianization: The Role of Cultural Difference in the Visual and Verbal Expression of Assyrian Ideology in the Reign of Ashshurnasirpal II (883–859 B.C.)." PhD diss., Columbia University.

Clancier, P. (2009). *Les Bibliothèques en Babylonie dans la deuxième moitié du Ier millénaire av. J.-C.* Münster.

Clancier, P. (2011). "Cuneiform Culture's Last Guardians: The Old Urban Notability of Hellenistic Uruk," in K. Radner and E. Robson, eds., *The Oxford Handbook of Cuneiform Culture.* Oxford and New York: 752–73.

Clancier, P. (2012). "Le šatammu, l'assemblée de l'Esagil, et les Babyloniens: Les notables de Babylone: du relais local à la marginalisation," in C. Feyel, J. Fournier, L. Graslin-Thomé, and F. Kirbihler, eds., *Communautés locales et pouvoir central dans l'Orient hellénistique et romain.* Nancy: 298–326.

Clarke, K. (2005). "Parochial Tales in a Global Empire: Creating and Recreating the World of the Itinerant Historian," in L. Troiani and G. Zecchini, eds., *La cultura storica nei primi due secoli dell'impero Romano.* Rome: 111–28.

Clarke, K. (2008). *Making Time for the Past: Local History and the Polis.* Oxford.

Clarysse, W. (2000). "Ptolémées et temples," in D. Valbelle and J. Leclant, eds., *Le Décret de Memphis. Colloque de la Fondation Singer-Polignac à l'occasion de la célébration du bicentenaire de la découverte de la Pierre de Rosette.* Paris: 41–65.

Clarysse, W. (2007). "A Royal Journey in the Delta in 257 B.C. and the Date of the Mendes Stele." *Chronique d'Egypte* 82: 201–6.

Clarysse, W., and G. van der Veken. (1983). *The Eponymous Priests of Ptolemaic Egypt: Chronological Lists of the Priests of Alexandria and Ptolemais with a Study of the Demotic Transcriptions of Their Names.* Leiden.

Clayden, T. (2009). "Eye-stones." *Zeitschrift für Orient-Archäologie* 2: 36–86.

Colburn, H. P. (2015). "Memories of the Second Persian Period in Egypt," in J. M. Silverman and C. Waerzeggers, eds., *Political Memory in and after the Persian Empire.* Atlanta:165–202.

Colditz, I. (2000). *Zur Sozialterminologie der iranischen Manichäer: Eine semantische analyse im Vergleich zu den nichtmanichäischen iranischen Quellen.* Wiesbaden.

Cole, E. (2015). "Interpretation and Authority: The Social Functions of Translation in Ancient Egypt." PhD diss., UCLA, Los Angeles.

Cole, S. W. (1996). *Nippur in Neo-Assyrian Times, c. 755–612 BC.* Helsinki.

Coles, R. A. (1966). *Reports of Proceedings in Papyri.* Brussels.

Collombert, P. (2000). "Religion égyptienne et culture grecque: L'Exemple de Dioskourides." *Chronique d'Egypte* 75: 47–63, 46 pl.

Collombert, P. (2008). "La 'Stèle de Saïs' et l'instauration du culte d'Arsinoé dans la chôra." *Ancient Society* 38: 83–100.

Compatangelo-Soussignan, R., and C.-G. Schwentzel, eds. (2007). *Étrangers dans la cité romaine: Actes du colloque de Valenciennes, 14-15 octobre 2005: "Habiter une autre patrie: des incolae de la république aux peuples fédérés du bas-empire."* Rennes.

Cornell, T. J. (1995). *The Beginnings of Rome.* London.

Cosgrove, D. (2003). "Globalism and Tolerance in Early Modern Geography." *Annals of the Association of American Geographers* 93/4: 852–70.

Coskun, A. (2009). *Bürgerrechtsentzug oder Fremdenausweisung? Studien zu den Rechten von Latinern und weiteren Fremden sowie zum Bürgerrechtswechsel in der Römischen Republik (5. bis frühes 1. Jh. v. Chr.).* Stuttgart.

Coulon, L. (2001). "Quand Amon parle à Platon (La statue Caire JE 38033)." *Revue d'Égyptologie* 52: 85–111.

Coulton, J. J. (1987). "Opramoas and the Anonymous Benefactor." *Journal of Hellenic Studies* 107: 171–8.

Daryaee, T. (2006). "The Sasanians and Their Ancestors," in A. Panaino and A. Piras, eds., *Proceedings of the 5th Conference of the Societas Iranologica Europae,* Vol. 1: *Ancient and Middle Iranian Studies.* Milan: 389–93.

de Blois, F. (1990). *Burzōy's Voyage to India and the Origin of the Book of Kalīlah wa Dimna.* London.

De Breucker, G. (2010). "Berossos (680)." In *Brill's New Jacoby Online.*

De Breucker, G. (2012). *De Babyloniaca van Berossos van Babylon. Inleiding, editie en commentaar.* PhD diss., Groningen.

De Breucker, G. (2013). "Berossos: His Life and His Work," in J. Haubold et al., eds., *The World of Berossos.* Wiesbaden: 15–28.

de Jong, A. (2005). "The First Sin: Zoroastrian Ideas about the Time before Zarathustra," in S. Shaked, ed., *Genesis and Regeneration: Essays on Conceptions of Origins.* Jerusalem: 192–209.

de la Vaissière, E. (2005). *Sogdian Traders: A History*. Leiden.

Debié, M. (2010). "L'Empire perse et ses marges," in J.-R. Armogathe, P. Montaubin, and M.-Y. Perrin, eds., *Histoire générale du christianisme des origins au XVe siècle*. Paris: 611–46.

Del Monte, G. F. (1997). *Testi dalla Babilonia Ellenistica I: Testi cronografici*. Pisa and Rome.

Delanty, G. (2012). *The Routledge Handbook of Cosmopolitanism Studies*. London.

Demetriou, D. (2010). "Τῆς πάσης ναυτιλίης φύλαξ: Aphrodite and the Sea." *Kernos* 23: 67–89.

Devijver, H. (1991). "The Geographical Origins of Equestrian Officers," in *Future of Roman Army Studies*, 107-126 (=*The Equestrian Officers of the Roman Imperial Army II*. Stuttgart, 109–128).

Dewar, M. (2014). *Leisured Resistance*. London.

Dietler, M. (2010). *Archaeologies of Colonialism: Consumption, Entanglement, and Violence in Ancient Mediterranean France*. Berkeley.

Dillery, J. (1999). "The First Egyptian Narrative History: Manetho and Greek Historiography." *Zeitschrift für Papyrologie und Epigraphik* 127: 93–116.

Dillery, J. (2005). "Greek Sacred History." *American Journal of Philology* 126: 505–26.

Dillery, J. (2013). "Berossos Narrative of Nabopolassar and Nebuchadnezzar II from Josephus," in J. Haubold et al., eds., *The World of Berossos*. Wiesbaden: 75–96.

Dillery, J. (2015). *Clio's Other Sons: Berossus and Manetho, with an Afterword on Demetrius*. Ann Arbor.

Doonan, O. P. (2004). *Sinop Landscapes: Exploring Connection in a Black Sea Hinterland*. Philadelphia.

Doyle, M. (1986). *Empires*. Ithaca.

Drews, R. (1975). "The Babylonian Chronicles and Berossos." *Iraq* 37: 39–55.

Dreyer, B., and P. F. Mittag. (2011). *Lokale Eliten und hellenistische Könige: Zwischen Kooperation und Konfrontation*. Berlin.

Droysen, J. G. (2008). *Geschichte der Epigonen, Geschichte des Hellenismus 3*. Darmstadt.

Duara, P. (2014). *The Crisis of Global Modernity: Asian Traditions and a Sustainable Future*. Cambridge.

duBois, P. (2014). *A Million and One Gods*. Princeton.

Dubovský, P. (2012). "King's Direct Control: Neo-Assyrian Qēpu Officials," in G. Wilhelm, ed., *Organization, Representation, and Symbols of Power in the Ancient Near East*. Winona Lake: 449–60.

Duindam, J., T. Artan, and M. Kunt, eds. (2011). *Royal Courts in Dynastic States and Empires: A Global Perspective*. Leiden.

Duncan-Jones, R. (1982). *The Economy of the Roman Empire: Quantitative Studies*. Cambridge.

Duncan-Jones, R. (2006). "Who Were the *Equites*?," in C. Deroux, ed., *Studies in Latin literature and Roman history* 13. Brussels: 183–223.

Dunn, J. (1988). "Trust and Political Agency," in D. Gambetta, ed., *Trust: Making and Breaking Cooperative Relations*. Oxford: 73–92.

Dusinberre, E. R. M. (2003). *Aspects of Empire in Achaemenid Sardis*. Cambridge.

Dusinberre, E. R. M. (2013). *Empire, Authority, and Autonomy in Achaemenid Anatolia.* Cambridge.

Eck, W. (1979). *Die staatliche Organisation Italiens in der hohen Kaiserzeit.* Munich.

Eck, W. (1995-8). *Die Verwaltung des römischen Reiches in der Hohen Kaiserzeit. Ausgewählte und erweiterte Beiträge,* ed. R. Frei-Stolba and M. A. Speidel. 2 vols. Basel.

Eck, W. (2000). "Emperor, Senate and Magistrates," in A. K. Bowman, P. Garnsey, D. Rathbone, eds., *The Cambridge Ancient History.* Vol. 11: *The High Empire,* AD 170–192. Cambridge: 214-37.

Eck, W. (2009). "Diplomacy as Part of the Administrative Process in the Roman Empire," in C. Eilers, ed., *Diplomats and Diplomacy in the Roman World.* Leiden: 193-207.

Edwards, C., and G. Woolf, eds. (2003). *Rome the Cosmopolis.* Cambridge.

Eich, P. (2005). *Zur Metamorphose des politischen Systems in der römischen Kaiserzeit: Die Entstehung einer "personalen Bürokratie" im langen dritten Jahrhundert.* Berlin.

Eilers, C., ed. (2009). *Diplomats and Diplomacy in the Roman World.* Leiden.

Eisenstadt, S. N. (1963). *The Political Systems of Empires.* New York.

El-Masry, Y., H. Altenmüller, and H. J. Thissen. (2012). *Das Synodaldekret von Alexandria aus dem Jahre 243 v. Chr.* Buske.

Emberling, G. (2014). "Ethnicity in Empire: Assyrians and Others," in J. McInerney, ed., *A Companion to Ethnicity in the Ancient Mediterranean.* London: 158-74.

Erskine, A. (1994). "The Romans as Common Benefactors." *Historia* 43: 70–87.

Euzennat, M., and J. Marion, eds. (1982). *Inscriptions antiques du Maroc.* Vol. 2: *Inscriptions latines.* Paris.

Fales, F. M. (1982). "The Enemy in Assyrian Royal Inscriptions: 'The Moral Judgement'," in H. J. Nissen, and J. Renger, eds., *Mesopotamien und seine Nachbarn: Politische und kulturelle Wechselbeziehungen im alten Vorderasien vom 4. bis 1. Jahrtausend v. Chr.* Berlin: 425-35.

Fales, F. M. (1990). "The Rural Landscape of the Neo-Assyrian Empire: A Survey." *State Archives of Assyria Bulletin* 4: 81-142.

Fales, F. M. (2009). "'To Speak Kindly to him/them' as Item of Assyrian Political Discourse," in M. Luukko, S. Svärd, and R. Mattila, eds., *Of God(s), Trees, Kings, and Scholars. Neo-Assyrian and Related Studies in Honour of Simo Parpola.* Helsinki: 27-40.

Fales, F. M. (2012). "After Ta'yinat: The New Status of Esarhaddon's *adê* for Assyrian Political History," *Revue d'assyriologie et d'archéologie orientale* 106: 133-58.

Fales, F. M. (2013). "Ethnicity in the Assyrian Empire: A View from the Nisbe. (I): Foreigners and "Special" Inner Communities," in D. S. Vanderhooft and A. Winitzer, eds., *Literature as Politics, Politics as Literature: Essays on the Ancient Near East in Honor of Peter Machinist.* Winona Lake: 47-74.

Fales, Frederick Mario (2015). "Idiolects and Identities in the Neo-Assyrian Epistolary Corpus," in S. Procházka, L. Reinfandt, and S. Tost, eds., *Official Epistolography and the Language(s) of Power.* Vienna: 91-100.

Falkenstein, A. (1941). *Topographie von Uruk.* Leipzig.

Feldman, M. (2014). *Communities of Style: Portable Luxury Arts, Identity and Collective Memory in the Iron Age Levant.* Chicago.

Fincke, J. (2004). "The British Museum's Ashurbanipal Library Project." *Iraq* 66: 55–60.

Fine, R. (2006). "Cosmopolitanism and Violence: Difficulties of Judgment." *British Journal of Sociology* 57: 49–67.

Finn, J. (2011). "Gods, Kings, Men: Trilingual Inscriptions and Symbolic Visualizations in the Achaemenid Empire." *Ars Orientalis* 41: 219–75.

Fischer-Bovet, C. (2014). *Army and Society in Ptolemaic Egypt*. Cambridge.

Fishwick, D. (1987–2005). *The Imperial Cult in the Latin West*. 6 vols. Leiden.

Foster, B. R. (1986). "Archives and Empire in Sargonic Mesopotamia," in K. R. Veenhof, ed., *Cuneiform Archives and Libraries*. Istanbul: 46–52.

Foster, B. R. (2015). "Centre et périphérie: Une perspective mésopotamienne," in C. Roche-Hawley and R. Hawley, eds., *Devins et lettrés dans l'orbite de Babylone*. Paris: 15–22.

Foucault, M. (2011). *The Government of Self and Others: Lectures at the College de France, 1982–1983*. New York.

Frahm, E. (2013). "Rising Suns and Falling Starts: Assyrian Kings and the Cosmos," in J. A. Hill, P. Jones, and A. J. Morales, eds., *Experiencing Power, Generating Authority: Cosmos, Politics, and the Ideology of Kingship in Ancient Egypt and Mesopotamia*. Philadelphia: 97–120.

Fraser, P. M. (1972). *Ptolemaic Alexandria*. Oxford.

Fulinska, A. (2012). "Arsinoe Hoplismene. Poseidippos 36, Arsinoe Philadelphos and the Cypriot Cult of Aphrodite." *Studies in Ancient Art and Civilisation* 16: 141–56.

Gabrielsen, V. (2005). "The Chronicle of Lindos. C. Higbie: The Lindian Chronicle and the Greek Creation of their Past." *Classical Review* 55: 319–22.

Gagné, R. (2006). "What is the Pride of Halicarnassus?" *Classical Antiquity* 25: 1–33.

Gandhi, L. (2014). *The Common Cause: Postcolonial Ethics and the Practice of Democracy, 1900–1955*. Chicago.

Garbarino, P. (1988). *Ricerche sulla procedura di ammissione al senato nel tardo impero Romano*. Milan.

Gardner, G. (2007). "Jewish Leadership and Hellenistic Civic Benefaction in the Second Century BCE." *Journal of Biblical Literature* 126: 327–43.

Gardner, J. F. (2001). "Making Citizens: The Operation of the *Lex Irnitana*," in L. de Blois, ed., *Administration, Prosopography and Appointment Policies in the Roman Empire*. Amsterdam: 215–29.

Garfinkle, S. (2013). "The Third Dynasty of Ur and the Limits of State Power in Early Mesopotamia," in S. Garfinkle and M. Molina, eds., *From the 21st century B.C. to the 21st Century A.D.: Proceedings of the International Conference on Sumerian Studies Held in Madrid 22–July 24 2010*. Winona Lake: 153–67.

Garnsey, P. (1970). *Social Status and Legal Privilege in the Roman Empire*. Oxford.

Garnsey, P. (2007). *Thinking about Property from Antiquity to the Age of Revolution*. Cambridge.

Garnsey, P., and R. P. Saller. (1987). *The Roman Empire: Economy, Society and Culture*. Berkeley.

Garrison, M. B. (1991). "Seals and the Elite at Persepolis: Some Observations on Early Achaemenid Persian Art." *Ars Orientalis* 21: 1–29.

Garsoïan, N. (1997). "Les Éléments iraniens dans l'Arménie paléochrétienne," in N. G. Garsoïan and J.-P. Mahé, eds., *Des Parthes au Califat: Quatre lemons sur la formation de l'identité arménienne*. Paris: 9–37.

Garsoïan, N. (2009). "La Politique arménienne des sassanides," in P Gignoux, ed., *Trésors d'Orient: Mélanges offerts à Rika Gyselen.* Paris: 67–79.

Gellner, E. (1969). *Saints of the Atlas.* London.

Gellner, E. (1981). *Muslim Society.* Cambridge.

Gellner, E. (1983). *Nations and Nationalism.* Oxford.

Gera, G., and S. Giglio (1984). *La tassazione dei senatori nel tardo impero romano.* Rome.

Giardina, A. (1986). "Le due Italie nella forma tarda dell'impero," in A. Giardina, ed., *Società romana e impero tardoantico 1: Istituzioni, ceti, economie.* Bari: 1–36.

Giglio, S. (2007). "Il "munus" della pretura a Roma e Costantinopoli nel tardo impero romano." *AnTard* 15: 65–88.

Gignoux, P. (1983). "Die religiöse Administration in sasanidischer Zeit: Ein Überblick," in H. Koch and D. N. Mackenzie, eds., *Kunst, Kultur, und Geschichte der Achämenidenzeit und ihr Fortleben.* Berlin: 253–66.

Gildenhard, I. (2007). *Paideia Romana: Cicero's Tusculan Disputations.* Cambridge.

Glassner, J.-J. (2005). *Mesopotamian Chronicles.* Leiden and Boston.

Gnoli, G. (1989). *The Idea of Iran: An Essay on its Origin.* Rome.

Go, J. (2011). *Patterns of Empire: The British and American Empires, 1688 to the Present.* Cambridge.

Goddio, F. (1998). *Alexandria: The Submerged Royal Quarters.* London.

Godwin, R. T. (2015). "Persian Christians at the Tang Chinese Court: The Xi'an Stele's Sasanian Heritage." PhD diss., School of Oriental and African Studies.

Goldstone, J. and Haldon, J. (2009). "Ancient States, Empires, and Exploitation: Problems and Perspectives," in I. Morris, and W. Scheidel, eds., *The Dynamics of Ancient Empires: State Power from Assyria to Byzantium.* Oxford: 3–29.

González, J. (1986). "The *Lex Irnitana*: A New Flavian Municipal Law." *Journal of Roman Studies* 76: 147–243.

Gorre, G. (2007). "Identités et représentations dans l'Egypte ptolémaïque." *Ktema* 32: 239–50.

Gorre, G. (2009). *Les Relations du clergé Égyptien et des Lagides d'après les sources privées.* Leuven.

Gorre, G. and Véïsse, A.-E. (forthcoming). 'La brève histoire des décrets sacerdotaux', in G. Gorre and S. Wackenier, eds., *Quand les vertus du prince ne font pas l'État: un renforcement de la monarchie lagide de Ptolémée VI à Ptolémée X ?* Paris.

Goulet-Cazé, M. (1982). "Un Syllogism Stoïcien sur la Loi dans la Doxographie de Diogène le Cynique à propos de Diogène Laërce VI 72." *Rheinisches Museum* 215: 214–40.

Goulet-Cazé, M. (1996). "Defacing the Currency: Diogenes' Rhetoric and the Invention of Cynicism," in R. B. Branham and M. Goulet-Cazé, eds., *The Cynics: The Cynic Movement in Antiquity and Its Legacy,* Berkeley: 81–104.

Goulet-Cazé, M. (2001). *L'Ascèse Cynique: Un Commentaire de Diogène Laërce VI 70–71.* Paris.

Gozzoli, R. B. (2006). *The Writing of History in Ancient Egypt during the First Millennium BC (ca. 1070–180 BC): Trends and Perspectives.* London.

Grayson, A. K. (1975). *Assyrian and Babylonian Chronicles.* Locust Valley.

Grayson, A. K. (1993). "Assyrian Officials and Power in the Ninth and Eighth Centuries." *State Archives of Assyria Bulletin* 7: 19–52.

Grey, C. (2011). *Constructing Communities in the Late Roman Countryside*. Cambridge.

Griffith, S. H. (1992). "Disputes with Muslims in Syriac Christian Texts: from Patriarch John (d. 648) to Bar Hebraeus (d. 1286)," in B. Lewis and F. Niewöhner, eds., *Religionsgespräche im Mittelalter*. Wiesbaden: 251–73.

Gruen, E. S. (2002). *Diaspora: Jews amidst Greeks and Romans*. Cambridge.

Gutas, D. (1998). *Greek Thought, Arabic Culture: The Graeco-Arabic Translation Movement in Baghdad and Early 'Abbāsid Society (2nd-4th/8th-10th centuries)*. London.

Habermas, J. (2001). *The Postnational Constellation*. Cambridge.

Habicht, C. (1958). "Die herrschende Gesellschaft in den hellenistischen Monarchien." *Vierteljahrschrift für Sozial- und Wirtschaftsgeschichte* 45: 1–16.

Habicht, C. (1992). "Athens and the Ptolemies." *Classical Antiquity* 11: 68–90.

Habicht, C. (2006). "The Ruling Class in the Hellenistic Monarchies," in *The Hellenistic Monarchies: Selected Papers*. Ann Arbor: 26–40.

Habicht, C., and C. P. Jones. (1989). "A Hellenistic Inscription from Arsinoe in Cilicia." *Phoenix* 43: 317–46.

Hainthaler, T. (2002). "Der persische Disputator Simeon von Bet Aršam und seine an-tinestorianische Positionsbestimmung," in A. Grillmeier, ed., *Jesus der Christus im Glauben der Kirche*. Vol. 2: *Die Kirchen von Jerusalem und Antiochien nach 451 bis 600*. Freiburg: 262–78.

Haldon, J. (1993). *The State and the Tributary Mode of Production*. London.

Halfmann, H. (1979). *Die Senatoren aus dem östlichen Teil des Imperium Romanum*. Göttingen.

Hall, J. A. (2013). *The Importance of Being Civil: The Struggle for Political Decency*. Princeton.

Hall, J. A. (2010). *Ernest Gellner. An Intellectual Biography*. London.

Hammond, M. (1957). "Composition of the Senate, A.D. 68–235." *Journal of Roman Studies* 47: 74–81.

Hannestad, L. (2013). "A Comparative Study of the Cultural Dynamics in Two Cities of the Eastern Seleucid Kingdom: Uruk and Ai Khanoum," in G. Lindström, S. Hansen, A. Wieczorek, and M. Tellenbach, eds., *Zwischen Ost und West: Neue Forschungen zum antiken Zentralasien*. Darmstadt: 99–113.

Hardt, M., and A. Negri (2001). *Empire*. Cambridge, MA.

Harris, W. V. (1989). *Ancient Literacy*. Cambridge, MA.

Harris, W. V. (2000). "Trade," in A. K. Bowman, ed., *The Cambridge Ancient History*. Vol. 11. *The High Empire, A.D. 70-192*. Cambridge: 710–40.

Hartmann, U. (2002). "Geist im Exile: Römische Philosophen am Hof der Sasaniden," in M. Schuol, U. Hartmann, and A. Luther, eds., *Grenzüberschreitungen: Formen des Kontakts zwischen Orient und Okzident im Altertum*. Stuttgart: 123–60.

Harvey, D. (2009). *Cosmopolitanism and the Geographies of Freedom*. New York.

Hatzopoulos, M. B. (1996). *Macedonian Institutions under the Kings*. 2 vols. Athens.

Hauben, H. (2011). "Ptolémée III et Bérénice II, divinités cosmiques," in P. P. Iossif, A. S. Chankowski, and C. Lorber, eds., *More Than Men, Less Than Gods—Studies on Royal Cult and Imperial Worship*. Leuven, Paris, Walpole: 357–88.

Hauben, H. (2013). "Callicrates of Samos and Patroclus of Macedon, Champions of the Ptolemaic Thalassocracy," in K. Buraselis, M. Stefanou, and D. Thompson, eds., *The Ptolemies, the Sea and the Nile: Studies in Waterborne Power.* Cambridge: 39–65.

Hauben, H., and A. Meeus. (2014). *The Age of the Successors and the Creation of the Hellenistic Kingdoms (323–276 B.C.).* Leuven.

Haubold, J. (2013a). *Greece and Mesopotamia: Dialogues in Literature.* Cambridge.

Haubold, J. (2013b). "'The Wisdom of the Chaldaeans': Reading Berossos, *Babyloniaca* Book 1," in J. Haubold, G. B. Lanfranchi, R. Rollinger, and J. Steele, eds., *The World of Berossos.* Wiesbaden: 31–45.

Haubold, J., G. B. Lanfranchi, R. Rollinger, and J. Steele, eds. (2013). *The World of Berossos.* Wiesbaden.

Hauser, S. (2005). "Die ewige Nomaden? Bemerkungen zu Herkunft, Militär, Staatsaubau und nomadischen Traditionen der Arsakiden," in B. Meißner, O. Schmitt, and M. Sommer, eds., *Krieg—Gesellschaft—Institutionen: Beiträge zu einer vergleichenden Kriegsgeschichte.* Berlin: 163–208.

Heather, P. (1994). "New Men for New Constantines: Creating an Imperial Elite in the Eastern Mediterranean," in P. Magdalino, ed., *New Constantines: The Rhythm of Imperial Renewal in Byzantium, 4th–13th Centuries.* Aldershot: 11–33.

Heather, P. (1998). "Senators and Senates," in A. M. Cameron and P. Garnsey, eds., *The Cambridge Ancient History.* Vol. 13: *The Late Empire, AD 337–425.* Cambridge: 184–210.

Heather, P. (2009). *Empires and Barbarians: Migration, Development and the Birth of Europe.* London.

Heinen, H. (2006). "Hunger, Not und Macht: Bemerkungen zur herrschenden Gesellschaft im ptolemäischen Ägypten." *Ancient Society* 36: 13–44.

Held, D. (2010). *Cosmopolitanism: Ideals and Realities.* Cambridge.

Held, W. (2002). "Die Residenzstädte der Seleukiden: Babylon, Seleukia am Tigris, Seleukia in Pieria, Antiocheia am Orontes." *Jahrbuch des Deutschen Archäologischen Instituts* 117: 217–49.

Henkelman, W. (2008). *The Other Gods Who Are: Studies in Elamite-Iranian Acculturation Based on the Persepolis Fortification Texts.* Leiden.

Henkelman, W., and M. W. Stolper. (2009). "Ethnic Identity and Ethnic Labeling at Persepolis: The Case of the Skudrians," in P. Briant and M. Chauveau, eds., *Organisation des pouvoirs et contacts culturels dans les pays de l'empire achéménide.* Paris: 271–329.

Henri, O. (2013). "Un exemple de l'interpretatio graeca : l'évolution du culte d'Apollon en Égypte ptolémaïque et romaine," in P. Schubert, ed., *Actes du 26e Congrès International de Papyrologie (Genève, 16–21 août 2010).* Geneva: 321–329.

Herman, G. (2012). *A Prince without a Kingdom: The Exilarch in the Sasanian Era.* Tübingen.

Heyden, K. (2009). *Die "Erzählung des Aphroditian": Thema und Variationen einer Legende im Spannungsfeld von Christentum und Heidentum.* Tübingen.

Higbie, C. (2003). *The Lindian Chronicle and the Greek Creation of their Past.* Oxford.

Himmelfarb, M. (1998). "Judaism and Hellenism in 2 Maccabees." *Poetics Today* 19: 19–40.

Himmelfarb, M. (1999). "Levi, Phinehas, and the Problem of Intermarriage at the Time of the Maccabean Revolt." *Jewish Studies Quarterly* 6: 1–24.

Hingley, R. (2005). *Globalizing Roman Culture: Unity, Diversity and Empire*. London and New York.

Höistad, R. (1948). "Cynic Hero and Cynic King: Studies in the Cynic Conception of Man." PhD diss., Uppsala.

Hölbl, G. (2001). *A History of the Ptolemaic Empire*. New York.

Hopkins, K. H. (1985). *Death and Renewal: Sociological Studies in Roman History 2*. Cambridge.

Horowitz, W. (1998). *Mesopotamian Cosmic Geography*. Winona Lake.

Hugonnard-Roche, H. (2004). *La Logique d'Aristote du grec au syriaque: Études sur la transmission des textes de l'Organon et leur interprétation philosophique*. Paris.

Hume, D. (1998). *The Natural History of Religion*, ed. J. C. A. Gaskin, *Principal Writings on Religion*. Oxford.

Hurlet, F., ed. (2008). *Les Empires: Antiquité et moyen âge, analyse comparée*. Rennes.

Hurrell, A. (2007). *On Global Order: Power, Values, and the Constitution of International Society*. Oxford.

Huss, W. (2001). *Ägypten in hellenistischer Zeit 332–30 v. Chr.* Munich.

Husson, S. (2011). *La République de Diogène: Une cité en quête de la Nature*. Paris.

Inglis, D., and R. Robertson (2011). "From Cosmos to Globe: Relating Cosmopolitanism, Globalization and Globality," in M. Rovisco and M. Nowicka, eds., *The Ashgate Research Companion to Cosmopolitanism*. Farnham, Surrey: 295–312.

Ingram, J. D. (2013). *Radical Cosmopolitics: The Ethics and Politics of Democratic Universalism*. New York.

Iossif, P. P., A. S. Chankowski, and C. Lorber, eds. (2011). *More Than Men, Less Than Gods—Studies on Royal Cult and Imperial Worship: Proceedings of the International Colloquium Organized by the Belgian School at Athens (November 1–2, 2007)*. Leuven, Paris, Walpole.

Isaac, B. (2004). *The Invention of Racism in Classical Antiquity*. Princeton.

Isager, S. (1998). "The Pride of Halikarnassos: Editio Princeps of an Inscription from Salmakis." *Zeitschrift für Papyrologie und Epigraphik* 123: 1–23.

Isager, S., and P. Pedersen, eds. (2004). *The Salmakis Inscription and Hellenistic Halikarnassos*. Odense.

Jacques, F. (1984). *Le Privilège de liberté: Politique impériale et autonomie municipale dans les cités de l'Occident romain (161–244)*. Rome.

Jakob, S. (2003). *Mittelassyrische Verwaltung und Sozialstruktur: Untersuchungen*. Leiden.

James, H. B. (2006). *The Roman Predicament: How the Rules of International Order Create the Politics of Empire*. Princeton.

Jany, J. (2012). "The Origins of the *Kalīlah wa Dimnah*: Reconsideration in Light of Sasanian Legal History." *Journal of the Royal Asiatic Society* 22: 505–18.

Joannès, F. (1988). "Le Titre de *ša rêš âli* (lú-sag uru-a)." *Nouvelles assyriologiques brèves et utilitaires*, no. 10.

Joannès, F. (1997). "Le Monde occidental vu de Mésopotamie, de l'époque néo-babylonienne à l'époque hellénistique." *Transeuphratène* 13: 141–53.

Jones, A. H. M. (1964). *The Later Roman Empire 284–602: A Social, Economic, and Administrative Survey*. 3 vols. Oxford.

Jursa, M. (2007). "The Transition of Babylonia from the Neo-Babylonian Empire to Achaemenid Rule," in H. Crawford, ed., *Regime Change in the Ancient Near East and Egypt: From Sargon of Agade to Saddam Hussein*. Oxford: 73–94.

Jursa, M. (2015). "Families, Officialdom, and Families of Royal Officials in Chaldean and Achaemenid Babylonia," in A. Archi, ed., *Tradition and Innovation in the Ancient Near East*. Winona Lake: 597–606.

Jursa, M., and J. Häckl (2011). "Rhetorics, Politeness, Persuasion and Argumentation in Late Babylonian Epistolography," *Imperium and Officium Working Papers*, University of Vienna, Institut für Orientalistik. Version 1 (June).

Jursa, M., J. Häckl, and M. Schmidl (2014). *Spätbabylonische Privatbriefe*. Münster.

Kaimio, J. (1979). *The Romans and the Greek Language*. Helsinki.

Kaiser, W. (1999). "Zur Datierung realistischer Rundbildnisse ptolemäisch-römischer Zeit." *Mitteilungen des Deutschen Archäologischen Instituts, Abteilung Kairo* 55: 237–63, pl. 235–9.

Kamesar, A., ed. (2009). *The Cambridge Companion to Philo*. Cambridge.

Kant, I. (1917). *Zum Ewigen Friede: Ein philosophischer Entwurf*, ed. K. Kehrbach. Leipzig.

Kant, I. (2006). "Toward Perpetual Peace: A Philosophical Sketch," in P. Kleingeld, ed. and trans. D. L. Colclasure, *"Toward Perpetual Peace" and Other Writings on Politics, Peace, and History*. New Haven: 67–109.

Kaser, M. (1955-9). *Das römische Privatrecht*. Munich.

Kayser, F. (2012). "Le Décret sacerdotal de 243 A.C.," in E. Delange, ed., *Les Fouilles françaises à Eléphantine (Assouan 1906-1911)*. Paris: 411–40.

Keay, S., and N. Terrenato, eds. (2001). *Italy and the West: Comparative Studies in Romanization*. Oxford.

Kelly, C. M. (2004). *Ruling the Later Roman Empire*. Cambridge, MA.

Khatchadourian, L. (2012). "The Achaemenid Provinces in Archaeological Perspective," in D. T. Potts, ed., *A Companion to the Archaeology of the Ancient Near East*. Malden: 963–83.

King, D. (2013a). "Grammar and Logic in Syriac (and Arabic)." *Journal of Semitic Studies* 58: 100–120.

King, D. (2013b). "Why Were the Syrians Interested in Greek Philosophy?" in P. Wood, ed., *History and Identity in the Late Antique Near East*. Oxford: 61–81.

Kleber, K. (2012). "Rhetorical Strategies in Letters of Babylonian officials." *Zeitschrift für Altorientalische und Biblische Rechtsgeschichte* 18: 221–37.

Kleingeld, P. (2011). *Kant and Cosmopolitanism. The Philosophical Ideal of World Citizenship*. Cambridge.

Klinkott, H. (2005). *Der Satrap: Ein achaimenidischer Amtsträger und seine Handlungsspielräume*. Frankfurt.

Klotz, D. (2009). "The Statue of the Dioikêtês Harchebi/Archibios. Nelson-Atkins Museum of Art 47–112." *Bulletin de l'Institut Français d'Archéologie Orientale* 109: 281–310.

Knauß, F. S., I. Gagošidse, and I. Babaev. (2013). "Karačamirli: Ein persisches Paradies." *Arta* 4: 1–29.

Koenen, L. (1993). "The Ptolemaic King as a Religious Figure," in A. Bulloch, E. S. Gruen, A. A. Long, and A. Stewart, eds., *Images and Ideologies: Self-Definition in the Hellenistic World*. Berkeley: 25–115.

Kokkinia, C. (2000). *Die Opramoas-Inschrift von Rhodiapolis: Euergetismus und Sociale Elite in Lykien.* Bonn.

Kokkinia, C. (2003). "Letters of Roman Authorities on Local Dignitaries: The Case of Vedius Antoninus." *Zeitschrift für Papyrologie und Epigraphik* 142: 197–213.

Kolb, A. (2000). *Transport und Nachrichtentransfer im Römischen Reich.* Berlin.

Kolb, F. (1987). *Diocletian und die erste Tetrarchie: Improvisation oder Experiment in der Organisation monarchischer Herrschaft?* Berlin and New York.

Kołodziejczyk, D. (2012). "Khan, Caliph, Tsar and Imperator: The Multiple Identities of the Ottoman Sultan," in P. F. Bang, and D. Kołodziejczyk, eds., *Universal Empire: A Comparative Approach to Imperial Culture and Representation in Eurasian History.* Cambridge: 175–93.

Konstan, D. (2009). "Cosmopolitan Traditions," in R. K. Balot, ed., *A Companion to Greek and Roman Political Thought.* Malden and Oxford: 473–84.

Koselleck, R. (2002). *The Practice of Conceptual History: Timing History, Spacing Concepts.* Stanford.

Kosmin, P. (2011). "Seeing Double in Seleucid Babylonia," in K. Radner and E. Robson, eds., *The Oxford Handbook of Cuneiform Culture.* Oxford and New York: 174–98.

Kosmin, P. (2013). "Seleucid Ethnography and Indigenous Kingship: The Babylonian Education of Antiochus I," in J. Haubold et al., eds., *The World of Berossos.* Wiesbaden: 199–212.

Kosmin, P. (2014a). *The Land of the Elephant Kings: Space, Territory, and Ideology in the Seleucid Empire.* Cambridge, MA, and London.

Kosmin, P. (2014b). "Seeing Double in Seleucid Babylonia: Rereading the Borsippa Cylinder of Antiochus I," in A. Moreno and R. Thomas, eds., *Patterns of the Past: Epitēdeumata in the Greek Tradition.* Oxford: 173–98.

Kuhlmann, P. (1994). *Die Giessener literarischen Papyri und und die Caracalla-Erlasse. Edition, Übersetzung und Kommentar.* Giessen.

Kuhrt, A. (1987). "Berossus' *Babyloniaca* and Seleucid Rule in Babylonia," in A. Kuhrt, and S. Sherwin-White, eds., *Hellenism and the East: Interactions of Greek and non-Greek Civilizations from Syria to Central Asia after Alexander.* London: 32–56.

Kuhrt, A. (2001). "The Achaemenid Persian Empire (c. 550–c. 332 BCE): Continuities, Adaptations, Transformations," in S. E. Alcock et al., eds., *Empires: Perspectives from Archaeology and History.* Cambridge: 93–127.

Kuhrt, A. (2014). "State Communications in the Persian Empire," in K. Radner, ed., *State Correspondence in the Ancient World: From New Kingdom Egypt to the Roman Empire.* Oxford: 112–40.

Kuhrt, A., and S. M. Sherwin-White (1991). "Aspects of Seleucid Royal Ideology: The Cylinder of Antiochus I from Borsippa." *Journal of Hellenic Studies* 111: 71–86.

Kuhrt, A., and S. M. Sherwin-White. (1993). *From Samarkhand to Sardis: A New Approach to the Seleucid Empire.* London.

Kurke, L. (2011). *Aesopic Conversations: Popular Tradition, Cultural Dialogue, and the Invention of Greek Prose.* Princeton.

Lambert, W. G. (2013). *Babylonian Creation Myths.* Winona Lake.

Lanciers, E. (2014). "The Development of the Greek Dynastic Cult under Ptolemy V." *Archiv für Papyrusforschung und verwandte Gebiete* 60: 375–83.

Lanfranchi, G. B. (2003). "The Assyrian Expansion in the Zagros and the Local Ruling Elites," in G. B. Lanfranchi, M. Roaf, and R. Rollinger, eds., *Continuity of Empire (?): Assyria, Media, Persia.* Padua: 79–118.

Lang, M., and R. Rollinger. (2010). "Im Herzen der Meere und in der Mitte des Meeres: Das Buch Ezekiel und die in assyrischer Zeit fassbaren Vorstellungen von der Grenzen der Welt," in R. Rollinger, B. Gufler, M. Lang, and I. Madreiter, eds., *Interkulturalität in der alten Welt: Vorderasien, Hellas, Ägypten und die vielfältigen Ebenen des Kontakts.* Wiesbaden: 206–64.

Langdon, S. (1912). *Die neubabylonischen Königsinschriften.* Leipzig.

Laniado, A. (2002). *Recherches sur les notables municipaux dans l'Empire protobyzantin.* Paris.

Larsen, M. T. (2000). "The City-States of the Early Neo-Babylonian Period," in M. H. Hansen, ed., *A Comparative Study of Thirty City-State Cultures.* Copenhagen: 117–27.

Latour, B. (2004). "Whose Cosmos, Which Cosmopolitics?" *Common Knowledge* 10: 450–68.

Lauinger, J. (2012). "Esarhaddon's Succession Treaty at Tell Tayinat: Text and Commentary." *Journal of Cuneiform Studies* 64: 87–123.

Lavan, M. (2013a). "The Empire in the Age of Nero," in E. Buckley and M. T. Dinter, eds., *A Companion to the Neronian Age.* Malden and Oxford: 65–82.

Lavan, M. (2013b). *Slaves to Rome: Paradigms of Empire in Roman Culture.* Cambridge.

Lavan, M. (2016). "The Spread of Roman Citizenship, 14–212 CE: Quantification in the Face of High Uncertainty." *Past and Present* 230: 3–46.

Legras, B. (2002). "Les Experts égyptiens à la cour des Ptolémées." *Revue Historique* 126: 963–91.

Leichty, E. (2011). *The Royal Inscriptions of Esarhaddon, King of Assyria (680–669 BC).* Winona Lake.

Lendon, J. E. (1997). *Empire of Honour: The Art of Government in the Roman World.* Oxford.

Lenger, M.-T. (1980). *Corpus des "Ordonnances" des Ptolémées.* 2nd ed. Brussels.

Lenzi, A. (2008). "The Uruk List of Kings and Sages and Late Mesopotamian Scholarship." *Journal of Ancient Near Eastern Religion* 8/2: 137–69.

Leprohon, R. J. (2013). *The Great Name: Ancient Egyptian Royal Titulary.* Atlanta.

Lévy, C. (2009). "Philo's Ethics," in A. Kamesar, ed., *The Cambridge Companion to Philo.* Cambridge: 146–74.

Lewis, M. E. (2006). *The Construction of Space in Early China.* Albany.

Lichtheim, M. (1980). *Ancient Egyptian Literature.* Vol. 3: *The Late Period.* Berkeley.

Lim, R. (1995). *Public Disputation, Power, and Social Order in Late Antiquity.* Berkeley.

Limet, H. (2005). "Ethnicity," in D. C. Snell, ed., *A Companion to the Ancient Near East.* Chichester and Malden: 370–83.

Lincoln, B. (2007). *Religion, Empire, and Torture: The Case of Achaemenian Persia, with a Postscript on Abu Ghraib.* Chicago.

Lincoln, B. (2010). "Human Unity and Diversity in Zoroastrian Mythology," *History of Religions* 50: 7–20.

Lincoln, B. (2012). *Happiness for Mankind: Achaemenian Religion and the Imperial Project.* Leuven.

Linssen M. J. H. (2004). *The Cults of Uruk and Babylon: The Temple Ritual Texts As Evidence for Hellenistic Cult Practice*. Leiden and Boston.

Liu, L. (1995). *Translingual Practices: Literature, National Culture, and Translated Modernity—China, 1900–1937*. Stanford.

Liverani, M. (1995). "The Medes at Esarhaddon's Court." *Journal of Cuneiform Studies* 47: 57–62.

Liverani, M. (1999–2001). "The Sargon Geography and the Late Assyrian Mensuration of the Earth." *State Archives of Assyria Bulletin* 13: 57–85.

Liverani, M. (2011). "From City-State to Empire: The Case of Assyria," in J. P. Arnason and K. A. Raaflaub, eds., *The Roman Empire in Context: Historical and Comparative Perspectives*. Malden: 251–69.

Liverani, M. (2014). "The King and His Audience," in S. Gaspa, A. Greco, D. Morandi Bonacossi, S. Ponchia, and R. Rollinger, eds., *From Source to History: Studies on Ancient Near Eastern Worlds and Beyond*. Münster: 373–85.

Llewellyn-Jones, L., and S. Winder (2011). "A Key to Berenike's Lock? The Hathoric Model of Queenship in Early Ptolemaic Egypt," in A. Erskine and L. Llewellyn-Jones, eds., *Creating a Hellenistic World*. Swansea: 247–69.

Lloyd-Jones, H. (1999 a and b). "The Pride of Halicarnassus." *Zeitschrift für Papyrologie und Epigraphik* 124: 1–14 and 127: 65–5 ("Corrigenda and Addenda").

Löhken, H. (1982). *Ordines dignitatum: Untersuchungen zur formalen Konstituierung der spätantiken Führungsschicht*. Cologne.

Long, A. A. (2002). *Epictetus: A Stoic and Socratic Guide to Life*. Oxford.

Long, A. A. (2008a). "The Concept of the Cosmopolitan in Greek and Roman Thought." *Daedalus* 138: 50–8.

Long, A. A. (2008b). "Philo on Stoic Physics," in F. Alesse, ed., *Philo of Alexandria and Post-Aristotelian Philosophy*. Leiden: 121–40.

L'Orange, H. P., R. Unger, and M. Wegner. (1984). *Das spätantike Herrscherbild von Diokletian bis zu den Konstantin-Söhnen, 284–361 n. Chr.* Berlin.

Lozano, F. (2011). "The Creation of Imperial Gods: Not Only Imposition Versus Spontaneity," in P. P. Iossif, A. S. Chankowski, and C. Lorber, eds., *More Than Men, Less Than Gods—Studies on Royal Cult and Imperial Worship*. Leuven, Paris, Walpole: 475–520.

Ma, J. (2002). *Antiochos III and the Cities of Western Asia Minor*. 2nd ed. Oxford.

Ma, J. (2003). "Kings," in A. Erskine, ed., *A Companion to the Hellenistic World*. Oxford: 177–96.

Ma, J. (2013). *Statues and Cities: Honorific Portraits and Civic Identity in the Hellenistic World*. Oxford.

MacCormack, S. (2007). *On the Wings of Time: Rome, the Incas, Spain and Peru*. Princeton.

Machinist, P. (1992). "Palestine, Administration of (Assyro-Babylonian)," in D. N. Freedman, ed., *Anchor Bible Dictionary*. Vol. 5. New York: 73.

MacKenzie, D. N. (1979). "Mani's Šābuhragān." *Bulletin of the School of Oriental and African Studies* 42: 500–534.

Macuch, M. (1995). "Herrschaftskonsolidierung und sasanidisches Familienrecht: Zum Verhältnis von Kirche und Staat unter den Sasaniden," in C. Reck and P. Zieme, eds., *Iran und Turfan: Beiträge Berliner Wissenschaftler, Werner Sundermann zum 60. Geburtstag gewidmet.* Wiesbaden: 149–67.

Macuch, M. (2004). "Pious Foundations in Byzantine and Sasanian Law," in A. Carile et al., eds., *La Persia e Bisanzio: Convegno internazionale, Roma 14-18 ottobre 2002.* Rome: 181–96.

Madreiter, I. (2013). "From Berossos to Eusebius: A Christian Apologist's Shaping of 'Pagan' Literature," in J. Haubold et al., eds., *The World of Berossos.* Wiesbaden: 255–76.

Maier, C. S. (2006). *Among Empires: American Ascendancy and Its Predecessors.* Cambridge.

Mairs, R. (2013). "Greek Settler Communities in Central and South Asia, 323 BCE to 10 CE," in G. Daswani and A. Quayson, eds., *A Companion to Diaspora and Transnationalism.* Oxford: 443–54.

Mairs, R. (2014). *The Hellenistic Far East: Archaeology, Language, and Identity in Greek Central Asia.* Oakland.

Manders, E. (2012). *Coining Images of Power: Patterns in the Representation of Roman Emperors on Imperial Coinage, A.D. 193–284.* Leiden.

Mann, M. (1986). *The Sources of Social Power.* Vol. 1: *A History of Power from the Beginning to A.D. 1760.* Cambridge.

Manning, J. G. (2003). *Land and Power in Ptolemaic Egypt: The Structure of Land Tenure.* Cambridge.

Manning, J. G. (2010). *The Last Pharaohs: Egypt under the Ptolemies 305-30 BC.* Princeton.

Martinez-Sève, L. (2003). "Quoi de neuf sur le royaume séleucide?" in F. Prost, ed., *L'Orient méditerranéen de la mort d'Alexandre aux campagnes de Pompée: Cités et royaumes à l'époque hellénistique.* Rennes: 221–42.

Martinez-Sève, L. (2014a). "The Spatial Organization of Ai Khanoum, a Greek City in Afghanistan." *American Journal of Archaeology* 118: 267–83.

Martinez-Sève, L. (2014b). "Remarques sur la transmission aux Parthes des pratiques de gouvernment séleucides: Modalités et chronologie." *Ktèma* 39: 123–42.

Marx, K. (1991). *Capital: A Critique of Political Economy.* Vol. 3. London.

Masuzawa, T. (2005). *The Invention of World Religions; or, How European Universalism Was Preserved in the Language of Pluralism.* Chicago.

Matthews, J. F. (1975/1990). *Western Aristocracies and Imperial Court, AD 364–425.* Oxford.

Matthews, J. F. (1989). *The Roman Empire of Ammianus.* London.

Mattila, R. (2000). *The King's Magnates: A Study of the Highest Officials of the Neo-Assyrian Empire.* Helsinki.

Mazover, M. (2012). *Governing the World: The History of an Idea.* New York and London.

McDonough, S. J. (2008). "Bishops or Bureaucrats?: Christian Clergy and the State in the Middle Sasanian Period," in D. Kennet and P. Luft, eds., *Current Research in Sasanian Archaeology, Art and History.* Oxford: 87–92.

McGing, B. (1997). "Revolt Egyptian Style: Internal Opposition to Ptolemaic Rule." *Archiv für Papyrusforschung* 43: 273–314.

Meadows, A. (2012). "Ptolemaic Possessions outside Egypt," in R. S. Bagnall, K. Brodersen, C. B. Champion, A. Erskine, and S. R. Huebner, eds., *The Encyclopedia of Ancient History.* New York: 5625–9.

Meeus, A. (2014). "The Territorial Ambitions of Ptolemy I," in H. Hauben and A. Meeus, eds., *The Age of the Successors and the Creation of the Hellenistic Kingdoms (323–276 B.C.).* Leuven: 263–306.

Menze, V. (2008). *Justinian and the Making of the Syrian Orthodox Church.* Oxford.

Meyer-Zwiffelhoffer, E. (2003). Πολιτικῶς ἄρχειν: *Zum Regierungsstil der senatorischen Statthalter in den kaiserzeitlichen griechischen Provinzen.* Stuttgart.

Michalowski, P. (1993). "Memory and Deed: The Historiography of the Political Expansion of the Akkad State," in M. Liverani, ed., *Akkad: The First World Empire.* Padua: 69–90.

Michalowski, P. (2010). "Masters of the Four Corners of the Heavens: Views of the Universe in Early Mesopotamian Writings," in K. A. Raaflaub and R. J. A. Talbert, eds., *Geography and Ethnography: Perceptions of the World in Premodern Societies.* Oxford: 147–68.

Millar, F. (1977). *The Emperor in the Roman world (31 BC–AD 337).* London.

Millar, F. (1988). "Government and Diplomacy in the Roman Empire during the First Three Centuries." *International History Review* 10: 345–77.

Millar, F. (2002). *Rome, the Greek World, and the East.* Vol. 1: *The Roman Republic and the Augustan Revolution,* ed. H. M. Cotton and G. M. Rogers. Chapel Hill.

Millett, M. (1990). "Romanization: Historical Issues and Archaeological Interpretation," in T. Blagg and M. Millett, eds., *The Early Roman Empire in the West.* Oxford: 35–41.

Moatti, C. (2006). "Translation, Migration, and Communication in the Roman Empire: Three Aspects of Movement in History." *Classical Antiquity* 25: 109–40.

Mokhtarian, J. (2015). *Rabbis, Sorcerers, Kings, and Priests: The Culture of the Talmud in Ancient Iran.* Oakland.

Moles, J. L. (1996). "Cynic Cosmopolitanism," in R. B. Branham and M. Goulet-Cazé, eds., *The Cynics: The Cynic Movement in Antiquity and Its Legacy.* Berkeley: 105–20.

Monerie, J. (2012). "Notabilité urbaine administration locale en Babylonie du sud aux époques Séleucide et Parthe," in C. Feyel, J. Fournier, L. Graslin-Thomé, and F. Kirbihler, eds., *Communautés locales et pouvoir central dans l'Orient hellénistique et romain.* Nancy and Paris: 327–52.

Monson, A. (2012). *From the Ptolemies to the Romans: Political and Economic Change in Egypt.* Cambridge.

Mooren, L. (1975). *The Aulic Titulature in Ptolemaic Egypt: Introduction and Prosopography.* Brussels.

Mooren, L. (1977). *La Hiérarchie de cour ptolémaïque: Contribution à l'étude des institutions et des classes dirigeantes à l'époque hellénistique.* Leuven.

Morony, M. (1974). "Religious Communities in Late Sasanian and Early Muslim Iraq." *Journal of the Economic and Social History of the Orient* 17: 113–35.

Morony, M. (1976). "The Effects of the Muslim Conquest on the Persian Population of Iraq." *Iran* 14: 41–59.

Morris, I., and W. Scheidel, eds. (2009). *The Dynamics of Ancient Empires: State Power from Assyria to Byzantium.* Oxford.

Mourgues, J.-L. (1995a). "Écrire en deux langues: Bilinguisme et pratique de chancellerie sous le Haut-Empire romain." *Dialogues d'histoire ancienne* 21: 105–29.

Mourgues, J.-L. (1995b). "Le Préambule de l'édit de Tiberius Julius Alexander, témoin des étapes de son élaboration." *Bulletin de correspondance hellénique* 119: 415–35.

Moyer, I. (2011a). "Finding a Middle Ground: Culture and Politics in the Ptolemaic Thebaid," in P. F. Dorfman and B. M. Bryan, eds., *Perspectives on Ptolemaic Thebes: Papers from the Theban Workshop 2006.* Chicago: 115–45.

Moyer, I. (2011b). "Court, Chora, and Culture in Late Ptolemaic Egypt." *American Journal of Philology* 132: 15–44.

Muthu, S. (2012). "Conquest, Commerce, and Cosmopolitanism in Enlightenment Political Thought," in S. Muthu, ed., *Empire and Modern Political Thought.* Cambridge: 199–231.

Mutschler, F.-H., and A. Mittag, eds. (2008). *Conceiving the Empire: China and Rome Compared.* Oxford.

Neesen, L. (1980). *Untersuchungen zu den direkten Staatsabgaben der römischen Kaiserzeit (27 v. Chr-184 n. Chr).* Bonn.

Neumann, H. (2014). "Altorientalische 'Imperien' des 3. und frühen 2. Jahrtausends v. Chr.: Historische Voraussetzungen und sozioökonomische Grundlagen," in M. Gehler and R. Rollinger, eds., *Imperien und Reiche in der Weltgeschichte: Epochenüb ergreifende und globalhistorische Vergleiche.* Vol. 1. Wiesbaden: 33–64.

Nickel, L. (2013). "The First Emperor and Sculpture in China." *Bulletin of the School of Oriental and African Studies* 76: 413–47.

Nissen, H. J., and J. Renger, eds. (1982). *Mesopotamien und seine Nachbarn: Politische und kulturelle Wechselbeziehungen im alten Vorderasien vom 4. bis 1. Jahrtausend v. Chr.* Berlin.

Nissinen, M. (2014). "Outlook: Aramaeans Outside of Syria: 1. Assyria," in H. Niehr, ed., *The Aramaeans in Ancient Syria.* Leiden: 273–96.

Nixon, C. E. V., and B. S. Rodgers (1994). *In Praise of Later Roman Emperors: The Panegyrici Latini.* Berkeley.

Nora, P. (1989). *Les Lieux de mémoire.* Vol. 2: *La Nation.* Paris.

Noreña, C. F. (2011). *Imperial Ideals in the Roman West: Representation, Circulation, Power.* Cambridge.

Novák, M. (2002). "The Artificial Paradise: Programme and Ideology of Royal Gardens," in S. Parpola and R. Whiting, eds., *Sex and Gender in the Near East.* Vol. 2. Helsinki: 443–60.

Noy, D. (2000). *Foreigners at Rome.* London.

Nussbaum, M. C. (1997). "Kant and Stoic Cosmopolitanism." *Journal of Political Philosophy* 5: 1–25, reprinted with minor changes as "Kant and Cosmopolitanism," in J. Bohman and M. Lutz-Bachmann, eds., (1997) *Perpetual Peace: Essays on Kant's Cosmopolitan Ideal* (Boston: 25–51) and in G. W. Brown and D. Held, eds., (2010) *The Cosmopolitan Reader.* Cambridge: 27–44.

Nussbaum, M. C. (2002). "The Worth of Human Dignity: Two Tensions in Stoic Cosmopolitanism," in G. Clark and T. Rajak, eds., *Philosophy and Power in the Graeco-Roman World: Essays in Honour of Miriam Griffin.* Oxford: 31–50.

Nylan, M. (2008). "The Rhetoric of 'Empire' in the Classical Era in China (323 BC–AD 316)," in F. Mutschler and A. Mittag, eds., *Conceiving the Empire: China and Rome Compared.* Oxford: 34–64.

Oelsner, J. (1986). *Materialen zur babylonischen Gesellschaft und Kultur in hellenistischer Zeit*. Budapest.

Oliver, J. H. (1989). *Greek Constitutions of Early Roman Emperors from Inscriptions and Papyri*. Philadelphia.

O'Meara, D. J. (2002). "Neoplatonic Cosmopolitanism: Some Preliminary Notes," in P. Manganaro, M. Barbanti, and G. R. Giardina, eds., *Henosis kai Philia*. Catania: 311–15.

Oppenheim, A. L. (1965). "On Royal Gardens in Mesopotamia." *Journal of Near Eastern Studies* 24: 328–33.

Oppenheim, A. L. (1968). "The Eyes of the Lord." *Journal of the American Oriental Society* 88: 173–80.

Osborne, R. (1981–3). *Naturalization in Athens: A Corpus of Athenian Decrees Granting Citizenship*. Brussels.

Pabst, A. (1989). *Symmachus: Reden*. Darmstadt.

Pagden, A. (2000). "Stoicism, Cosmopolitanism, and the Legacy of European Imperialism." *Constellations* 7: 3–22.

Pagden, A. (2003). "Human Rights, Natural Rights, and Europe's Imperial Legacy." *Political Theory* 31: 171–99.

Pagden, A. (2005). "Imperialism, Liberalism and the Quest for Perpetual Peace." *Daedalus* 134: 46–57.

Palagia, O. (2013). "Aspects of the Diffusion of Ptolemaic Portraiture Overseas," in K. Buraselis, M. Stefanou, and D. Thompson, eds., *The Ptolemies, the Sea and the Nile: Studies in Waterborne Power*. Cambridge: 153–69.

Panaino, A. (2010). "The Astronomical Conference of the Year 556 and the Politics of Xusraw Anōšāg-ruwān," in H. Börm and J. Wiesehöfer, eds., *Commutatio et contentio: Studies in the Late Roman, Sasanian, and Early Islamic Near East*. Düsseldorf: 293–306.

Panciera, S., ed. (1982). *Atti del Colloquio internazionale AIEGL su Epigrafia e ordine senatorio, Roma, 14–20 maggio 1981*. 2 vols. Rome.

Pappi, C. (2012). "Religion and Politics at the Divine Table: The Cultic Travels of Zimrī-Līm," in G. Wilhelm, ed., *Organization, Representation, and Symbols of Power in the Ancient Near East*. Winona Lake: 579–90.

Parpola, S. (1993). "The Assyrian Tree of Life: Tracing the Origins of Jewish Monotheism and Greek Philosophy." *Journal of Near Eastern Studies* 52/3: 161–208.

Paton, W. R. R. B., F. W. Walbank, and C. Habicht. (2011). *Polybius, The Histories*. Cambridge, MA, and London.

Paul, S. (1969). "Sargon's Administrative Diction in II Kings 17:27." *Journal of Biblical Literature* 88: 73–74.

Paulus, S. (2014). "Babylonien in der 2. Hälfte des 2. Jts. v. Chr.—(K)ein Imperium? Ein Überblick über Geschichte und Struktur des mittelbabylonischen Reiches (ca. 1500-1000 B.C.)," in M. Gehler and R. Rollinger, eds., *Imperien und Reiche in der Weltgeschichte: Epochenübergreifende und globalhistorische Vergleiche*. Vol. 1. Wiesbaden: 65–100.

Paykova, A. V. (1968). "O Proiskhozhdenii Drevnesiriiskoi Versii Sbornika 'Kalīla wa Dimna.'" *Vestnik Drevnei Istorii* 17: 110–20.

Payne, R. E. (2011). "The Emergence of Martyrs' Shrines in Late Antique Iran: Conflict, Consensus, and Communal Institutions," in M. dal Santo and P. Booth, eds., *An Age of Saints? Conflict and Dissent in the Cult of Saints (300-1000 AD)*. Leiden: 89–113.

Payne, R. E. (2013). "Cosmology and the Expansion of the Iranian Empire, 502-628 CE." *Past and Present* 220: 3–33.

Payne, R. E. (2014). "The Reinvention of Iran: The Sasanian Empire and the Huns," in M. Maas, ed., *The Cambridge Companion to the Age of Attila*. Cambridge: 282–99.

Payne, R. E. (2015). *A State of Mixture: Christians, Zoroastrians, and Iranian Political Culture in Late Antiquity*. Oakland.

Peachin, M. (1990). *Roman Imperial Titulature and Chronology: AD 235-284*. Amsterdam.

Pearson, A. C. (1905). "Review: Von Arnim's Stoic Fragments." *Classical Review* 19/9: 454–8.

Pedde, F. (1991). "Frehat en-Nufeǧi: Zwei seleukidenzeitliche Tumuli bei Uruk." *Baghdader Mitteilungen* 22: 521–35.

Pedde, F. (1995) "Seleukidische und parthische Zeit," in R. M. Boehmer, F. Pedde and B. Salje, eds., *Uruk: Die Gräber*. Mainz: 140–99.

Perdue, P. C. (2007). "Erasing the Empire, Re-racing the Nation: Racialism and Culturalism in Imperial China," in A. L. Stoler, C. McGranahan, and P. C. Perdue, eds., *Imperial Formations*. Santa Fe: 141–69.

Peremans, W. (1985). "Notes sur les traductions de textes non littéraires sous les Lagides." *Chronique d'Égypte* 60: 248–62.

Perikhanian, A. (1979). "Ordalya i Klyatva v Sudoproizvodstve Doislamskovo Irana." *Peredneaziatskii Sbornik* 3: 182–92.

Perpillou-Thomas, F. (1993). *Fêtes d'Égypte ptolémaïque et romaine d'après la documentation papyrologique grecque*. Leuven.

Petrie, C. (2002) "Seleucid Uruk: An Analysis of Ceramic Distribution." *Iraq* 64: 85–123.

Pfeiffer, S. (2004). *Das Dekret von Kanopos (238 v. Chr.). Kommentar und historische Auswertung einer dreisprachigen Synodaldekretes der ägyptischen Priester zu Ehren Ptolemaios' III. und seiner Familie*. Munich.

Pfeiffer, S. (2010). "Das Dekret von Rosette: Die ägyptischen Priester und der Herrscherkult," in G. Weber, ed., *Alexandreia und das ptolemäische Ägypten: Kulturbegegnungen in hellenistischer Zeit*. Berlin: 84–108.

Pines, Y. (2002). "Changing Views of *Tianxia* in Pre-Imperial Discourse." *Oriens Extremus* 43: 101–16.

Pirngruber, R. (2013). "The Historical Sections of the Astronomical Diaries in Context: Developments in a Late Babylonian Scientific Text Corpus." *Iraq* 75: 197–210.

Pitts, J. (2010). "Political Theory of Empire and Imperialism." *Annual Review of Political Science* 13: 211–35.

Pitts, J. (2012). "Empire and Legal Universalisms in the Eighteenth Century." *American Historical Review* 117: 92–121.

Plantzos, D. (2011). "The Iconography of Assimilation: Isis and Royal Imagery on Ptolemaic Seal Impression," in P. P. Iossif, A. S. Chankowski, and C. Lorber, eds., *More Than Men, Less Than Gods—Studies on Royal Cult and Imperial Worship*. Leuven, Paris, Walpole: 417–56.

Plischke, S. (2014). *Die Seleukiden und Iran: Die seleukidische Herrschaftspolitik in den östlichen Satrapien.* Wiesbaden.

Pocock, J. G. A. (2005). *Barbarism and Religion.* Vol. 3: *The First Decline and Fall.* Cambridge.

Podany, A. H. (2010). *Brotherhood of Kings: How International Relations Shaped the Ancient near East.* Oxford.

Pollock, S. (1998). "The Cosmopolitan Vernacular." *Journal of Asian Studies* 57/1: 6–37.

Pollock, S. (2006a). *The Language of the Gods in the World of Men: Sanskrit, Culture, and Power in Premodern India.* Berkeley.

Pollock, S. (2006b). "Empire and Imitation," in C. Calhoun, F. Cooper, and K. W. Moore, eds., *Lessons of Empire: Imperial Histories and American Power.* New York: 175–88.

Pollock, S. (2013). "Cosmopolitanism, Vernacularism, and Premodernity," in S. Moyn and A. Sartori, eds., *Global Intellectual History.* New York: 59–80.

Ponchia, S. (2012). "Administrators and Administrated in Neo-Assyrian Times," in G. Wilhelm, ed., *Organization, Representation, and Symbols of Power in the Ancient Near East.* Winona Lake: 213–24.

Ponchia, S. (2014). "The Neo-Assyrian Adê Protocol and the Administration of the Empire," in S. Gaspa, A. Greco, D. Morandi Bonacossi, S. Ponchia, and R. Rollinger, eds., *From Source to History: Studies on Ancient Near Eastern Worlds and Beyond.* Münster: 502–25.

Pongratz-Leisten, B. (2001). "The Other and the Enemy in the Mesopotamian Conception of the World," in R. M. Whiting, ed., *Mythology and Mythologies: Methodological Approaches to Intercultural Influences.* Helsinki: 192–232.

Pongratz-Leisten, B. (2013). "All the King's Men: Authority, Kingship, and the Rise of the Elites in Assyria," in J. A. Hill, P. Jones, and Antonio J. Morales, eds., *Experiencing Power, Generating Authority: Cosmos, Politics, and the Ideology of Kingship in Ancient Egypt and Mesopotamia.* Philadelphia: 285–309.

Porter, B. N. (2000). "The Anxiety of Multiplicity: Concepts of Divinity as One and Many in Ancient Assyria," in B. N. Porter, ed., *One God or Many? Concepts of Divinity in the Ancient World.* Casco Bay: 211–72.

Postgate, N. (2007). "The Invisible Hierarchy: Assyrian Military and Civilian Administration in the 8th and 7th Centuries BC," in J. N. Postgate, ed., *The Land of Assur & the Yoke of Assur: Studies on Assyria, 1971-2005.* Oxford: 331–60.

Postgate, N. (2014). *Bronze Age Bureaucracy: Writing and the Practice of Government in Assyria.* Cambridge.

Potter, D. S. (2004). *The Roman Empire at Bay, AD 180–395.* London.

Potter, D. S., and R. J. A. Talbert, eds. (2011). "Classical Courts and Courtiers." *American Journal of Philology*, Special issue, 132/1.

Pourshariati, P. (2008). *Decline and Fall of the Sasanian Empire: The Sasanian- Parthian Confederacy and the Arab Conquest of Iran.* London.

Price, S. (1984). *Rituals and Power: The Roman Imperial Cult in Asia Minor.* Cambridge.

Pucci Ben Zeev, M. (1998). *Jewish Rights in the Roman World: The Greek and Roman Documents Quoted by Josephus Flavius.* Tübingen.

Purcell, N. (2006). "Romans in the Roman World," in K. Galinsky, ed., *Cambridge Companion to the Age of Augustus.* Cambridge: 85–105.

Radice, R. (2009). "Philo's Theology and Theory of Creation," in A. Kamesar, ed., *The Cambridge Companion to Philo*. Cambridge: 124–45.

Radner, K. (2000). "How Did the Neo-Assyrian King Perceive His Land and Its Resources?" in R. M. Jas, ed., *Rainfall and Agriculture in Northern Mesopotamia*. Leiden: 234–46.

Radner, K. (2011). "Royal Decision-making: Kings, Magnates, and Scholars," in K. Radner and E. Robson, eds., *The Oxford Handbook of Cuneiform Culture*. Oxford: 358–79.

Radner, K. (2012). "After Eltekeh: Royal Hostages from Egypt at the Assyrian Court," in H. D. Baker, K. Kaniut, and A. Otto, eds., *Stories of Long Ago: Festschrift für Michael D. Roaf*. Münster: 471–9.

Radner, K. (2013). "Assyria and the Medes," in D. Potts, ed., *The Oxford Handbook of Ancient Iran*. Oxford: 442–56.

Radner, K. (2014a). "The Neo-Assyrian Empire," in M. Gehler and R. Rollinger, eds., *Imperien und Reiche in der Weltgeschichte: Epochenübergreifende und globalhistorische Vergleiche*. Vol. 1. Wiesbaden: 101–19.

Radner, K. (2014b). "An Imperial Communication Network: The State Correspondence of the Neo-Assyrian Empire," in K. Radner, ed., *State Correspondence in the Ancient World: From New Kingdom Egypt to the Roman Empire*. Oxford: 64–93.

Radner, K. (2015). "Royal Pen Pals: The Kings of Assyria in Correspondence with Officials, Clients, and Total Strangers (8th and 7th Centuries BC)," in S. Procházka, L. Reinfandt, and S. Tost, eds., *Official Epistolography and the Language(s) of Power*. Vienna: 61–72.

Radner, K., ed. (2014c). *State Correspondence in the Ancient World: From New Kingdom Egypt to the Roman Empire*. Oxford.

Ramelli, I. (2009). *Hierocles the Stoic: Elements of Ethics, Fragments, and Excerpts*. Atlanta.

Rawlinson, H. C., and T. G. Pinches. (1884). *The Cuneiform Inscriptions of Western Asia*. Vol. 5: *A Selection from the Miscellaneous Inscriptions of Assyria and Babylonia*. London.

Rees, R. (2004). *Diocletian and the Tetrarchy*. Edinburgh.

Richardson, S. (2007). "Death and Dismemberment in Mesopotamia: Discorporation between the Body and the Body Politic," in N. Laneri, ed., *Performing Death*. Chicago: 189–208.

Richardson, S. (2010). "Writing Rebellion Back into the record: A Methodologies Toolkit," in S. Richardson, ed., *Rebellions and Peripheries in the Cuneiform World*. Ann Arbor: 1–27.

Richardson, S. (2011). "Mesopotamia and the 'New' Military History," in L. Brice and J. T. Roberts, eds., *Recent Directions in the Military History of the Ancient World*. Claremont: 11–51.

Richardson, S. (2012). "Early Mesopotamia: The Presumptive State." *Past & Present* 215: 3–49.

Richardson, S. (2014a). "The First 'World Event': Sennacherib at Jerusalem," in I. Kalimi and S. Richardson, eds., *Sennacherib at the Gates of Jerusalem: Story, History and Historiography*. Leiden: 429–505.

Richardson, S. (2014b). "Mesopotamian Political History: The Perversities." *Journal of Ancient Near Eastern History* 1/1: 61–93.

Richardson, S. (2016). "Exercising Sympathy: On Mesopotamian Letters," in R. Talbert and F. Naiden, eds., *Mercury's Wings: Exploring Modes of Communication in the Ancient World*. Oxford.

Richter, D. S. (2011). *Cosmopolis: Imagining Community in Late Classical Athens and the Early Roman Empire*. Oxford and New York.

Ricketts, L. M. (1982–3). "The Epistrategos Kallimachos and a Koptite Inscription: SB V 8036 Reconsidered." *AncSoc* 13–14: 161–5.

Rigsby, K. J. (1996). *Asylia: Territorial Inviolability in the Hellenistic World*. Berkeley.

Ristvet, L. (2011). "Travel and the Making of North Mesopotamian Polities." *BASOR* 361: 1–31.

Ritter, N. (2005). "Had the Sasanians Been Interested in Roman Culture?" *Altorientalische Forschungen* 32: 182–99.

Rivaroli, M., and L. Verderame (2005). "To Be A Non-Assyrian," in R. Kalvelagen, D. Katz, and W. H. Van Soldt, eds., *Ethnicity in Ancient Mesopotamia*. Leiden: 290–305.

Robbins, B. (2012). *Perpetual War: Cosmopolitanism from the Viewpoint of Violence*. Durham.

Robinson, D. M. (1906). *Ancient Sinope*. Chicago.

Rochberg, F. (1993). "The Cultural Locus of Astronomy in Late Babylonia," in H. D. Galter, ed., *Die Rolle der Astronomie in den Kulturen Mesopotamiens. Beiträge zum 3. Grazer Morgenländischen Symposion (23.-27. September 1991)*. Graz: 31–45.

Rochberg, F. (2004). *The Heavenly Writing: Divination, Horoscopy, and Astronomy in Mesopotamian Culture*. Cambridge.

Rochberg, F. (2011). "Observing and Describing the World through Divination and Astronomy," in K. Radner and E. Robson, eds., *The Oxford Handbook of Cuneiform Culture*. Oxford: 618–36.

Roller, M. B. (2001). *Constructing Autocracy: Aristocrats and Emperors in Julio-Claudian Rome*. Princeton.

Rollinger, R. (2012). "From Sargon of Agade and the Assyrian Kings to Khusrau I and Beyond: On the Persistence of Ancient Near Eastern Traditions," in G. B. Lanfranchi, D. Morandi Bonacossi, C. Pappi, and S. Ponchia, eds., *Leggo! Studies Presented to Frederick Mario Fales on the Occasion of his 65th Birthday*. Wiesbaden: 725–43.

Root, M. C. (2000). "Imperial Ideology and Achaemenid Persian Art: Transforming the Mesopotamian Legacy." *Bulletin of the Canadian Society for Mesopotamian Studies* 35: 19–27.

Rösch, G. (1978). *Onoma basileias: Studien zum offiziellen Gebrauch der Kaisertitel in spätantiker und frühbyzantinischer Zeit*. Vienna.

Rostovtzeff, M. I. (1941). *The Social and Economic History of the Hellenistic World*. Oxford.

Rowe, G. (2002). *Princes and Political Cultures: The New Tiberian Senatorial Decrees*. Ann Arbor.

Rowlandson, J. (1998). *Women and Society in Greek and Roman Egypt*. Cambridge.

Runciman, G. (2011). "Empire as a Topic in Comparative Sociology," in P. F. Bang and C. A. Bayly, eds., *Tributary Empires in Global History*. Basingstoke: 99–107.

Runia, D. T. (2009). "Philo and the Early Christian Fathers," in A. Kamesar, ed., *The Cambridge Companion to Philo*. Cambridge: 210–30.

Ruzicka, S. (2012). *Trouble in the West: Egypt and the Persian Empire, 525-332 BCE.* Oxford.

Ryholt, K. (2009). "Egyptian Historical Literature from the Greco-Roman Period," in M. Fitzenreiter, ed., *Das Ereignis: Geschichtsschreibung zwischen Vorfall und Befund.* London: 231-8.

Ryholt, K. (2012). *Narrative Literature from the Tebtunis Temple Library.* Copenhagen.

Sachs, A., and H. Hunger, eds. (1988-2006). *Astronomical Diaries and Related Texts from Babylon.* 6 vols. Vienna.

Sachs, A. J., and H. Hunger. (1988). *Astronomical Diaries and Related Texts from Babylon.* Vol. 1: *Diaries from 652 BC to 262 BC.* Vienna.

Sallaberger, W., and I. Schrakamp. (2015). "Philological Data for a Historical Chronology of Mesopotamia in the 3rd Millennium," in W. Sallaberger and I. Schrakamp, eds., *Associated Regional Chronologies for the Ancient Near East and the Eastern Mediterranean.* Vol. 3: *History & Philology.* Turnhout: 1-136.

Saller, R. P. (1982). *Personal Patronage under the Early Empire.* Cambridge.

Saller, R. P. (1994). *Patriarchy, Property, and Death in the Roman Family.* Cambridge.

Salway, B. (1994). "What's in a Name? A Survey of Roman Onomastic Practice from c. 700 B.C. to A.D. 700." *Journal of Roman Studies* 84: 124-45.

Salzman, M. R. (2002). *The Making of a Christian Aristocracy: Social and Religious Change in the Western Roman Empire.* Cambridge, MA.

Sarris, P. (2011). *Empires of Faith: The Fall of Rome to the Rise of Islam, 500-700.* Oxford.

Sassen, S. (2006). *Territory, Authority, Rights: From Medieval to Global Assemblages.* Princeton.

Savalli-Lestrade, I. (1998). *Les "philoi" royaux dans l'Asie hellénistique.* Geneva.

Scheidel, W. (2004). "Human Mobility in Roman Italy, I: the Free Population." *Journal of Roman Studies* 94: 1-26.

Scheidel, W. (2005). "Human Mobility in Roman Italy, II: The Slave Population." *Journal of Roman Studies* 95: 64-79.

Scheidel, W., ed. (2009). *Rome and China. Perspectives on Ancient World Empires.* Oxford.

Scheidel, W., ed. (2015). *State Power in Ancient China and Rome.* Oxford.

Schenkeveld, D. M., and J. Barnes. (2007). "Language," in K. Algra, J. Barnes, J. Mansfeld, and M. Schofield, eds., *The Cambridge History of Hellenistic Philosophy.* Cambridge: 177-228.

Schironi, F. (2013). "The Early Reception of Berossos," in J. Haubold et al., eds., *The World of Berossos.* Wiesbaden: 235-54.

Schmidt-Hofner, S. (2006). "Die städtische Finanzautonomie im spätrömischen Reich," in H.-U. Wiemer, ed., *Staatlichkeit und politisches Handeln in der römischen Kaiserzeit.* Berlin: 209-48.

Schmidt-Hofner, S. (2014). "Der *Defensor civitatis* und die Entstehung des städtschen Notabelnregiments in der Spätantike," in M. Meier and S. Patzold, eds., *Chlodwigs Welt: Organisation von Herrschaft um 500.* Stuttgart: 488-522.

Schofield, M. (1999). *The Stoic Idea of the City.* Chicago.

Schwartz, D. R. (2009). "Philo, His Family, and His Times," in A. Kamesar, ed., *The Cambridge Companion to Philo.* Cambridge: 9-31.

Schwartz, S. (2001). *Imperialism and Jewish Society, 200 BCE to 640 CE*. Princeton.

Schwartz, S. (2009). *Were the Jews a Mediterranean Society? Reciprocity and Solidarity in Ancient Judaism*. Princeton.

Secunda, S. (2011). "The Talmudic *Bei Abedan* and the Sasanian Attempt to 'Recover' the Lost *Avesta*." *Jewish Studies Quarterly* 18: 343–66.

Selz, G. (2004). "Composite Beings: Of Individualization and Objectification in Third Millennium Mesopotamia." *Archiv Orientální* 72: 33–53.

Shaked, S. (1969). "Esoteric Trends in Zoroastrianism." *Proceedings of the Israel Academy of Sciences and Humanities* 3: 175–221.

Shaked, S. (1990). "Administrative Functions of Priests in the Sasanian Period," in G. Gnoli and A. Panaino, eds., *Proceedings of the First European Conference of Iranian Studies*. Part I: *Old and Middle Iranian Studies*. Rome: 261–73.

Shaked, S. (1999). "Quests and Visionary Journeys in Sasanian Iran," in J. Assmann and G. G. Stroumsa, eds., *Transformations of the Inner Self in Ancient Religions*. Leiden: 65–86.

Shaked, S. (2008). "Religion in the Late Sasanian Period: Eran, Aneran, and Other Religious Designations," in V. S. Curtis and S. Stewart, eds., *The Sasanian Era: The Idea of Iran*. Vol. 3. London: 103–17.

Shaked, S. (2010). "Human Identity and Classes of People in the Pahlavi Books," in C. G. Cereti, ed., *Iranian Identity in the Course of History: Proceedings of the Conference Held in Rome, 21-24 September 2005*. Rome: 331–45.

Shen, S. (2009). *Cosmopolitan Publics: Anglophone Print Culture in Semi-Colonial Shanghai*. Piscataway.

Sherk, R. K. (1969). *Roman Documents from the Greek East*. Baltimore.

Sherk, R. K. (1988). *The Roman Empire: Augustus to Hadrian*. Cambridge.

Sherwin-White, A. N. (1973). *The Roman Citizenship*. 2nd ed. Oxford.

Sherwin-White, S., and A. Kuhrt. (1993). *From Samarkhand to Sardis: A New Approach to the Seleucid Empire*. Berkeley.

Sinopoli, C. M. (2001). "Imperial Integration and Imperial Subjects," in S. E. Alcock et al., eds., *Empires: Perspectives from Archaeology and History*. Cambridge: 195–200.

Skinner, A. (2013). "Political Mobility in the Later Roman Empire." *Past and Present* 218: 17–53.

Smallwood, E. M. (1967). *Documents Illustrating the Principates of Gaius, Claudius and Nero*. Cambridge.

Smith, K. (2015). *Constantine and the Captive Christians of Persia: Martyrdom and Religious Identity in Late Antiquity*. Oakland.

Smith, R. R. R. (1985). "Roman Portraits: Honours, Empresses, and Late Emperors." *Journal of Roman Studies* 75: 209–21.

Smith, R. R. R. (1997). "The Public Image of Licinius 1: Sculptured Portraits and Imperial Ideology in the Early Fourth Century." *Journal of Roman Studies* 97: 170–202.

Sogno, C. (2006). *Q. Aurelius Symmachus: A Political Biography*. Ann Arbor.

Solans, B. (2014). *Poderes colectivos en la Siria del Bronce Final*. Barcelona.

Spawforth, A. J. S. (2012). *Greece and the Augustan Cultural Revolution*. Cambridge.

Spawforth, A. J. S., ed. (2007). *The Court and Court Society in Ancient Monarchies*. Cambridge.

Steele, J. M. (2011). "Astronomy and Culture in Late Babylonian Uruk." *Proceedings of the International Astronomical Union* 7: 331–41.

Steinert, U. (2012). *Aspekte des Menschseins im Alten Mesopotamien: Eine Studie zu Person und Identität im 2. und 1. Jt. v. Chr.* Leiden.

Steinkeller, P. (1991). "The Administration and Economic Organization of the Ur III State: The Core in the Periphery," in M. Gibson and R. D. Biggs, eds., *The Organization of Power: Aspects of Bureaucracy in the Ancient Near East.* Chicago: 19–41.

Steinkeller, P. (1993). "Early Political Development in Mesopotamia and the Origins of the Sargonic Empire," in M. Liverani, ed., *Akkad: The First World Empire.* Padua: 107–29.

Steinmetz, G. (2008). "The Colonial State as a Social Field: Ethnographic Capital and Native Policy in the German Overseas Empire before 1914." *American Sociological Review* 73: 589–612.

Stevens, K. (2014). "The Antiochus Cylinder, Babylonian Scholarship and Seleucid Imperial Ideology." *JHS* 134: 66–88.

Stolper, M. W. (1984). "The Neo-Babylonian Text from the Persepolis Fortification." *Journal of Near Eastern Studies* 43: 299–310.

Stolper, M. W. (1987). "Bēlšunu the Satrap," in F. Rochberg-Halton, ed., *Language, Literature, and History: Philological and Historical Studies Presented to Erica Reiner.* New Haven: 389–402.

Stolper, M. W. (1989). "The Governor of Babylon and Across-the-River in 486 B.C." *Journal of Near Eastern Studies* 48: 283–305.

Stoneman, R., ed. (2007). *Il Romanzo di Alessandro.* Vol. 1. Milan.

Stoneman, R. (2008). *Alexander the Great: A Life in Legend.* New Haven.

Striker, G. (1983). "The Role of Oikeiosis in Stoic Ethics." *Oxford Studies in Ancient Philosophy* 1: 145–67.

Strootman, R. (2007). *The Hellenistic Royal Court: Court Culture, Ceremonial and Ideology in Greece, Egypt and the Near East, 336–30 BCE.* PhD diss., Utrecht.

Strootman, R. (2011). "Hellenistic Court Society: The Seleukid Imperial Court under Antiochos the Great, 223-187 BCE," in J. Duindam, T. Artan, and M. Kunt, eds., *Royal Courts in Dynastic States and Empires: A Global Perspective.* Leiden: 63–89.

Strootman, R. (2014a). *Courts and Elites in the Hellenistic Empires: The Near East after the Achaemenids, c. 330-30 BCE.* Edinburgh.

Strootman, R. (2014b). "Hellenistic Imperialism and the Idea of World Unity," in C. Rapp and H. A. Drake, eds., *The City in the Classical and Post-Classical World: Changing Contexts of Power and Identity.* Cambridge: 38–61.

Svärd, S. (2012). "Differences in Ancient Assyria: Some Methodological Questions," in A. Kajanus and M. Meincke, eds., *Perspectives on Difference: Makings and Workings of Power.* Helsinki: 123–45.

Svärd, S. (2015). *Women and Power in Neo-Assyrian Palaces.* Helsinki.

Swain, S. (1996). *Hellenism and Empire.* Oxford.

Tadmor, H. (1991). "On the Role of Aramaic in the Assyrian Empire," in M. Mori, H. Ogawa, and M. Joshikawa, eds., *Near Eastern Studies Dedicated to H. I. H. Prince Takahito Mikasa on the Occasion of His Seventy-Fifth Birthday.* Wiesbaden: 419–26.

Tannous, J. (2013). "You Are What You Read: Qenneshre and the Miaphysite Church in the Seventh Century," in P. Wood, ed., *History and Identity in the Late Antique Near East*. Oxford: 83–102.

Thiers, C. (2006). "Égyptiens et Grecs au service des cultes indigènes: Un aspect de l'évergétisme en Égypte lagide," in M. Molin, ed., *Les Régulations sociales dans l'Antiquité*. Rennes: 275–301.

Thiers, C. (2007). *Ptolémée Philadelphe et les prêtres d'Atoum de Tjékou: Nouvelle édition commentée de la "stèle de Pithom" (CGC 22183)*. Montpellier.

Thiers, C. (2009). *La Stèle de Ptolémée VIII Évergète II à Héracléion*. Oxford.

Thomason, A. K. (2001). "Representations of the North Syrian Landscape in Neo-Assyrian Art." *BASOR* 323: 63–96.

Thompson, D. J. (1984). "The Idumaeans of Memphis and the Ptolemaic Politeumata," in M. Manfredi, ed., *Atti del XVII Congresso internazionale di papirologia. Napoli, 19–26 maggio 1983*. Naples: 1069–75.

Thompson, D. J. (2012). *Memphis under the Ptolemies*. Princeton.

Thomson. R. W. (2004). "Armenian Ideology and the Persians," in A. Carile, L. Cracoo Ruginni, G. Gnoli, G. Pugliese Carratelli, and G. Scarcia, eds., *La Persia e Bisanzio: Convegno internazionale, Roma 14–18 ottobre 2002*. Rome: 373–89.

Toral-Niehoff, I. (2014). *Al-Ḥīra: Eine arabische Kulturmetropole im spätantiken Kontext*. Leiden.

Turner, B. S. (2006). "Classical Sociology and Cosmopolitanism: A Critical Defence of the Social." *British Journal of Sociology* 57/1: 133–51.

van Bladel, K. (2009). *The Arabic Hermes: From Pagan Sage to Prophet of Science*. Oxford.

van Bladel, K. (2011). "The Bactrian Background of the Barmakids," in A. Akasoy, C. Burnett, and R. Yoeli-Tlalim, eds., *Islam and Tibet—Interactions along the Musk Routes*. Farnham: 43–88.

van der Spek, R. J. (1993). "The Astronomical Diaries as a Source for Achaemenid and Seleucid History." *Bibliotheca Orientalis* 50: 91–102.

van der Spek, R. J. (2000). "The šatammus of Esagila in the Seleucid and Parthian periods," in J. Marzahn and H. Neumann, eds., *Assyriologica et semitica. FS Joachim Oelsner*. Münster: 437–46.

van der Spek, R. J. (2009). "Multi-ethnicity and Ethnic Segregation in Hellenistic Babylon," in T. Derks and N. Roymans, eds., *Ethnic Constructs in Antiquity: The Role of Power and Tradition*. Amsterdam: 101–16.

Van Dijk, J. J. A. (1962). "Die Inschriftenfunde," Vorläufiger Bericht über die von dem Deutschen Archäologischen Institut und der Deutschen Orient-Gesellschaft aus den Mitteln der Deutschen Forschungsgemeinschaft unternommenen Ausgrabungen in Uruk-Warka 18. Berlin: 44–51.

Van Dijk, J. J. A., and W. Mayer. (1980). *Texte aus dem Rēš-Heiligtum in Uruk-Warka*. Berlin.

van Nuffelen, P. (2014). "The End of Open Competition? Religious Disputations in Late Antiquity," in D. Engels and P. Van Nuffelen, eds., *Religion and Competition in Antiquity*. Brussels: 148–71.

Vasunia, P. (2013). *The Classics and Colonial India*. Oxford.

Véïsse, A.-E. (2004). *Les "Révoltes Égyptiennes": Recherches sur les troubles intérieurs en Egypte du règne de Ptolémée III Evergète à la conquête romaine.* Leuven.

Verboven, K. (2009). "Resident Aliens and Translocal Merchant Collegia in the Roman Empire," in O. Hekster and T. Kaizer, eds., *Frontiers in the Roman World. Proceedings of the Ninth Workshop of the International Network Impact of Empire (Durham, 16-19 April 2009).* Leiden: 335–48.

Verbrugghe, G., and J. Wickersham, eds. (1996). *Berossos and Manetho: Native Traditions in Ancient Mesopotamia and Egypt.* Ann Arbor.

Viviers, D. (2011). "Une cité crétoise à l'épreuve d'une garnison lagide: L'Exemple d'Itanos," in J.-C. Couvenhes, S. Crouzet, and S. Péré-Noguès, eds., *Pratiques et identités culturelles des armées hellénistiques du monde méditerranée.* Bordeaux: 35–64.

Waerzeggers, C. (2012). "The Babylonian Chronicles: Classification and Provenance." *Journal of Near Eastern Studies* 71: 285–98.

Waerzeggers, C. (2014). *Marduk-Rēmanni: Local Networks and Imperial Politics in Achaemenid Babylonia.* Leuven.

Waldron, J. (2000). "What is Cosmopolitanism?" *Journal of Political Philosophy* 8: 227–43.

Walker, J. (2004). "Against the Eternity of the Stars: Disputation and Christian Philosophy in Late Sasanian Mesopotamia," in A. Carile, L. Cracoo Ruginni, G. Gnoli, G. Pugliese Carratelli, and G. Scarcia, eds., *La Persia e Bisanzio: Convegno internazionale, Roma 14–18 ottobre 2002.* Rome: 510–37.

Walker, J. (2006). *The Legend of Mar Qardagh: Narrative and Christian Heroism in Late Antique Iraq.* Berkeley.

Wang Hui (2010). *Sheng zhi shan e: shenme shi Qimeng? Chongdu Lu Xun de Po Esheng Lun* 声之善恶：什么是启蒙？——重读鲁迅的《破恶声论》. *Kai fang shidai* 10: 84–115.

Wang Hui (2014). *China from Empire to Nation-State.* Cambridge, MA.

Watanabe, K. (2014). "Esarhaddon's Succession Oath Documents." *Orient* 49: 145–70.

Watts, E. J. (2005). "Where to Live the Philosophical Life in the Sixth Century? Damascius, Simplicius, and the Return from Persia." *Greek, Roman and Byzantine Studies* 45: 285–315.

Watts, E. J. (2006). *City and School in Late Antique Athens and Alexandria.* Berkeley.

Wegner, M. (1979). *Gordianus III bis Carinus.* Berlin.

Weil, P. (2012). *The Sovereign Citizen: Denaturalization and the Origins of the American Republic.* Philadelphia.

Weissbach, F. H. (1911). *Die Keilinschriften der Achämeniden.* Leipzig.

Weisweiler, J. (2012). "From Equality to Asymmetry: Honorific Statues, Imperial Power and Senatorial Identity in Late-Antique Rome." *Journal of Roman Archaeology* 25: 319–50.

Weisweiler, J. (2014). "Domesticating the Senatorial Elite: Universal Monarchy and Transregional Aristocracy in the Fourth Century AD," in J. Wienand, ed., *Contested Monarchy: Integrating the Roman Empire in the Fourth Century AD.* Oxford: 17–41.

Welles, C. B. (1934). *Royal Correspondence in the Hellenistic Period: A Study in Greek Epigraphy.* New Haven.

Westenholz, A. (1999). "The Old Akkadian Period: History and Culture," in W. Sallaberger and A. Westenholz, eds., *Mesopotamien: Akkade-Zeit und Ur III-Zeit.* Göttingen: 17–117.

White, P. (1993). *Promised Verse: Poets in the Society of Augustan Rome.* Cambridge, MA.

White, R. (1991). *The Middle Ground: Indians, Empires, and Republics in the Great Lakes Region, 1650–1815.* Cambridge.

Whitmarsh, T. (2001a). *Greek Literature and the Roman Empire: The Politics of Imitation.* Cambridge.

Whitmarsh, T. (2001b). "'Greece is the World': Exile and Identity in the Second Sophistic," in S. Goldhill, ed., *Being Greek under Rome: Cultural Identity, the Second Sophistic and the Development of Empire.* Cambridge: 269–305.

Whitmarsh, T., ed. (2010). *Local Knowledge and Microidentities in the Imperial Greek World.* Cambridge.

Whittaker, C. R. (1994). *Frontiers of the Roman Empire: A Social and Economic Study.* Baltimore.

Whittow, M. (1990). "Ruling the Late Roman and Early Byzantine City: A Continuous History." *Past & Present* 129: 3–29.

Wiesehöfer, J. (2009). "The Achaemenid Empire," in I. Morris, and W. Scheidel, eds., *The Dynamics of Ancient Empires: State Power from Assyria to Byzantium.* Oxford: 66–98.

Wiesehöfer, J. (2010). "The Late Sasanian Near East," in C. Robinson, ed., *The New Cambridge History of Islam.* Vol 1: *The Formation of the Islamic World, Sixth to Eleventh Centuries.* Cambridge: 98–152.

Williams, W. (1975). "Formal and Historical Aspects of Two New Documents of Marcus Aurelius." *Zeitschrift für Papyrologie und Epigraphik* 17: 37–78.

Winnicki, J. K. (1994). "Carrying Off and Bringing Home the Statues of the Gods: On an Aspect of the Religious Policy of the Ptolemies Towards the Egyptians." *Journal of Juristic Papyrology* 24: 149–90.

Winterling, A. (1997). *Zwischen "Haus" und "Staat": antike Höfe im Vergleich.* Munich.

Winterling, A. (1999). *Aula Caesaris: Studien zur Institutionalisierung des römischen Kaiserhofes in der Zeit von Augustus bis Commodus (31 v. Chr.–192 n. Chr.).* Munich.

Winterling, A. (2005). "Dyarchie in der römischen Kaiserzeit: Vorschlag zur Wiederaufnahme der Diskussion," in W. Nippel and B. Seidensticker, eds., *Theodor Mommsens langer Schatten: Das römische Staatsrecht als bleibende Herausforderung für die Forschung.* Hildesheim: 177–98.

Winterling, A. (2009). *Politics and Society in Imperial Rome.* Malden.

Witschel, C. (2011). "Der Kaiser und die Inschriften," in A. Winterling, ed., *Zwischen Strukturgeschichte und Biographie: Probleme und Perspektiven einer neuen Römischen Kaisergeschichte, 31 v. Chr.–192 n. Chr.* Munich: 45–112.

Woods, C. (2006). "Bilingualism, Scribal Learning, and the Death of Sumerian," in S. L. Sanders, ed., *Margins of Writing, Origins of Culture.* Chicago: 95–124.

Woolf, G. (1994). "Becoming Roman, Staying Greek: Culture, Identity and the Civilizing Process in the Roman East." *Proceedings of the Cambridge Philological Society* 40: 116–43.

Woolf, G. (1995). "The Formation of Roman Provincial Cultures," in J. Metzler, M. Millett, N. Roymans, and J. Sloistra, eds., *Integration in the Early Roman West: The role of Culture and Ideology*. Luxembourg: 9–18.

Woolf, G. (1998). *Becoming Roman: The Origins of Provincial Civilization in Gaul*. Cambridge.

Woolf, G. (2009a). "Found in Translation: The Religion of the Roman Diaspora," in O. Hekster, S. Schmidt-Hofner, and C. Witschel, eds., *Ritual Dynamics and Religious Change in the Roman Empire*. Leiden: 239–52.

Woolf, G. (2009b). "World Religion and World Empire in the Ancient Mediterranean," in H. Cancik and J. Rüpke, eds., *Die Religion des Imperium Romanum: Koine und Konfrontationen*. Tübingen: 19–35.

Woolf, G. (2011). *Tales of the Barbarians: Ethnography and Empire in the Roman West*. Malden.

Woolf, G. (2012). *Rome: An Empire's Story*. Oxford.

Yarshater, E. (1983). "The Iranian National History," in E. Yarshater, ed., *The Cambridge History of Iran*. Vol 3(1): *The Seleucid, Parthian, and Sasanian Periods*. Cambridge: 359–477.

Yates, R. (2001). "Cosmos, Central Authority, and Communities in the Early Chinese Empire," in S. E. Alcock, T. N. D'Altroy, K. D. Morrison, and C. M. Sinopoli, eds., *Empires: Perspectives from Archaeology and History*. Cambridge: 351–68.

Zaccagnini, C. (1982). "The Enemy in the Neo-Assyrian Royal Inscriptions: The 'Ethnographic' Description," in H. J. Nissen, and J. Renger, eds., *Mesopotamien und seine Nachbarn: Politische und kulturelle Wechselbeziehungen im alten Vorderasien vom 4. bis 1. Jahrtausend v. Chr*. Berlin: 409–24.

Zamazalová, S. (2013). "Claiming the World: Geographical Conceptions and Royal Ideology in the Neo-Assyrian Empire, with Focus on the Reign of Sargon II (721-705 BC)." PhD diss., University College London.

Zawadski, S. (1995). "Hostages in Assyrian Royal Inscriptions," in K. van Lerberghe and A. Schoors, eds., *Immigration and Emigration within the Ancient Near East: Festschrift E. Lipinski*. Leuven: 449–58.

Zhaoming, X. (2014). "The Hepu Han Tombs and the Maritime Silk Road of the Han Dynasty." *Antiquity* 88: 1229–43.

Zielonka, J. (2006). *Europe as Empire: The Nature of the Enlarged European Union*. Oxford.

Zuiderhoek, A. (2009). *The Politics of Munificence in the Roman Empire: Citizens, Elites and Benefactors in Asia Minor*. Cambridge.

Index